EMMET FIELD HORINE, M. D.

Dr. Emmet Field Horine, a Louisville heart specialist, has long been an ardent admirer and student of Daniel Drake. After undergraduate work at Emory University, he received his medical degree in Louisville in 1907, and he has practiced and taught there in the half century since, with a brief interlude for military service in 1917 to 1919.

The present volume is the result of many years of study of Dr. Drake's career, and represents a definitive biography of the medical pioneer. Dr. Horine's own career has, in many respects, followed the pattern of his admired predecessor. He has been on the faculty of the University of Louisville and has written on a wide variety of medical and historical topics. He is a Fellow of the American College of Physicians, and is affiliated with numerous other national and local associations.

In addition to many published articles concerning heart disease, Dr. Horine has written a large number of essays in the field of medical history. He wrote the *Introduction* to Daniel Drake's *Letters on Slavery* (1850) and also the *Introduction* to Drake's *Inaugural Discourse on Medical Education* (1820). Dr. Horine was the Editor of the latest edition (1948) of Dr. Drake's *Pioneer Life in Kentucky*. As the historian of the Kentucky State Medical Association, Dr. Horine wrote its history and edited its centennial volume (1952). He is the author of over twenty-five biographical sketches of early presidents of the Kentucky State Medical Association published in its programs.

DANIEL DRAKE (1785-1852)

Pioneer Physician of the Midwest

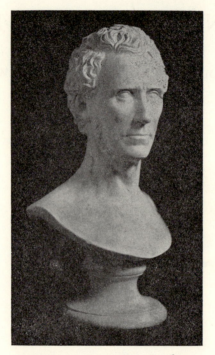

DANIEL DRAKE, M.D., *aet.* 65.
*Bust by Charles Bullett (1824-73),
in author's collection.*

DANIEL DRAKE (1785-1852)

Pioneer Physician of the Midwest

by

Emmet Field Horine, M.D.

Introduction by J. Christian Bay, Litt.D.
Librarian Emeritus
The John Crerar Library

Philadelphia ❧ University of Pennsylvania Press

Published in Great Britain, India, and Pakistan
by the Oxford University Press
London, Bombay, and Karachi

Printed in the United States of America

TO MY WIFE, HELEN, &

who with this biography

as with other under-

takings, has been of the

greatest assistance.

Contents

Illustrations Ꝑ

The following illustrations appear as a group after page 256.

Preface ॐ

THIS BIOGRAPHY has been thirty-two years in preparation. In 1927 material was somewhat hurriedly gathered for an address before the Ohio Valley Medical Association.[1] Unfortunately, few primary sources were at hand and much of the secondary material proved woefully inaccurate. In this biography I am attempting to set the record straight about one of the most distinguished of American physicians.

With all known aspects of Drake's life under consistent scrutiny for thirty-two years, there emerges the image of a man possessing commanding talents. By some he has been called a genius. He had an unusual, almost prophetic, vision, a philanthropic outlook, an abiding philosophy, as well as a scientific and inquisitive mind. Drake was a thunderer to his enemies yet the "most loving-hearted" of men.

Readers previously interested in Daniel Drake will find here statements at variance with or contradictory to those made by my predecessors. For serious students references are made to primary sources and placed at the bottom of each page. It seems especially fitting that this book is being published in such a scholarly manner by the University of Pennsylvania Press. Drake and many of the physicians herein mentioned were graduated from the Medical Department of the Univer-

[1] Emmet F. Horine: "Biographical Sketch of Daniel Drake (1785-1852)," *Journal of Medicine* (Cincinnati), IX:159-62, June 1928.

sity of Pennsylvania, the first medical school in the United States, established 3 May 1765.

All known books, pamphlets, addresses, and manuscript material by Drake have been consulted. In addition, all extant issues of Cincinnati newspapers from 1800 through 1852 were read. Likewise, the newspapers of Philadelphia, Lexington, and Louisville have been consulted for the periods of Drake's sojourn in those cities.

Over the years, a vast amount of material concerning Drake, his associates, and his period has been accumulated. With such a collection at hand the composition of this book has been one of selection. To have covered all of Drake's varied activities in detail, the work would have been extended to at least three volumes. It is hoped that no significant point in his life has been omitted.

Drake's interests were so numerous that he often appeared to be managing alone a multi-ringed circus. Therefore, it has seemed better at times to discuss the performance in one "ring" to its end instead of chronologically combining several acts. This plan may prevent confusing the reader. Shuttling "back and forth between several major themes," as one early critic aptly said, becomes unnecessary.

Despite some readers' aversion to quotations ("I hate quotations. Tell me what you know."), and impatience with bibliographical apparatus, paraphrase has often been avoided here. Aside from the fact that some of the quoted material is not easily accessible, the exact words give a more precise picture of the man and Daniel Drake's writings *are* worth reproducing. Further it appears incontrovertible that a statement by an eyewitness carries much greater weight than any paraphrase. Hence, I have deliberately made this an anthological biography and, thereby, attempted to add life, color, and piquancy.

Many biographies are inaccurate, frequently through carelessness, though some biographers deliberately fabricate. Writers on Drake to an extraordinary degree, with the exception of Charles D. Meigs, seem to have been guilty of both carelessness and resort to fiction.

The earliest of numerous brief biographies of Daniel Drake was written by his friend, Samuel D. Gross (1805-84), Professor of Surgery in the Medical Department of the University of Louisville. Delivered at a public meeting in the main auditorium of the university, 27 January 1853, the *Discourse* is highly eulogistic and reveals Gross's genuine admiration.[2] Although based on an intimate acquaintance of eighteen years and much manuscript material it is not entirely free of errors. The date of Drake's death is incorrectly given as "6" November 1852, which, of course, should have been Friday, 5 November 1852. Some thirty years later in his *Autobiography*, Gross again shows his admiration though he makes additional misstatements which could be laid only to a decaying memory.[3]

The first book-length biography was written by a cousin of Drake's wife, a lawyer, author, and editor, Edward D. Mansfield (1801-80).[4] He had access to all of Drake's manuscripts, many of which were either lost or destroyed after use. Despite the wealth of material Mansfield carelessly supplied errors of fact and much fiction for those who wrote after him. Fully half of the "Chronological Data" (page v) in Mansfield's biography is erroneous. Lunsford Pitts Yandell, Sr. (1807-78), long-time friend and associate of Drake, commented thus on Mansfield's book:

[2] Samuel D. Gross: "A Discourse on the Life, Character, and Services of Daniel Drake," *Louisville Journal* (Louisville), 1853.

[3] Samuel D. Gross: *Autobiography* (2 vols. Philadelphia: George Barrie, 1887).

[4] Edward D. Mansfield: *Memoirs of . . . Daniel Drake* (Cincinnati: Applegate & Co., 1855). Reissued, Ohio School Library, 1860.

So far as the memoirs consist of Dr. Drake's own narrative of his life and the contributions of his friends, they are exceedingly interesting; so far as they are the production of his biographer, they are intolerably tedious and vapid. Unfortunately the former bear to the latter only the proportion that the spots of verdure in a desert bear to the interminable waste of sands. As a life of Dr. Drake, the volume is inaccurate, unsatisfactory and meagre; as a history of everything in which it is not supposed that the reader of Dr. Drake's memoirs feels the slightest interest, it is full to satiety—*usque ad nauseam.*[5]

The second attempt at a full length biography, *Daniel Drake and his Followers,* was by Otto Juettner (1865-1922), a Cincinnati physician.[6] He unquestionably did an enormous amount of research but failed to document most of his statements. The actual biography of Drake fills 77 pages whereas 409 of Juettner's text are devoted to sketches of many Cincinnati physicians, to medical schools, periodicals, hospitals, etc. Juettner has copied Mansfield's errors and added some of his own. Since the compilers of the various biographical dictionaries merely followed these writers, errors are numerous in *Appleton's Cyclopaedia of American Biography* (1888, Vol. II:223); *Dictionary of American Biography* (1930, V:426-27); *The Encyclopedia Americana* (1957, IX:300); and Kelly-Burrage: *Dictionary of American Medical Biography* (1928, pp. 344-45).

Embarrassed by the errors in my biographical sketch of Drake in 1927, I determined thenceforth to use primary sources. A biography based on original material, as this is, *may* contain errors while one relying on secondary sources *is certain* to be replete with them.

[5] Lunsford P. Yandell, Sr.: Review, *Memoirs* . . . by Edward D. Mansfield, *Louisville Review,* I:1-25, May 1856.

[6] Otto Juettner: *Daniel Drake and his Followers* (Cincinnati: Harvey Publishing Co., 1909).

As long-time librarian of the John Crerar Library and especially as an eminent authority on western Americana, no one seemed more capable than Dr. J. Christian Bay of evaluating Drake and his milieu. I am deeply grateful to him for his fine Introduction.

In my opinion there is no other group of more uniformly conscientious, unselfish, and dedicated persons than librarians. They have been always extremely helpful in answering numerous questions and in furnishing either typed copies, photostats, or microfilms of important items. This book could not have been written without their assistance.

Undoubtedly the best Drake collection open to the public is owned by the Historical and Philosophical Society of Ohio. Not only do they have many manuscripts, books, and pamphlets by Drake and his associates but also a unique collection of the newspapers of Cincinnati. To the former librarian there, Miss Eleanor Wilby, to the present librarian, Mrs. Norris Hook, and her assistant, Miss Lillian Wuest, I am sincerely grateful. The late librarian of Transylvania College, Mrs. Charles F. Norton, was extremely helpful as has been her successor, Miss Roemol Henry. Notable manuscript material, including the original letters of Drake's *Pioneer Life in Kentucky*, is housed in the Medical Library of the Cincinnati General Hospital. The former librarian there, Miss Eva G. Kyte, and the present incumbent, Miss Alice E. McCaffrey, have been of great assistance. Miss Ludie J. Kinkead, formerly curator of The Filson Club, the present assistant curator, Miss Evelyn R. Dale, and Miss Mable C. Weaks of the staff have lightened my work. I am indebted to Miss Blake Beem, librarian, and her assistants, Miss Lucy Addams and Mrs. Kenton Atwood, of the Jefferson County-University of Louisville Medical Library, for help on numerous occasions.

The librarians of many other institutions have been uniformly courteous and helpful, including those of the Louisville Free Public Library, University of Louisville Library, Cincinnati Public Library, Lexington Public Library, University of Kentucky Libraries, the Lloyd Library (Cincinnati), Library of Congress, National Library of Medicine, New York Public Library, New York Academy of Medicine Library, Henry E. Huntington Library and Art Gallery, Frick Art Reference Library, Boston Public Library, Harvard University Library, Yale University Library, University of Pennsylvania, Wisconsin Historical Society, Miami University Library, Marietta College, Ohio State Archaeological and Historical Society, Missouri State Historical Society, American Antiquarian Society, American Philosophical Society, Library of the College of Physicians of Philadelphia, Presbyterian Historical Society, John Crerar Library, University of Edinburgh, and the Chattanooga Public Library.

I would recognize with appreciation the help of Miss Millicent Sowerby, Dr. Lawrence S. Thompson, Dr. Harry R. Stevens, Mr. Ted Langstroth, Dr. Walter Havighurst, Dr. William E. and Ophia D. Smith, Mr. Edward H. Dwight, Miss Marie Dickoré, Miss Elizabeth L. Mitchell, Dr. Nelson F. Adkins, Dr. John Francis McDermott, and the Reverend Frederic B. Atkinson.

Several descendants of Dr. Drake have lent important items. It has been stimulating to have met them either personally or by correspondence: Mrs. Daniel B. Ruggles (Alice McGuffey Morrill), Miss Marion C. Bridgman, and Mr. Kingsland Drake McGuffey. A very distant relative, Mr. Oliver D. Drake, was most helpful in allowing unrestricted use of his unpublished "Drake Genealogy" and in answering questions concerning New Jersey.

Mr. Henry Schuman, publisher of Drake's *Letters on Slavery, Pioneer Life in Kentucky,* and the *Inaugural Discourse* (1820), has been interested in this biography almost from its inception. He has read critically and helpfully several chapters. Among other early readers of certain chapters were Dr. Walton B. McDaniel II and Dr. William B. Bean to whom I am indebted for important suggestions. The late Dr. Thomas L. Butler, grandson of Dr. Charles Wilkins Short, gave me several significant letters formerly belonging to his ancestor. Likewise, Dr. George A. Robertson donated three letters from Dr. Drake to his grandfather, Dr. John F. Henry. Dr. Charles F. Wood, great-grandson of Dr. Lunsford P. Yandell, Sr., allowed access to the fragment of his ancestor's contemplated history of Kentucky medicine.

Certain chapters have been read and helpfully criticized by my son, Field, and by my son-in-law and daughter, Dr. and Mrs. Carleton B. Chapman. The entire manuscript was read and many important suggestions were made by another son-in-law and daughter, Professor and Mrs. Herbert E. Arntson, by Miss Dorcas Ruthenburg, and by Dr. Walter Dean. Mrs. Nina H. Robinson meticulously typed the whole manuscript and made many useful suggestions. To all those named and to the many other friends who have encouraged me I am sincerely grateful.

Introduction ℈

DANIEL DRAKE at the age of 62 casually mentioned that as a child he was precocious. But we may safely believe that what he terms the original principle of his nature had its roots in a very circumspect and purposeful parental attention. Pioneers at the time of Drake's birth (1785) of necessity were wide-awake, even though lacking in some forms of conventional culture. Boys quickly grew to man's estate at all new frontiers. Amidst primitive surroundings many people led constructively intellectual lives, and set latent forces free.

When the Drakes came into the scene of the regions West of Cumberland Gap, this country was awaiting the fulfilment of a prophecy, not a conquest. Settlements naturally bloomed by gradual organization, but indifferently as to imported wealth. Wildernesses were tamed by the people and in time took form and character consonant with the landscape, with natural necessity, native resource. In this way the Ohio River country by degrees became host to that powerful, creative spirit which marked and fulfilled our colonial people's hope, backing its recollections and memories with healthy activity and, above all, framing its unconscious impressions into a will toward a free but responsible life. Traditions persisted inevitably, good and bad, anchored at the Atlantic coast settlements and in remote forms of life over the seas. But present ever and overwhelming was the necessity created by immediate demands, of coming to reasonable terms with the land that had lain untouched since Creation. This land, while being subdued and drawn into service, naturally and of itself would contribute much enlightening and even educational stimulus to the mind of young Daniel Drake. His imagined precosity is readily explained by the hearty response which he brought to the new life that claimed him and his folks. Philadelphia, center of colonial culture, in 1805, when Drake went there to study medicine, was eighteen days' journey on horseback from Cincinnati. Chronologically the distance might be measured in fantastic figures. The cultural distance need not be emphasized.

The traditional element in the Atlantic seacoast provinces was strongly traditional, while the western frontier organized itself intellectually by a native ingenuity more than it benefited by historical example. Considering the Ohio Valley in its advance from 1800 to 1850, Daniel Drake, at the age of 65, confesses that in looking backward he is facing an intellectual mirage in which the scene is lighted by that constructive impulse which is one of the traits of our national character.

As a child he had entered a scene at a time when unwittingly we were facing the task of compressing all previous periods of growth into the shortest possible compass, to meet emergencies. The world of his youth was far from a chaos, for wild nature has its own organization, but to make it respond to man's needs called for skill. Tradition often proved inadequate to afford a working method, a safe base for operation. An *ingenium* was needed where experience failed. Then would operate prophecy, vision, skill.

The Drake family was well fitted for its chosen task as settlers in a new, primitive region. They were children of our War of Independence, inured to physical effort and enlightened, and capable of turning the activities of their children into purposeful, happy channels. Isaac Drake planned well when he brought his son, then but fifteen years old, from Mays Lick to Cincinnati and apprenticed him to Dr. Goforth to be educated for the practice of medicine. It must have been the result of a decision unusual in the cabins of the settlers, yet prompted by a conviction of the boy's leanings, even though the example of the cousin John had long animated young Daniel to pursue serious studies and to look to medicine as a life interest. We may take it that in those days, as now, a medical career attracts the unusual person rather than the average. Service, a much-abused term, goes before personal preference and self-assertion among the truly unusual. Daniel Drake verified this in several ways.

Precocious—hardly. In retrospect it may have seemed so, but actually every normal child, inspired by parental attention and by an unexplored Eden for a background, will readily discover the world—some world—for himself. Let nobody deny that the grade school, high school, college (med. prep.) are necessary steps toward the study of medicine in this day and age. But give me a fifteen-year-old boy, ardent for learning, sound in mind and direction, and I might vote for apprenticing him to some contemporary Goforth, trusting him to respond in a felicitous way. Knowledge absorbed before the age of twenty, all factors considered, never fades from man's memory. Anyway, at the age of twenty Daniel Drake was considered by his preceptor fully qualified for the practice of medicine.

As this service developed under his hand and eye, his attention was drawn to many things that the ordinary practitioner might easily overlook in an effort to make his living. In the first place, local history and events in and about Cincinnati caught his attention. But he also began to consider the medical needs, especially of the Ohio Valley, as determined by specific conditions of health and its preservation, of illness and its prevention. We may surmise that the local experience of him-

self and his colleagues quite early in his career directed his
attention to the relationship between locality and the variations in the forms of known and unknown diseases. As his
region possessed its specific characters, a difference of many
pathological phenomena from those known elsewhere became
obvious. Pictures of diseases would differ from those recorded
in textbooks as known in older lands where the medical
sciences had accumulated for centuries. Drake's interest in
topographic research quickly asserted itself in his *Notices
Concerning Cincinnati,* which was published in 1810 and
contains reflections tending toward medical topography: the
relationship between weather and locality and climate, on one
side, and health and disease and their management, on the
other.

From this nucleus of observation he proceeded gradually
toward researches and inquiries which extended further and
further, until they had covered the entire interior valley of our
continent—a feat of investigation which we have not yet
intelligently used, or even studied as it deserves.

Intelligent observation comes with training, but a wide view
is a gift of the gods. Daniel Drake's possession of both fitted
him admirably for that career in medical education which
came to set deep marks in Ohio and Kentucky; in fact it went
far beyond the field of medicine. As a humanist, a student, an
explorer, but always a medical practitioner, he faced, however,
a task harder than that of his spiritual children and successors
of later decennia, who inherited his curiosity, initiative, and
energy. The period of the experimental method in science and
medicine burst into bloom just about the time when Drake's
*Systematic Treatise . . . on the Principal Diseases of the In-
terior Valley of North America* began to beg for readers, and
Edward D. Mansfield (in 1855) gave us the first extensive
biography of our great scientific pioneer. Then a generation
passed before we began to give earnest attention to the history

of the medical sciences on our own continent Samuel D. Gross—and in later years Otto Juettner, Fielding H. Garrison, Wm. Osler, with the classical groups at Philadelphia and Baltimore—quite effectively roused an interest in Drake's literary, medical, and educational work. There followed a widespread interest in our local history of science, medicine, and the technical arts; the genius of pioneer times was recognized. Still, fifty years ago a "first" Beaumont went begging for a purchaser in Chicago. Gradually, however, medical historians discovered how very applicable, even to modern needs and ideas, were Drake's inaugural and other addresses on medical education. His *Pioneer Life in Kentucky* became recognized as a classic among works on western forms of life, and in time librarians found food for their thoughts in his *Discourses before the Cincinnati Medical Library Association* (1852), which, incidentally, contains observations of fundamental value in the analysis of our national characteristics.

So now, a full century after his departure from our valley, Drake faces us as not merely an interesting figure of a period of cultural progress. Like Lincoln, he belongs to the ages. In medical sciences, in midwestern topography, in professional philosophy, in method generally, he has been proved one of the masters. With due regard to his previous biographers, editors, and commentators who have paved the way for posthumous recognition of Daniel Drake's position in American science and letters, we recognize that the most painstaking, persistent, and exhaustive study of the great pioneer's life and influence is being accomplished by Dr. Emmet Field Horine, himself a Kentuckian and historian of medicine. Dr. Horine's annotated critical edition of Drake's *Pioneer Life in Kentucky*, his numerous papers on medical events and episodes in the Middle West, his critical edition of Drake's famous address of 1820 on medical education entitle Dr. Horine to come before us now with what we shall hail as the definitive biography of that Nestor of medical men whose inspiration we wish to preserve. This task covers a round hundred years of American life, during which our people hastened through several collective centuries of development and growth. The picture is truly western and solemnly uplifting—in spite of the element of impatience that Drake attributes to us—and the uplift is this: A mite of a boy coming out of the wilderness, seemingly isolated from the benefits of sheltering culture and traditional liberal education, but winning this and all else by his native inheritance, his ability, zeal, and readiness of effort. Winning in time, as Dr. Horine will show, the quality of mastership that inspires a desire of emulation and makes it clear that constructive work involves not only the agreeable and hopeful task of looking forward as each new day dawns, but also the quality of being historically minded.

J. CHRISTIAN BAY.

Daniel Drake (1785-1852)

Pioneer Physician of the Midwest

1

Such is the stock I spring from.
Plautus (*ca.* 251-184 B.C.)

Ancestry, 1654-1785

THIS IS the chronicle of a man who rose from the poverty of a pioneer Kentucky family to pre-eminence among American physicians; a man of innate ability, indomitable will, tireless energy, and great ambition; a man whose keen sensitivity sometimes led to controversy and who was, on occasion, apparently neither conciliatory nor diplomatic.

New Jersey, the birthplace of Daniel Drake, had a more diverse group of settlers than any other of the thirteen colonies. Many Dutch had come from New Amsterdam to settle in its eastern part. During the first half of the seventeenth century Sweden had established one fort on the east bank of the Delaware River in what is now New Jersey and two others on the west side. These were never materially augmented and were ultimately surrendered to the Dutch, though most of the colonists remained. Quakers purchased the greater part of west Jersey in 1763 and began settling there seven years before William Penn acquired Pennsylvania. Judging by the name of New Limerick, called also Tow Town, there was an Irish settlement near what is now Plainfield, New Jersey. Possibly New Limerick was settled by a portion of a company of Baptists from the County of Tipperary, which in 1683 "arrived at Amboy and proceeded toward the interior parts." [1]

[1] Morgan Edwards: *Materials towards a History of the American Baptists* (12 Volumes, Philadelphia: Thomas Dobson, 1792, New Jersey), Vol. II, p. 10.

Still other groups, largely English and Scotch, although other European countries were represented, came from the Puritan Massachusetts Bay Colony. Perhaps they had sought to escape the rigors of its climate, physical, spiritual, and moral.

Thus the early settlers of New Jersey represented many different countries and cultures. Their diversity of origin was undoubtedly advantageous. Different farming and domestic skills from their several nations were introduced. The acceptance likewise of varied social patterns made human equality more manifest. The inhabitants acquainted themselves with one another's customs both in the field and in the home. The result was that techniques best adapted to the environment came into general use more rapidly than in the other colonies. Emigrants from New Jersey to Kentucky were said to possess a knowledge of the domestic arts superior to that of those from either Maryland or Virginia. This was attributed to the fact that the Virginians and Marylanders had slaves while those from New Jersey possessed very few.[2] Granting the validity of the influence of slavery, it also appears logical that intermingling of many nationalities in New Jersey and its resultant pooling of knowledge were factors as potent as the lack of slave labor.

Even as early as 1600, many religious denominations were represented among the Jerseymen. In 1664, when Lord Berkeley and Sir George Carteret purchased the colony, they immediately formed a constitution which provided for "full liberty of conscience to all religious sects that should behave well." [3] In view of the diversity of beliefs there existed a surprising degree of liberalism in marked contrast to the intolerance of Puritan New England. However, within the various sects strict obedience to their own rules and articles of faith

[2] Daniel Drake: *Pioneer Life in Kentucky, 1785-1800*, edited by Emmet F. Horine, M.D. (New York: Henry Schuman, 1948), p. 180.
[3] Edwards: *op. cit.*, p. 10.

was demanded. The emphasis was upon theology rather than morality. Among the Baptists even minor deviations from the rules were punishable by "excommunication." Likewise the Quakers often "read" nonconformists out of their society.

Beverages containing high percentages of alcohol, known as "ardent spirits," were freely consumed in the colonies and New Jersey was no exception. Whiskey was cheap, four to seven shillings a gallon. At this period in New Jersey, the value of a dollar in sterling was seven shillings and six pence. No harvest, cornhusking, houseraising, wedding, or funeral was held without "the bottle, a symbol of hospitality." The Methodists were an exception since they did not deal in or drink whiskey, although it was sometimes said of them that "no doubt they drank behind the door." [4]

A century and a half after the period we have been describing, Daniel Drake in a letter to his children stated that his parents "belonged, as had their ancestors . . . to the country, and were labourers on the farm." [5] He mentioned also the family tradition of descent from Sir Francis Drake (1540?-96), but otherwise knew nothing of his ancestry except the names of his grandparents. He lacked time, though probably not the inclination, to delve further into the history of his forebears. A biographer cannot shirk this task. He may not thereby solve the riddle of heredity but certain influences may be traced which could have played some part in the molding of the man.

Samuel Gardner Drake (1798-1875), well-known author and Boston's first antiquarian book dealer—apparently unrelated to Daniel Drake—stated that John and Robert Drake and their families came from England to Boston in 1630. In one genealogical record [6] he also stated that Nathaniel, son of

[4] Drake: *Pioneer Life* . . . , p. 84.
[5] *Ibid.*, p. 5.
[6] Samuel Gardner Drake: *Genealogical and Biographical Account of the Family of Drake in America* (Boston: George Coolige, Aug. 1845), p. 28.

Robert, left no children, but in another account he intimates
that this same Nathaniel was "probably the founder of the
New Jersey family of Drake." [7] There can be no question that
this latter statement is incorrect.

Daniel Drake's first ancestor in America of whom we have
certain knowledge was named Francis. This name is at least
suggestive of descent from the famous seafarer in the time of
Queen Elizabeth. On 17 April 1654, Francis Drake was
granted a house lot on Roger Knight's island "at the mouth
of the fresh marsh creeke" in Portsmouth, New Hampshire.[8]
He was a landowner, a surveyor, a selectman of Strawberry
Bank (Portsmouth), and an "Ensigne" of the militia. In
1665 he was one of the signers of the petition to King Charles
II complaining about the government of the Bay Colony.[9]
On 5 August 1668, "Francis Drake of Portsmouth, yeoman,
and Mary his wife" disposed of 164 acres "more or less" of
land in Portsmouth Township for 114 pounds, 10 shillings.[10]

Hugh Dunn, a son-in-law of Francis Drake, with several
others had left New Hampshire in 1666 and settled on a grant
of land in New Jersey.[11] Here the town of New Piscataway
was founded, named after the Piscataqua River upon which
the Drakes and Dunns had lived in New Hampshire. Francis
Drake, after the sale of his land in New Hampshire, moved
with his family to New Jersey. Here he was granted, on
15 July 1673, a license to keep an "Ordinary" (tavern).[12] The
next year he was one of a committee to investigate the
"meadows on the other side of the Raritan River." At the
same time he was appointed constable for New Piscataway.

---

[7] Samuel G. Drake: *Drake of Hampton, New Hampshire*, Genealogical
chart (Boston, Apr. 1867).

[8] Oliver D. Drake: "Drake Genealogy" (unpublished MS which indicates a
vast amount of research through primary sources).

[9] *Ibid.*, p. 1.

[10] *Ibid.*

[11] *Ibid.*, p. 2.

[12] *Ibid.*, p. 3.

In 1675, he was commissioned captain of the militia, and later he was successively justice of the peace and a member of the Grand Jury. Thus, Captain Francis Drake was prominent in the early annals of the Piscataway neighborhood of New Jersey. Here he died on 23 October 1687, leaving an estate valued at several hundred pounds.[13]

Of the children of Captain Drake, two sons and a daughter, we are especially interested in John, the youngest and the great-great-grandfather of Daniel Drake. He was born about 1655, while the family was still in New Hampshire, and died in New Jersey in 1741. He became one of the organizers and the first pastor of the New Piscataway Baptist Church which he served for fifty years.[14] Not only was he the religious leader of the town but he was also a justice of the peace, legislator, assistant judge of common pleas for Middlesex and Somerset Counties. In fact he was probably the most prominent citizen of New Piscataway. His first wife was Rebecca Trotter whom he married on 7 July 1677. Of the children of this union our special interest lies in Isaac, the great-grandfather of Daniel, born 12 January 1687/8 at New Piscataway.

Isaac turned from the varied activities of his father and grandfather to devote himself to farming. This proved rewarding. In time he acquired three plantations in Essex and Middlesex Counties, New Jersey. Isaac and his wife, Hannah (Blackford) Drake, had five sons and a daughter. At his death in 1759, each of the three surviving sons was given a farm. That of the youngest, Nathaniel (1725-1801), comprised 111 acres and was part of the area upon which the town of Plainfield, New Jersey, now stands. Nathaniel, also a successful farmer, built a home which today houses the Plainfield Historical Society. On the death of his brother Daniel (1717-77), he took over a portion of the latter's property through which

[13] *Ibid.*
[14] Edwards: *op. cit.*, p. 25.

the stream, Bound Brook, ran and where there was a grist-mill.[15]

Nathaniel, like his forebears, was a staunch Baptist. A member and later a deacon (1788) of the Scotch Plains Baptist Church, he married a fellow communicant, Dorithy[sic] Rattan.[16] Of this union there were three sons who concern us: Abraham (born 27 November 1751), Cornelius (b. 20 April 1754), and Isaac (b. 18 January 1756). The year of Isaac's birth was that in which England was combating uprisings among the Bengalese in India and encountering discontent elsewhere. The stage was being set for the American Revolution. It was the year during which William Pitt (1708-78) first came into power and forced King George II to issue the latter's epochal declaration "captivating to the people." [17] America was to be aided and defended, a national militia was recommended, and the sufferings of the poor were to be mitigated. This declaration which had been written by Pitt ushered in a new era for the British empire.

That Abraham, Cornelius, and Isaac Drake must have had some schooling is shown by their ability in later years to read and write.[18] While they were growing up, momentous events were occurring. Their elders were chafing under the despotic rule of King George III (1738-1820), who became sovereign of Great Britain in 1760.

The Molasses Act of 1733 had never been enforced, but the Sugar Act of 1764 was more comprehensive and its attempted enforcement created widespread dissatisfaction. William Pitt, champion of the American colonists, was no longer in power and George III with his new advisers passed the Stamp Act in 1765. Complaints increased, cries of "taxation without

[15] Oliver D. Drake: *op. cit.*
[16] Drake: *Pioneer Life* . . . , p. 5.
[17] J. C. Long: *Mr. Pitt and America's Birthright* (New York: Frederick A. Stokes Co., 1940), p. 247.
[18] Drake: *Pioneer Life* . . . , p. 8.

representation" were heard everywhere, and open rebellion against such tyranny was advocated. The Stamp Act was repealed in 1766 because of alarm over the course of events and probably as a result of William Pitt's statement in Parliament on 14 January 1766 that he rejoiced "that America has resisted. Three millions of people, so dead to all the feelings of liberty, as voluntarily to submit to be slaves, would have been fit instruments to make slaves of the rest. . . ." [19] The grievances of the colonies were ably outlined by John Dickinson (1732-1808), lawyer, publicist, private in the Continental Army, subsequently a brigadier general, and later the leader in the foundation of Dickinson College (Carlisle, Pennsylvania). In his *Letters from a Farmer in Pennsylvania*, he wrote of excise taxes as follows:

> . . . He gets something *visible* and *agreeable* for his money; and tax and price are so confounded together, that he cannot separate or does not chuse to take the trouble of separating them.
>
> This mode of taxation is the method suited to arbitrary and oppressive governments . . .
>
> This policy did not escape the cruel and rapacious NERO . . . [20]

Dickinson's *Letters* were first published in the *Pennsylvania Chronicle* (Philadelphia) and reprinted in most of the colonial newspapers. Later, issued in book form, they became a best seller. [21]

Repeal of the Stamp Act was followed by an indirect tax approach in 1667 through the Townshend Acts. These were resisted so effectively that they also were repealed with the

---

[19] [Anonymous]: *Anecdotes of the Life of William Pitt*, (4 vols., London: J. S. Jordan, 1792), Vol. II, p. 135.

[20] John Dickinson: *Letters from a Farmer in Pennsylvania* (Philadelphia: William and Thomas Bradford, 1769, 3rd ed.), p. 49.

[21] Frank Luther Mott: *Golden Multitudes* (New York: Macmillan Co., 1947), p. 50.

exception of the duty on tea. The new Tea Act of 1773 pro-
voked the Boston Tea Party, closing of the Port of Boston in
1774, the first Continental Congress (1774), and hostilities
at Lexington and Concord on 19 April 1776.

Published 10 January 1776, six months before the Declaration of Independence, *Common Sense*, by Thomas Paine
(1736-1809), exerted a tremendous influence in its appeal for
the formation of an American republic. In rousing words
Paine stressed the multiple factors of colonial dissent, both
social and economic. He spoke "a language the people *had
felt but not thought*." It has been estimated that "within a
year probably 150,000 copies had been sold: which on the
basis of increased population, would represent a distribution
today of close to eight million copies." [22]

Nathaniel Drake was a Whig who hated despotism and
was in sympathy with colonial aims for independence. Doubtless with his encouragement, the three sons, Abraham, Cornelius, and Isaac, along with a son-in-law, Benjamin Manning, enlisted. Abraham and Isaac were privates in the New
Jersey militia.[23] It has been found impossible to determine
the number of enlistments each had or the battles in which
they were engaged. Cornelius Drake was in the Continental
line first as a private, later as a corporal. The deposition for
his pension discloses that he first enlisted on 14 February
1776 for one year.[24] He re-enlisted and continued in the Continental Army until his regiment, that of Colonel Chas. Dayton, was disbanded in 1783. Cornelius stated that he "was
present at the affair of the Short Hills in Essex County, State
of New Jersey in the year 1777, that he was engaged in the
Battles of Brandywine, Germantown and Monmouth and

---

[22] *Ibid.*, p. 51.
[23] William S. Stryker: *Official Register of the Officers and Men of New
Jersey in the Revolutionary War* (Trenton: Wm. T. Nicholson & Co., 1872),
pp. 578-79.
[24] National Archives, U.S.A., Cornelius Drake, S45336.

that he was present at the taking of Cornwallis at York-
town. . . ." Altogether there were thirty of the Drake name,
including Colonel Jacob Drake from New Jersey, who fought
in the Army of the Revolution.[25]

Lying between New York, which early (1776) fell to British arms, and Philadelphia, the first seat of government for
the Federation of the Colonies, New Jersey came to be called
the "battle ground of the Revolution." Invading and defending forces marched across the area and the invaders usually
pillaged as they went. Unquestionably, Jerseymen suffered the
devastation of war more acutely than did the inhabitants of
any other of the thirteen colonies. We hear much of the
suffering at Valley Forge but it was probably no greater there
than in the encampment of the New Jersey Militia at "the
Blue Hills," occupying a portion of the present site of Plainfield [26] to which the name "Pinch-gut" was applied during the
Revolution. Nathaniel Drake's farm bounded the Blue Hills
encampment on the east, and tradition has it that his home
was for a while the headquarters of General Washington.

Essential supplies were wholly inadequate, especially food,
clothing, and bedding. Further, the troops were paid in a
currency which by 1780 had depreciated 75 to 1, to the point
where "a soldier's pay for an entire year was worth only about
a dollar in silver." [27] Unfortunately, study of the history of
this Continental paper reveals evidence of both public and
private frauds. That there was not widespread mutiny similar
to the brief episodes of January 1781 at Morristown and
Pompton, New Jersey,[28] is indicative of unsurpassed patience,
endurance, and fortitude on the part of the troops.

[25] Stryker: *loc cit.*
[26] Cornelius C. Vermeule: *The Revolutionary Camp Ground at Plainfield,
New Jersey* (No place, no pub., 1923).
[27] Carl Van Doren: *Mutiny in January* (New York: The Viking Press,
1943), p. 34.
[28] *Ibid.*

Early in the war, Thomas Paine, using a drum for a desk and a flickering campfire for light, had written the first of his papers comprising *The American Crisis*. Almost every American will recall the opening sentences of his immortal composition:

> These are the times that try men's souls. The summer soldier and the sunshine patriot will, in this crisis, shrink from the service of their country; but he that stands it *now*, deserves the love and thanks of man and woman. Tyranny, like hell, is not easily conquered; yet we have this consolation with us, that the harder the conflict, the more glorious the triumph. What we obtain too cheap, we esteem too lightly; it is dearness only that gives everything its value. Heaven knows how to put a proper price upon its goods; and it would be strange indeed if so celestial an article as FREEDOM should not be highly rated.

With the surrender of Lord Cornwallis on 19 October 1781, the weary soldiers began to return home. Among them were the three Drake boys who found many changes upon their arrival. On 10 February 1781, Dorithy [sic] (Rattan) Drake, their mother, had died and had been buried in the Scotch Plains Baptist Church Cemetery.[29] There was now a stepmother, the former Mrs. Elizabeth Bishop, who had no love for the soldier sons and made no effort to conceal her feelings. No doubt young Isaac, always mischievous, was especially irritating because of his pranks and practical jokes. He now went to work on his father's farm and was assigned the task of tending the gristmill on the property formerly owned by his uncle Daniel.

Some four miles from Nathaniel Drake's home place there lived a farmer, Benjamin Shotwell (1731-1797), whose first wife had been Elizabeth Manning (Bonney?), the mother of his ten children. The Shotwells had been farmers for several

[29] Oliver D. Drake, *op. cit.*

generations and were members of the Society of Friends. In accordance with Quaker pacifist views, Benjamin Shotwell did not enter the army, though his sympathies were apparently with the aims of the federation since he supplied the Army of the Revolution with beef cattle. For these he was paid in Continental currency, the value of which soon vanished. He was further impoverished by the fact that after a battle which was fought in his orchard the British soldiers entered his home and "destroyed nearly all the furniture." [30]

The fifth of the Shotwell children was Elizabeth, born 20 September 1761. Five years younger than Isaac Drake, she had probably known him since childhood. Elizabeth's mother had died during the war (18 June 1777) and her stepmother, far from affectionate, was not even civil. Elizabeth Shotwell was "pretty if not beautiful," with a "most delicate" complexion, a cheerful disposition, unusual patience, piety, and fortitude.[31] Though she had little formal schooling, she possessed a remarkable knowledge of the simple domestic arts, which in those days were so necessary in the making of a home.

We know nothing of the details of Isaac's courtship but it is not surprising that he should have fallen in love with the talented Elizabeth Shotwell. Though inclined to be mischievous, he was honest, refined, dependable, "seeking an honorable place in society." As a member of the Society of Friends Elizabeth realized that in marrying outside her faith she would be "disowned." Regardless of such consequences, she and Isaac were married by the Reverend Mr. Benjamin Woodruff (1733?-1803) in the Presbyterian Church in Westfield, New Jersey, on Thursday, 8 August 1782.[32] Why they

[30] Drake: *Pioneer Life* . . . , p. 5.
[31] *Ibid.*, p. 112.
[32] William K. McKinney, Chas. A. Philhower, and Harry A. Kniffin: *Commemorative History of the Presbyterian Church in Westfield, New Jersey, 1782-1928* (Westfield, N.J.: Presbyterian Church, 1929), p. 441.

chose to marry at the Westfield Presbyterian and not at the Scotch Plains Baptist Church, several miles nearer home, is not known. As stated, Isaac's father was an influential member and later a deacon in the Baptist church. It is barely possible that Nathaniel Drake objected to his son's marriage, though the more probable reason was that the Scotch Plains Baptist Church was temporarily without a regular pastor. The Reverend Benjamin Miller, the incumbent there since 1748, had died on 14 January 1781.

Elizabeth and Isaac first occupied a log cabin near the site of the gristmill on Bound Brook where he worked. Here their first child, Phoebe, was born on 23 May 1784. Nothing is known of her except that she died on 20 January 1785 and was buried in the Scotch Plains Baptist Church Cemetery. Their next child, a boy, was born 20 October 1785. They named him Daniel Drake for his mother's eldest brother.

Three happenings during Daniel's first two and a half years he set down thus for his children:

> 1st I was *precocious*, and that too, in the feet, rather than the head, for when I was in my 8th month I could waddle across the cabin floor, when held up and led on by one hand. 2d When older & locomotive enough to totter over the doorsill and get out on the grass, as I was sitting there one day, a mad dog came along: and what do you think I did? Strangle him, as Hercules did the two big snakes which crawled so rashly into his cradle? No; more than that! I looked at the mad animal, and he thought it prudent to pass me by, and attack a small herd of cattle, several of which died from his bite! 3d As soon as I could run about I made for the mill but whether from the instinct of the anserine tribe or a leaning towards the trade of a miller, doth not appear. Whatever impulse prompted my visits, they were not without danger, and gave my mother, who had no servant, a great deal of trouble.[33]

[33] Drake: *Pioneer Life* . . . , pp. 6-7.

Isaac Drake's earnings at the gristmill were probably meager and he, Abraham, and Cornelius "were not contented with their condition, in New Jersey and thought of emigrating." [34] Concerning New Jersey at this time, John F. D. Smyth, a loyalist with the British forces there, published an account of the post-revolutionary situation in which he stated: "This province has suffered extremely by the war much more in proportion than any other; and it must be many years before it can possibly recover its former flourishing state." [35] To this situation were added the facts that land in the South and West was cheap and more fertile and that the climate was milder. Also taxes, which were high after the Revolution in the eastern states, could be avoided. Then too there were the challenge of adventure and the promise of wealth in a newly developing territory. At first the Drake brothers considered emigrating to the older portion of Virginia, but after investigation the County of Kentucky was selected because of the glowing accounts of that paradise.

In the spring of 1788 the three sons of Nathaniel Drake, together with Lydia Shotwell who was a sister of Isaac's wife, and her cousins, David Morris and John Shotwell, with their families, set out for Kentucky.[36] The journey was made in two-horse "Jersey" wagons for approximately four hundred miles to Red Stone Old Fort (Brownsville, Pennsylvania) and from there by flatboat to Limestone (now Maysville), Kentucky, on the Ohio River. Crowded into Isaac's wagon along with their furniture and other possessions were his wife, Daniel and his baby sister, Elizabeth, and Lydia Shotwell.

Although Daniel was too young to remember any details of the tiresome and dangerous journey there are contemporaneous accounts of similar ones. On 27 September 1787,

[34] *Ibid.*, p.7.
[35] J. F. D. Smyth: *A Tour of the United States* (2 vols., London: G. Robinson, 1784), Vol. II, p. 401.
[36] Drake: *Pioneer Life* . . . , pp. 8ff.

approximately six months before the Drakes started from New Jersey, Mrs. Mary Dewees had left Philadelphia. She travelled by wagon and, on 9 October 1787, wrote in her diary:

> Crossed Sidlinghill and were the greatest part of the day in performing the Journey,—the roads being so excessive steep, sidling and Stony, that it seemed impossible to get along. We were obliged to walk the greatest part of the way up, tho' not without company; there was five waggons with us all them moving to different parts. This night our difficulties began; we were obliged to put up at a Cabin at the foot of the hill, perhaps a dozen logs upon one another with a few slabs for a roof, and the earth for a floor, and a Wooden Chimney Constituted this extraordinary Ordinary. The people very kind but amazing dirty. There was between twenty and thirty of us; all lay on the floor, except Mrs. Rees, the children and your Maria, who by our dress or address or perhaps both, were favored with a bed, and I Assure you that we thought ourselves lucky to escape being flead alive.[37]

McKee's Ferry, "just below mouth of Youghiogeny which empties into the Monongahela" was reached on 18 October, 1787. At this point she took a flatboat and on 26 November 1787, arrived at Limestone (now Maysville, Kentucky) on the Ohio River.

Mrs. Dewees with about twenty other travellers left Limestone at 9:00 A.M. on November 28 and that evening arrived in Washington, only four miles south on the road to Lexington! Washington was left before daylight the following morning and by noon "Mary's Lick," eight miles away, was reached.[38] Pressing on, about four miles were covered by

---

[37] "Mrs. Mary Dewees's Journal from Philadelphia to Kentucky, 1787-1788," *The Pennsylvania Magazine of History and Biography* (Philadelphia), XXVIII: 1821-98, 1904.

[38] Mrs. Dewees should have written "May's Lick" not "Mary's Lick." Daniel Drake in *Pioneer Life in Kentucky* thought that this hamlet was named

nightfall and they encamped. "We made our bed at the fire, the night being very cold, and the howling of the wolves, together with its being the most dangerous part of the road, kept us from enjoying much repose that night. . . ."

Almost a quarter of a century later another traveller from the east encountered similar hardships. She wrote: "We found the roads bad past description,—worse than you can possibly imagine—Large stones & deep mud holes every step of the way. We were oblig'd to walk as much as we possibly could, as the horses could scarcely stir the waggon the mud was so deep & the stones so large—" [39]

Sixty years later Daniel Drake wrote of the journey: "The only incident to which tradition testifies is, that while on the Alleghenies, when descending the steep & rocky side of a mountain, I clambered over the front board of the wagon, and hung on the outside by my hands, when I was discovered & taken in, before I had fallen, to be crushed, perhaps by the wheels. . . ." [40]

The journey down the river, doubly hazardous because of Indian hostility, was made in safety. Together with the boats belonging to the Drakes and their relatives were those of the Reverend John Gano (1727-1804), which carried his thirteen children, some of them with their husbands or wives. Also with the Ganos was "Dr." William Goforth (1766-1817) whose sister had married a Gano. Goforth was presumably in flight from the "Doctors Mob" which is described in Chapter 3.

The flat boats, sometimes called "arks," in which the party descended the river were from twelve to fourteen feet

---

by the emigrants from New Jersey (p. 14). He is of course mistaken, since Mrs. Dewees passed through the village, May's Lick, more than six months before the arrival of the Drakes. Consult also the Harry Innes advertisement.

[39] Margaret van Horn Dwight: *A Journey to Ohio in 1810* (New Haven: Yale University Press, 1912), pp. 46-47.

[40] Drake: *Pioneer Life* . . . , p. 9.

wide and forty to seventy feet in length. A rude cabin in which they slept and stored such possessions as might be damaged by rain was usually built at the forward end of the boat. The loaded wagon to which the horses and other livestock were tied was usually placed near the center of the boat. Oars were rarely used, the arks merely floating along with the current guided by a rudder attached to a long pole. One of the boats belonging to the Reverend Gano "overset" and its passengers narrowly escaped. They saved their horses only by cutting their ropes.[41]

Sprightly, blue-eyed Daniel with his curly auburn hair attracted the attention of twenty-two year old "Dr." Goforth. He suggested to the parents that Daniel become a physician. This idea, implanted in their minds, seems to have struck firm roots and, with simple faith, they nourished it.

During the journey Isaac Drake sprained his ankle so severely that, on arrival at Limestone (Maysville) on 10 June 1788, he had to be carried ashore. Daniel, in later years, wrote that his father "was not very heavy: for he had in his pocket but one dollar and that was asked for a bushel of corn." [42] From Limestone, Isaac took his family to Washington, Kentucky, where they occupied "a covered pen or shed, built for sheep." While waiting for a place to settle permanently, Isaac became a teamster and is known to have hauled at least one wagonload of goods from Limestone to Lexington, a distance of sixty-six miles.[43]

[41] The Reverend John Gano wrote in his *Biographic Memoirs . . . , Written Principally by Himself* (New York: Southwick and Hardcastle, 1806), p. 118, that "We landed at Limestone on 17 June 1787." Daniel Drake stated unequivocally that the landing was made on 10 June 1788. Gano's year, 1787, is wrong since there are so many contemporary proofs to verify the 1788 date. The records of the Baptist Church at Scotch Plains, N.J., state that the Drakes were given "Letters of dismission" on 12 April 1788. The land purchased by Drake and Morris was not offered for sale until 22 March 1788.

[42] Drake: *Pioneer Life . . . ,* p. 10.

[43] *Ibid.,* p. 12.

The first and only newspaper in the West at that time was the *Kentucke Gazette,* a weekly consisting of a single sheet of three columns, started at Lexington on 11 August 1787. There appeared in it on 22 March 1788 an advertisement by Colonel Harry Innes (1752-1816) offering for sale 1400 acres of land lying on the main road leading south from Limestone and twelve miles distant.[44] This advertisement was continued almost every week until 12 July 1788.

It is evident from the advertisement that a village, "Mays

FOR SALE

A tract of land containing 1400 acres on the waters of the north fork of Licking, lying on the road from Limestone to the lower blue licks; being Mays settlement and preemp ion and includes Mays lick, good bonds on persons in this district or on persons in the Eastern, part of Virginia will be received in payment, and I will warrant the title.

tf   b 30   HARRY INNES

Fig. 1. Advertisement: "For Sale." Kentucke Gazette. March 22, 1788.

lick," existed on this boundary. The inhabitants most likely consisted of squatters, occupying cabins or sheds in the immediate vicinity of the saline impregnated spring (a "salt lick"), the source of a most important and necessary commodity.

The 1400 acres had originally been staked out by an earlier settler, William May. Subsequently it was acquired by a one-time conscientious student of medicine turned adventurer, General James Wilkinson (1757-1825), for whom Innes was acting as attorney. Wilkinson had reached Kentucky in 1781

[44] Harry Innes: "For Sale," *Kentucke Gazette* (Lexington), No. XXX: p. [1]—c. [3], Mar. 22, 1788.

where he began a series of speculations in land and commodities, court actions, and intrigues with the Spaniards for which he became notorious. Wilkinson's real estate "deals" must have been extensive. He once wrote that he had control of 1,950,000 acres and was willing to sell tracts of any extent, "not exceeding 60,000 acres." [45] On another occasion he said "I shall by next May have Patents for 100,000 Acres, which I shall be able to sell for 6d. per acre. . . ." [46]

Extensive search in the court records at Maysville, Paris, and Lexington, Kentucky, has failed to turn up a record of the deed for the transfer of this tract of land. However, an advertisement in the *Kentucke Gazette* for 7 November 1789 reveals that David Morris and Abraham Drake (acting no doubt for the others) had purchased the May tract on 15 July 1788, by giving their bond for "two hundred thirty-eight pounds eighteen shillings and six pence, Virginia currency," and wished to complete payment.[47] The tract was so divided that each section had a corner at the salt spring which was within a few feet of the main road from Limestone (Maysville) to Lexington, now U.S. Highway 68. For mutual protection against Indians, they selected the point of convergence of their tracts for the erection of their cabins.[48] The name "Mays Lick" was retained and is, at the present time, a town with a population of approximately 310.

Of the 1400, Isaac Drake could afford only 38¼ acres. Even so he was unable to make a final payment and thus obtain a deed for this small acreage until two years later, on 24 August 1790.[49] Before the arrival of winter in 1788, the

[45] Gen. James Wilkinson: "Letters of Gen. James Wilkinson addressed to Dr. James Hutchinson, of Philadelphia," *Pennsylvania Mag. of History and Biography* (Philadelphia, 1888) XII:59.

[46] *Ibid.*, p. 64.

[47] David Morris and Abraham Drake: "Notice," *Kentucke Gazette* (Lexington), III, No. IX:p. [1]—c. [4], Oct. 24, 1789.

[48] Drake: *Pioneer Life* . . . , p. 14.

[49] Deed from David Morris and Abraham Drake to Isaac Drake, dated 24

Drakes, Morrises, and Shotwells had sufficiently completed their rude cabins to permit their occupation.

Neither Isaac Drake nor his wife ever returned to New Jersey. Probably neither wished to encounter a spiteful stepmother. Nor is there evidence that there was any correspondence between the Drakes in Kentucky and their New Jersey relatives. It is known that on two occasions news from home reached them. About 1796, Manning Shotwell visited his sister, Elizabeth (Isaac's wife), and remained three weeks. Shotwell had walked from New Jersey to Pittsburgh, thence had come by flatboat to Limestone (Maysville). From that point he had walked the twelve miles to Mays Lick.[50] Shortly after the visit of Manning Shotwell, a more distinguished visitor came, the Reverend William Van Horne (1747-1807) who had been the pastor of the Scotch Plains (New Jersey) Baptist Church which the Drakes had attended. Each family entertained him in turn and, of course, he preached in the log church they had erected.[51]

Nathaniel Drake, father of Isaac, left him no portion of his estate. Nathaniel was buried in the Scotch Plains Baptist churchyard between his wives. The inscription on his tombstone reads:

> This stone is erected to the
> memory of Deacon Nathaniel
> Drake who died Octr. 2^d.
> 1801 in the 76th. year of
> his age.

Farewell good man—
A blessed subject thou of heavenly grace.
Thy life was holy and thy end was peace,

August 1790, in Deed Book A, Clerk's Office, Mason County, Maysville, Ky., pp. 159-60.

[50] Drake: *Pioneer Life* . . . , p. 221.

[51] *Ibid.*, pp. 223-24.

Thy warfare's o'er, and in good old age,
Hast thou concluded well thy pilgrimage.
What pungent grief the doleful tidings spread,
When thou wast numbr'd with the pious dead,
Insatiate death! What inroads dids't thou make
And forc'd from our embrace, our honor'd DRAKE.

2 ⚘

*It is happiness to be borne and framed
unto vertue, and to grow up from the
seeds of nature rather than the inoculation and forced grasses of education.*
Sir Thomas Browne (1605-82.)[1]

Boyhood in Kentucky, 1788-1800

REMINISCING IN his sixtieth year, Daniel Drake described his
boyhood in a series of letters to his children. Although they
were not written with any thought of publication, his son
Charles, after making many alterations and deletions, published these letters in 1870 under the title of *Pioneer Life in
Kentucky*.[2] A second edition appeared in 1907.[3] Recognizing
their unique character Mr. Henry Schuman of New York
issued a new edition on 22 June 1948.[4] The Schuman publication was edited from the original manuscript letters without alteration. Depicting the Kentucky pioneer's log cabin
and fireside in sympathetic terms, the book has become a
classic. It has been called "the greatest of all Kentucky books"
by Dr. J. Christian Bay.

Extracts from the Schuman edition of *Pioneer Life in*

[1] Sir Thomas Browne: *A True and full coppy of that which was most
imperfectly and Surreptitiously printed before under the name of Religio
Medici* (London, Printed for Andrew Crooks, 1643), p. 136.
[2] Daniel Drake: *Pioneer Life in Kentucky*. A series of reminiscential letters
from Daniel Drake, M.D., of Cincinnati, to his children. Edited with notes
and a biographical sketch by his son, Charles D. Drake (Cincinnati: Robert
Clarke & Co., 1870). Ohio Valley Historical Series, No. 6.
[3] *Ibid.*, copyright by the Robert Clarke Co., 1907.
[4] Drake: *Pioneer Life in Kentucky* (New York: Henry Schuman, 1948).

Kentucky make up the remainder of this chapter. In it Daniel
Drake describes his life in Kentucky from 1788 to 1800. The
digits which are italicized are the page numbers of the Schuman edition. The digits enclosed in brackets are the approxi-
mate dates.

15. [September 1788] . . . Now fancy to yourself a log
cabin of the size of Dove's [his daughter's] dining room—one
story high—without a window—with a door opening to the
south—with a half finished wooden chimney—with a roof on
one side only—without any upper or lower floor—and fancy,
still further, a man and two women stepping from sleeper to
sleeper (poles laid down to support the floor when [my fa-
ther] should find time to split the puncheons,) with two children—a brother & sister—sitting on the ground between
them, as joyous as you ever saw . . . and you will have the
picture which constitutes *my first memory*. The mordant
which gave permanence to the tints of this domestic scene
was a sharp rebuke from my father, for making a sort of
whooping, guttural noise (which is still ringing in my ears),
for the amusement of my sister Lizzy, then I believe about a
year old, while I was a little rising three. Thus, my first memory includes an act of discipline by my father, and well would
it have been for many who have grown up unimpelled and
uncontrolled by parental admonition, if they had been subjected in due time to a parental sway as firm and gentle as
that which presided over my childhood. . . .

24. On the morning the first duty was to ascend the ladder
which always stood, leaning behind the door, to the loft and
look through the cracks for Indians lest they might have
planted themselves near the door, to rush in when the strong
crossbar should be removed, and the heavy latch raised from
its resting place. But no attack was ever made on his [that of
my father] or any other of the five cabins which composed
the station [Mayslick].

25. I well recollect that in the spring of 1790 when I was
4½ years old . . . the Indians one night attacked a body of

travellers, encamped a mile from our village on the road to
Washington Ky. They were sitting quietly around their camp
fires, when the Indians shot among them, and killed a man
whose remains I remember to have seen brought, the next
day, into the village on a rude litter. The heroic presence of
mind of a woman saved the party. She broke open a chest in
one of the wagons with an axe, got out the ammunition,
gave it to the men and called upon them to fight. This with
the extinction of their Camp fires, led the Indians to re-
treat. . . .

28. Thro' the period of which I have been speaking & for
several years afterwards, as I well recollect, nearly all my
troubled or vivid dreams included either Indians or snakes—
the copper colored man and the copper headed snake, then
extremely common. Happily I never suffered from either (except in dread.) My escape from the latter I ascribe to cow-
ardice or, to express it more courteously, to a constitutional
cautiousness beyond the existence of which my memory run-
neth not. This original principle of my nature, which
throughout life has given me some trouble & *saved* me from
some was, perhaps, augmented by two causes. 1st For a good
while, I had no male companions. The sons of my uncles were
too old to play with me. . . . My cousin Osee Drake, uncle
Abraham's oldest daughter, afterwards Mrs. Robert Taylor,
and cousin Polly Drake, uncle Cornelius's daughter, now
Mrs. Chinn, both a little older than me, were, for 4 or 5
years, my chief companions. We agreed well for they were
good children and while they contributed to soften my manners and quicken my taste for female companionship, they
no doubt increased my natural timidity. 2^{d} My mother was,
by nature and religious education, a noncombatant and
throughout the whole period of her tutelage, that is, till I
went from home to study medicine, sought to impress on me
not to fight. Father had, constitutionally, a great amount of
caution but was personally brave and, as I can now recollect,
did not concur in the counsels of my mother.

29. The first illness I remember (and the only one in those

days) was indeed both severe and protracted. It arose from a fall on the ice (I think) and produced an inflammation with fever on the lower part of the spine. It terminated in an abscess and an ulcer that continued for a long time. I was attended by Dr. Goforth of W.[ashington, Ky.] and distinctly remember how anxious I used to feel for his visits, and at the same time, how much I dreaded his probe. On the voyage down the river, he and my father had become, as the saying is, swornfriends. Father thought him on many points a very weak man, and knew that he was intemperate, but believed him a great physician. Already when 5 years old, I had been promised to him as a student and among my remembrances of that period is my being called Dr. Drake . . . !

Soon after the settlement of Mayslick, all the people being . . . adherents to the Baptist Church, a log meeting house was built about a quarter of a mile up The Road to the South and parson Wood of Washington frequently came out to preach. He was often at my father's and used to take me between his knees and talk to me on religious subjects. At length he brought with him a catechism and when I was about 6 years old and could read a little, I was put to its study. It opened with the doctrines of the Trinity which so perplexed me that I retain a prejudice against all catechisms to this hour. This parson Wood was the father of Mrs Doctor Goforth, and I afterwards lived 4 years and a half in her family. . . .

33. The first money I ever had, as far as I can recollect, came to me in the following manner. A man (I know not who—some acquaintance of father's) had lodged all night with us, and the next morning lost a silver knee buckle (at that time an indispensable article) in the snow, near the door of our cabin. I was set to hunt for it, and father at length came to my assistance with a rake. I do not remember which found it, but I got the reward—a piece of cut money,[5]

---

[5] The money of this period in the United States had a variable and uncertain value. Change was made by cutting coins, occasionally bills, into

at that time the circulation medium of Virginia & Kentucky. My joy was unbounded, and ever since I have had it reproduced by the receipt of money. Then, it was the mere *possession* that threw me into rapture. Since I grew up, it was the idea of appropriating it to the payment of some debt that gave me pleasure. . . .

My first school master had the Scotch name of McQuitty, but whether he was from the "land o'cakes," I can not tell. He taught in a very small log cabin in sight of father's, up [34] the creek which flows through Mayslick. . . . My dim recollections suggest that I was about 5 years old when I was his pupil for a short time. . . . His successor was master Wallace, whose name again suggests a Scottish origin. Under his tuition I presume I made progress, for in 1792 and 3, I was a pretty good reader, and maintained my place respectably when we stood up to spell, before school was "let out" in the evening. My teacher then was Hiram Miram Curry. . . . I went to him as late as 1794, and had begun to write before I left him.

35. As years rolled on Father began to conclude (very justly) that he should aim at a larger farm. . . . Uncle Abraham Drake, moreover, was anxious to own the little tract on which father resided, as it so immediately adjoined his own. He had purchased 200 [36] acres of one Shannon, lying about a mile directly West of Mayslick, and offered to exchange it for the place on which father resided. A bargain was at length concluded . . . in the summer of 1794, when I was in my 9th year. . . .

This was a new era in my life. The land acquired was covered with an unbroken forest, which must be cleared away, and a new cabin erected. Father was still too poor to hire a labourer for steady work, and was, himself, far from being a robust and vigorous man. My health was good and my spirit willing—I might, therefore, render some assistance in his

---

pieces, ergo, "cut money." A silver dollar was usually divided into five pieces, each passing as a quarter. The person doing the cutting retained one piece as compensation.

new enterprise; and accordingly master Curry's hickory and myself parted, never to meet again. I was provided with a small axe—father had a larger, and a mattock for grubbing. Thus equipped, with some bread & meat wrapped in a towel, we charged upon the beautiful blue ash and buckeye grove, in the midst of which he proposed to erect his cabin.

37. Shrubs and bushes were grubbed up; trees under a foot were cut down, and those of a larger diameter "girdled," except such as would make good logs for the projected cabin, or could be easily mauled into rails. It was father's business, of course, to do the "heavy chopping;" mine, to "hack" down saplings, and cut off the limbs of trees and pile them into brush heaps. . . .

38. The brush was of course burnt up as fast as it was cut, and of all the labours in the forest, I consider that of dragging and burning the limbs of trees the most delightful. To me it made toil a pleasure. The rapid disappearance of what was thrown upon the fire gave the feeling of progress—the flame was cheering—the crackling sound imparted animation —the columns of smoke wound their way upwards, in graceful curves, among the tall green trees left standing; and the limbs & twigs of the hickory sent forth a balmy and aromatic odor, which did not smell of the school house.

[1794] In due time a "log rolling" frolic was gotten up. . . . The ground being prepared, and the logs collected and hewed on one side, the new cabin, a considerable improvement over the old, was "raised" and brought to some degree of finish; though glass could not be afforded, and a kitchen could not be put up till a stable had been first built. At length the day for removal arrived, and we left the village and public roadside . . . for the loneliness of the woods. . . . Thence forth for 6 years I passed a happy life of diversified labour. . . .

64. The *new* soils of Kentucky were not good for wheat and the weavel, moreover, in "them" days (to speak in the dialect of the field) "done" great injury to that grain. Father & mother, however, like other immigrants, longed for wheat

bread and, as soon as practicable, wheat was sown. . . . The ground had to be plowed with the shovel plow and until I was 12 years old it was my function to ride the horse & have both legs stuck with Spanish needles up to my knees. Having no shoes & stockings (superfluous things in early autumn) & tow trousers, which would slip half way up to the knees, the service was not the most enviable. After my 12th year I was able to hold the plow & guide the horse. . . .

Harvest was a social labour, a frolic, a scene of excitement and, therefore, a much more desirable era than that of seeding. My first labour in that field was to carry the sheaves to the place on which they were to be shocked. The next was to bind up the handfuls of cut wheat, a more difficult task for a small boy. My ambition was to wield the sickle. The maxim of the harvest field was that no boy becomes a good reaper till he cuts his left hand. Notwithstanding my characteristic cautiousness I cut mine several times. . . .

69. Among the labours of the latter 3 years of my country life [1797-1800] was that of mauling rails. This was generally done in winter and, although a most laborious work, I took delight in it and still recollect it with pleasure. A *green blue*-ash was my choice, for it was easy to chop and easy to split; but I often had to encounter a dead locust in the field which was a very different affair. When I was 14 I could "cut & split" 75 rails a day out of the former and from 40 to 50 out of the latter. Still I was not large for my age; but was inured to labour, and (why I cannot explain) was willing to pursue it either alone or with father. When I got [70] a tough log the wedges & "gluts" would fly out on being struck a hard blow. Gentle taps were necessary to get them well entered. I have often observed since that many failures occur, in the enterprises of human life, from want of patience in giving the gentle taps which are necessary in beginning them. . . .

83. Fond of horses, I should perhaps, have become an expert, and for one of cautious temperament an adventurous horseman, but for an event which came nigh destroying my life. I was about 11 years old when father placed me on a

young horse which was supposed to be tolerably well
"broken." He and another man were walking near me up the
lane, and presently I found them lifting me up from the
hard road. I had been thrown by the animal over his head
so suddenly that I was never able to recollect the fact. Being
very seriously injured, I was ever afterwards "afeard" of wild
and wicked horses.

84. Throughout the period [1795-97] of which I write,
Father aimed at raising horses for sale; and one of them
proved to be very fine. Not satisfied with any price offered
him at home, Father resolved to try a *foreign* market, & it
was no other than the *adjoining* county of Bourbon. There
he sold him to M^r afterwards Col. Garrard, a son of old
Governor Garrard. In part pay, he took a hundred gallons of
whiskey. When it arrived we felt quite rich. A barrel was
immediately tapped, and the "tin quart" scoured bright as
possible, and put in requisition. Our customers were of course
the neighbors, most of whom regarded it a duty to their families and visitors, not less than themselves, to keep the whiskey
bottle well replenished. For a friend to call and find it empty
was a real mortification to one party, and quite a disappointment to the other. . . .

85. The sale of the whiskey devolved largely on me. I had
learned, moreover, to write a little, and mother made a small
blank book on which I charged most that I measured out.
Thus I was once a sort of bar keeper or, at least, commenced
my mercantile career by retailing whiskey. At 7 this evening
in the midst of the letter in which I am recording this early
history, I had to lay down my pen, and deliver in the University[6] before our Physiological Temperance Society a lecture on the diseases produced by excessive drinking. I took
care not to tell the audience that I was once engaged in
selling whiskey to a whole neighbourhood, and felt very glad
when I saw a boy coming with his junk bottle or half gallon

---

[6] The University of Louisville, School of Medicine. At the time the letter
was written (1847) Dr. Drake was professor of pathology and the practice
of medicine.

jug. The price was "eighteen pence"—25 cents—a quart. The price of a yard of coarse India muslin in those days was from one & six pence to two shillings; that of a bushel of corn from 9 pence to one and thrippence . . . ![7]

93. Up to the time of my leaving home at the age of 15, my mother never had a "hired girl" except in sickness; and father never purchased a slave for two substantial reasons: *first*, he never had the means; & *second*, was so opposed to slavery that he never would have accepted the best negro in Kentucky, as a gift, provided he would have been compelled to keep him as a slave. Now & then, he hired one, male or female, by the day, from some neighbouring master (white hirelings were scarce), but he or mother never failed to give something to the slave in return for the service. In this destitution of domestic help, and with from 3 to 6 children, of which I was the oldest, you will readily perceive that she had urgent daily & nightly need of all the assistance I could give her. To this service, I suppose, I was *naturally* well adapted; for I do not recollect that it was ever repugnant to my feelings. At all events, I acquiesced in it as a matter of duty—a thing of course—for what could she [94] do—how get on—without my aid . . . ?

I have already spoken of grating and pounding corn, toting water from a distant spring, holding the calf by the ears at milking time, going to the pond on wash days, and divers other labours with which mother was intimately connected. But my domestic occupations were far more [95] extensive than these. To chop, split and bring in wood; keep up the fire, pick up chips in the corn basket for kindlings in the morning, and for light, through the long winter evenings when "taller" was too scarce to afford sufficient candles, and "fat" so necessary for cooking, that the boat-lamp, stuck into one of the logs of the cabin over the hearth, could not always be supplied, were regular labours. . . . To slop the cows,

[7] Thomas Senior Berry: *Western Prices before 1861* (Cambridge, Mass.: Harvard University Press, 1943), pp. 357 ff. This book gives the best discussion of prices of the first half of the nineteen century which I have found.

and, when wild, drive them into a corner of the fence, and
stand over them with a stick while mother milked them, was
another. Occasionally I assisted her in milking, but sister Lizy
was taught that accomplishment as early as possible, seeing
that it was held by the whole neighbourhood to be quite too
"gaalish" for a boy to milk; and mother, quite as much as
myself, would have been mortified, if any neighbouring boy
or man had caught me at it. . . .

99. I was happy in the days of childhood which I am describing, [100] and have lived long enough to find happiness
in recurring to them. . . . [101] When I look back upon the
useful arts which mother and I were accustomed to practice,
I am almost surprised at their number and variety. Although
I did not regard them as anything but incidents of poverty
and ignorance, I now view them as knowledge—as elements
of mental growth. Among them was *colouring*. A "standing"
dye stuff was the inner bark of the white walnut, from which
we obtained that peculiar & permanent shade of dull yellow
—the "Butternut," so common in these days. The "hulls" of
the *black* walnut gave us a rusty black. Oak bark, with copper
as a mordant (when father had money to purchase it) afforded a better tint of the same kind, and supplied the ink
with which I learned to write. Indigo, which cost eighteen
pence an ounce, was used for blue; and madder, when we
could obtain it at three shillings a pound, brought out a
dirty red. In all these processes I was once almost an adept.
As cotton was not then in use in this country (or in Europe)
and flax can with difficulty be coloured, our material was
generally wool or linsey or linsey woolsey. . . .

104. I became quite a nurse—[105] I like the society of
little children, and their amusements around me excite and
interest me. . . . In a log cabin, one story high, 16 by 20 feet
and without a partition, the distance from the nursery to
the kitchen is not very great; and hence I am brought by a
natural transition from nursing to cooking . . . ! [107] I
know of no scene in civilized life more primitive than such a
cabin hearth as that of my mother. In the morning, a buckeye

backlog & hickory forestick resting on stone andirons, with
a Jonny [*sic*] cake on a clean ash board, set before it to bake,
a frying pan with its long handle resting on a split bottomed
turner's chair, sending out its peculiar music, and the tea
kettle swung from a wooden "lug pole" with myself setting
the table, or turning the meat, or watching the Jonny [*sic*]
cake, while mother sat nursing the baby. . . .

109. The time *has* been (perhaps should be still), when I
looked back upon the years thus spent as *lost*. Lost as it respects my destiny in life—lost as to distinction in my profession—lost as to influence in the generation to which I belong.
But might I not have been rocked in the cradle of affluence,
been surrounded by servants and tutors, exempt from every
kind of labour, and indulged in every lawful [110] gratification, and yet have at last fallen short of the limited and
humble respectability which I now enjoy? In the half century
which has elapsed since I began to emerge from those duties,
I have certainly seen many who, enjoying all that I have
named, still came to naught—were blighted, and if they did
not fall from the parent bough, could not sustain themselves
after the natural separation, but perished when they were
expected to rise in strength and beauty. Who can tell that
such might not have been my fate? The truth is, that I was
the whole time in a school (I will not *any longer* say, of
adversity, but) of probation and discipline, and was only
deprived of the opportunities afforded by the school of letters. Great and precious as these are to him who is afterwards to cultivate literature and science, they are not the
whole. They impart a certain kind of knowledge and
strengthen the memory, but they leave many important principles of our nature undeveloped, and, therefore, can not
guarantee future usefulness or fame. . . .

111. My mother comprehended the principles of domestic
and Christian duty, and sought to inculcate them. This she
never did by protracted lectures, but mixed them up with our
daily labours. Thus my mother was always by my side, and
ready with reproof, or admonition, or rewarding smile, as

occasion required or opportunity arose. Unlike many (so
called *wiser*) teachers, she instructed me as to what was *sin.*
Her theory of morals was abundantly simple—*God has said
it!* The Bible forbids this, and commands that. . . . How
often did I, and my sisters and brothers hear that impressive
word *wicked* fall from her lips in the midst of her toilsome
and never ceasing household duties! How seldom does it fall
on the ears of many children, born under what are called
happier auspices! It was wicked to treat anything which had
life with cruelty—it was wicked to neglect the cattle or forget
the little lambs in winter—it was wicked to waste or throw
away bread or meat—it was wicked to strike or quarrel with
each other. . . . [112] It was wicked to be lazy—to be dis-
obedient—to get drunk, or to fight. . . .

119. If I were to write a recipe for making great and good
men and women, I would direct the family to be placed in
the woods—reared on simple food—dressed in plain clothes
—made to participate in rural and domestic enjoyments—allowed to range through the groves & thickets, but *required
a part of every day to give themselves up to the instruction
of competent and accomplished teachers,* till they were 14
or 16 years of age. In my case the last element was wanting;
and, therefore, you must not judge of my system by myself. . . . [120] The very loneliness of our situation led me to
seek for new society & amusement in the woods, as often as
opportunity offered. But they were, in themselves, attractive.
To my young mind there was in them a kind of mystery.
They excited my imagination. They awakened my curiosity.
They were exhaustless in variety. There was always something
ahead. Some new or queer object *might be* expected, and thus
anticipation was sustained. To go from the family fireside—
from the midst of large and little babies, and cats and kittens
—into the woods for society, may seem to you rather para-
doxical, but it was not so in fact. Familiar objects lost their
wonted effect, and we may become solitary in their midst.

But, to find men in trees, and women in bushes, and children in the flowers, and to be refreshed by them, one must

be a little imaginative, and so I was, as I *now* know, though
I did not know it then. To frequent the woods from motives
of *mere utility* is *mere occupation*, and all the feeling raised
by it is connected with business. With this also I was well
acquainted, for I was often sent to search for a tree or sapling
for some special purpose, as, to make a helve or a basket (of
which I have plaited many, & could now earn my living by
it); or bottom a chair (which I have often done); or to make
a broom (of which I have already bragged). But an excursion
in spring to gather flowers was a very different affair. I am
unable to analyse the emotions which these excursions raised
in me; but the pleasure on finding a new flower was most
decided. . . . [121] The Claytonias, Pulmonaries, Phloxes,
Trilliums. & Fringillarias, whose annual reappearance I had
greeted in each succeeding spring of my boyhood, were my
favorite subjects of botanical investigation later in life. . . .

Summer had its charm not less than spring. Its flowers, its
luxuriant herbage, its blackberries & wild cherries, its endless
variety of green leaves, its deep and cool shade, with bright
gleams of sunshine, its sluggish & half dried brooks, of which,
like other boys, I would lie down and drink (first looking out
for snakes), and then turn over the flat stones, to see if there
were any crawfish beneath. . . .

126. The "Fall," as we always called it, not less than spring
and summer, brought its sylvan scenes and pleasures . . .
and often called me to the woods . . . [127] to gather those
wild fruits which were so precious to us in the absence of the
cultivated. . . .

133. Of winter scenes in the woods, I have spoken in some
preceding letter, and will not chill you with any more. But,
as it is still autumn, you must gaze for a moment at the hues
in which the woods are so gloriously attired. . . . [134] In
this affecting display of mingled tints (which has no equal in
nature, save that sometimes made in the clouds, for a moment, by the setting sun), a living green, here and there, still
smiles upon us. The brown and withered leaves, which are already strewn around us, tell too plainly the end to which all

are hastening. They have but gone to rest, and the hand of
destiny is suspended over all. . . . [135] We may see in the
series of autumnal events the care with which God has provided for the preservation and perpetuation of the forest
races, by an endless multiplication of germs, and their dependence on the parent tree for life: on its leaves for protection, and the influence of air, to them the "breath of life";
—thus illustrating, in the midst of surpassing beauty & solemn
grandeur, the relations of child and parent, and showing all
to be the workmanship of one wise & almighty Hand. Such
are some of the autumnal lessons taught in the great school
house of the woods. . . .

143. The general rule as to my going to school was, to
attend in winter, & stay at home for work the other parts of
the year; but this was not rigidly observed. . . . I have mentioned the names of McQuitty, Wallace & Curry, as my
teachers till I was 9 years old. Father then removed from the
village and my schooling was suspended. At the time it was
broken off, I had luckily learned to read, and had begun to
write. . . . Thus I was able to make some progress at
home. . . .

In a year or two after our removal a small log schoolhouse
was erected by the joint labour of several neighbours. . . .
[144] The first teacher, who wielded the hickory mace in this
academy was *Jacob Beaden.* . . . His function was to teach
spelling, reading, writing and cyphering as far as the rule of
three; beyond which he could not go. . . . [151] My next
school master was Kenyon, a Yankee! At that time an *avis
rara,* in Kentucky. . . . Under him I made some progress. . . . [152] Continuing to cypher, I reached the "Double
rule of Three" and came at length to a sum which *neither* of
us could work. . . . Of grammar, geography & definitions, I
presume he knew nothing; still he was of superior scholarship
to Beaden. . . . Sometime afterwards I returned for awhile to
the old sylvan Academy, which now had a new Domino—
Master *Smith.* . . . [153] With him, I began my classical
studies. True, he knew nothing of grammar, etymology, geog-

raphy, or mathematics; but he had picked up a dozen lines of Latin poetry, which I had an ambition (carried out) to commit to memory. I was much taken with the sounds of the words—the first I had ever heard beyond my native tongue. From the few I now recollect, I presume the quotation was from the eclogues of Virgil. Master Smith changed his locality, and another long vacation ensued. . . .

156. My next and last tutor before beginning the study of medicine, was my old Master Smith, who now *ruled* the boys and girls in another log school house, under a great shell bark hickory among the haw trees. . . . To him I was sent, more or less, through the spring, summer, & early autumn of the year 1800, when I was in my 15th year. As my destiny to the profession of medicine was now a "fixed fact," I was taking the finishing touches; and yet spelling, reading, writing, and cyphering constituted the *curriculum* of Master Smith's college. . . .

160. In the midst of this last effort, however, a family affliction arose, which greatly interrupted my studies. Father got a severe injury to his foot . . . and three or four of the children were taken down with the ague & fever. . . . When the care of *every* thing turned on mother and myself, my heart grew big with the emotions which such calamities naturally inspire. The feeling of responsibility that was quite natural produced in my actions their proper fruits. . . . What a precious reward (referring to this life only) there is in striving to do what trying occasions require of us. As old age is ruminant, youth ought to prepare for it as many savory cuds as possible. . . .

161. Of our own *library* I have already spoken incidentally. A family Bible, Rippon's Hymns, Watts' hymns for children, the Pilgrims [162] progress, an old Romance of the days of Knight Errantry, primers, with a plate representing John Rogers at the stake, spelling books, an arithmetic & a new almanac for the new year, composed all that I can recollect. . . . When I was 12 or 13 years old, Father purchased of a neighbour . . . a copy of Love's Surveying, which I well

remember afforded me great pleasure. . . . Another book
which fell into my hands (I can not tell how) . . . was
Guthrie's Grammar of Geography. . . . [164] I feel grateful
to Mr. Guthrie for his patient teachings of so dull a pupil,
and would like to meet him again.

Before I fell in with the Grammar of Geography, I was
advanced from Dilworth's to Webster's spelling book. I was
greatly interested in the new & hard words, and in the
new reading it afforded. . . . A couple of years, or there-
abouts, before leaving home, I got Entick's (a pocket)
dictionary which was, of course a [165] great acquisition. I
also obtained Scott's lessons, which afforded me much new
reading, and I used to "speak" pieces from it at Master
Smith's school, when I went to him the second time. In
addition (but not to my school library), father purchased
I remember (when I was 12 or 13) the Prompter, Esop's
Fables, & Franklin's Life—all sterling books for boys. . . .
A puzzle growing out of the last was his being called doctor,
when he had not studied physic!

Occasionally, father borrowed books for me of Dr Goforth. Once he brought me the Farmer's Letters, a work
by Dickinson. . . . Much of it was above my comprehen-
sion. . . . Another book from the same source . . . was Lord
Chesterfield's Letters to his son, inculcating politeness. This
fell in mighty close with my tastes, and not less with those
of father and mother, who cherished as high and pure an
idea of the duty of good breeding as any people on earth.
. . .[8] [167] The Life of Robinson Crusoe (greatest of Auto-
biographies) was among my early readings. I have not read
it for 45 or 50 years, but long and often *threaten* to do it
yet. . . .

170. As to my actual attainments in learning, they were

[8] Since the original edition of Chesterfield's *Letters to His Son* contains a
curious commingling of etiquette with dissimulation and immorality, Drake's
opinion was undoubtedly based on an expurgated edition, probably that of
1775 by Dr. John Trusler which was reprinted at Portsmouth, New Hampshire, in 1786. Samuel Johnson said: "Take out the immorality, and it should
be placed in the hands of every gentleman."

certainly quite limited, & yet I could read & examine a dictionary for the meaning of words, & here is the starting point of all improvement. . . .

189. All the first settlers of Mays Lick were, either by association or profession, Baptists, and had belonged to the Church at Scotch Plains, of whom the Revd William Van Horne was the worthy pastor. At what time after their immigration, a house of public worship was erected, I do not remember, but recollect to have attended public worship in Mr. Morris' barn. It happened that most of the Jersey & Virginia families, around the village, were likewise [*190*] Baptists, & therefore it was the predominant sect. Hence all my early ideas of Christian doctrine, worship & deportment, were derived from that denomination. The "Meeting House," as it was always called, was built on a ridge a quarter mile south of the village, hard by the great road leading to Lexington. A couple of acres surrounding it constituted the "burying ground" for the station and its neighbourhood. . . .[9]

236. The long talked of project—that of "making me a doctor"—had at length been finally settled in the affirmative. I was [*237*] to enter on the study in a few months with my cousin, Dr John Drake, whose education was then nearly completed, and whose genius was only equalled by his great moral purity. With this prospect before me, he was taken ill in July with typhus fever, and died in August. This was my first disappointment, and a real misfortune to me, for *he* would have been a *good* preceptor, and I could have studied at home, & thus saved father an expense which he was in no way prepared to meet. He courageously persevered, however, in his cherished purpose, and I had to submit; although (on his account) I would have preferred being bound to a trades man; and had actually selected a master, Mr Stout, of Lexington, a sadler, to whom some of my cornfield companions had already gone.

But my preparatory education was not yet completed.

[9] All traces of the "Meeting House" have disappeared but the Mays Lick Cemetery adjoining it is on "the great road," now U.S. Highway 68.

. . . As a reader, I was equal to any in what I regarded as the highest perfection—a loud & tireless voice. . . . In [238] chirography I was *so so*, in geography obscure, and in history, o. In arithmetic, I had gone as far as the double rule of 3, practice, tare & tret, interest, and even a fraction in decimals. My greatest acquirement—that of which I was rather proud—was some knowledge of Surveying, acquired from Love (I mean to name the Author as well as my taste), but which I have long since forgotten. Of grammar I knew nothing, and unfortunately there was no one within my reach who could teach it. . . .

239. Meanwhile . . . other arrangements were making for the life before me, such as knitting socks, making coarse India muslin Shirts instead of tow linen, providing a couple of cotton pocket hand kerchiefs, and purchasing a white roram hat (which to my grief, was stolen in less than a month after I reached C.)[10]

Father visited Dr Goforth in Cincinnati and on his return, [240] announced that all was arranged, and that I was to go down before the setting in of winter. I was to live in the Doctor's family, and he was to pay $400, provided I remained, as it was expected I would, four years, by which time, I was to be transmuted into a doctor, as I should then be 19! My whole time, however, was not to be given up to the study of medicine; for the D^r was to send me to School for two quarters, that I might learn Latin. But as was sagely decided, it was not to be done *before* I began the study of medicine, but at some future time. . . .

241. I was fond of study, but not passionately so, and if I had any aspirations, they were not intense, and several circumstances conspired to countervail them. 1st I had looked into the medical books of my cousin, and found them so learned, technical, & obscure, that I was convinced my education was too limited. 2^d My father was too poor to pay for what he had undertaken, and was too ailing to dispense

[10] The roram hat, also spelled "rorum," was in vogue from about 1790 to 1840. These hats were made of a heavy woolen material faced with fur.

with my labours on the farm. . . . 3ᵈ I was a great home-body; had never been out of the family more than a day or a night "at a time"; felt timid about going among strangers in a town, and mingling with the "quality." Finally, I was distressed at the idea of an absence of 4 or 5 months. At length, all arrangements were made. . . .

243. The morning of the 16 Decʳ 1800 at length arrived, and the parting came with it. Lizzy was 13, Lydia 10, Benʲ 6, Lavinia 3 or 4, & Livingston about one. There we all were in the cabin where more than half had been born, where I had carried the younger ones in my arms, and amused them with the good old cow brindle, as she drank her slop at the door while mother milked her. . . . The parting over, we mounted, and I took a farewell look at the little cabin, then wiped my eyes. . . .

Our first halt, at noon, was in a village of a dozen cabins [244] and 2 or 3 frames, called Germantown, where we stopped to feed, and dine at Dʳ Donaphan's. . . . After dinner we put off, and passing in the next 14 miles a few solitary cabins, by night reached Leathers' cabin and ferry, on the banks of the river Ohio opposite the mouth of Bull Skin creek. . . .

Mʳ Leathers' pennsylvania dutch Hotel consisted of a log cabin of one room, which was made to answer for bar, dormitory, refectory, and family apartments. . . . [245] In the hope of reaching C. [Cincinnati] the next day, we made an early start. The river was about as high as it is now, and abounded in cakes of floating ice. I had not been on it before since I could remember, and had not yet learned to swim. Our ferry boat was of small size, and my fears were very large. Our crew consisted of the old man & his daughter, a good looking, rosy faced damsel of 16 or 17. They toiled and twisted and dodged. My confidence increased as the voyage continued. We approached the shore of Ohio, and I (greatly delighted) escaped the perils of the deep. . . .

We mounted, and not only left the water, but the valley in which it flows. Our first halt was at Bohannon's, which was

about 12 or 14 miles. There we dined & fed. We had not
passed a house on the way. . . . Next, we halted and refreshed at John's mill on 15 mile creek. . . . Then we came
to the mouth of the little Miami, and had to travel up it a
mile, before we could ford it. . . . A mile further brought
us into the then village of Columbia, and also brought twilight. . . . In the center of the place was a tavern, kept [246]
in a two story log house, and we "put up" for the night.
. . . At daylight next morning we were off, intending to
breakfast at Dr Goforth's. It rained, and the mud had
become deep. Between the lower end of Col.[umbia] and
the upper end of Cin.[cinnati] (below Deer Creek bridge),
there were two cabins. . . . We passed the post office . . .
and made our way to Peach Grove [home of "Dr." Goforth].
. . . Father remained a day, when to my dismay, he took
leave of me, and I took to Chesselden's [*sic.*] Anatomy.[11]

[11] William Cheselden (1688-1752), English surgeon and author of the
widely used *Anatomy of the Human Body*. In England, thirteen editions
appeared between 1713 and 1792. It was translated into German in 1790.
There were at least two editions of Cheselden published in the United States:
1795 and 1806.

3 ꙮ

Know the true value of time; snatch, seize, and enjoy every moment of it. No idleness, no laziness, or procrastination: never put off till tomorrow what you can do today. Lord Chesterfield: "Letters to his son," Dec. 26, 1749.[1]

Becoming a Physician, 1800-06

IN 1800 WHEN Daniel Drake, a lad of fifteen, began the study of medicine, the concepts of Galen (130-200 A.D.) and other classical and medieval physicians were to a considerable extent still given credence. In Great Britain, even as late as the 1830's, Celsus' (53 B.C.-7 A.D.) *De medicina,* which has passed through more than fifty separate editions since the first printing in 1478, was one of the texts upon which the candidate in medicine was examined. Medical examining boards required a knowledge of Celsus, partly to acquaint the student with a medical classic and also, since it was in Latin, to "exact from young gentlemen destined for the medical profession a more respectable and liberal education." [2]

The ancient "fathers" in medicine largely disregarded disease entities, about which they knew little, to concentrate on the theoretical changes in body fluids, i.e., humoralism. They

[1] In H. L. Mencken: *A New Dictionary of Quotations* (New York: Alfred A. Knopf, 1942), p. 587. Search has revealed similar admonitions but none with the exact wording used by Mencken. (Concerning Chesterfield's *Letters,* see reference 8, Chapter 2.)

[2] Aulus Cornelius Celsus: *On Medicine, in eight books,* Latin and English, translated by Alex. Lee (2 vols., London: E. Cox, 1831), Vol. I, p. vii.

believed that disease arose when the four humors—blood, phlegm, yellow bile, and black bile—became defective or improperly mixed. Some there were who opposed humoralism and argued verbosely that disease was the result merely of an imbalance between constriction and relaxation in the tissues (solidism). The pulse was meticulously studied in order to determine the humoral or other changes. The Englishman Sir John Floyer (1649-1743) went so far as to believe, as did the Chinese, that there was a unique pulse for each disease— that even the sex of the unborn child might be determined by carefully studying the character of the mother's pulse! [3]

The well-known time lag between an epochal scientific discovery and its general acceptance is well illustrated by that of the circulation of the blood. Prior to William Harvey (1578-1657), physicians thought that the blood ebbed and flowed as the tides. In 1616, Harvey began teaching and proved experimentally that the blood was propelled by the heart in a circular pathway through the body. Although his epoch-making book[4] announcing and proving his discovery was published in 1628, a quarter of a century elapsed before Harvey's teachings were generally accepted.

In the seventeenth century, Thomas Sydenham (1624-89) re-emphasized the Hippocratic approach through clinical observation and personal experience. This "English Hippocrates" added noteworthy clinical descriptions of many diseases though he adhered to humoral teachings. In the eighteenth century, William Heberden, Sr. (1710-1801) unequivocally rejected the prevalent fantastic doctrines of the pulse and enunciated modern concepts.[5]

The leaven of Harvey's discovery had been working during

---

[3] Emmet F. Horine: "An Epitome of Ancient Pulse Lore," *Bulletin of the History of Medicine* (Baltimore) X:209-49, July 1941.

[4] William Harvey: *Exercitatio Anatomica de motu cordis et sanguinis in animalibus* (Francofurti: Guilielmi Fitzeri, 1628).

[5] Horine, *op. cit.*, p. 248.

the latter half of the seventeenth and the whole of the eighteenth centuries. A new concept of the physical origin of disease and its treatment (iatrophysics) had begun to emerge. These ideas along with the new chemical concepts (iatrochemistry) began to replace the ancient ones. The older physicians did not readily accept the newer ideas and some sought a way out by evolving fanciful theories to explain the nature of disease. Thus Drake's pupilage began at a time when the ancient doctrines were being slowly discarded. Out of the confusion there was developing an independence of thought and action which initiated the spectacular and revolutionary changes distinguishing the nineteenth century.

Throughout the early colonial period few physicians were graduated in medicine. It has been estimated that even at the time of the Revolution fewer than 400 of the more than 3500 practitioners held degrees in medicine.[6] By the beginning of the nineteenth century the proportion of those holding degrees to those without them had probably been greatly reduced as the result of the suspension of the few medical schools in America during the Revolution.

The plan of medical training customarily followed at this time was an arrangement whereby the young doctor-to-be spent a considerable period of apprenticeship under some established and successful older physician. Under this "preceptorship" plan, at the end of four or more years, the student was thought to have absorbed the necessary knowledge and he then assumed the title of "doctor." Medical examining and licensure regulations were enacted generally at a much later date. It may be stated in passing, however, that the City of New York should be given credit for inaugurating such regulations (1760) in the United States,[7] followed by

[6] Joseph M. Toner: *Contributions to the Annals of Medical Progress and Medical Education in the United States* (Washington: Government Printing Office, 1874), p. 106.

[7] New York: *The Colonial Laws of* . . . (Albany, 1894) Vol. IV, pp. 455-56.

Louisiana in 1770,[8] and New Jersey in 1772.[9] In order to begin practice the young "doctor" obtained a quantity of calomel, Peruvian bark and a few other drugs, saddlebags, and a horse. He then announced the location of his "shop" which would be open at all hours except when he was out on calls. Due to the shortage of practitioners, especially west of the Allegheny Mountains, patients soon came. Judging by the record of many of the men trained under the preceptorship plan it was by no means ineffectual as will be evident by the accomplishments of Drake and of others who could be cited.

William Goforth, Drake's preceptor in the village of Cincinnati, was born in New York City in 1776. Like so many other physicians of his day Goforth held no degree although he had grown up in one of the few American cities of this period which could boast of a medical college. The Medical Department of King's College, which later became Columbia University, had been established in 1769 but was suspended during the Revolution and was not re-organized until 1792. During this interval, in 1783, Goforth began the study of medicine in the office of Joseph Young (1733-1814), a graduate of the Medical Department of the University of New York and a prominent New York physician.[10] He had been one of the surgeons in the Army of the Revolution and was the author of a book on astronomy which had two appendices, one on physiology and the other on treatment.[11]

Later Goforth studied anatomy and surgery under Charles

[8] Douglas C. McMurtrie: "A Louisiana Decree of 1770 Relative to the Practice of Medicine and Surgery," *New Orleans Medical Journal*, 86:7-11, July 1933.

[9] Francis R. Packard: *The History of Medicine in the United States* (Philadelphia: J. B. Lippincott Co., 1901, pp. 462-64.

[10] "Historical Account of the Medical Department of the University of New York," *New York Medical Journal*, VII:312 (1828).

[11] Joseph Young, M.D.: *A New Physical System of Astronomy . . . To which is Annexed a Physiological Treatise* (New York: Geo. F. Hopkins, 1800).

McKnight (1750-91), a graduate (A.M., 1774) of Princeton and an army surgeon during the Revolution. McKnight's preceptor had been William Shippen Jr. (1736-1808). About 1790, McKnight successfully operated on a case of extra-uterine pregnancy.[12] This operation antedated by nineteen years the ovarian operation performed by the Danville, Kentucky, surgeon, Ephraim McDowell (1771-1830) and preceded by thirty-seven years the first successful Caesarian section in the United States. As mentioned, Young held a degree in medicine but McKnight practiced without one. Yet, judging by their publications and the success attending their efforts, they were both well grounded in the principles of medicine and surgery.

Goforth had probably completed the course of study for the practice of medicine by 1788, and may have planned to locate in New York City. Then the celebrated "Doctors Mob" occurred which markedly influenced his future. Prior to the last quarter of the nineteenth century when prejudice against anatomical studies waned, such investigations were greatly hampered by laws which restricted the procurement of corpses. In accordance with an early law in Massachusetts, only those killed in a duel or those executed for such a homicide could be dissected. Judges in some of the other states were allowed to decree dissection as part of the death sentence. Upon consent of the owner, the body of a slave dying from natural causes might be used for anatomical studies. The resulting scarcity of anatomical material necessitated the use of devious methods for the procurement of bodies, such as theft of corpses recently interred. The "resurrectionist" (grave robber) might be the college or hospital janitor, although often it was the student himself, or even the pro-

---

[12] Charles McKnight: "Case of Extra Uterine Abdominal Foetus Successfully Extracted by an Operation," *Memoirs of the Medical Society of London*, IV:342-47 (London: Charles Dilly, 1795).

fessor of anatomy. In mid-April 1788, a boy whose mother had recently died, climbed a ladder to peep into the window of a New York hospital. He saw several students dissecting a cadaver which he took to be that of his mother. Rushing to his father, a stonemason employed nearby, he described what he had seen. The father and a large party of fellow laborers, armed with their tools, stormed the hospital, destroying books, skeletons, laboratory apparatus, and furniture. The corpses, they carted away for reburial. Four of the suspected "body snatchers" were caught by the mob and would, no doubt, have been seriously injured, possibly killed, had they not been rescued by the mayor of New York, the sheriff, and others. For protection the anatomists were placed in jail over night. The following day, the rioters besieged the jail and visited "every physician's house in town." [13] The militia had to be called out and it was three days before the rioters could be dispersed and then only after many casualties and the loss of several lives.

Goforth, either during or immediately after his contact with the mob, fled to New Jersey. There he joined his brother-in-law, John S. Gano, who with his father's family, the Drakes, and some other relatives were preparing to start for Kentucky. Drake once mentioned that Goforth left New York as a result of the mob but furnished no details.[14]

"Dr." Goforth began the practice of medicine at Washington, the second largest town in the District of Kentucke then a part of Virginia. He married a daughter of the prominent Baptist minister in Washington, the Reverend William Wood.

In the meantime Goforth's father had emigrated to Columbia, near Cincinnati, and in 1799 "Dr." Goforth moved there.

[13] Jules C. Ladenheim: "The Doctor's Mob of 1788," *Journal of History of Medicine and Allied Sciences* (New York) V:23-43, Winter 1950.
[14] Daniel Drake: *Discourses . . . before the Cincinnati Medical Library Association* (Cincinnati: Moore & Anderson, 1852), p. 38.

In the spring of 1800, Cincinnati's most popular early physician, Richard Allison (1757-1816), left and Goforth took over his home, "Peach Grove," as well as his extensive practice. Drake described "Dr." Goforth as having

> The most winning manners of any physician I ever knew, and the most of them. Yet, they were all his own, for in deportment he was quite an original. The pains taking and respectful courtesy with which he treated the poorest and humblest people of the village, seemed to secure their gratitude; and the more especially as he dressed with precision, and never left his house in the morning till his hair was powdered by our itinerant barber, John Arthurs, and his gold-headed cane was grasped by his gloved hand. His kindness of heart was as much of a part of his nature, as hair powder was of his costume; and what might not be given through benevolence, could always be extracted by flattery, coupled with professions of friendship, the sincerity of which he never questioned. In conversation he was precise yet fluent, and abounded in anecdotes, which he told in a way that others could not imitate. He took a warm interest in politics of what was then the North Western Territory, being at all times the earnest advocate of popular rights. . . .[15]

Cincinnati or Losantiville, as it was originally named, was twelve years old in 1800 when Daniel Drake arrived as its first student in medicine. It was the site of a palisaded United States stronghold, Fort Washington, established in 1789 as a base for operations against the Indians in the Northwest Territory, i.e., northwest of the Ohio River. At times the garrison outnumbered the citizens and, as a matter of fact, for many years the name Fort Washington was more frequently used to designate the settlement than Cincinnati. The population in 1800, exclusive of the garrison which varied greatly, was estimated at 600. The town had but a single brick home,

[15] *Ibid.*, p. 39.

on the northwest corner of Fifth and Main Streets; all others were of logs or of simple frame construction. "The great eastern mail was brought once a week from Maysville, Kentucky, in a pair of saddle-bags." [16] There were two newspapers, *Freeman's Journal* and *The Western Spy and Hamilton Gazette*, until March 1800, when the former was moved to Chillicothe, the newly designated capital of the territory.

The "doctors" at the time, in Cincinnati proper, in addition to Goforth, were Robert McClure, John Sellman (1764-1827), and John Cranmer (Dranmore?, died 1832). In the immediate vicinity was John C. Winans who announced in *The Western Spy and Hamilton Gazette* for 17 December 1800, that: "Lately arrived from Elizabeth Town, New Jersey, with a general assortment of medicine, he respectfully tenders his service to the public in the line of his profession as physician and surgeon. Those who may have occasion, and are disposed to call on him may find him at the Rev. Mr. Kamper, on Turtle Creek, where he has opened shop, and is now in a capacity to serve &c." In this same issue of the *Spy*, 17 December 1800, appeared the latest news "By Monday's Mail," i.e. of 15 December. "The Foreign Intelligence" was dated from 19 September to 10 October and the American news was as late as 22 November 1800. The news included the speech delivered on that date "before both houses in congress in the senate chamber" by President John Adams.

On 20 December 1800 Daniel Drake started his medical studies:

> My first assigned duties were to read Quincy's Dispensatory and grind quicksilver into *unguentum mercuriale;* the latter of which, from previous practice on a Kentucky hand mill, I found much easier of the two. But few of you have seen the genuine, old Doctor's shop of the last century; or regaled your olfactory nerves in the mingled odors which, like in-

[16] *Ibid.*, p. 29.

cense to the God of Physic, rose from brown paper bundles, bottles stopped with worm-eaten corks, and open jars of ointment, not a whit behind those of the Apothecary in the days of Solomon; yet such a place is very well for a student. However idle, he will be always absorbing a little medicine; especially if he sleep beneath the greasy counter. . . . It was my alloted task to commit to memory Chesselden [*sic*] on the bones, and Innes on the muscles, without specimens of the former or plates of the latter; and afterwards to meander the currents of humoral pathology, of Boerhaave and Vansweiten; without having studied the chemistry of Chaptal, the physiology of Haller, or the Materia Medica of Cullen.[17]

From these statements it would appear that Goforth's library was meagre and that he had no skeleton with which to teach osteology. It also seems quite unlikely that he suggested any dissecting. Perhaps his experience with the mobs which dispersed the students of anatomy in New York in 1788 had been sufficient to deter him from taking risks in a new community.

Studies were frequently interrupted by the necessity of performing many other tasks, in fact doing anything the preceptor wished. As part of Drake's duties he was expected to feed, water, curry, and saddle the horse, as well as watch and sweep the "shop."

It was my function during the first three years of my pupilage thus to put up and distribute medicines over the village. . . . In this distribution when my preceptor was, I may say, the principal physician of the village, fleetness was often necessary to the safety of patients; and as there were no pavements, the shortest way through a mud-hole, seemed to boyish calculation the best, and although half a century has rolled away, such is the influence of early impressions, that I have not yet gotten rid of the conviction. . . .[18]

[17] *Ibid.*, pp. 55-56.
[18] *Ibid.*, p. 54.

The prices at which these medicines were sold, differed widely from those of the present day. Thus an emetic, a Dover's powder, a dose of Glauber's salt, or a night draught of Paregoric and Antimonial Wine, *haustus anodynus* as it was learnedly called, was put at twenty-five cents, a vermifuge or blister at fifty, and an ounce of Peruvian bark at seventy-five for pale and a dollar for the best red or yellow. On the other hand personal services were valued very low. For bleeding, twenty-five cents—for sitting up all night, a dollar, and for a visit, from twenty-five to fifty cents, according to the circumstances or character of the patient. . . .[19]

Every physician was then a country practitioner and often rode twelve or fifteen miles on bridle paths to some isolated cabin. Occasional rides of twenty and even thirty miles were performed on horse-back, on roads which no kind of carriage could travel over. I recollect that my preceptor started early, in a freezing night, to visit a patient eleven miles in the country. The road was rough, the night dark, and the horse brought for him not (as he thought) gentle; whereupon he dismounted after he got out of the village, and, putting the bridle into the hands of the messenger, reached the patient before day on foot. The ordinary charge was twenty-five cents a mile, one-half being deducted, and the other paid in provender for his horse, or produce for his family. These pioneers, moreover, were their own bleeders and cuppers, and practiced dentistry not less, certainly, than physic—charged a quarter of a dollar for extracting a single tooth, with an understood deduction if two or more were drawn at the same time. . . .[20]

Goforth began the use of vaccination against smallpox as soon as he heard of its value, only three years after the publication by Edward Jenner (1749-1823) of his epochal book.[21] Drake gives the story with simple directness:

[19] *Ibid.*, p. 53.
[20] *Ibid.*, p. 52.
[21] Edward Jenner: *An Inquiry into the Causes and Effects of Variolae Vaccinae* (London: S. Low, 1798).

To Dr. Goforth the people were indebted, for the introduction of the Cow-pock, at an earlier time, I believe, than it was elsewhere naturalized in the West. Dr. Benjamin Waterhouse, of Boston, had received infection from England in the year 1800, and early in 1801 Dr. Goforth received it, and commenced vaccination in this place [Cincinnati]. I was myself one of his first patients, and seeing it has extended its protecting influence through fifty years, I am often surprised to find medical gentlemen shying off from a case of smallpox.[22]

Drake is not correct in his belief that Goforth deserved sole credit for the introduction of vaccination in the West. At Lexington, Dr. Samuel Brown (1769-1830) and "Dr." Frederick Ridgley (1757-1824) had in May 1801 vaccinated two young men.[23] In January 1802, "Dr." Isaac E. Gano of Frankfort, Ky., reported that he would in a few days "be prepared to inoculate any number." [24] François A. Michaux (1770-1855), who was in Lexington during the first week of August 1802, stated that the people there were indebted to Dr. S. Brown "for the introduction of cow-pock. He has already vaccinated upwards of a hundred and fifty people at Kentucky. . . ." [25]

In 1802, John Stites, Jr., who had studied medicine in Philadelphia under Dr. Charles Caldwell (1772-1853), located in Cincinnati and formed a connection with Goforth. Thus Stites became one of Drake's teachers and introduced him to the memoirs and other writings of Caldwell as well as to the "fresh and captivating works of Professor Rush." [26]

[22] Drake: *Discourses . . .* p. 40.
[23] John Bradford: Editorial concerning vaccination, *The Kentucky Gazette* (Lexington), XIV, No. 766:p. [2]—c. [4]. May 25, 1801.
[24] Isaac E. Gano: [Letter], "From the Guardian of Freedom. To the Public." *The Kentucky Gazette* (Lexington) XV, No. 804:p. [2]—c. [2-3]), February 12, 1802.
[25] F. A. Michaux: *Travels to the West of the Allegheny Mountains . . . in the Year 1802* (London: B. Crosby and Co. 1805), p. 160.
[26] Drake: *Discourses . . . ,* p. 45.

The uniquely egotistical Charles Caldwell became, in later years, a teacher in Transylvania University, Lexington, as will be mentioned elsewhere in this book.

The teachings of Benjamin Rush were widely accepted by physicians in Europe, though for many years Goforth derided them. He even forbade Drake's reading the few of Rush's works in his library. Later, when Drake had access to the newer volumes by Rush which Stites furnished him, Goforth evinced surprise at the knowledge acquired by his pupil.

After Stites left Cincinnati in 1803, Goforth began to rely more and more on Drake and, on 18 May 1804, made him his partner.[27] This partnership added to Drake's responsibilities without offering commensurate returns. On 31 July 1804, Drake wrote his father that their practice had increased rapidly and that they *charged* from three to six dollars per day, but it was doubtful whether more than a fourth could be collected. He continued:

> The Doctor trusts everyone who comes as usual. I can get but a small share in the management of our accounts, or they would be conducted more to our advantage. . . . An execution against the Doctor, for the medicine he got three years since, was issued a few days ago, and must be levied and returned before the next general court, which commences the 1st of September. This execution has thrown us all topsy-turvy. . . . I am heartily sick and tired of living in the midst of so much difficulty and embarrassment. . . . I get but little time to study now-a-days, for I have to act the part of both physician and student, and likewise assist him every day in settling his accounts.[28]

Drake's first known entrance into civic affairs occurred in October 1804 when with thirty-five prominent citizens he

---

[27] *Ibid.*, p. 56.
[28] Mansfield: *Memoirs* . . . , p. 63.

signed, with a flourish, a petition addressed to President Jefferson. It was pointed out that the condition of the Indians in the West might be ameliorated by the propagation of Christianity among them. Hitherto, missionaries had accomplished little because of distrust but as agents of the government their message would carry greater weight. Should the President adopt the suggestion, the Reverend William Wood was recommended "as a person well qualified for this purpose." Among prominent persons signing the petition were Edward Tiffin (1766-1829), physician, clergyman, first governor of Ohio, and surveyor-general of the Northwest Territory; David E. Wade, prominent early pioneer from New Jersey; General Henry Lee (1758-1846), lawyer and Kentucky pioneer; General John S. Gano, one of the founders of Columbia, Ohio; the Reverend John W. Browne, early minister and publisher of Cincinnati; and Drake's preceptor, William Goforth.[29]

The financial affairs of the firm of Goforth and Drake had improved somewhat by November 1804. Then Drake wrote his father that although money was scarce, improvement could be expected shortly: "We have plenty owing."

Early in 1805, Drake decided it was time to seek further training in medicine at the University of Pennsylvania. As Drake prepared to leave, Goforth, unsolicited, gave his first Cincinnati pupil a certificate of proficiency, probably the first medical "diploma" issued west of the Alleghenies:

> I do hereby certify that Mr Daniel Drake has pursued under my direction for four years, the study of Physic, Surgery, and Midwifery. From his good Abilities and marked Attention to the Prosecution of his studies, I am fully convinced, that he is well qualified to practice in the above branches of his Profession.

[29] Original petition owned by The Henry E. Huntington Library and Art Gallery, San Marino, Cal.

Wm Goforth, Surg^n Gen^1 1st Division, Ohio Militia. Cincinnati, State of Ohio, August 1st 1805.[30]

Where Drake obtained the money with which to defray his expenses in Philadelphia is not definitely known. No doubt he received aid from his father. There were also undoubtedly funds accruing from the partnership with Goforth. Mansfield states that Drake received some money "from a Mr. Taylor, of whom he always spoke with gratitude and kindness." [31] This was probably Robert Taylor of Mason County, Ky., who had married Drake's cousin, Osee, oldest daughter of his Uncle Abraham.[32]

Drake reached Philadelphia on 9 November 1805, after a journey of eighteen days on horseback. Mansfield states that his funds were so low he was unable to pay for more than four courses of lectures, those of Professors Rush, Woodhouse, Wistar; and Physick.[33] In this respect, as in so many others, Mansfield is in error. Drake specifically mentions the fact that he signed Professor Barton's register "in the Fall of 1805." [34] Benjamin Smith Barton (1766-1815) was professor of materia medica, botany, and natural history, subjects of special interest to Drake. It seems most unlikely that he would have failed to take advantage of instruction in these subjects. If additional proof were needed, the "Common place-book" begun by Drake on "Jany 22nd 1805 [6]" discloses many quotations from the lectures of Barton.[35]

With five other students Drake lodged with a Mrs. Brown, where board including candles, firewood, etc., cost five dollars per week. This was the usual cost for accommodations. His

[30] Property of the University of Cincinnati, College of Medicine.
[31] Mansfield: *op. cit.*, p. 66.
[32] Drake: *Pioneer Life* . . . , p. 28.
[33] Mansfield: *op. cit.*, p. 67.
[34] Drake: *Pioneer Life* . . . , p. 158.
[35] Daniel Drake: *"Medical diary, or Common place-book,"* "Philadelphia. Jany 22nd 1805 [6]." Original owned by the National Library of Medicine.

roommate was from Brunswick, New Jersey, but his name is not known. Of his classmates from Kentucky three are known: John Todd, a second cousin by blood and an uncle by marriage of Mrs. Abraham (Mary Todd) Lincoln; Bernard Gaines Farrar, Sr. (1784-1849), later the first president of the Missouri Medical Society of St. Louis; and William H. Richardson (died 1845), who located in Lexington, and became professor of obstetrics, diseases of women and children in the Medical Department of Transylvania University. Another classmate, William Paul Crillon Barton (1786-1856), a graduate of Princeton, was mentioned as being especially friendly. In the graduating class, though attending the same lectures with Drake, were William Potts Dewees (1768-1841), afterwards professor of midwifery in the University of Pennsylvania, and Benjamin Winslow Dudley (1785-1870), who in later years was to be associated with Drake as one of the professors in Transylvania University, Lexington.

With unusual energy and endurance, Drake took advantage of his precious opportunities, as is evident in a letter to his parents:

> I try not to lose a single moment, seeing I have to pay so dear for leave to stay in the city a few months. . . . I attend the lectures, and then study till two in the afternoon. After dinner apply myself closely to book; call for candles, and sit up till one, sometimes two, in the morning. . . . I only sleep six hours in the twenty-four. . . . I had not money enough to take a ticket at the Hospital library, and therefore had to borrow books. Several of my fellow-students, Dr. Dewees and Dr. Barton, were very kind to me in this way. . . . I go to different churches every Sunday. . . . The play-house has been open ever since the last of November. I have only been once, and shall only go once more while I stay here.[36]

[36] Mansfield, *op. cit.*, pp. 68, 69.

It is impossible to judge the degree to which Drake's sensitive and discerning nature was stimulated by his experience in Philadelphia. Possibly Benjamin Rush (1745-1813) made the most profound impression. Rush was a graduate of the University of Edinburgh (M.D. in 1768), a signer of the *Declaration of Independence*, early professor of chemistry and later of physiology and the practice of medicine in the University of Pennsylvania. He had the reputation of being one of the best lecturers of his day. Although sometimes referred to as the "Sydenham of America," Rush, apparently steeped in medieval tradition, did not carry on the traditions of the justly celebrated English clinician. Instead, Rush believed in the *unity of disease* and taught that, regardless of apparent differences, there was but one underlying disease.[37] He also insisted that there was but one type of fever consisting of twelve states which must be treated heroically with depletive drugs and repeated bloodlettings. The accomplished American medical philosopher and teacher, Elisha Bartlett (1804-55), stated that Rush's theory was "not merely abstract, gratuitous and unintelligible, but in direct and manifest opposition to all common sense, to all true philosophy, and to all correct observation."[38]

When Drake went to Philadelphia in 1805, Rush was in his sixtieth year and at the zenith of his career. A few years before he had won an important victory in his suit for libel against his detractor, William Cobbett (1763-1835), and he occupied the most important medical post in the University of Pennsylvania. Although Rush's dogmas of the unity of disease and of fever did not long endure, his writings on insanity, his insistence upon the noncontagiousness of yellow fever, and his advocacy of the necessity for the removal of decayed

---

[37] Benjamin Rush: *Medical Inquiries and Observations* (4 vols, 5th ed., Philadelphia: M. Carey & Son), Vol. III, pp. 1-36.

[38] Elisha Bartlett: *An Essay on the Philosophy of Medical Science* (Philadelphia: Lea & Blanchard, 1844), p. 225.

teeth have stood the test of time. Despite an exceedingly complex personality, difficult of analysis, as his autobiography reveals, he was a great man and, from all accounts, a convincing lecturer. The first paragraph of Rush's "Introductory Lecture" of 21 November 1805, to which Drake listened, strikes a modern note:

> Man is said to be a compound of soul and body. However proper this language may be in religion, it is not so in medicine. He is, in the eye of a physician, a single and indivisible being, for so intimately united are his soul and body, that one cannot be moved, without the other. The actions of the former upon the latter are numerous and important. They influence many of the functions of the body in health. They are the causes of many diseases; and if properly directed, they may easily be made to afford many useful remedies. Under the impression of this belief I shall employ the time allotted for an introductory lecture, in pointing out the utility of a knowledge of the faculties and operations of the human mind to a physician.[39]

In Drake's "Common place-book" there are occasional quotations from lectures given by Philip Syng Physick (1768-1837), professor of surgery, by his assistant, John Syng Dorsey (1783-1818), and by James Woodhouse (1770-1809), professor of chemistry. William Shippen (1736-1808) had been professor of anatomy, surgery, and midwifery since the inception of the medical school in 1768 and, on 23 January 1792, Caspar Wistar (1761-1818) was appointed his adjunct. On 5 June 1805, surgery was separated from anatomy and midwifery, with Wistar continuing as adjunct to Shippen, the professor of the two latter subjects. Judging by Drake's notes, Shippen occasionally lectured though it appears that the bulk

[39] Benjamin Rush: *Sixteen Introductory Lectures* (Philadelphia: Bradford and Innskeep, 1811), pp. 256-73: Lecture XI, "On the Utility of a knowledge of the faculties and Operations of the Human Mind, to a Physician."

of the teaching devolved on Wistar. Interesting among Drake's comments is the following:

> Feby 14th 1806. We this day saw the female organs of generation, elegantly prepared by Dr. Chovet—The woman died during the act of coitios [*sic*] & the fimbries [*sic*] of the right fallopian tube is grasping the ovarium very firmly— This preparation, together with many others purchased of Dr. Chovet's heirs & many superbly colored engravings presented by Dr Fothergill belongs to the Pennsylvania Hospital.[40]

The lectures closed early in March 1806 and Drake with three classmates, John Todd, William H. Richardson, and Bernard G. Farrar, Sr., began their return journey to Kentucky. Reaching Pittsburgh, they secured a flatboat in which to descend the Ohio to Maysville, Ky. Having been taught to cook by his mother in their Kentucky cabin and having a "repugnance to a disorderly kitchen and dirty cooks," Drake was easily persuaded to take over the scullery. In later life he related another incident of the voyage down the river.

> When we were approaching Maysville, we began to dress up and prepare for landing. Each put on his best clothes, and I recollect that your friend, Dr Farrer [*sic*] especially exerted himself, because, as I suppose, he had relatives in the neighborhood of the town. I also put on *my best coat*—that is—my *coat*, worn on a horseback journey of 18 days in the fall— for four months in Phil^a, and over the mountains to Pittsburg in the spring, to say nothing of cooking in it through a flatboat voyage of 10 days. The contrast it made with theirs gave me a feeling of mortification, which I have occasionally *recollected* ever since.[41]

Acting as cook on a flatboat voyage was probably a unique experience for a medical student but a restricted wardrobe

[40] Drake: "Medical diary. . . ."
[41] Drake: *Pioneer Life* . . . , p. 106.

was not. In later years, having become the most widely
known physician in the West, Drake no doubt recalled his
early embarrassment when he wrote:

> [19 January 1848, reception in home of Dr. Samuel D.
> Gross, Louisville, Ky.]
> I wore my new clothes. How amazingly cheering it is to
> be dressed up now and then! The *philosophy* of *dressing* is
> not better understood than many other philosophies. To
> understand it well, a man must have been a poor boy, and
> known the happiness conferred by an occasional new wool
> hat, or new pair of brass "slee' buttons"—price nine pence;
> and having known this, possess the means and time to dress
> up occasionally in after life. . . .
> It appeared to me that I was better dressed than any other
> gentleman in the room and I had a good opportunity for
> judging. While they were busy, talking with each other, I
> now and then took a walk up and down the long drawing
> room, in a natural kind of way, as if I were thinking of some-
> thing important, so that they should not surmise my object.
> While doing so, I carelessly glanced at the great opposite
> mirrors and was thus able to compare my image with that of
> each of the party. Being a little (I hope not unjustifiably)
> elated by this comparison. . . .[42]

Having been separated from his parents and relatives for six
years, Drake doubtless found it only logical to open his "shop"
at Mays Lick in Kentucky. Here he began in April 1806.
Widely known, he soon acquired an extensive practice. It was
at Mays Lick that Drake observed an epidemic which he
described as "A fever of the typhous or typhoid kind attended with bilious symptoms, which prevailed in every house
in the village, and in many in its vicinity." After briefly allud-
ing to the topography of Mays Lick, he recorded fifteen
clinical observations, then discussed the weather during the

[42] *Ibid.,* pp. 222-23.

course of the epidemic and finally enumerated the insects observed. These notes were embodied in a letter to his former teacher, Dr. Benjamin Smith Barton, then editor of *The Philadelphia Medical and Physical Journal.* Barton published the communications under the title, "Some Account of the Epidemic Diseases which prevail at Mays-Lick, in Kentucky." [43] This was Drake's first contribution to medical literature. Original in concept and giving proof of keen powers of

---

X. *Some Account of the Epidemic Diseases which prevail at Mays-Lick, in Kentucky. In a letter to the* EDITOR, *from Dr.* DANIEL DRAKE.

TO fill up this sheet, I will copy from my common-place-book some observations on the topography and diseases of that part of Kentucky in which I lived, after my return from Philadelphia, till about three months ago. The village in which I lived is 12 miles from the Ohio. It is remote from any marsh, pond, or considerable stream of water; the land is fertile and rolling; the

---

Fig. 2. *Daniel Drake's earliest published contribution to medical literature.*

observation, it was the first of a series culminating in his exhaustive and monumental treatise on the diseases found in the Mississippi Valley which will be described later.

Thus Daniel Drake, less than seven years after his first contact with medical science, was already a successful practitioner as well as an author and was moving quickly along the road that was to lead him to a position of pre-eminence among American physicians.

[43] Daniel Drake: "Some Account of the Epidemic Diseases which Prevail at Mays-Lick in Kentucky," *The Philadelphia Medical and Physical Journal,* III, Part I: 85-90 (1808).

The young physician is not aware how soon his elementary knowledge—much of which is historical and descriptive, rather than philosophical—will fade from his mind, when he ceases to study. That which he possesses can only be retained by new additions.[1]

Cincinnati, 1807-14

THAT DRAKE was happy at Mays Lick, among relatives, friends, and the scenes of his boyhood is certain. He constantly followed the precepts given in the above quotation. Not only was he reviewing and adding to his fund of medical knowledge but he continued the study of Latin and English literature.

Since his preceptor, "Dr." Goforth, owned no human skeleton and the textbook in his library on anatomy (Cheselden) had only ten illustrations of the bones, Drake's knowledge of the human osseous system must have been meagre. He was too poor during his stay in Philadelphia to have purchased a human skeleton even had one been available, an unlikely possibility at that period. About 1795, the corpse of a vagrant discovered in the edge of a wooded tract near Mays Lick was buried where found. More than ten years later, after his return from his first course of medical lectures at the University of Pennsylvania, Drake one night surreptitiously opened the shallow grave and removed the skeleton, all that

[1] Daniel Drake: *Practical Essays on Medical Education, and the Medical Profession* (Cincinnati, Roff & Young, 1832), p. 61. A facsimile edition was issued in 1952 by the Johns Hopkins Press.

remained of the vagrant. Drake's thirst for knowledge was rewarded though his act, according to the stringent Kentucky statutes against anatomical studies at the time, might have brought a penitentiary sentence. A long-time friend, associate, and great admirer of Drake, Dr. George W. Bayless (1816-73), once told of the above incident, though he erroneously assumed its occurrence at an earlier date.[2]

Though happy in his work at Mays Lick, Drake's ambitions prompted a desire to relocate in a larger and faster growing community. Mansfield states that in the summer of 1806, he formally proposed partnership with his preceptor, "Dr." Goforth, in Cincinnati.[3] It has been impossible to verify this statement; certainly nothing came of it. Although Cincinnati's busiest and leading physician, Goforth's restless spirit demanded a change of location, the third in his brief career. Enamored of French customs, he decided to move in 1807 to Louisiana, purchased from France by the United States only four years earlier.

Goforth was "fond of schemes and novelties." For years he had been a patron to those seeking precious metals in the Northwest Territory. His gullibility was as great as his generosity, since he entertained the prospectors until the specimens were analyzed—the specimens included fool's gold and other minerals of no greater value. The exportation of ginseng (*aralia quinquefolium*) to China attracted his attention and again money was lost.[4]

At considerable expense in 1803, Goforth excavated at Big Bone Lick, Ky., a large assortment of bones of prehistoric animals, bones of great archaeological interest and of con-

---

[2] G. W. Bayless: *Reminiscences of the Medical College: being an Introductory Address* . . . *October 1st, 1866* (Louisville: Courier Steam Book & Job Printing Establishment, 1866), p. 42.

[3] Mansfield: *Memoirs* . . . , p. 70.

[4] Drake: *Discourses* . . . , p. 41.

siderable value.* The collection was later trustingly placed in the hands of "that swindling Englishman, Thomas Ashe, alias, Arville, who sold them in Europe and embezzled the proceeds."[5] Thomas Ashe (1770-1835) wrote, among other works, a book of *Travels in America*[6] and *Memoirs and Confessions,*[7] each containing obvious plagiarism, the grossest exaggerations, and many falsehoods. In his *Travels,* Goforth, who entertained Ashe in Cincinnati, is cited several times (p. 203: "a very skilful physician, and a true lover of learning and science"; pp. 206, 213, and 214). There is no mention of the mammoth bones. Ashe in his *Memoirs* has "forgotten" Goforth entirely and brags of the successful visit to the United States:

> I made a magnificent collection of stupendous bones; I conquered every difficulty that lay in my way; arrived at New Orleans, and embarked for Liverpool, with six tons weight of the first-rate curiosities ever heard of carefully packed on board. To acquire them, I spent the whole of my eleven hundred pounds, and traversed countries, and navigated waters, to the extent of ten thousand miles.[8]

Arriving at Liverpool, Ashe had trouble with customhouse officials which finally necessitated disposal of the bones "for the miserable and contemptible sum of two hundred pounds."[9] It appears that the collection of bones was ex-

---

* These Pleistocene mammals have been classified as *mammut americanum* (pleistocene mastodon), *elephas primigenius* (small Siberian mammoth), and the *elephas calumbi* (large American mammoth).

[5] *Ibid.,* p. 41.

[6] Thomas Ashe: *Travels in America, Performed in 1806* (Newburyport: Wm. Sawyer & Co., 1808).

[7] Captain [Thomas] Ashe: *Memoirs and Confessions . . .* (3 vols., London: Henry Colburn, 1815).

[8] *Ibid.,* Vol. II, pp. 207-8.

[9] *Ibid.,* Vol. II, p. 215.

hibited at the Liverpool museum since Ashe wrote a fanciful and garbled description of them.[10]

On 1 December 1806, Caspar Wistar, Jr., on behalf of the American Philosophical Society, wrote Goforth requesting that information be given to the president of the society, Thomas Jefferson, concerning the mammoth bones. Goforth's reply,[11] in which he described the collection and mentioned having "unfortunately entrusted them to the care of a person . . . ," is his only extant writing I have located with the exception of the previously mentioned "diploma."

In the spring of 1807, Goforth went to Louisiana where he was

> . . . appointed a parish judge, and subsequently elected by the Creoles of Attacapas to represent them in forming the first Constitution of the state of Louisiana; soon after which he moved to New Orleans. During the invasion of that city by the British, he acted as surgeon to one of the regiments of Louisiana volunteers. By this time his taste for French manners had been satisfied, and he determined to return to this city [Cincinnati] which he had left in opposition to his friends and patients. On the first of May, 1816, he left New Orleans, with his family on a keel boat; and on the 28th. day of the next December, after a voyage of eight months, he reached our landing. He immediately reacquired business; but in the following spring he sunk under hepatitis, contracted by his summer sojourn on the river.[12]

Goforth's departure from Cincinnati furnished Drake with an opportunity which he immediately seized. On 10 April

---

[10] Th. Ashe: *Memoirs of Mammoth, and Various other Extraordinary and Stupendous Bones, or Incognita* (Liverpool: G. F. Harris, 1806).

[11] [Zadok Cramer]: *The Navigator, Containing Directions for Navigating the Ohio and Mississippi Rivers* (12th ed., Pittsburgh: Cramer & Speer, 1824), pp. 204-6. The Goforth communication appeared originally in the eighth ed. (1814) of *The Navigator*. It is in each subsequent edition, up to the twelfth, the latest one available to me.

[12] Drake: *Discourses . . .* , p. 44.

1807, he became a Cincinnatian, and was welcomed by the many friends made during his previous residence. Within a short time his practice became extensive. Despite the demands of his profession, he participated in an unbelievable number of extraprofessional activities.

With other young men he formed an amateur theatrical group and the Cincinnati Debating Society. Nothing has been found concerning the activities of these groups but probably the outgrowth of the latter was the Cincinnati Lyceum. Drake's first address before the Lyceum was entitled "Observations on Debating Societies & the Duties of the Members," delivered in 1807.[13] Even so early in his career, the address exhibited evidence of an unusual ability to assemble facts logically and present them with clarity and cogency.

Practically every member of the Lyceum attained local fame and three of them, in addition to Daniel Drake, became national figures. In this group was John McLean (1785-1861), lawyer, postmaster general of the United States (1823-29), associate justice of the U.S. Supreme Court (1830), and, later, a candidate for the presidency. Another member was Thomas Sidney Jessup (1788-1860), a lieutenant of infantry in the War of 1812, quartermaster general of the army (1818), and a brevetted major general ten years later. Joseph Gilbert Totten (1788-1864), graduate (1805) of West Point, an expert in military engineering who attained the rank of major general, an authority on conchology, one of the first regents (1846) of the Smithsonian Institution, and, in 1863, was named by Congress as one of the corporate members of the National Academy of Sciences. Totten had come to Cincinnati as secretary to his uncle, Captain Jared Mansfield (1759-1830), who had, on 1 November 1803, been appointed surveyor-general of the Northwest Territory with orders to

---

[13] Daniel Drake: "Observations on Debating Societies," MS owned by the Historical and Philosophical Society of Ohio in Cincinnati.

continue the systematic survey of the area northwest of the Ohio River.

Through friendship with Totten, Drake visited in the home of Captain Mansfield whom he came to regard as a foster father. Jared Mansfield, after graduating from Yale College, taught mathematics, navigation, and the classics there, and later at Philadelphia. He entered the U.S. Army, Corps of Engineers, with the rank of captain. For over a year he was acting professor of mathematics at West Point, whence to Cincinnati, Ohio.

It was in Captain Mansfield's home at Ludlow's Station, just outside of Cincinnati, that Drake met Harriet Sisson (1787-1825). She was a niece of Captain Mansfield, the daughter of James and Sarah (Mansfield) Sisson.

> In person she was of middle stature or rather less, with a comely though not beautiful form, but erect, elastic and dignified: In countenance animated, forceful, expressive; free from affected looks and gestures; inclining to an aspect of honest and native pride. The great charm of her presence was simplicity. . . . Her opportunities for acquiring knowledge, particularly scholastic learning, had been limited; but her observation of those about her and of society was acute and discriminating. . . .[14]

Thus Drake described the woman to whom he was married at the home of the Mansfields on Sunday, 20 December 1807, by the Reverend James Kamper, after a courtship which was "not coy, nor formal, nor protracted. . . . Our marriage was from love; our love from mutual respect and esteem." [15]

Reminiscing after her death, Drake wrote:

[14] Daniel Drake: "Emotions, Reflections and Anticipations, 1826-27," MS destroyed by his son, Charles D. Extracts were quoted in the biographical sketch of the 1870 edition of *Pioneer Life in Kentucky*.

[15] *Ibid.*, pp. xiv-xv.

We began the world in love and hope and poverty. It was all before us, and we were under the influence of the same ambition to possess it; to acquire not wealth merely, but friends, knowledge, influence, distinction. We had equal industry and equal aspirations. She devoted herself to every duty of her station, and might have been a model to those much older and, in bodily powers, much abler than herself. . . . Her mind was highly inquisitive, and she soon manifested a rising interest in my studies and literary pursuits. . . . She seldom wrote, but soon manifested that she was an excellent judge of composition. She not only sat at my side conversing, more or less, while I wrote at various times the most I have written, but my constant practice was to exhibit to her inspection whatever I wrote. She saw the first draughts [sic] and criticized with taste, judgment, severity, and love. We were thus together personally and spiritually, in most of my domestic hours. When abroad for social enjoyment, we seldom were without each other. I had no separate social or sensual gratifications, no tavern orgies, no political club recreations, no dissipated pleasures nor companions. Society was no society to me without her presence and co-operation.

. . . .

We journeyed much together. At various times we had traveled with each other more than five thousand miles by land and water. This was not all. Many years ago she began to ride with me in my gig while I was engaged on professional business, and this practice had at last grown into a confirmed habit. It was a daily custom—a sort of afternoon recreation, and was often kept up till bed time. In the coldest nights of winter she sometimes traversed with me the town and its vicinity in every direction. . . . When asked where was her home, she often answered, "In the gig."

A more devoted mother never lived. The love of her offspring was at once a passion and a principle. After her husband, all her solicitude, her ambition, and her vanity were for her children. She loved them tenderly—she loved them practically, but she loved them with discretion, and was jealous of whatever could impair their qualities, manners or physical constitution. Her tenderness was without frailty, her fondness without folly, her care without sickliness. Her affection begat vigilance, and modified the indulgence which maternal love too often sanctions, to the ruin of its object. . . .[16]

Drake's studiousness, imagination, ability, and laudable ambition would certainly have insured success, but without doubt he was greatly stimulated and assisted by his wife. It is regrettable that so small a fragment of the 214 manuscript pages he wrote concerning her has been saved. His son, Charles D., might well have altered the extracts, since we have proof of the liberties he took with the letters in his father's *Pioneer Life in Kentucky*.[17] As I have said elsewhere, "it is tragic that Daniel Drake's immediate descendants, while revering him, seem not to have realized his full stature nor the interest of posterity in every memento of him." [18]

Although Drake recognized the limitations of his wife's scholastic training, he appreciated her interests and abilities which had led her to read widely in the classics including Homer, Vergil, and Ovid in addition to Milton, Johnson, and many other writers. She had musical talent sufficient to be in demand at parties. She painted in oils as evidenced by the fact that in 1818 Drake had requested John D. Clifford of Lexington, Ky., to purchase paints for his wife either in Philadelphia or London.[19] I have been unable to locate any canvases which can be attributed to her.

The children of Daniel and Harriet Sisson Drake, three of

[16] *Ibid.*, pp. xiii-xvii.
[17] Drake: *Pioneer Life in Kentucky*, pp. ix, 30, 222-23.
[18] Emmet F. Horine: "Daniel Drake and the Missing Lincoln Letter," *Manuscripts* (New York), IX:31-34, Winter 1957.
[19] Daniel Drake: ALS to William H. Richardson, June 24, 1818. Owned by the Presbyterian Historical Society, Philadelphia.

whom will be mentioned later, were: Harriet, born 24 October 1808 and died 20 September 1809; Charles Daniel, b. 11 April 1811, d. 1 April 1892; John Mansfield, b. 1 July 1813, d. 5 February 1816; Elizabeth Mansfield, b. 31 May 1817, d. 9 November 1864; Harriet Echo, b. 19 July 1819, d. 9 September 1864.

Throughout his life Drake was an indefatigable student and made use of even the briefest intervals between many pressing duties. "It has happened, not unfrequently, that he was found sitting by his wife with an infant in one hand and writing with the other, by the dim light of a dipped candle. . . . Fixed hours of study he could not have, and many of those in which he accomplished most, were at the midnight time. . . ." [20]

From 1807 through the year 1839, when Drake left Cincinnati to accept a professorship in the Louisville Medical Institute (now the School of Medicine of the University of Louisville), he was either the leader or an active participant in every movement of importance for the improvement of Cincinnati. Sir William Osler (1849-1919), the eminent book collector, student of the history of medicine, erudite teacher, and clinician, once wrote that Drake "founded nearly everything that is old and good in Cincinnati." [21]

In 1808, Drake became one of the subscribers to a proposed circulating library, a project which had its inception on 13 February 1802. He was greatly interested in the library movement, and, at the first meeting of the subscribers on 2 January 1809, he acted as chairman. [22] An application to the General Assembly of Ohio for a charter was not favorably acted on until 1812 and it was not until 1814 that the Circulating

---

[20] Mansfield: *Memoirs* . . . , p. 111.

[21] Sir William Osler: *Aequanimitas with other Addresses* (3rd ed., Philadelphia: P. Blakiston's Son & Co., 1932), p. 307.

[22] Daniel Drake, Chairman, Library, *Liberty Hall and Cincinnati Mercury*, V, No. 215:p. [3], Jan. 5, 1809.

Library of Cincinnati was opened with Daniel Drake as its president.[23]

Early in the last century many physicians in the United States operated drug stores. Thus it was no innovation for Drake to announce the opening on 2 May 1810 of a drug store under the firm name of Daniel Drake & Co. The "company" was at this time his sixteen-year old brother, Benjamin, who had made his home with Drake since 1807.[24] The firm must have prospered because, within five months, it was necessary to secure a larger building. Groceries, paints, surgical instruments, stationery, and books (school, medical, and philosophical) were stocked in addition to drugs.[25] On 28 September 1811, announcement was made that Daniel Drake & Co. "had purchased the drug store of Mr. David C. Wallace" which would be operated in addition to the original establishment. The various advertisements of Daniel Drake & Co. reveal the extent to which barter was used at this period, since "whiskey, tallow, beeswax, lard, black or Virginia Snakeroot, Seneca Snakeroot, country linen and sugar" were accepted in lieu of cash. Cincinnati at this time had a population of 2500 but supported the two establishments owned by Drake in addition to the Philadelphia Cash Drug Store operated by Robert Harris, Jr.[26]

Not content with professional, civic, and commercial pursuits, Drake was at the same time actively engaged in the preparation of a book which proved to be the foundation of

[23] [Daniel Drake]: A *Systematic Catalogue of Books belonging to the Circulating Library Society. To which are prefixed an historical preface, the Act of Incorporation* (Cincinnati: Looker, Palmer and Reynolds, 1816).

[24] Daniel Drake & Co. [Ad.], *Liberty Hall* . . . (Cincinnati), VI, No. 284: p. [3]—c. [2], May 2, 1810.

[25] Daniel Drake & Co., [Removal], *ibid.*, VI, No. 303:p. [3]—c. [4], Sept. 12, 1810.

[26] Daniel Drake & Co. [Ad.], *ibid.*, VII, No. 358: p. [3]—c. [4], Oct. 2, 1811.

Fresh Drugs & Medicines.

DANIEL DRAKE & CO.

HAVE juft received from Philadelphia, and are now opening, near the court-houfe, oppofite the Wheat-Sheaf Hotel, an

EXTENSIVE ASSORTMENT OF GENUINE

Drugs & Medicines,

which they offer for fale at the moft reduced prices for cafh *only.*

Among the other articles, are cloves, cinnamon, mace, nutmegs, tamarinds, fago, tapioca, Pruffian blue, oil of juniper, red precipitate, Venice turpentine, and a variety of patent medicines.

As they intend procuring regular fupplies, they will be able and happy to furnifh country practitioners, (whofe remote fituations render their purchafing at Philadelphia inconvenient) with whatever they may want of medicines, furgeon's inftruments, or fhop furniture, and are determined to do it on fuch terms as will make it unneceffary for them to import.

N. B. The fubfcriber continues to keep his fhop for practice at the ufual place, where he is very anxious to fee all thofe indebted to him.

DANIEL DRAKE.

Cincinnati, May 2, 1810.   849

Fig. 3. Advertisement. Liberty Hall (*Cincinnati*), *Vol. VI, No. 284: p.* [3]*-c.* [2], *May 2, 1810.*

his international reputation. As early as 1808, he had begun a careful record of observations of meteorological phenomena and a detailed study of the vegetation in the vicinity of Cincinnati. The book which bore the simple title, *Notices Concerning Cincinnati,* was thus based on meticulous personal

observation.[27] Drake's early biographer, and his cousin by marriage, Edward D. Mansfield (1801-80), even accused him of always having *"too great a regard to accuracy."* [28] Mansfield himself was somewhat careless in writing and though trained as a lawyer seems not to have appreciated the scientific ideals and honesty of Drake.

Notices Concerning Cincinnati was the *first* book with a medical section to be printed west of the Allegheny Mountains, the *first* comprehensive account of a midwestern town, and the *first* to list the indigenous plants. The "Prefatory Remarks" are dated 1 May 1810, and the first section of twenty-eight pages with a four-page appendix was published either on, or a few days before, 18 June 1810. In the appendix there is under the heading "New Disease" the *first* description of a hitherto undescribed local malady, now called trembles or milk sickness.*

In each copy of the first part of the *Notices*, so far examined, there is the following notation in Drake's handwriting: "The printing of the Sect. of memoranda respecting our diseases is postponed for a few months." However, almost a year elapsed before the second section appeared.[29] In it there was a description of the town, its population, its diseases, and other features. It is unlikely that more than one or, at the most, two hundred copies of *Notices Concerning Cincinnati* were printed. Today it appears that only eight complete

[27] Daniel Drake: *Notices Concerning Cincinnati* (Cincinnati: John W. Browne & Co., 1810).

[28] Mansfield: *Memoirs* . . . , p. 110.

* Milk sickness (trembles), now quite rare, affects animals as a result of poisoning by white snakeroot (*Eupatorium urticaefolium*), or the rayless goldenrod (*Aplopappus heterophyllus*). The disease is transmitted to man and many other animals through ingestion of milk, butter, and flesh of those poisoned. The mother of Abraham Lincoln died of milk sickness.

[29] Extracts from the second portion of *Notices Concerning Cincinnati, The Western Spy* (Cincinnati), I, June 1, 1811:p. [3]—c. [2-3].

NOTICES

CONCERNING

CINCINNATI.

———◆———

BY DANIEL DRAKE.

———◆———

CINCINNATI:

PRINTED FOR THE AUTHOR,

AT THE PRESS OF JOHN W. BROWNE & CO.

———◆———

1810.

Fig. 4. Title page of Daniel Drake's first book.

copies are in existence.[30] Although this was a limited edition, intended solely for distribution among his friends, several reviews appeared. One stated: "The present composition is replete with information concerning the physical constitution of the new and rising state of Ohio. We hope the industrious and ingenious author will continue his researches; for, from one who has done so well, we naturally expect more. . . ." [31] Isaac G. Burnet (1784-1856), editor of *The Ohio Centinel* (Dayton), on the other hand quipped: "We advise the doctor to annex a glossary to the next edition. What is more disgusting than pedantry?" [32] Today, most writers would, I believe, dismiss any such sarcasm as an effort to gain attention. But not Drake! He instantly reacted with a scathing retort which revealed him as a master of invective. This is the first controversy in which Drake is known to have participated, and it should be noted that he entered the lists only upon provocation. He wrote:

> Your ill nature, sir, seems very much to have outstripped your judgment, when you apply the epithet *pedantic* to a *necessary* use of certain words.
>
> Pedantry certainly consists in the misplaced or untimely use of words or criticism and not in the proper employment of either. If this were not the case, the Lawyer, the Mathematician, the Astronomer and every other man of science, to avoid the lash of pedantic satirists, would be obliged to cease using the terms necessary to express the principles of his science, and seek for vulgarisms. If one science abounds in technical expressions beyond another, its votaries are not necessarily pedants. . . . Unless, therefore, you show, that in the article alluded to, there are *more* scientific terms than are requisite to convey to Botanists the information intended,

[30] Report from the Director of the Union Catalog, Library of Congress, supplemented by the author's investigation.
[31] *The Medical Repository* (New York), 3rd Hexad, II:169-75(1811).
[32] [Isaac G. Burnet, editor]: *The Ohio Centinel* (Dayton), I, No. 11: p. [3]—c. [1], July 12, 1810.

your criticism must fall to the ground, neither its incivility nor its lampoon can hold it up.

The pamphlet, sir, which has given you so much offense, was not written to instruct the people, nor to waste the time and energy of newspaper reviewers. It was designed for distribution among gentlemen attached to physical researches, by whom alone its merits and demerits can be appreciated.[33]

The editor of *The Ohio Centinel* attempted further criticism,[34] as did one of his friends;[35] but Drake again replied with devastating effect.[36] An anonymous admirer, "Justice," defended Drake.[37] The controversy finally ended in abject defeat for the editor.[38]

Drake was apparently never reluctant to call attention to errors whenever found. This trait may have been in part due to his predilection for debate but it was also the result of his love of truth. In a section captioned "Science" in *The Port Folio* (Philadelphia),[39] Drake pointed to several errors made by the celebrated French professor of history and traveler, Count C. F. C. de Volney (1757-1820), in his *View of the United States*.[40] These errors were based partly on statements made by Thomas Jefferson (1748-1826). Drake admitted his temerity in disagreeing with such authorities as Count de

---

[33] Daniel Drake: To Isaac G. Burnet, Esq., *Liberty Hall* . . . (Cincinnati), VI, No. 295:p. [3]—c. [2], July 18, 1810.
[34] [Isaac G. Burnet, editor]: *The Ohio Centinel* I, No. 14: p. [3]—c. [2-4], Aug. 2, 1810. No. 16:p. [3]—c. [2-3], Aug. 16, 1910. No. 18:p. [3]—c. [3-4], Aug. 30, 1810.
[35] *Ibid.*, No. 20:p. [3]—c. [2-4], Sept. 13, 1810.
[36] Daniel Drake: To Isaac G. Burnet, *Liberty Hall* . . . , VI, No, 299: p. [1]—c. [4] and p. [2]—c. [1-2], Aug. 15, 1810. No. 304: p. [3]—c. [1-2], Sept. 17, 1810.
[37] "Justice," *ibid.*, No. 295:p. [3]—c. [2-4], July 18, 1810.
[38] *Ibid.*, No. 298, Aug. 8, 1810, and continued in No. 299:p. [2]—c. [2-3], Aug. 15, 1810.
[39] Daniel Drake: "Science," *The Port Folio* (Philadelphia), V:320-24, Apr. 1811.
[40] C. F. de Volney: *A View of the Soil and Climate of the United States*, translated by C. B. Brown (Philadelphia: J. Conrad & Co., 1804).

Volney and President Jefferson. One of the errors concerned supposed differences in the temperature between the western states and those of the eastern seaboard of the same latitude. Drake assumed that their error in this respect resulted from publication of "their inquiries before a sufficient number of observations had been made, to support unequivocally any opinion." As usual, in this article, Drake exhibits a wide acquaintance with observations, past and immediate, made in relation to the subject. In this communication as in many others, because of his enthusiasm for the West, he was an excellent advertising agent and promoter of emigration. Later, writing in *The Western Spy* (Cincinnati), all the criticisms against the western climate are reviewed. Of these Drake insists that only two deserve consideration, namely the heat and the sudden daily changes from heat to cold. He continues:

> Those, therefore, who may wish to emigrate to this desirable country, from any of the Atlantic states which lie nearly in its latitude need apprehend no injury from the effect of heat. . . . Dr. Ramsey of Charleston, S.C., Thomas Jefferson (*Notes on Virginia*), Dr. Rush and others are quoted as admitting sudden violent changes in temperature in the Atlantic states. From these respectable authorities, it appears, that the diurnal changes from heat to cold are actually of greater extent, in the Eastern than Western States.[41]

In 1812 Drake was active in securing from the General Assembly of Ohio an authorization for the establishment of the First District Medical Society. He became the first secretary of this society. No doubt, Drake either introduced or was instrumental in having the following bylaws presented before the First District Medical Society on 1 June 1812:

[41] [Daniel Drake]: "Climate," *The Western Spy* (Cincinnati), I, June 15, 1811:p. [3]—c. [2-3].

1. It shall be the duty of every member to procure and transmit to the society as early as possible, specimens of the roots, leaves, flowers and seeds of those vegetables indigenous to this state, which he may know to be reputed useful in Medicine or the Arts; together with such information concerning their qualities and virtues as he can collect.

2. It shall be the duty of each member to make a quarterly report concerning the Diseases of the district in which he practices accompanied with such topographical and meteorological observations as may be necessary to illustrate their causes.[42]

There are no records to indicate whether these plans were adhered to but their adoption indicated an awareness of the possibilities for original scientific research.

Drake was a gifted speaker, being in demand at public dinners, Fourth of July celebrations, and various gatherings as shown by the newspapers of the period. With the declaration of war against England in 1812 much patriotism was evidenced by Cincinnatians. At a dinner on 4 July 1812 in honor of his friend, Governor (later President) William Henry Harrison, Drake proposed the following toast: "May our contributions to foreign nations be taken from our saltpetre caverns and lead mines."[43] Such a sentiment expressed in 1812 was considered, without doubt, highly patriotic. Another toast by Drake is as follows: "Our institutions of learning, science and humanity dim specks in a dark horizon, may they speedily ascend and shed over us a flood of light and glory."[44]

In addition to the many activities already mentioned Drake took an additional one by entering politics. On 5 April 1813, he was elected one of the seven trustees of the Corpora-

---

[42] Daniel Drake, Secretary, *Liberty Hall* . . . (Cincinnati), VIII, No. 394: p. [3]—c. [3], June 9, 1812.
[43] [News items], *ibid.*, No. 399:p.[3]—c. [1], July 14, 1812.
[44] Daniel Drake, 4 July 1818, celebration, *Liberty Hall* . . . , XIV, No. 793: p. [3]—c. [1], July 7, 1818.

tion of Cincinnati.[45] At the first meeting he was selected as the clerk. Previous to Drake's election it is evident that the trustees had neglected sanitation. It now became one of their prime concerns, which was wise, since filth had been accumulating for fifteen years! Pigs, cows, chickens, and other stock had been permitted to roam at will. Later, Cincinnati, with its ubiquitous pigs, its many slaughter houses, and pork-packing establishments, came to be known as "Porkopopolis." The first sanitary measure adopted by the trustees specified that owners of lots, yards, or cellars were required to remove all filth. It was further decreed that pits or ponds created by the excavation of material for bricks must be either filled up or drained.[46] It is probable that civic pride may have been wounded by Drake's aggressiveness in demanding sanitary measures. Another ordinance unquestionably fathered by him made it obligatory to report all deaths within two days.[47] This was probably the first vital statistics act in the Northwest Territory.

With the Treaty of Greenville in 1795, between the U.S. government and the Indians, peace was restored. The need for Fort Washington at Cincinnati ceased and the garrison was gradually transferred. In 1808, the land was sold and Drake bought five lots, one of which "included the S. E. Angle and Block house" of the fort.[48] Upon the "blockhouse" site Drake began the erection, in 1811, of an imposing three-story dwelling of brick which was ready for occupancy the following year.* This house was on Third near the intersection of

[45] Cincinnati Election, *Liberty Hall*, IX, No. 442: p. [1]—c. [4], Apr. 20, 1813.

[46] Daniel Drake (Clerk), Ordinances, *ibid.*, No. 445:p. [2]—c. [2], May 11, 1813.

[47] "An Ordinance Forming Bills of Mortality," *The Western Spy* (Cincinnati), III, May 22, 1813:p. [3]—c. [3].

[48] Robert Ralston Jones: *Fort Washington at Cincinnati, Ohio* (Cincinnati: Society of Colonial Wars in the State of Ohio, 1902), p. 92.

* In the autumn of 1952, during excavation for a building at Third Street

Ludlow Street, and for many years the area was called "Drake's Corner." His wife's uncle, Jared Mansfield, who had on 25 February 1808 been promoted to Lieutenant Colonel in the U.S. Corps of Engineers, erected a home nearby. These well-built houses are still in good condition (1959), the present number of Drake's old home being 429 East Third Street. He lived there from 1812 to 1823 when he went to Lexington to teach at Transylvania University for the second time.

Even this early Drake had a national reputation. His *Notices Concerning Cincinnati* had been extremely well received in the Altantic states. Johnson and Warner, publishers and booksellers of Philadelphia, requested that he and his friend, Jared Mansfield, prepare the article on Ohio for insertion in their geography. Drake wrote:

> Mr Mansfield & myself will be glad to receive the rest of the books mentioned to Mr Warner, at as early a period as convenient. We have concluded to comply with your proposition concerning the article "Ohio" for your Geography. Young men are generally to [*sic*] sanguine, however, and we find already, that we shall not be able to make that article what we desire & what we at first expected. Such as it will be, however, you shall be welcome to it, whenever your work is ready for the press; which we hope will not be the case for several months. . . .[49]

---

and Broadway, Cincinnati, the shovels uncovered logs, fifteen feet below the surface. The foreman, with remarkable acumen, realized that an historic find had been made and notified the Director of the Historical and Philosophical Society of Ohio. Investigators concluded that the remains of the powder magazine under the southwest blockhouse of Fort Washington had been uncovered. With the powder magazine as a guide, an attempt was made to determine the exact location of the fort. Two different theories emerged about which we are not concerned. Whichever construction is correct, it appears that Drake was mistaken in believing that his home had been erected on the SE corner of the fort. (Consult *Bulletin of the Historical and Philosophical Society of Ohio*, XI, No. 1, January 1953, and No. 2, April 1953.)

[49] Danl Drake: ALS, Cincinnati, 10 Dec. 1811, to Messrs. Johnson & Warner, booksellers, Philadelphia. In the author's collection.

It happened that Lieutenant Colonel Mansfield was ordered from Cincinnati on 7 October 1812 to become professor of natural and experimental philosophy at the U.S. Military Academy, and the article on Ohio may not have been
written. To date, I have been unable to find it.

Succeeding Colonel Mansfield to the post of surveyor-general of the Northwest Territory, there came another highly
educated graduate of Yale, Josiah Meigs (1757-1822), who
immediately became a friend and admirer of Drake. These
two men along with Peyton Short Symmes (1793-1861), one
of the earliest poets of the West, and several other prominent
Cincinnatians established a literary group with the ambitious
name of the School of Literature and the Arts. The organization met fortnightly under the presidency of Josiah Meigs,
with Peyton Short Symmes as secretary. Drake took a leading
part in the proceedings and read at least three essays before
the group during the first year: "On the Earthquakes of 1811,
1812 and 1813," "Notices of the Aurora Borealis of the 17th
of April and 11th September 1814," and *"Geology of Cincinnati and its Vicinity."* In addition to the above papers, Drake,
in the absence of President Meigs who had been transferred
to Washington, D.C., delivered the Anniversary Address on
23 November 1814. Except for a few newspaper comments
and a letter from the secretary, this oration is the only source
of our knowledge of the School of Literature and the Arts.[50]

Since he was the substitute speaker, Drake prepared the
address in haste. Therefore, it is all the more remarkable in its
ringing challenge to the possibilities which lay ahead of the
organization. First he fittingly enumerates the papers presented during the preceding year. With philosophical clarity
and insight Drake balances against one another the oppor-

---

[50] [Daniel Drake]: *Anniversary Address, Delivered to the School of Literature and the Arts, at Cincinnati, November 23, 1814* (Looker and Wallace,
1814). This is a "separate" of *Liberty Hall* . . . , Dec. 27, 1814.

tunities afforded by areas of long-established culture with those of a newly developing country. He exhorts his listeners to address themselves to such studies as will benefit them and, in turn, the community as a whole. In his brief outline of possible subjects for study Drake displays a remarkable knowledge in numerous fields not strictly medical, such as geology, mineralogy, meteorology, botany, zoology, agriculture, and astronomy. He sought to inspire his audience with a desire for learning, not necessarily as an end in itself but in order to improve conditions in agriculture, manufacture, commerce, society, and politics. He rises to a climax with an urgent plea for the recording of the history of the region while it was still possible to interview those who participated in its making. Many sections of this address are worthy of quotation but the following is illustrative: "In new countries, the empire of prejudice is comparatively insignificant; and the mind, not depressed by dogmas of licensed authority, nor fettered by the chains of inexorable custom, is left free to expand, according to its original condition." [51]

One of the Cincinnati newspapers, *Liberty Hall*, obtained a copy of Drake's oration and published it as a separate to its issue for Tuesday, 27 December 1814. Drake's name did not appear on the title page. The editors of the *National Intelligencer* (Washington) republished the address in its entirety with the following comment: "The following little tract is ushered to the world, with peculiar modesty, the more commendable because of its rarity, unaccompanied even with the name of the Author. It affords, as well in the substance as in the manner of the Address, flattering proof of the progress of the arts in a quarter which a very few years past was an untravelled forest." [52]

[51] *Ibid.*, pp. 5-6.
[52] Gales & Seaton: *National Intelligencer* (Washington), XVI, No. 2268: p. [2]—c. [1-4], April 6, 1815.

In 1812, a Presbyterian clergyman and friend of Drake, the Reverend Joshua Lacy Wilson, heard of the so-called Lancasterian system of instruction and attempted to start a school of this type in Cincinnati. His efforts were unsuccessful as were those independently undertaken by the Methodist Church. In 1814, Daniel Drake joined with Wilson, and together with Edmund Harrison of the Methodist Church, secured pledges amounting to $9000. Their institution was named the Cincinnati Lancaster Seminary. Drake was secretary of the board of trustees for several years and had much to do with the success of the institution.[53] A commodious building was erected. The opening of the school, scheduled for 27 March 1815, was delayed until 17 April 1815, on account of the illness of the teacher. Within less than two weeks 420 pupils had been enrolled and for a while subsequent applicants had to be rejected because of lack of accommodations.[54] The seminary continued in successful operation until 1819 when Drake obtained a charter for Cincinnati College into which the Cincinnati Lancaster Seminary was merged, as will be mentioned later.

Although the name of Joseph Lancaster (1778-1838) is ordinarily attached to the system of instruction in which the older pupils teach the younger, he was, while not its originator, certainly its advocate and promoter. Lancaster thus deserves great credit for arousing interest in public education. The monitorial plan (the Madras system of education) stressed by Lancaster apparently was conceived by the Reverend Andrew Bell (1753-1832) who first used it in Madras, India, and later brought it to the attention of Lancaster and the English-speaking world.[55]

[53] Daniel Drake, Secretary, Cincinnati Lancaster Seminary, *The Western Spy*, IV, April 23, 1814:p. [3]—c. [2].
[54] Daniel Drake: *Natural and Statistical View, or Picture of Cincinnati* (Cincinnati: Locker and Wallace, 1815), p. 157.
[55] *Concise DNB* (Oxford University Press, 1930), p. 84.

The Reverend Joshua L. Wilson, the "frontier contro-versialist" as he has been called, deserves more than passing notice.[56] The son of a physician, Wilson was born in Bedford County, Virginia, 22 September 1774 and died in Cincinnati, 14 August 1846. He studied law for a short time but was attracted to the ministry and pursued his theological studies under the Reverend James Vance who lived near Louisville. Wilson held but two charges during his forty-four years as a Presbyterian clergyman. His first pastorate (1802-8) was at Bardstown, Ky., where his salary consisted of a small amount of cash with the balance paid in wheat, pork, linen, potatoes, and whiskey! [57] The restless spirit of Wilson sought a wider field and though there were few Presbyterians in Cin-cinnati, Ohio, he agreed to accept the pastorate there at the annual stipend of $350! Here he became a friend of Drake whom he warmly admired. The most unusual copy of Drake's *Notices Concerning Cincinnati* is a presentation copy to Wilson, now owned by the Library of the University of Cin-cinnati. On the recto of the leaf preceding the title page is the following inscription: "For/The Rev. J. L. Wilson with the compliments/of his friend & most/ob^t sev^t/The Au-thor./Thankfully rec^d from/the author June 18. 1810./"

Wilson was professor of moral philosophy and logic in Cincinnati College during its first few years but resigned on 26 March 1823. He spoke out against slavery but, at the same time, decried the actions of the abolitionists which he thought could only lead to conflict.[58] In this respect, too, he held beliefs similar to those of Drake as will be mentioned later. In other ways these men were much alike, especially in their intensity of purpose, their driving and indefatigable

[56] R. L. Hightower: "Joshua L. Wilson, Frontier Controversialist (Ph.D. thesis, U. of Chicago, 1933).
[57] Edward A. Henry, librarian, the General Library, University of Cincin-nati, Letter to the author, 16 March 1945.
[58] Hightower: *loc. cit.*

energy and fearlessness. Instrumental in founding Lane Theological Seminary, Wilson charged its first president, Lyman Beecher (1775-1863), with heresy. Wilson well deserved the appellation of "controversialist" and his rigid Calvinistic views frequently led to disputes, especially since he "divided his acquaintances into two classes, friends and foes." [59]

[59] *Ibid.*

Professional fame, is the capital of a physician, and he must not suffer it to be purloined, even should its defence involve him in quarrels.[1]

Cincinnati, Philadelphia, Lexington, 1815-18

THE ACCLAIM accorded *Notices Concerning Cincinnati* prompted Drake to prepare an expanded version. In August 1813 the following editorial appeared in *Liberty Hall*:

LITERATURE OF THE BACK WOODS

It affords us much pleasure to learn that Doctor Drake intends shortly to issue proposals for publishing by subscription, a STATISTICAL WORK, relative to CINCINNATI and its vicinity, to be illustrated with engravings. We understand it will embrace sketches of the Topography, Geology and Botany of the town and adjoining country; observations on our climate and diseases; a view of the improvement of the town, its progress in manufacture, commerce, &c.

In this undertaking we hope to see the superior advantages of this quarter exhibited in their proper light; and from a conviction that the work will prove highly beneficial to the place of which it treats, the author has our best wishes for success.[2]

A month later, Drake issued a prospectus of his contemplated book, to cost subscribers one dollar. Apparently he

[1] Drake: *Practical Essays on Medical Education*, p. 99.
[2] [Editorial] "Literature of the Back Woods," *Liberty Hall* . . . (Cincinnati), IX, No. 460:p. [3]—c. [1], Aug. 24, 1813.

hoped to attract emigrants, and certainly should be termed Cincinnati's first and most persistent publicity agent. He wrote:

> The principal object of the work is to furnish those persons desirous of knowing the comparative advantages of different sections of the western country, with a body of facts and observations respecting Cincinnati and its vicinity. . . . The *plan* of the work, will not be novel; being modelled after that of the pictures and statistical accounts of several of our Atlantic cities. . . .[3]

Advance subscriptions were not entirely satisfactory. Drake, with his customary zeal, completed the manuscript by October 1814. An announcement was then made that the work "is now in press."[4] This notice seems to have been quite premature as is shown by the following:

> We are requested by Dr. Drake, to offer an apology to the subscribers for this work, for the delay in its publication. This has in part arisen from the unexampled progress of population and improvement in the town and its vicinity, rendering it difficult to give an account that would not be found defective; and partly from an extension of the work beyond the original plan and limits. The printing is now in rapid execution, and the latest period to which the publication will be deferred, is the middle of the coming autumn.[5]

Further progress was noted in the newspapers; and *Niles Weekly Register* at Baltimore quoted extracts from a sheet of the book which it had received through a friend.[6] Delay in the executing of the maps in Philadelphia also retarded

---

[3] Daniel Drake: Prospectus, *ibid.*, IX, No. 465:p. [3]—c. [3], Sept. 28, 1813.
[4] [News item]: Picture of Cincinnati, *ibid.*, XI, No. 521: p. [3]—c. [3], Oct. 25, 1814.
[5] *Ibid.*, No. 557:p. [3]—c. [4], June 26, 1815. Also in *The Western Spy* (Cincinnati), N.S., I, June 30, 1815:p. [3]—c. [2].
[6] *Niles Weekly Register* (Baltimore), IX:35-36, Sept. 16, 1815.

publication. In October 1815, one of the Cincinnati newspapers printed, with special permission, the portions of Chapter III which described "Manufactures, Commerce and Education." [7] Although the date of copyright was 6 September 1815, and the title page bears the date, 1815, the *Picture of Cincinnati* was not ready for delivery to subscribers until 16 February 1816.[8]

The title of Drake's second book was: *Natural and Statistical View, or Picture of Cincinnati and the Miami Country, Illustrated by maps. With an appendix Containing Observations on "The late Earthquakes, the Aurora Borealis and the South-west Wind."* * The dedication was in part as follows:

> To Lieutenant-Colonel Jared Mansfield, Professor of Natural and Experimental Philosophy in the United States Military Academy
>
> Dear Sir—
>
> I trust you will pardon my inscribing to you, without permission, the following work; when I avow that my chief inducement for using your name, is the opportunity it affords of expressing the unmingled pleasure with which I cherish the recollection of your instructive converse, while sojourning, with your family, in the vicinity of Cincinnati.

This book was widely acclaimed in the Atlantic states as well as in the Central West, and it helped to establish

[7] [Editorial column] "Statistical," *Liberty Hall* . . . , XII, No. 575, p. [3]—c. [2], Oct. 30, 1815.

[8] [Ad.]: Just published, Daniel Drake: Natural and Statistical View, or Pictures of Cincinnati, *The Western Spy*, N.S., II, No. 83:p. [3]—c. [4], Feb. 16, 1816.

* In using *Picture of Cincinnati*, as part of his title, Drake was merely following precedent. Probably he had seen a copy of *The Picture of London for 1806* (price five shillings). Undoubtedly he was familiar with Dr. Samuel Latham Mitchell's *Picture of New York* (1807) and also with Dr. James Mease's *Picture of Philadelphia* (1811). Drake was a correspondent both of Mitchell and of Mease. Drake's *Picture* has steadily risen in price from five dollars, the sum my first copy cost in 1935, to fifty dollars in 1958.

Drake's reputation as a physician, scientist, and author. One Cincinnati reviewer wrote: "On its diction, tho perfectly simple and modest, we rest, without hesitation, the literary reputation of our town." [9] A Baltimore writer said: "Cincinnati has reason to be proud of the specimen which is here given of her literature, whatever the modesty of the author may have led him to say to the contrary; and we congratulate the United States upon a valuable addition to their stock of native literature. . . ." [10]

From Philadelphia came the following comment by the editor of *The Port Folio*, Dr. Charles Caldwell, who was usually hypercritical:

> But the principal value of the book arises from the number and importance of the facts it contains, derived from the personal observation of the author. In this respect it is abundantly rich. On the whole, we recollect no work written in the United States, which, within an equal compass, gives so able and satisfactory a view of the climate and statistics. . . . Without meaning to speak of Dr. Drake in the language of flattery, from which we feel persuaded his modesty would shrink, we think it but justice to state, as our candid opinion, that he is entitled to be proud of his book, and Cincinnati to be proud of him.[11]

In October 1815, after correcting proofs of his book and selling his drug store, Drake left Cincinnati for Philadelphia, accompanied by his wife. His father and mother, who had been persuaded to move to Cincinnati, took over the Drake household and the care of the two sons, Charles and John Mansfield. Although at the time many physicians were prac-

[9] [Editorial] Drake's Picture of Cincinnati: *Liberty Hall* . . . , XII, No. 592:p. [3]—c. [2], Feb. 19, 1816.

[10] [Review], Natural and Statistical View or Picture of Cincinnati, *The Portico* (Baltimore), I:265-76, Apr. 1816.

[11] [Review] Natural and Statistical View . . . , *The Port Folio* (Philadelphia), XV:25-38, Jan. 1816.

ticing without a degree in medicine, Drake was not content to follow the majority and he recognized the low standards in medicine at that period:

> You are well apprized of the necessity there exists, in a literary and professional point of view, of my visiting Philadelphia in order to obtain a degree. That necessity I find every day to increase. You know no business can be conducted without renovating the capital stock, as it becomes wasted. It is now eight years since I commenced the practice of physic, which is a trade in ideas, and I begin seriously to feel an exhaustion of funds. You will be surprised that I have not felt it before. In truth I have, but not being able to replenish them, I said but little, being willing, like all others, to support my credit as long as it was practicable.[12]

When less than a third of the distance to Philadelphia, Mrs. Drake became ill with what was termed "bilious fever" and they were delayed three weeks at Zanesville, Ohio. Classes in the Medical Department of the University of Pennsylvania had started more than two weeks before Drake's arrival. Such a handicap was overcome by the strictest attention to his studies and attendance at the remaining lectures. Mansfield states that Drake was apprehensive about his examination for a degree. In this instance, Drake's modesty is clearly evident (as revealed in an incident to be shortly mentioned). The fact is that, of the seventy members of the class of 1816, Drake was the only one with a national reputation at the time. Biographies of only two other of Drake's classmates are to be found in Kelly and Burrage: *Dictionary of American Medical Biography* (1928). The two who attained distinction were Henry Rutledge Frost (1790-1866), a professor of materia medica in Charleston, South Carolina, and Joseph Kinnersley Swift (1798?-1871) of Phila-

---

[12] Mansfield, *op. cit.*, p. 112.

delphia, the first to apply strips of adhesive plaster in fractures necessitating extension.

As soon as the printing of his *Picture of Cincinnati* was completed, several hundred unbound sheets were sent to Drake in Philadelphia. He had these bound and it is probable that copies were available there by the time others were ready for delivery in Cincinnati, 16 February 1816. Drake sent copies immediately to his friend, Josiah Meigs, who had

JUST PUBLISHED,
AND FOR SALE AT THE
Book-bindery of Wm. Poundsford,
Main street, in front of the Spy Office,
AND AT THE OFFICE OF
Liberty Hall & Cincinnati Gazette,
THAT VALUABLE WORK ENTITLED
NATURAL AND STATISTICAL VIEW,
OR
PICTURE OF CINCINNATI
AND THE
MIAMI COUNTRY.
ILLUSTRATED BY MAPS.

BY DANIEL DRAKE.

☞ Subscribers living in the country,
who can make it convenient, will please
to call for their books.
February 16.

Fig. 5. Advertisement: in The Western Spy *(Cincinnati), N.S., II, No.
83: p. [3]-c. [4], Feb. 16, 1816.*

been transferred in 1814 from Cincinnati to Washington to the post of commissioner of the General Land Office of the U.S. Instead of sending a copy directly Drake, with evident modesty, requested that Meigs forward one to Thomas Jefferson. A portion of Meigs's letter of transmittal, dated 1 March 1816, is as follows:

> My friend Doctor Daniel Drake of Cincinnati, Ohio, has requested me to transmit to you a Copy of his work, en-

titled "*Picture of Cincinnati.*" I presume it will gratify you as an elegant and valuable work.

The author is a native of New Jersey, from which state his Father, after having served in the Revolutionary War, emigrated to Kentucky—he has acquired a valuable fund of Literature & Science—propio Marto with steady industry—without the aid of Schools or Colleges—he is a sincere and faithful friend of our free Institutions. It is pleasant to know that the best distinguished minds are supporters of these Institutions.[13]

From Monticello on 7 April 1816, Jefferson replied to Meigs:

I have referred [*sic*] asking the favor of you to return my thanks to Dr Drake for the copy of his account of the state of Ohio which he has been so kind as to send me until I could have time to peruse it. I have done this with great pleasure and may now express my gratification on this able addition to the knoledge [*sic*] we possess of our different states; and I may say with truth that were all of them as well delineated as that which is the subject of this volume, we should be more accurately and scientifically known to the rest of the world. With my thanks for this mark of attention be pleased to accept the assurance of my great esteem & respect.

Th: Jefferson[14]

In 1816, the professor of anatomy at the University of Pennsylvania was Caspar Wistar, Jr. (1761-1818), a graduate in medicine (1786) of the University of Edinburgh. In 1815, he succeeded Thomas Jefferson to the presidency of the American Philosophical Society, an office he continued to hold until his death. From him the beautiful climbing plant, the wisteria, gets its name. During the winter months his house was thrown open to scientists, travellers, students, and Phila-

[13] and [14] Owned by the Library of Congress which kindly furnished photostats.

delphia intellectuals. Drake attended the Wistar parties regularly. He was somewhat disappointed in that the literary zeal of the Philadelphians did not seem as great as he had expected. To his uncle, Lieutenant Colonel Mansfield, he wrote:

> There are, however, some gentlemen of extensive and very respectable attainments. Dr. Wistar . . . is both a scholar and a philosopher; not, perhaps, of the first order, but of a grade which entitles him to distinction. He occupies, however, the very first rank as the patron of literature and science. . . . I have spent many evenings with him, and always with pleasure and improvement. We generally have the Abbe Correa, of whom you have probably heard something, and who I wish you could see. He is unquestionably a man of very great attainments, with powers of understanding unusually strong. He is a Portuguese, and has been in the United States about four years. But I will reserve these details for the happy hours I promise myself in your society.[15]

As a result of his acquaintance with Wistar, Drake was invited to the meetings of the American Philosophical Society, which he attended regularly.

Between lectures, Drake visited various wholesalers and made large purchases of stationery, books, dry goods, drugs, paints, hardware, and staple groceries. With remarkable foresight, he also purchased a complete outfit for the manufacture of soda water.* He planned to place his father and his brother Benjamin in charge of the new and greatly enlarged store in Cincinnati. In February 1816, Benjamin came to Philadelphia for the purpose of arranging for shipment of the merchandise. On 26 April 1816, announcement was made of the new store, Isaac Drake & Co.:

[15] Mansfield, *op. cit.,* p. 114.

* John Hart, a Quaker druggist in Philadelphia, is usually credited with having devised, at the suggestion of the Rev. Joseph Priestley (1733-1804), an apparatus for the preparation of soda-water.

[They] respectfully inform the public that they have formed a mercantile establishment at the well known stand heretofore exclusively occupied as a Drug store by Dr. Drake, where they are now opening a general assortment of Dry Goods, Hardware, Groceries &c. . . . Their stock of Fancy Goods, especially, is extensive and elegant.

They have received also, and will continue to keep a large supply of Genuine Medicines, Paints, Dyes, Patent Medicines and Stationery. . . .[16]

It was announced that the preparation of artificial mineral waters would be resumed upon completion of a special "Recess" which it was expected would become "a fashionable resort." On 10 May 1816, the manufacture of "Artificial Mineral Waters" began.[17] Thus, in Drake's newly stocked general store, there was opened the first soda-water fountain west of the Allegheny Mountains.

At the close of the 1815-16 medical lectures at the University of Pennsylvania, Drake and his wife went to West Point, New York, to visit Lieutenant Colonel and Mrs. Mansfield. Notification of the exact date set for the final examinations and commencement failed to reach them. He found on returning to Philadelphia that the graduating exercises were over. The news also reached him that his only son, Charles, had broken his thigh. Under the impression that the coveted degree might not be granted by the University, Drake immediately applied for an honorary one from the College of Physicians and Surgeons of New York. Meanwhile the trustees authorized a special investiture, the only one in the long and brilliant history of the University of Pennsylvania. The following entries appear in the "Minutes of the Board of Trustees" for Tuesday, 7 May 1816:

[16] [Ad.] New Store, Isaac Drake & Co., *The Western Spy* (Cincinnati), N.S., II, No. 93:p. [3]—c. [4], Apr. 26, 1816.
[17] Ibid., No. 95:p. [3]—c. [5], May 10, 1816.

The Medical Faculty having represented that Daniel Drake one of the students in medicine, had, from unavoidable accidents, been absent from the last examination of the Medical Class, and had since been examined and approved, and that it would be greatly inconvenient to him to attend at the examination in the next year: they therefore recommend his case to the consideration of the Trustees and pray that he may be admitted to the degree of Doctor in Medicine.

Resolved, that in consideration of the particular circumstances of Doctor Drake a commencement be held on Tuesday next, and that the Degree of Doctor of Medicine be then conferred upon him.

Adjourned to Tuesday next.

Tuesday May 14, 1816.

Present: Mr. Chief Justice Tilghman, Mr. McKean, Mr. Chew, Mr. Gibson, General Cadwalader, Mr. Levy, Mr. Lewis, Mr. Binney, Mr. Fox, Mr. Burd, Mr. Rawle.

The Degree of Doctor of Medicine was conferred on Daniel Drake of the State of. [Either the secretary was interrupted or did not know where Dr. Drake came from.][18]

One of the prerequisites for graduation at the University of Pennsylvania at the time was the submission of a thesis on a medical subject "in the candidate's own handwriting." This thesis was referred to one of the professors for review and "general bad spelling, or general inattention to the rules of grammar," would preclude the candidate's examination for a degree.[19] In the case of Drake there is no record this requirement was enforced. The probable explanation is that his *Picture of Cincinnati* which contained a medical section was

---

[18] TLS from Philip Soule, Secretary, U. of Pennsylvania, March 22, 1946, to William Pepper, M.D., who kindly sent it to the author on 25 March 1946.

[19] University of Pennsylvania: *Catalogue of the Medical Graduates of . . . with an Historical Sketch.* (2nd ed., Philadelphia: Lydia R. Bailey, 1839), pp. 103-4.

accepted in lieu of a thesis. In fact, Chapter V of that book, which discussed medical conditions in and around Cincinnati, had appeared in *The Eclectic Repertory* . . . , Philadelphia, April 1816.[20]

After receiving his coveted degree, Drake returned at once to Cincinnati. Having been away seven months there was much to be done before he could resume practice. The firm of Isaac Drake and Co. was finding it increasingly difficult to compete with the flood of cheaper goods coming from abroad. During the War of 1812, importations had been cut off and prices of domestic goods had risen. It had been Daniel Drake's idea that goods bought in Philadelphia could be sold at a good profit in Cincinnati. He had not taken into consideration that less than two years after the treaty of peace at Ghent on 4 December 1814, foreign goods would flood the market with subsequent disruption of prices. Local manufacturing firms were beginning to feel pressure for similar reasons.

On 22 November 1813, the Cincinnati Manufacturing Co. was organized with Drake as a member of the charter group and a shareholder.[21] Initially the firm was engaged in the manufacture of broadcloth and woolens but soon added the processing of white and red lead to their activities, in addition to running an oil mill for grinding paints. The company prospered but Drake found it necessary to sell his stock in order to help the firm of Isaac Drake and Co. On 18 June 1816, Drake announced he had "resumed the practice of Medicine and Surgery at his former shop in Main-street." [22]

His patients returned but the year 1816 had been a harass-

---

[20] Daniel Drake: "Medical Topography" (from the *Natural and Statistical View or Picture of Cincinnati and the Miami Country*), *The Eclectic Repertory and Analytical Review* (Philadelphia), VI:137-49, Apr. 1816.

[21] Hamilton County Ohio Deed Book F3, p. 135.

[22] Daniel Drake: "Medical Notice," *The Western Spy* (Cincinnati) N. S., II, No. 101:p. [3]—c. [3], June 21, 1816.

ing one. While in Philadelphia, he had received word that his younger son, John Mansfield, three years of age, had died of croup (diphtheria?) on 5 February 1816. Returning to Cincinnati, business worries and reverses were encountered. He was concerned over the state of his wife's health. His cousin, Edward D. Mansfield, states that Drake now developed "dispepsia" and lost weight. With exercise, a restricted diet, and regular hours for rest, improvement was rapid. Early in January 1817, he was encouraged by notification of his election to a professorship in the Medical Department of Transylvania University, Lexington. His letter of acceptance is interesting:

Cincinnati Jan[y] 7th 1817

Gentlemen:

Your polite favor of the 14th ultimo, announcing my election to the professorship of Materia Medica and Botany in the Transylvania University was received and has been attentively considered.

In accepting the appointment I beg leave to offer thro you to the Trustees of the University, an acknowledgment of thanks for the distinction they have conferred on me.

Whether I shall be able to discharge the duties of the professorship in such a manner as not to impede the progress of the medical school can only be known by making the experiment; but if I should not succeed I hope to prove that my failure is neither attributable to indolence nor a want of devotion to the interests of the institution.

I have the honor to be gentlemen

with the highest respect
your very obed[t] serv[t]
Dan Drake[23]

The first medical college west of the Allegheny Mountains and the sixth* in the United States was created by Transyl-

---

[23] Original owned by Transylvania College, Lexington, Ky.

* The earlier schools, according to Garrison (3rd ed., p. 422) were: Medi-

vania University on 8 January 1799.[24] Efforts to activate this department were made from time to time, desultory lectures were delivered, but it was not until the fall of 1817 that all of the medical chairs were filled and accredited courses began.[25] The professors were as follows: Benjamin W. Dudley (1785-1870), professor of anatomy and surgery; James Overton (1785-1865), professor of the theory and practice of medicine; Daniel Drake, professor of materia medica and medical botany; William H. Richardson (d. 1845), professor of obstetrics and diseases of women and children; and the Reverend James Blythe (1765-1842), professor of chemistry. Thus Drake, the first student of medicine in Cincinnati, the first Cincinnatian to receive a diploma in medicine, and the first medical author in the West, also became a member of the first accredited faculty of the first medical institution west of the Alleghenies.

"Dr." Goforth returned to Cincinnati on 28 December 1816, and Drake immediately suggested a partnership which began on 1 January 1817. Since Drake had not fully recovered from his illness, Goforth was doubtless of great assistance. After a few months, Goforth sickened and died on 12 May 1817. This was still another blow to Drake, especially in view of his commitment to teach in Lexington during the ensuing winter. On 9 July 1817, Drake formed a partnership with Coleman Rogers (1781-1855) who received an honorary degree of M.D. from the University of Pennsylvania on 10 April 1818. In the announcement of the partnership it

---

cal Dept., University of Pennsylvania, 1765; King's College, N.Y., 1767 (became Columbia 1792); Harvard University, 1782; College of Philadelphia, 1790; and Medical School of Dartmouth, 1798.

[24] Transylvania University: *Records of the Proceedings of the Board of Trustees* (1799-1810), Vol. I Second Section, p. 3, Jan. 8, 1799.

[25] Emmet F. Horine: "Early Medicine in Kentucky and the Mississippi Valley. A Tribute to Daniel Drake," read before the Centennial Meeting (1947), American Medical Association, *Journal of the History of Medicine* (New York), III:263-78.

was stated that arrangements had been made for the instruction of medical students "in any number that may apply." [26]
The editors of the Cincinnati newspapers congratulated
Lexington on the establishment of a medical school but be-
moaned the fact that Kentucky had gotten ahead of Ohio.
After deploring the suspension of Miami University, one
editor concluded: "It must be peculiarly mortifying to see the
College of a neighboring state attract from us both students
and Professors to assist it whilst our own is thrust into the
gloom of the Beach-Wood-Flats where the footsteps of enlightened and liberal patronage cannot penetrate, and from
whence not a ray of Science will be reflected for a century." [27]
Drake reached Lexington early in November 1817. At the
organizational meeting of the medical faculty the dissension,
present from the time of its formation, erupted. It continued
throughout the term. Benjamin W. Dudley, professor of
anatomy and surgery, and James Overton, professor of the
theory and practice of medicine, disliked Wm. H. Richardson, professor of obstetrics. They objected to him on the
ostensible grounds that he held no degree in medicine. The
trustees would have awarded Richardson a degree but his
foes blocked this plan by their violent objections. It was
agreed that Richardson be allowed to teach provided he
signed no diplomas. Drake, now, with customary zeal on behalf of friends, immediately wrote David Hosack, M.D., of
the college of Physicians and Surgeons of New York, requesting that an honorary degree be given Richardson. In time
the request was granted with the proviso that Richardson
appear in person and undergo an examination. He received
his degree on 6 April 1819. [28]

[26] [Ad.] Doctors Drake and Rogers, *The Western Spy* N.S., III, No. 150:
p. [3]—c. [3], July 11, 1817.
[27] M. T. Williams and James M. Mason (editors), "Medical Instruction in
the West," *The Western Spy* (Cincinnati), N.S., IV, Oct. 3, 1817, p.
[3]—c. [1].
[28] Estelle Brodman: "An Unpublished Letter of Daniel Drake to the Col-

Twenty students composed the class of the first recognized course in Transylvania University. The first lecture, an introductory one to the course on the "institutes and practice of medicine," was delivered by the professor of those subjects on 10 November 1817, in the Market Street Presbyterian Church. The other members of the faculty delivered their introductories on succeeding days. Concerning Drake's introductory on Wednesday, 12 November 1817, John Norvell, editor of the *Kentucky Gazette*, wrote: "Of Dr. Drake's lecture, we may truly pronounce that it was one of the most finished performances we have ever witnessed, and showed him to be a master of his branches of the profession, and a man of general science." [29]

Another appraisal of this lecture was likewise laudatory:

> Dr. Drake introduced us into the garden of nature, and delighted us with a display of the endless variety, inimitable beauty and exquisite arrangement of its several objects. He gave us a general view of the several departments of natural science, which he arranged with admirable perspicuity and skill, and concluded with a brief historical sketch of the rise and progress of the knowledge of materia medica.[30]

Drake's valedictory to his class was a sincere exhortation to studiousness throughout life:

> When you leave the medical school, your studies are merely begun. The germ of your future professional knowledge is yet a tender seedling, which neglected by you must inevitably perish. Watch over it then unceasingly—foster it with tenderness—supply it with liberality, and you will elevate it in time to a magnificent tree. Its balmy exhortation

---

lege of Physicians and Surgeons in New York," *Bull. Hist. Med.* (Baltimore), XVIII:338-48, Oct. 1945. Also, *ibid.*, XX:467-69, Oct. 1946.

[29] John Norvell: "Introductory Lectures," *Kentucky Gazette* (Lexington), XXXI, Nov. 15, 1817:p. [3]—c. [1].

[30] (Copied from the *Monitor*). Medical Lectures, *The Western Spy* (Cincinnati), N.S., IV, Nov. 28, 1817:p. [2]—c. [2].

will diffuse health and comfort among the wretched victims
of disease;—the *golden fruit* of its wide spreading branches
will supply your numerous wants, and in the shade of its ever
green foliage you will glide serenely down the vale of declining life. . . .

On one account, gentlemen, I may be supposed to feel
sensations more acute at leaving you, than you experience at
separating from each other: You part with the intention of
reassembling: I leave you with no very sanguine expectation
of another meeting; and in the presentment that this is the
last time that I shall ever have the pleasure of addressing
you, I beg leave to express my earnest desire for your personal and professional welfare.[31]

At the close of the session, early in March 1818, there was
only one successful candidate for the degree of M.D., John
Lawson McCullough (1793-1825), the first graduate of the
first school of medicine west of the Allegheny Mountains.

Drake at once returned to Cincinnati and resumed practice
in partnership with Dr. Coleman Rogers. In order that the
trustees of Transylvania University might have ample time to
select a successor, Drake resigned his professorship on 24
March 1818. The dislike of Dudley for his associates burst
into the open, resulting in the Richardson-Dudley duel. Dr.
Robert Peter (1805-94) is responsible for publishing the
often repeated, but erroneous, story that Dudley challenged
Drake who refused to fight and that Richardson fought for
him.[32] Peter's error is based on letters from Dr. Christopher
Columbus Graham (1784-1885), hazily reminiscing in his
ninety-second year.[33] Had Dr. Peter consulted the "sharp

---

[31] Daniel Drake: "Extract from Professor Drake's Valediction," *Kentucky
Reporter* (Lexington), XI, No. 11:p. [2]—c. [1-3], Mar. 11, 1818.

[32] Robert Peter: *The History of the Medical Department of Transylvania
University*, Filson Club, Publication No. 20 (Louisville: John P. Morton &
Co., 1905), pp. 24-25.

[33] C. C. Graham: ALS to "Doct. Robert Peter," Louisville, Feb. 2 and
Feb. 12, 1876. Owned by Transylvania College.

pamphlets" mentioned in his story of the duel, his blunder would have been impossible.

On 2 April 1818, Drake learned from his friend, Richardson, that Dudley was openly accusing Drake of breaking a promise to remain in Lexington two years. Drake immediately wrote Dudley, denying the accusation and requesting correction. Dudley's reply through Drake's intermediary, Captain Bain, reiterated this charge and added that Drake's "conduct had been illiberal and ungentlemanly," and that he sought to destroy the medical school. Drake now obtained letters from Dr. Richardson and the Reverend Blythe refuting Dudley's charges. These letters were sent to the board of trustees accompanied by a letter in which Drake emphatically denied Dudley's accusation. Deeming the controversy out of their jurisdiction, the trustees did not reply. Dudley, having access to this correspondence, wrote Drake an abusive letter on 30 June 1818, in which is amply demonstrated Peter's estimate that, "He [Dudley] was not ready with his pen; because, probably, of early neglect in the practice of composition." [34]

The portion of Dudley's letter to Drake which is of special significance concerned Dr. Richardson and the Reverend Blythe:

> The Contents of your two friends letters have been duly appreciated; that of Doctor Blythe is in perfect Character with the man; his memory is tenacious in retaining everything agreeable to his wishes while he has the peculiar faculty of forgeting [*sic*] all which would prejudice his views either in relation to money, to Politics, or to the Church— The letter of Doctor Richardson amounts to all that could have been expected. I am well assured, had the students attacked my Professional deficiency in a publication; had they represented my incapacity to the board of Trustees as good cause of disgrace and removal had my associate Profes-

[34] Peter: *The History . . . T. U.*, p. 21.

sors objected to me as an unqualified teacher in the medical
school, I should not only have been insensible to the pledges
you gave but my feelings would have entirely disqualified me
for the detail he has drawn—

. . . .

I therefore do not hesitate to say that you have designedly
withheld the truth & that you have been regardless of the
honor & the principles of a Gentleman & for this I am responsible—

respectfully
B. W. Dudley[35]

Instead of challenging Dudley to a duel or entering into
a newspaper controversy as was so often done at this period,
Drake published a pamphlet (10 July 1818) addressed to
the citizens of Lexington. Included in it were his letter to
the board, the supporting letters, and Dudley's reply. He
stated: "The object of the Author of the following pages is
not so much to retort invective on his aggressor, as to vindi-
cate himself from the charge of having made an attempt to
destroy the Medical College of the Transylvania University,
while a Professor in that Institution." [36]

Continuing, each of Dudley's charges was discussed in detail and refuted. He concluded:

I have on this occasion had but a single object in view,
that of proving all my conduct relative to the University to
have been correct and honorable; and have not therefore
stepped aside to inflict chastisements for insults, which, my
principal object being accomplished, must fall harmless at
my feet. How far the preceding facts are adequate to this
end, is not for me to decide. But I may be permitted to re-
mark, that in proportion as they establish my innocence,

[35] [Daniel Drake]: *An Appeal to the Justice of Intelligent and Respectable
People of Lexington* (Cincinnati: Looker, Reynolds & Co., 1818), pp. 9-10.
[36] *Ibid.* [2].

they inevitably demonstrate Dr. Dudley to be a base and unprincipled villain, who has wantonly and wickedly attempted to destroy my reputation. For this outrage, my feelings require no other, and can have no higher satisfaction, than the favorable award of an impartial and intelligent public.

I have now finished a necessary but disgusting task, and shall with great difficulty be reexcited to another of the same kind. Although I cannot, like the Grecian Hercules, boast of having vanquished a monster, I may at least claim some praise for having ferreted out one of the vermin which infest our modern Attica.

DANIEL DRAKE.[37]

The reactions of Dr. Richardson and of the Reverend Blythe to Dr. Dudley's aspersions, as quoted above, were distinctive:

> The former, abandoning his characteristic moderation, demanded, as an atonement for the outrage on his character, that satisfaction which the fashionable world erroneously call the highest that can be given. The latter, with as little delay, resigned his Professorship, and in a letter at once temperate and energetic, has shown to society with what indignation he resented the imputation of dishonesty.[38]

Dudley accepted Richardson's challenge and selected pistols as the weapons. Several days elapsed between the challenge and the date set for the duel. During this time, according to Dr. Graham, Dudley carefully practiced handling his pistol. He decided to wear a coat greenish in color from which all buttons were removed. Stringent laws against duelling had been passed in Kentucky as early as 1799. As too well known, these statutes did not prevent duelling but certainly they

---

[37] *Ibid.*, pp. 22-23.
[38] Daniel Drake: *A Second Appeal to the Justice of the Intelligent and Respectable People of Lexington.* (Cincinnati: Looker, Reynolds & Co., 1818), pp. 5-6.

necessitated secrecy. The Richardson-Dudley duel was fought not earlier than 20 July and not later than 5 August 1818.

Dudley told Graham that his shot: "Cut Richardson's inguinal artery, and he would have soon bled to death, but for Dudley's aid, who knowing exactly where the artery passed over illum [*sic*] he with the pressure of his thumb checked the blood while Richardson's surgeon ligated the artery. . . ." [39]

Dr. Peter adds that this act of Dudley converted "his deadly antagonist into a lifelong friend." [40] At a later date, they may have become less antagonistic but certainly there was no friendship immediately after the duel. At the time of the encounter, Richardson was Grand Master of the Grand Lodge (Masonic) of Kentucky and Dudley was a Past Master. At the meeting of the Grand Lodge begun in Lexington on 31 August 1818, the duellers were censured for conduct entirely repugnant to the principles of masonry and cited to appear before it on 3 September 1818. Claiming jurisdiction over the duellists, some of the members strongly urged expulsion. On motion of Henry Clay (1777-1852) a committee of five was appointed with instructions to attempt reconciliation. The committee was successful and though the Grand Lodge condemned the duellists in the strongest terms, they were merely "suspended from the privileges of Masonry during the pleasure of the Grand Lodge." A year later, 3 September 1819, as a result of "the reconciliation which has happily taken place between said brothers," they were restored to all rights and privileges of the order. [41]

More than two months elapsed before Dudley answered

---

[39] Graham: ALS, Feb. 2, 1876.
[40] Peter: *op. cit.*, p. 25.
[41] Grand Lodge of Kentucky: *Proceedings begun* . . . 31 August 1818 (Lexington, Ky.: Worsley & Smith, 1818), p. 10. *Proceedings* . . . (1819), p. 21.

Drake's "sharp" pamphlet of 10 July 1818. Dudley had been busy preparing for the meeting with his challenger. Then too composition was at all times difficult for him. On 25 September 1818, Dudley replied *To Dr. Drake* in a pamphlet of eighteen pages.[42] He not only again accused Drake of many misdemeanors, adding new ones, but also unmercifully castigated the Reverend Blythe. Strangely enough, however, he failed to mention Richardson. Of him, he had had enough: a second demand for "personal satisfaction" might have been forthcoming.

Eleven days from the date of Dudley's pamphlet, Drake issued his *Second Appeal*.[43] In its unanswerable logic, its witticisms, and quaint humor, it is fully equal if not superior to any controversial article Drake ever wrote. Refuting Dudley's new and former charges, Drake then taunts him, declaring:

> I acknowledge that in going to Lexington I anticipated something from his society. I had heard, it is true, that he once failed to get into practice in that town, and, abandoning the profession, established himself in the trade of a commission merchant at New Orleans; but I was so credulous, as to suppose that a voyage to Europe, even for commercial purposes, might have added something to his natural inanity. In this, however, I was disappointed. In my first interview, I perceived the ensigns of Paris foppery to have nearly obscured the slender stock of intellect on which they were engrafted;—while a closer inspection soon convinced me, that egotism, ignorance and sycophancy had formed within him an unholy alliance, and alternately guided the helm of his destinies. The obligations of official duty might compel me to associate with such a man; but nature would defend me against his friendship.[44]

[42] [B. W. Dudley]: *To Dr. Drake* [No imprint, signed on p. 18: "B. W. Dudley, Lexington, K., September 25, 1818."].

[43] Drake: *A Second Appeal. . . .*

[44] *Ibid.*, p. 21.

He proceeds to expose Dudley's labored and ineffectual style with biting sarcasm. Dudley had complained that his letter had been published without punctuation. Drake's retort was: ". . . if he wished me to do this, he should have added a postscript to that effect." A letter of 18 July 1818 is quoted, clearly indicating that a challenge to a duel from Dudley would be accepted. Drake comments: "Dr. Dudley could not fail to be convinced, that while from policy, as well as principle, I might expose his falsehoods, as the surest mode of punishment, the further outrage of a *call* would be resented by an acceptance." [45]

Dudley neither sent a challenge nor attempted rebuttal, remaining silent in his defeat.

[45] *Ibid.*, p. 24.

Cincinnati, 1818-23

BY THE publication of the *Notices* (1810) and the *Picture
of Cincinnati* (1815), Drake became Cincinnati's best-known
citizen. Visitors either had letters of introduction to him or
sought an interview without one. He was gracious to all. Since
a discussion of his reception of travellers and their reactions
is reserved for a subsequent chapter, two visitors only will be
mentioned here.

Thomas Nuttall (1786-1859), scientist, author, and professor of natural history in Harvard University, visited Cincinnati during the summer of 1816. Drake arranged for a party
and invited, among others, J. C. Short, Dr. Charles Wilkins
Short, and General (later President) William Henry Harrison.[2] On a later visit, 13 November 1818, Nuttall wrote:
"To-day, I arrived in Cincinnati, and was again gratified by
the company of my friend, Doctor Drake, one of the most
scientific men west of the Allegheny Mountains." [3]

Bishop Philander Chase (1775-1852) of the Episcopal
Church wrote of his first visit to Cincinnati:

[1] Daniel Drake: *An Oration on the Causes, Evils and Prevention of Intemperance* (Columbus, Ohio: Olmstead & Bailhache, 1831), p. 8.
[2] Daniel Drake: ALS, Wednesday noon, 1816, to Messers. J. C. & C. W.
Short. In the Charles Wilkins Short Collection, the Filson Club, Louisville.
[3] Thomas Nuttall: *A Journal of Travels into the Arkansa Territory* (Philadelphia: Thomas W. Palmer, 1821), p. 32.

Arrived in Cincinnati, Saturday, May 17, 1817.

Dr. Drake, whose book, descriptive of that rising city, had attracted the writer's notice, received him kindly, and made provision that he should preach in the brick meeting-house with two steeples the next day. [The First Presbyterian Church of which the Reverend Joshua L. Wilson was pastor.] The congregation was large and attentive, and at the close of the service the writer observed that if there were any present friendly to the Episcopal Church and desirous of forming a parish attached to her Communion in that city, he would be glad to see them at Dr. Drake's immediately after the sermon. Repairing thither, there was a goodly number of the most respectable inhabitants, and among the rest was our late chief magistrate, his excellency the president of the United States, then known by his favorite name, "General Harrison. . . ." [4]

This group organized Christ Church of which Drake's wife was a charter member. Years later in Louisville, Dr. Drake united with the Episcopal Church.

Recognition of Drake's scientific achievements by national organizations came six months after his thirty-second birthday. On 17 April 1818, he was elected to membership in the American Philosophical Society. The American Antiquarian Society on 15 April 1818 made him a regular member and, in 1819, a "corresponding member." In accepting the latter honor, he wrote: "I am at this time engaged, in conjunction with some other gentlemen, in attempting to lay the formation of a museum of natural and artificial curiosities from the Western Country." The American Antiquarian Society owns another letter from him, 25 February 1820, in which he offered to send a description of the "remains of antiquity" in

[4] [Philander Chase], *Bishop Chase's Reminiscences to A. D. 1847* (2 vols., Boston: James B. Dow, 1848), Vol. I, p. 132. Consult also William Henry Venable: *A Centennial History of Christ Church, Cincinnati 1817-1917* (Cincinnati: Stewart Kidd Company, 1918).

Cincinnati. The director of the American Antiquarian Society states that Drake never sent the description.[5]

Early in February 1818, Drake was appointed one of the directors of the Office of Discount and Deposit of the Bank of the United States (Cincinnati Branch).[6] He served until 1820.

In the editorial column of *The Western Spy* for 30 May 1818 will be found the first newspaper reference to the museum mentioned by Drake in his letter to the American Antiquarian Society. The editors prophesied that: "Full cooperation could be expected from a community which abounds with liberality towards every undertaking that has a tendency to promote the extension of science in our newly settled country."[7]

Some writers have stated that Drake, after having visited museums in the East, conceived the plan of establishing one in Cincinnati. Though the most industrious worker and, in fact, the driving force behind the institution, the idea did not originate with him. This fact is unequivocally acknowledged in the dedication to the Cincinnati merchant, William Steele, in the printed version of Drake's discourse delivered at the formal opening of the museum:

> To Mr. William Steele, of Cincinnati.
> Dear Sir,
>   As you had the honor of first proposing the establishment of a permanent Museum in this city, and have contributed more liberally than any other person to its organization and support, I cannot forego the pleasure, as an act of common

---

[5] Clarence S. Brigham, Director, American Antiquarian Society, TLS to the author, 25 July 1958.

[6] *The Western Spy* (Cincinnati), N.S., IV, Feb. 14, 1818: p. [3]—c. [1].

[7] [Editorial], "A Museum of Natural Curiosities," *The Western Spy*, N.S., VI, May 30, 1818: p. [3]—c. [1].

justice, of inscribing to you the following humble but well
meant effort to promote its interests and utility.[8]

Associated with merchant Steele and Drake as managers
were the Reverend Elijah Slack, General James Findlay, attorney, early mayor of Cincinnati, and congressman from
Ohio (1825-33); and Jesse Embry, a land agent. In a few
weeks the managers obtained subscriptions amounting to
$45,000. Had Drake, the secretary of the board of managers,
not been ill in July, it is probable that detailed plans for the
museum would have been announced earlier than 15 September 1818. In their appeal for specimens the managers requested all types in the following groups:

> 1. Our metals and minerals generally, including petrefac-
> tions.
> 2. Our indigenous animals, embracing the remains of
> those which are now extinct.
> 3. The relicks of the unknown people who contributed
> the ancient works of the Western Country.
> 4. The various articles manufactured for ornament or use
> by the present savage tribes.[9]

As a nucleus, Drake gave the society his extensive collections of minerals, bones of the mammoths, and antiquities
of the West. It is evident that the managers planned, in
addition to the above, comprehensive collections of animals
(both living and extinct), birds, fish, insects, reptiles, fossils, remains of the prehistoric inhabitants, and the weapons,
utensils, and trinkets of all the contemporary Indian tribes.
It was also proposed: "In due time to open a gallery of paint-
ings, and thus offer to the lovers and cultivators of the fine

[8] Daniel Drake: *An Anniversary Discourse, on the State and Prospects of
the Western Museum Society* (Cincinnati, Ohio, The Society, 1820), p. 3.
[9] Daniel Drake *et al.*, Managers: "An Address to the people of the Western
Country," *Liberty Hall* . . . , *Cincinnati Gazette*, XIV, No. 733:p. [2]—c.
[2], Sept. 15, 1818. Also in *The American Journal of Science* (New York-New
Haven), I:203-6 (1818).

arts, a few of those models which are absolutely necessary to the gratification and improvement of their taste."

For a town with a population of 9120 in 1818, the managers' vision of such a comprehensive institution seems impractical. Yet within less than three years, the dream became a flourishing reality.

As secretary of the Board of Managers of the Western Museum Society, Drake was in charge of arrangements. Exhibit space in the south wing of the Cincinnati College building was secured. In August 1819, Drake appointed as curator, on a full-time basis, Robert Best, a young watch and instrument repairer. It is clearly apparent that this selection was wise since Best showed considerable imagination and ingenuity in preparing and arranging the exhibits. During the winter of 1819-20, he was sent into the northwest whence he returned with many pelts of the wild animals and numerous articles used by various Indian tribes.

Probably as a result of keen interest in his wife's artistic talents, Drake went out of his way to befriend artists. Late in 1819, he learned of the interest in art, ornithology, and taxidermy of John James Audubon (1785?-1851), then in Louisville. He was penniless, following the most recent of his several failures in business. Audubon was immediately employed as taxidermist and artist on a part-time basis.

Audubon's work in Cincinnati under Drake, as suggested by Donald Culross Peattie, could have been the spark which started him on his career as "the portraitist of all the birds of America." [10] In his *Anniversary Discourse*, Drake, in comparing the work of Alexander Wilson (1766-1813) and of Audubon, suggests that additional ornithological studies be made:

> It would be an act of injustice to speak of our ORNI-
> THOLOGY, without connecting with it the name of Alex-

[10] Donald Culross Peattie: *Audubon's America* (Boston: Houghton Mifflin Co., 1940), pp. 13-14.

ander Wilson. To this self taught, indefatigable and ingenious man we are indebted for most of what we know concerning the natural history of our Birds. His labours may have nearly completed the Ornithology of the middle Atlantic states, but must necessarily have left that of the Western imperfect. When we advert to the fact, that most birds are migratory, and that in their migrations they are not generally disposed to cross high mountains, but to follow the courses of rivers; when we contemplate the great basin of the Mississippi, quite open to the north and south, but bounded on the east and west by ranges of lofty mountains, while the river itself stretches through twenty degrees of latitude, connecting Lake Superior and the Gulf of Mexico, it is reasonable to conjecture, that many birds annually migrate over this country which do not visit the Atlantic states, and might, therefore, have escaped the notice of their greatest ornithologist in the single excursion which he made to the Ohio. As a proof of this supposition, it may be stated that Mr. Audubon, one of the excellent artists attached to the Museum, who has drawn from nature, in colored crayons, several hundred species of American birds, has, in his port folio, a large number that are not figured in Mr. Wilson's work, and many which do not seem to have been recognized by any naturalist.[11]

The suggestion that Wilson's work be supplemented could not have failed to influence Audubon. After his connection with the Western Museum Society, Audubon never again engaged in business. Audubon's *Journals* show that he wrote Dr. Drake for at least a year after leaving Cincinnati.

In one of his *Journals*, Audubon mentions Mr. Best's "great talent" stating that, "So industrious were Mr. Best and I that in about six months we had augmented, arranged and finished all we could do for the museum." [12] With reference

[11] Drake: *An Anniversary Discourse* . . . , pp. 9-10.
[12] Maria R. Audubon: *Audubon and his Journals* (2 vols., New York: Charles Scribner's Sons, 1897), Vol. I, p. 37.

to his employment, Audubon wrote in his journal: "My salary was large, and I at once sent for your mother to come [to Cincinnati] . . . I found, sadly too late, that the members of the College museum were splendid promisers and very bad paymasters." [13]

It is obvious that Audubon was confused as to his employers: Cincinnati College or the Western Museum Society. In one place Drake is referred to as president of Cincinnati College while in another as president of the museum. He was, of course, neither. Audubon's memory was "untrustworthy" according to some biographers. He gleefully deceived a fellow naturalist, Constantine S. Rafinesque (1783-1842), with "tall" tales of grotesque birds and fish. Rafinesque attributed their "discovery" to Audubon to his embarrassment.

In *Audubon and his Journals*, it is stated that "no money was received from Dr. Drake." This statement is modified by its footnote: "Mrs. Audubon afterwards received four hundred dollars, of the twelve hundred dollars due, the remainder was never paid." [14] Herrick, who found many errors in previous accounts of Audubon's life, states in his authoritative biography: "The published accounts of the Cincinnati experience are strangely confused, and have led to aspersions of bad faith which were, we believe, quite undeserved. . . ." [15]

Audubon taught an art class and made hundreds of portraits in Cincinnati. Black chalk was his favorite medium, although ink, water color, and pencil were employed. Several years later oils were used. Only a few portraits of the Cincinnati period are known. Of the Drake family, one is of Isaac and another of his wife, Elizabeth. A third sketch in pencil is owned by Mrs. Samuel B. McPheeters of St. Louis,

[13] *Ibid.*
[14] *Ibid.*, p. 49.
[15] Francis Hobart Herrick: *Audubon the Naturalist* (New York: D. Appleton & Co., 1917), p. 303.

Missouri. It is of a man in his twenties which greatly resembles a recently discovered portrait of Drake's brother, Benjamin.

Coincidentally, with completion of the work for the Western Museum, his art classes dwindled. Study of ornithology now took precedence over all else. Audubon left Cincinnati by flatboat for New Orleans on 12 October 1820, thus beginning his voyage to international fame.

In July 1818, a lad of sixteen with a letter of introduction came to Cincinnati from Maysville, near Drake's Kentucky home. Recognizing the artistic talents of Aaron Houghton Corwine (1802-30), Drake befriended him. Corwine's previous training had been obtained by sketching portraits and scenes on barns and board fences, occasionally aided by itinerant artists. He sought more formal training and, at Drake's suggestion, a number of Cincinnatians paid for their portraits in advance in order to defray the expenses of a course under the famous Philadelphia artist, Thomas Sully (1783-1872). Returning to Cincinnati in 1822, Corwine made the portraits previously promised and many others. These are today acclaimed the best ever executed there. One of the most remarkable is that of Dr. Drake's son, Charles D., in the uniform of a U.S. midshipman (October 1827).

A contemporary estimate of Corwine by Benjamin Drake and Edward D. Mansfield was: "In Portrait painting we may indeed boast of a young artist* who has but a single rival in the Western Country./ *Mr. A. H. Corwine, a native of Kentucky." [16] To the director of the Milwaukee Art Center, Edward H. Dwight, belongs the credit for "rediscovering" and for locating more than two dozen portraits by Corwine.[17]

---

[16] B. Drake and E. D. Mansfield: *Cincinnati in 1826* (Cincinnati: Morgan, Lodge, and Fisher, Feb., 1827), p. 88. The rival of Corwine was probably Matthew Harris Jouett (1787-1827) of Lexington.

[17] Edward H. Dwight: "Aaron Houghton Corwine," *Antiques* (New York), LXVII:502-4, June 1955 and [Edward H. Dwight]: *Rediscoveries in Ameri-*

Corwine was in Philadelphia at the time of the formal opening of the exhibits of the Western Museum Society. It has been impossible to determine whether he was ever directly connected with the Western Museum, though several portraits in oil by him were exhibited there.

Mention should here be made of the earliest contact of Constantine S. Rafinesque with the Western Museum Society. On 8 July 1820, he wrote Drake, the secretary, offering to send some marine shells, botanical specimens, and books he had published, in exchange for mounted birds and quadrupeds of the West.[18] Drake answered on 29 August 1820. This reply has not been found though its contents may be safely surmised from Rafinesque's reaction in one of his many extraordinarily tactless comments:

> [Of institutions in Ohio]: Many of their puffs are mere tricks, for instance, they have established a Museum, which has issued proposals of exchange; but when applied to, they had nothing to give, but were very greedy to receive!
>
> . . . .
>
> You will perhaps be glad to hear that there are two writers of some talent in Ohio: Dr. Drake of Cincinnati and Mr. Atwater of Circleville. The former has shown himself an author of capability in his first work called Picture of Cincinnati; although that work is not free from defects and even errors: but he has not published anything since, except small rhetorical pamphlets; he aims at knowledge however, and if he does not know how to reach it, it is perhaps because he has a share of the unfortunate shortsight.[19]

---

can Painting (Cincinnati, Ohio), The Cincinnati Art Museum, 3 Oct. to 6 Nov. 1955.

[18] Constantine S. Rafinesque: ALS, 8 July 1820, to Daniel Drake. In Library of Harvard University.

[19] C. S. Rafinesque: "Fragments of a Letter to Mr. Bory St. Vincent," *Western Minerva* (Lexington), I:74, 7 Jan. 1821.

In the only known issue of *Western Minerva*, suppressed apparently before distribution because of many caustic comments, Rafinesque reviewed western publications of 1820: "An Anniversary Discourse on the state and prospects of the Western Museum Society, delivered in Cincinnati at the opening of the Museum, on June 10th, 1820. By Dr. Daniel Drake—Cincinnati, pamphlet, in 48.—An elaborate oration on a commendable subject and occasion; it would be well if the author could unite practice to theory." [20]

Rafinesque wrote "The Monkeys.—No. 1," signed "P. Hystrix, M.D." The following are excerpts:

> On the important art of distorting every thing to suit a peculiar purpose. Drs. Dragon and Sourlip.
>
> . . . .
>
> The Art of Cudgelling, and disturbing the sleep or rest of our neighbors. Dr. Fairplay.
>
> . . . .
>
> On the necessity of importing friends, when none are at home. By Dr. Stilts.
>
> Notes on 150 errors, misnomers, oversights, blunders and mistakes, in a picture of a town on the banks of the Ohio. By Dr. Telescope.[21]

It appears improbable that the quips quoted above were aimed at anyone other than Drake. He is likewise satirized in the "Future Epitaph" by "Doctor Porcupine Hystrix":

> Under this black stone
> Lies a body without a soul!
> Cleon Dragon, M.D.
> Who departed this life, the 5th January, 1823,

[20] *Western Minerva*, p. 66.
[21] *Ibid.*, pp. 68-69.

> At the early age of 35 years.
> Mourn Ohio! weep Cincinnati!
> Alas! your greatest pride is gone.
> But he has left you a picture
> Worthy of you and him.
> Alive he had no friends—
> Has he any below?
> Do not come too near
> Lest the gall of his bones
> Should yet reach you.
> Away! Away! Away! [22]

Rafinesque's ire can be readily understood since several satirical articles concerning him had appeared in Cincinnati newspapers. These were anonymous, though he apparently attributed them to the best-known writer there. Some were possibly by Drake, though "Ode XII" by "Horace in Cincinnati" was written by Thomas Peirce. This "Ode" is addressed "To C. S. Rafinesque: alias, *Professor Muscleshellorum, of Transylvania University, Lexington, Ky.*" The second of nine stanzas reads:

> What I may write you, cannot much surprise,
>   Since your own yankee friends have *guess'd* and *reckon'd*
> That you must be a Newton in disguise,
>   Or downright Quixote—not the first but second:
> And I, too, think your feats, harangues, disasters
> And writings, much resemble Sancho's master's.[23]

In two of the eight explanatory notes, Peirce stated that:

> Prof. Raf. travelled from Wheeling, Va. to Henderson, Ky. in a skiff, as fast as two men could row him. During that journey he discovered from 100 to 200 new species of fishes.

[22] *Ibid.*, pp. 69-70.
[23] [Thomas Peirce]: *The Odes of Horace in Cincinnati; as published in the "Western Spy and Literary Cadet" during the year 1821* (Cincinnati: Harrison's Press, 1822), pp. 22-23.

The oldest inhabitants of Cincinnati have not seen more than 30!!!!

Prof. Raf. during a short visit to the Island of Sicily, was so fortunate as to discover 1000 new species of plants; the whole of which were lost by shipwreck on his return to the U. States. His memory however being excellent, he has since his arrival been enabled to give a minute description of the whole. See his Flora Sicula.[24]

In every enterprise with which Drake was connected is seen a striking degree of organizational ability. He took advantage of all possible avenues of publicity. He early conceived the idea of creating honorary members to the Western Museum Society. Certificates were sent to prominent physicians, scientists, and editors throughout the Ohio Valley, the eastern and the southern states.

The certificate to Dr. Samuel Hildreth (1783-1863), prominent physician, historian, and scientist of Marietta, Ohio, is an example of many in existence:

Cincinnati, Ohio, July 23[d] 1819

Sir,

I have the honor to inform you, that on the pres't inst. you were elected an honorary member of the Western Museum Society.

The plan and object of this institution you will see displayed in the preceding address by the Managers. Any contributions which you may be able to make to our Museum will be thankfully received; and any expense you may incur in procuring and forwarding what you may regard as curiosities, will be promptly reimbursed by the Society

With great respect, I am, sir
your very obedient servant
Dan Drake, M. D. Secretary.

[24] *Ibid.*, p. 105.

Dr Sir

If you have any antiquities from the ancient works at Marietta, which you would part with our society would be greatly indebted to you for them. I am sir your servant

Very respectfully
Dan Drake.[25]

The activities of the Western Museum Society were not limited to the collection and exhibition of curiosities, but a library was started. On the 3 August 1819, it was stated that "Mr. George Charters and Doctor Drake, are the only persons who have yet made donations to the library . . ." An organ was installed, probably made by the curator, Robert Best. On 10 December 1819, another activity was announced: "Two courses of popular lectures will be delivered during the winter in the Western Museum at the College Edifice. The first by Dr. Drake, on MINERALOGY and GEOLOGY, with particular reference to the *minerals* and *formations* of the Ohio countries. The second by President Slack on the Elements of Natural Philosophy. . . ." [26]

The editors of the *Western Spy* commented:

On Tuesday evening the 14th inst. [i.e., Dec. 1819] Doct. Drake delivered in the College Hall to a numerous and respectable audience a lecture preparatory to the course instituted by the managers of the Western Museum Society. In this lecture he enumerated the various religious, charitable and literary institutions of this city, and after dwelling with considerable interest upon their character, utility and the improvement which they indicated in society, he closed his remarks with some admonitory exhortations to the members.

[25] Owned by the Library of Marietta College, through whose courtesy a photostat was obtained.
[26] J. Embree, Secretary, pro tem, Announcement, Lectures before the Western Museum Society, *Liberty Hall* . . . , I, Dec. 10, 1819:p. [3]—c. [3].

On Saturday evening, the 18th, he delivered in the Museum room his *introductory* lecture on the utility and pleasures of the study of mineralogy and geology, a copy of which by the request of the class, was furnished for publication, and we very much regret that for want of room it cannot appear in this day's paper. It will appear in our next.[27]

With his customary logic, Drake gave many reasons for the usefulness of the study of mineralogy and geology:

We are all endued with a disposition to enquire into the nature and relations of the things that surround us, & are led to gratify this disposition as liberally as possible in relation to works of art, and to the animal and vegetable kingdom; but why should we stop at these? Why not penetrate the thin covering which conceals from our prying eyes the multitudinous subjects of the mineral world? Its boundless variety of forms; its secret and silent decompositions and transformations, its beautiful petrefactions, and astonishing arrangement of parts. So inexhaustible are these wonders, that curiosity may feast to satiety and inquisitiveness exhaust itself in the most delightful scrutinies. Why then should we not devote a small portion of time to the studies which may claim our attention, and add to our catalogue of subjects for rational investigation those which our mother so liberally furnishes to her enquiring children? [28]

Francis Mason (1799-1874), a journeyman shoemaker, later a Baptist missionary, was in Cincinnati in 1819. He thought Cincinnati a "pretty place" and mentions in a single sentence the Indian "earthwork walls and gateways" which were visible. He devotes a whole paragraph to Dr. Drake:

[27] [James M. Mason and Thomas Palmer, editors]: "Introductory Lectures," *Western Spy and Cincinnati General Advertiser*, N.S. VI, Dec. 24, 1819: p. [3]—c. [4].
[28] Daniel Drake: "An Introductory Lecture on the Utility and Pleasures of the Study of Mineralogy and Geology," *Liberty Hall* . . . , N.S., I, No. 85:p. [2]—c. [1-4], Dec. 28, 1819.

In those days more interest was taken in geology than antiquities. Dr. Drake started a museum and delivered lectures on geology of the western country, illustrating his statements by many fossils that had been dug up in the neighborhood. I attended some of them, but the audience was small, owing to there being an entrance fee of twenty-five cents.[29]

The lectures by Drake on mineralogy were concluded on 26 February 1820, at which time he discussed copper, lead, antimony, tin, and mercury. During the course he had covered a wide range of subjects including Sir Humphry Davy's analytical studies on the earths and alkalies, limestones, marl, iron, slate, various gems, etc. Drake's lectures on mineralogy were followed by a series on geology, his last one, 1 April 1820, being on "Geological Theories and on the Conformity of Geological Facts to the Mosaic Account of the Creation and the Deluge."

Though organized primarily for the establishment of a museum, the Western Museum Society sought to influence Cincinnati culturally and scientifically. Through Drake's example and encouragement other Cincinnatians lectured on natural history, astronomy, chemistry, medical jurisprudence, aerostation, and ornithology. John Cleves Symmes (1780-1829), nephew and namesake of the pioneer owner of 1,000,000 acres of Ohio lands, lectured on his utterly fantastic theory of "concentric spheres," asserting that the earth was hollow, habitable within and open at the poles. The concentric sphere theory was ably refuted before the society by T. J. Matthews, civil engineer and onetime professor of mathematics at Transylvania University.

As an added attraction to the lectures, beginning 10 Feb-

[29] Francis Mason, D.D.: *The Story of a Working Mans Life* (New York: Oakley, Mason & Co.), p. 100.

ruary 1821, and for seven years afterward, nitrous oxide (laughing gas) was manufactured. Venturesome persons wishing a thrill were allowed to inhale it. "Laughing gas parties" had been started in England by Sir Humphry Davy (1778-1829) as early as 1798. James Gillray (1757-1815), caricaturist, made a striking drawing (23 May 1802) of a demonstration, labeled "Scientific Researches." In Gillray's caricature were shown Davy, Count Rumford, Isaac Disraeli, the Marquis of Stafford, Lord Stanhope, and other notables, some in ludicrous positions.[30]

Davy enlisted many friends including the poets Robert Southey (1774-1843) and Samuel Taylor Coleridge (1772-1834) as participants in his experiments. Since injuries to persons inhaling laughing gas caused no pain, Davy asserted (1800) that it might be advantageously used during surgical operations.[31] That the era of surgical anesthesia was delayed almost half a century after Davy's suggestion is one of the enigmas in the history of medicine. Drake was necessarily an interested observer of the Western Museum "laughing gas parties." No comments by him have been found.

The Western Museum Society under ordinary circumstances should have become a permanent institution. The founders had foresight, were zealous and indefatigable. Foreign visitors and those from other sections of the country considered the natural history collections the best in the United States.

After the War of 1812, rapid expansion of business and inflation of real estate began, especially in the West. There were untold millions in paper money, though probably not more than a million dollars in coins in circulation west of

[30] Thomas Wright: *The Works of James Gillray* (London: Chatto and Windus, n.d.), p. 289.

[31] Humphry Davy: *Researches, Chemical and Philosophical; chiefly concerning Nitrous Oxide* (London: J. Johnson, 1800), p. 556.

the Allegheny Mountains.[32] The paper money was of uncertain value, depending on the supposed solvency of the bank or firm issuing it.

The Bank of the United States, re-established in 1816, had a branch in Cincinnati. Its home office (Philadelphia) in 1818 drastically revised the procedure for the acceptance of paper money. This action forced the privately owned Cincinnati banks to suspend specie payments on 5 November 1818. Efforts on the part of Drake and other directors of the Cincinnati branch to secure a more realistic approach to the local problems by the Philadelphia office failed. The story, long and involved, need not be told here. The efforts of the Cincinnati directors merely resulted in their not being re-appointed at the end of their terms in 1820.

Business in Cincinnati stood still. Private citizens held rallies for devising means of meeting the emergency. It was even proposed that tea and coffee be dispensed with. Drake is reported to have favored retrenchment but objected to the banning of tea possibly because he believed it had medicinal value.

On 20 October 1820, the Cincinnati branch of the Bank of the United States was closed and an agent appointed for liquidation. Payment in specie—an impossible stipulation—was demanded on all loans. The other banks were closed. Many of the most prominent citizens lost their savings: Jacob Burnet, leader of the bar; Daniel Drake; and Martin Baum, wealthy businessman and financier. General William Henry Harrison lost heavily. Ironically, the real estate obtained by foreclosure was held for several years by the U.S. branch bank and then sold at a handsome profit. The names of those against whom foreclosure proceedings were instituted read like a Who's Who. Drake personally, and as security for

[32] [Editorial], *Western Spy and Literary Cadet* (Cincinnati), VII; Dec. 28, 1820.

relatives, owed more than fifty thousand dollars.[33] Ultimately he repaid his entire debt.

By the latter part of 1822, the Western Museum Society had accumulated debts amounting to fifteen hundred dollars. This deficit could have been met easily had several delinquent subscribers made good their pledges. In December 1822, the curator, Robert Best, agreed to buy the museum. Some shareholders being dissatisfied, Best surrendered his contract. Notice was then given that the collections would be sold at auction.[34] Apparently no bidders appeared and the institution was turned over to Joseph Dorfeuille (1791?-1840), a local scientist who had frequently lectured in the museum. It appears that the only proviso was that the original members of the society and their families have the privilege of visiting the exhibits.

From 1823, the institution became known as Dorfeuille's Museum. He commercialized it and added features entirely foreign to the original plans. These included the exhibition of wax and plaster figures of noted and notorious persons, the "Infernal Regions," and various undignified surprise features. The scientific exhibits gradually disappeared and their present location is unknown. In 1839, Dorfeuille went to New York City where the "Infernal Regions" were rebuilt in a building later operated by Barnum. Such was the fate of the first natural history museum in the West, to which Drake and the other managers had devoted so much thought and effort.

In 1819, a "humane society" was formed, of which Drake was second vice-president and one of the medical assistants. The purpose of this group was the rescue and resuscitation of persons apparently drowned. Cincinnati newspaper announce-

---

[33] Bank of the United States against Daniel Drake *et al.*, recorded in the Office of the Clerk of the U.S. District Court, Cincinnati, Ohio.
[34] The Western Museum for Sale [Ad.], *Liberty Hall* . . . , V; Mar. 18, 1823:p. [3]—c. [5].

ments of the society gave the location of the boats, drags, resuscitation apparatus, and directions.

Philanthropic projects in early Cincinnati took precedence over all others and Drake took part in most of them. The Cincinnati Society for the Promotion of Agriculture, Manufactures and Domestic Economy was established in 1819 with General William Henry Harrison, president. Drake was appointed a member of a standing committee of nine.[35] At the first regular meeting Drake read a paper: "Observations on the Means and Importance of Preserving Fruit and Forest Trees." This is the first discussion of forest conservation by an American writer which I have been able to locate. It antedated by seventy-three years the earliest systematic attempt in forestry in the United States, that of Gifford Pinchot (1865-1946).

Drake said:

> There are many persons, who will smile on any proposition that has for its object the preservation of a forest, which 30 years ago was the habitation of wild beasts. They consider all recommendations of the kind as applicable to the Eastern states or Europe, where timber trees are rare and valuable; but they forget, that this rarity and high price, have chiefly arisen from the neglect in those countries of these very recommendations. Had the people of Europe, in former times, been more provident and enlightened on this subject, their posterity of the present day would not be compelled to devote so large a portion of time to the cultivation of forest trees. . . .
>
> This wanton destruction of an invaluable heritage, this unnecessary waste of our future resources, must like every other species of improvidence, materially injure the interests of posterity.[36]

[35] "Agricultural and Economical Society," *Western Spy*, N.S., VI, Aug. 28, 1819:p.[2]—c. [1-2].

[36] Daniel Drake: "Observations on the Means and Importance of Preserving Fruit and Forest Trees," *Western Spy*, N.S., VI, Oct. 23, 1819:p. [2]—c. [4-6] and p. [3]—c. [1-2].

Drake deplored especially the destruction of trees around the farmstead which, if left standing, "would have not only afforded inexhaustible supplies in the center of the plantation, but contributed greatly to its picturesque appearance." He advised that wounds made in tapping sugar maples be treated with the protective cement formulated by the English gardener, William Forsyth (1737-1804). Likewise injuries to other important forest and fruit trees should receive the same treatment.

Thirty-one years before Drake's address, the spot from which he spoke was part of a heavily wooded wilderness. Here John Filson (?-1788), surveyor, schoolteacher, author of the first book describing Kentucky, and part owner of the land upon which Cincinnati stands, was killed by Indians. Almost a hundred years ahead of his time, Daniel Drake was advocating forest conservation, tree surgery, and landscape gardening.

7 ✌ *The establishment of medical schools is a prolific source of discord in the profession.*[1]

Medical College of Ohio, 1818-21

DRAKE'S INITIAL success in teaching in Transylvania University during the winter of 1817-18 made him ambitious to continue as a professor of medicine. Shortly after his return to Cincinnati from Lexington, the following notice appeared in *The Western Spy:*

LECTURES ON BOTANY

Dr. Drake proposes to deliver a course of *botanical* lectures, to commence about the first of May—should a competent number of Ladies and Gentlemen express their desire to become members of the class.

Public notice will be given of the time and place of the introductory lecture.[2]

More than forty subscribers enrolled and Drake delivered the introductory lecture on Friday evening, 8 May 1818, "at candle light in the First Presbyterian Church." Newspaper comment indicated that the lecture was of much interest, and "it was truly gratifying to see so numerous and respectable an audience, at the first attempt of the kind in the Western Country. . . ."[3]

[1] *Drake: Practical Essays on Medical Education,* p. 98.
[2] *The Western Spy,* N.S., IV, Apr. 4, 1818, p. [3]—c. [1].
[3] "Botanical Lectures," *Liberty Hall* . . . , XIV, No. 716:p. [2]—c. [4], May 20, 1818.

Writing to his friend Wm. H. Richardson of Lexington, Drake confided: "I have so far succeeded much better than I expected, though am still very imperfect. I lecture ex tempore and frequently use no notes at all. By next summer I hope to deliver a pretty good course." [4]

On 27 May 1818, Drake, Dr. Coleman Rogers, and the Reverend Elijah Slack ("late Vice-President, Professor of Mathematics and Natural Philosophy and Teacher of Chemistry, Princeton College") inserted an advertisement in the Cincinnati newspapers. A postscript requested fourteen other newspapers of the central west and south to copy it:

MEDICAL INSTRUCTION

The undersigned beg leave to inform those young gentlemen of the Western Country who are desirous of studying Medicine, that they have made the following preparations and arrangements for the instruction of private pupils:

1. They have collected an extensive medical, surgical and philosophical library, which includes all the journals of medicine and the physical sciences hitherto published, or now issuing in the U. States, with some of the principal magazines of Europe.

2. Dr. Drake will every spring and summer deliver a course of lectures on BOTANY; and every winter another one of MATERIA MEDICA and the PRACTICE OF PHYSIC; the latter course to be preceded by a series of lectures on PHYSIOLOGY, and illustrated with specimens of our *native medicines*.

3. Dr. Rogers will, in the winter season, deliver a course on the principles and practice of Surgery, illustrated with *operations and* ANATOMICAL *demonstrations*.

4. Mr. Slack will, during the same season, deliver a course on theoretical and practical CHEMISTRY embracing

---

[4] Daniel Drake: ALS to Willam H. Richardson, June 24, 1818. Owned by the Presbyterian Historical Society, Philadelphia, Pa.

PHARMACY; and the analysis of *Animal and Vegetable* substances.

5. Dr. Rogers and Drake will in conjunction, deliver annually a series of demonstrative OBSTETRICAL lectures.

6. They will be able to afford all who study with them, frequent opportunities of seeing Clinical practice both in Physic and Surgery.

The price of tuition including all the lectures, will be, as heretofore, fifty dollars a year.

Should any young gentlemen wish to attend the lectures without becoming private pupils, they will be admitted to all the courses for forty dollars.

Decent boarding and lodging can be procured for three dollars per week.[5]

In accordance with the advertised plans of Drake, the Reverend Slack, and Dr. Rogers, the lectures began early in November 1818. Drake's introductory to his course on materia medica and the practice of physic was delivered in the hall of the Lancasterian Seminary at "candle light" on 10 November 1818. His lecture was immediately followed by that of the Reverend Slack on chemistry and pharmacy. Dr. Rogers' course on surgery and surgical anatomy began the following day at noon in his lecture room.

Extracts of Drake's lecture and that of the Reverend Slack were carried in the newspapers. The historical portion of Drake's address revealed an unusual degree of knowledge of early materia medica in addition to ancient history.[6] The editor commented favorably on both lectures: "We cannot omit in this place to add our feeble testimony to the ardor

[5] D. Drake, C. Rogers, E. Slack: [Ad.], "MEDICAL INSTRUCTION," *Liberty Hall* . . . , XIV, No. 717:p. [3]—c. [1], May 27, 1818, and in subsequent issues for six weeks.

[6] [Extracts of Dr. Drake's Introductory]: *Inquisitor Cincinnati Advertiser,* I, No. 22:p. [2]—c. [3-5], Nov. 17, 1818 and No. 23:p. [2]—c. [1-6], Nov. 24, 1818.

and persevering enterprise of Doctor Drake, to introduce among us a taste for scientific pursuits. His incipient steps towards the establishment of a medical school here, eminently entitle him to the respect and consideration of the public." [7]

The medical lectures started by Dr. Rogers, the Reverend Slack, and Drake "attracted more students from a distance, than have at any time been brought to one of our western towns for a similar purpose." This success prompted Drake (December 1818) to go before the General Assembly of Ohio to ask for charters for two educational institutions. Without a dissenting vote charters were granted Cincinnati College and the Medical College of Ohio.[8]

Cincinnati College was to replace the Lancasterian Seminary previously mentioned. It was authorized to confer "all or any of the degrees that are usually conferred in any college within the United States." Twenty prominent citizens were designated trustees of Cincinnati College while the governing body of the Medical College of Ohio was its faculty. With the broad powers given Cincinnati College there would seem to have been no need for another institution conferring medical degrees exclusively. Possibly Drake thought that lay trustees could not manage a department of medicine as well as could physicians. The name, "Medical College of Ohio," might to him have seemed more likely to attract medical students than "Cincinnati College" with a medical department. Whatever the reason, Drake made a serious mistake in designating the medical college faculty as the governing body.

Cincinnati College immediately took over the affairs of the Lancasterian Seminary and occupied its partially completed

[7] "Chemical Lectures," *Liberty Hall* . . . , XIV, No. 746:p. [2]—c. [1-2], Dec. 15, 1818.
[8] Ohio: *Acts of General Assembly* (Chillicothe, Ohio: Geo. Nashee, 1819), Vol. XVII, pp. 37-40, 46-50.

building. Daniel Drake had been designated one of the trustees. At a meeting of the trustees on 30 March 1819, his brother Benjamin Drake was elected secretary. Cincinnati College continued its activities until 1826, when, as a result of the bank failures previously mentioned, it was suspended. Drake in 1835, resuscitated it with medical, academic, and law departments.

The legislative act establishing the Medical College of Ohio designated Daniel Drake as president and professor of the institutes and the practice of medicine. The same act named Coleman Rogers vice-president and professor of surgery; Elijah Slack, registrar, treasurer, professor of chemistry and pharmacy; and Samuel Brown, professor of anatomy. Drake's efforts in establishing the Medical College of Ohio led to a series of controversies which continued intermittently for almost thirty years.

John P. Foote (1783-1865), early book dealer, publisher, and author, once stated that "A history of the Medical College of Ohio may not inaptly be styled—'a history of the Thirty Years War.' " [9] He also wrote:

> The medical profession has always been remarkable for the belligerent propensities of its professors; and Cincinnati has furnished as eminent examples in this branch of medical practice as in the doctrines taught in the text-books of the other departments of medical science.
>
> It is a general characteristic of mankind to be willing to fight in behalf of whatever is considered of paramount importance to their well-being, present or prospective, and the religion whose first announcement and most important precept is, "peace on earth," has always had more professors who were ready to fight in its cause than obey its precepts—

[9] John P. Foote: *The Schools of Cincinnati and Its Vicinity* (Cincinnati: C. F. Bradley & Co.'s Power Press, 1855), p. 141.

enough always ready to die in its defence, but a marvellously small number who were willing to defend and diffuse its doctrines by living in conformity with them. The Christian religion is of the highest importance to mankind spiritually. The medical profession is so influential upon their physical well-being, that it is next in power to stimulate combativeness, and cause the sacrifice of great good to the evil principle of our nature.[10]

Before his appointment by the General Assembly of Ohio to a professorship, Dr. Samuel Brown (1769-1830), a Kentuckian then in Philadelphia, had sent a signed letter of acceptance. But when Drake notified him of the action of the General Assembly, Brown made no reply for eight months. He then refused the position, explaining that he had obtained a much better contract from President Holley of Transylvania University. Brown's failure to answer promptly the letter notifying him of the appointment places him in an unfortunate light which suggests duplicity or, at least, carelessness. Drake clearly stated that he did not censure Brown for not having accepted the position but for "withholding an expression of refusal. . . ." [11] Brown's rejection of the offer, received on 10 September 1819, thwarted Drake's hope of opening the college that year.

To make matters worse, his erstwhile partner, Dr. Coleman Rogers, although designated by Drake as vice-president and professor of surgery, had lauded and nominated Brown for honorary membership in the Cincinnati Medical Society.[12] To the sensitive Drake, this action of Rogers was nothing short of treason. At a faculty meeting immediately afterward

[10] *Ibid.*, p. 137.
[11] Daniel Drake: "Medical College of Ohio," *Liberty Hall* . . . , I, Oct. 19, 1819:p. [3]—c. [2-3].
[12] Daniel Drake: Letter to *The Western Spy* (Cincinnati), N.S., VI, Jan. 29, 1820:p. [3]—c. [3].

Drake and Slack voted to dismiss Rogers. On 23 February 1820, Drake and Rogers dissolved partnership.[13]

In a newspaper statement detailing the reasons for the failure to open the Medical College of Ohio as planned, Drake placed the sole blame on the defection of Dr. Samuel Brown.[14] Drake incidentally stated that the plans for the faculty "required six professors, three supplied by Cincinnati and it was necessary to obtain the other three elsewhere." A clique of physicians in Cincinnati immediately seized upon the latter sentence as a slur upon them. Learning of this, Drake at once published a letter of explanation in which he denied any intentional derogation of local physicians. He stated that while some local physicians *"have exercised a lively and honorable interest in the success of the project, there are none among those who have complained, that were at any time disposed to participate in its execution."* And he concluded: In common with many enlightened citizens I have felt an earnest desire that it [the college] should succeed, and for the glory of the profession, I have ventured to indulge the expectation that something beneficial to the interests of science and humanity might be accomplished:— The desire can never be extinguished." [15]

Drake's explanation only incited the opposition to greater fury. It is apparent that those participating in the attacks sought to ruin not only the medical college but also its sponsor. Dr. Oliver B. Baldwin, whose name survives solely because of his enmity to Drake, attempted to publish a derogatory statement in the two leading Cincinnati newspapers: *Liberty Hall and Cincinnati Gazette* and the *Inquisitor Cincinnati Advertiser.* Their editors refused publication unless

---

[13] "Dissolution of Partnership," *Inquisitor Cincinnati Advertiser,* I, No. 36: p. [3]—c. [5], Feb. 23, 1819.
[14] Drake: "Medical College of Ohio," *op. cit.*
[15] Daniel Drake: "An Explanation," *Liberty Hall . . . ,* I, Oct. 26, 1819: p. [3]—c. [1].

the article were first altered. However, the editor of the newly established *Literary Cadet* agreed to publish it.

Early on the morning of 27 December 1819, Drake went to the lodgings of Baldwin who described the visit:

> This morning when it was scarcely light, while I was in bed asleep, my boy having gone for some fire and left my office door unlocked, Dr. Drake entered with club in his hand, and drew a note from his pocket, ordering me to sign it, holding at the same time the club over my head. The substance of the note was, that I withdraw the piece about to appear in answer to him in today's paper. This I refused; he seized me, unarmed and in bed, by the throat, and said I should; at the same time raising the club in the act of striking me. I immediately seized the club, and endeavored to protect myself; in doing so, he dragged me out in the street, and tore the shirt nearly off my back; at the same time my wrist was injured so that I could not defend myself; I then left in haste, to procure some weapon and dress myself. As soon as I had done so, I returned, and found he had disappeared.[16]

Drake is known to have carried a cane. His description of the incident follows:

> Dr. Baldwin had me indicted by the grand jury of the City Court, for *unlawfully entering his house with intent to do mischief*, and for committing upon him an *assault* and *battery*. It appeared, however, in evidence on the trial, that I went in a peaceable manner, to remonstrate against the publication which has already been referred to; that I did not unlawfully enter his house; that while in it I did *not* commit an assault and battery upon him; but he got alarmed at my insisting that he stop his intended publication, "and left in haste" for an adjoining tavern; and that when he started from his own door I ran a few steps after him to get him fairly

[16] Oliver B. Baldwin: *The Literary Cadet* (Cincinnati), I, No. 6:p. [2]—c. [2-3] and p. [3]—c. [1-2], Dec. 27, 1819.

under way. For this the jury, not on his testimony, but that of bystanders, convicted me of an *assault* only, and the Court fined me ten dollars.[17]

Further investigation of this clash seems impossible since fire, in 1849, destroyed the courthouse and its records. The statements of the participants permit us to reach our own conclusions.

The Cincinnatians enjoyed the comedy, as is shown by a commemorative "Ode" by "Horace in Cincinnati." Thomas Peirce (1786-1850), a businessman with poetic inclinations, wrote thirty-one "Odes" concerning various happenings of local interest. The odes appeared anonymously in a newspaper and were later published in book form. The following two stanzas from "Ode XXIV" describe the Baldwin-Drake comedy:

> Our Aesculapian jars
>   Of all are much the oldest;
> Ergo, in paper wars
>   Physicians are much the boldest.
> They're resolute—to think,
>   They're desperate—in writing;
> And while they shed but ink,
>   There can't be bloody fighting.
> *The town can never thrive,*
>   *But when we have a squabble*
> *To keep the bards alive*
>   *And titillate the rabble.*
>
> The warfare was begun
>   Long ere we shook with laughter
> To see *Pillgarlic* run
>   And *Doctor Pompous* after:—
> It was a fearful strife

---

[17] Daniel Drake: "To the Editors," *The Western Spy*, N.S., VI, Feb. 19, 1820:p. [3]—c. [2-5].

As some have stated, sighing
Who saw, to save his life
The former shirtless flying.
The town can never thrive, &c.[18]

The venom of Oliver B. Baldwin is shown by a later attack
in which he referred to Drake as "that common disturber of
the peace" who has an "ungovernable passion for broils and
newspaper abuse" and who attempts to screen his character
by "effusions of stupid vulgar wit." He continues:

> And neither the local popularity which he may acquire
> with a few unacquainted with Natural Science, by his plagia-
> rised lectures; nor the more extended reputation which he may
> have attached to his name by laboriously and *mechanically*
> collecting and publishing in a book, the knowledge and ob-
> servations of others, will save him from the contempt due to
> his arrogance, malignity and meanness.[19]

No reply to this latter attack has been found. Drake may
have felt it was too absurd to require a reply.

On 5 January 1820, Dr. Coleman Rogers challenged Drake
to a duel.[20] Following the duel in Lexington between Richardson and Dudley and his published defiance of the latter,
Drake had apparently decided, in 1818, in the light of his
"education, habit and principle," never to accept a challenge.
He had discussed this decision with many friends, including
Rogers, who was then his office partner. Hence when Rogers
in 1820 accused him of *aggression* and demanded *satisfaction,*

---

[18] Peirce: *The Odes of Horace*, p. 67. The appellation, "Dr. Pompous,"
given Drake by "Horace" was probably apt, since he was said to give directions to his patients "very much as though he were delivering a discourse on
the doctrine of election." (Annie Fields: *Life and Letters of Harriet Beecher
Stowe* [Boston: Houghton, Mifflin & Co., 1897], p. 79.)

[19] Oliver B. Baldwin: "To the Editors," *The Western Spy and Cincinnati
General Advertiser*, N.S., VI:p. [3]—c. [4], Feb. 5, 1820.

[20] Daniel Drake: "To the Editors," *ibid.*, N.S., VI:p. [3]—c. [2-5], Feb.
19, 1820.

Drake refused the challenge, asserting that the only aggression was that of Rogers himself in having lauded Brown, thus securing his election to the Cincinnati Medical Society. Therefore Drake left the matter with his "considerate fellow citizens" to decide: "If Dr. Rogers did not challenge me under a perfect conviction that I would not accept it; and whether under any circumstances this was the proper mode of atoning to the people of Ohio, for a desertion of the interest of an institution, in which our legislature had given him a professorship?" [21]

Thus ended the Rogers-Drake affair. Shortly thereafter, Rogers moved to Newport, Kentucky, and later to Louisville (1823) where he practiced for the remainder of his life.

Drake was now attacked by a recently arrived Irish emigrant, John Moorhead (1784-1873), a medical graduate of the University of Edinburgh. Moorhead was palpably influenced by at least four motives: desire for publicity, apparent friendship for Baldwin, jealousy of the most capable and prominent western physician, and his own well-known bellicosity. It has been impossible to determine Coleman Rogers' influence in this and in the other disputes of this period.

Although not even a member of the Cincinnati Medical Society, Moorhead demanded in an angry letter whether he were included among those accused of seeking to destroy the medical college. His language was so offensive that Drake did not reply. Next, Moorhead wrote a note to Dr. Drake's father, who answered that he had heard his son say: "I did not even think of Dr. Moorhead." Regardless of this, Moorhead immediately published a diatribe of four newspaper columns in which he laboriously set himself up as Drake's implacable enemy. He vehemently denies that he is a "conspirator" adding: "Never hope, Sir—never dare to hope that till thou

[21] *Ibid.*

shalt have made a full and humble retraction, war on my side open, vehement war shall ever cease between us." [22]

It is most unfortunate that Drake did not ignore an attack from such a source. However, Moorhead's vulnerability proved too great a temptation. Instead of making accusations, Drake ingeniously posed thirty-nine "problems." Some of these seem irrelevant, but others were so telling that Moorhead was apparently furious.[23]

In two installments of nine verbose and frequently incoherent columns, Moorhead corroborates rather than controverts the barbed insinuations. In "Problem 34," Drake had asked: "Whether, in a few months after the Drs. arrival in America, if he had not left Nashville by stealth, he would have been mobbed for abusing the character of General Jackson."

Moorhead replied:

> In Knoxville not in Nashville, I happened on the evening of my arrival to fall in conversation with some gentlemen in the bar-room. . . . [Next morning I learned] that my observations had given deep offense. . . . Friendly advice placed me on my guard. . . . Having transacted my business and after listening awhile to the debates of the legislature, I departed about noon, fearlessly in the face of open day from Knoxville—a place which I shall ever remember, as having first introduced me to a knowledge of such characters as Dr. Drake—to a knowledge of Rowdies, who are zealous by clubs and violence to proscribe in the name of their country the liberty of speech.[24]

[22] J. Moorhead: "To Daniel Drake, M.D.," *The Western Spy*, N.S., VI, Jan. 15, 1820:p. [3]—c. [2-6].
[23] Daniel Drake: "To the Editors," *The Western Spy*, N.S., VI, Jan. 22, 1820:p. [3]—c. [4-6].
[24] J. Moorhead: "To Daniel Drake, M.D.," *Liberty Hall* . . . , N.S., I, No. 96:p. [2]—c. [1-4], Feb. 4, 1820 and No. 98:p. [2]—c. [1-5], Feb. 11, 1820.

Months later, Moorhead, clumsy and resembling a wrestler in build, met Benjamin Drake (1794-1841), younger brother of the doctor, on the street. Moorhead attempted to whip him when Benjamin, undaunted, pulled a knife and routed his assailant. "Horace" sang:

> And t'other day we find
> (Here none can think me bouncing)
> *Professor Pill* design'd
> To give "one Ben" a trouncing.
> Though furious as a Turk
> The lad seem'd not to mind him,
> But promptly drew a dirk,
> And popt it in behind him.
> *The town can never thrive, &c.*[25]

The newspapers published several additional letters from Moorhead to which Drake replied. Finally the editor of *The Western Spy* announced:

> We have been applied to by Dr. Drake to publish a reply to Dr. Moorhead's last piece, including the certificates of four gentlemen, going to substantiate Dr. Drake's statement that Dr. Moorhead made an apology to him for the letter which is referred to in that publication; but having nothing more, we have been under the necessity of refusing this answer an insertion. It therefore remains in the hands of the author where, we are requested to say, it may be seen by any gentleman who may desire to read it.[26]

The malignity of Moorhead toward Drake continued unabated for thirty years. Moorhead never became a U.S. citizen and Drake, therefore, designated him as "that foreigner." There are two apocryphal stories concerning physical encounters between them. In one, after Drake had inflicted a scalp

[25] Peirce: *The Odes* . . . , p. 68.
[26] [Editorial], *The Western Spy*, N.S., VI, No. 302:p. [3]—c. [3], Mar. 18, 1820.

wound and blackened Moorhead's eye, bystanders separated them. Another tale was that having met on the street, they exchanged angry words and Moorhead knocked Drake unconscious by a blow on the head with a sack filled with silver dollars. He then casually continued on his way to the bank. Juettner states[27] that Moorhead challenged Drake to a duel, which, if true, was undoubtedly ignored.

Obituaries and eulogies may sometimes be quite at variance with facts. In 1873, the Academy of Medicine of Cincinnati held a meeting to express the sense of the profession on the death of Moorhead. One speaker bore testimony "to his remarkable truthfulness, to his bright integrity of purpose, and his singular freedom from little meannesses *such as dirty attacks in the newspapers upon his professional brethren.*" [28] The italicized portion of the quotation should be compared with the facts.

Elsewhere, notably in Louisville, the early attempt to establish a medical school (1833-37) resulted in opposition on the part of certain members of the medical profession. In Louisville at that time there was no Drake with a ready pen and no Moorhead to doggedly pursue the attack. In 1842, several years after Drake had accepted a professorship in the Louisville Medical Institute, the professors were again subjected to criticism.[29] By this time Drake was less sensitive, and since the assault was directed against all members of the faculty, he seems to have ignored it.

In 1818, the Cincinnati Medical Society was organized. When Dr. Samuel Brown, whose failure to accept a professorship prevented the immediate opening of the Medical

[27] Juettner, *op. cit.*, p. 62.
[28] [E. B. Steven, editor], "Death of Dr. Morehead [should be Moorhead]," *The Cincinnati Lancet and Observer*, N.S., XVI:562-64, Sept. 1873.
[29] Emmet F. Horine: "A Collector Goes to the Race Track Bookishly Inclined," *The Filson Club History Quarterly* (Louisville, Ky.), XVIII: 203-23, Oct. 1944.

College of Ohio, was elected to honorary membership, Drake and the Reverend Elijah Slack, its president, resigned. Shortly thereafter, a rival medical society was formed: The Medico-Chirurgical Society of Cincinnati. Drake was elected president and Slack became the senior vice-president.[30] At about the same time, Drake issued proposals for the establishment of a medical journal. Though over two hundred subscribers were obtained, other duties prevented its start.

Despite continued opposition and intrigues of his enemies, Drake persisted in efforts to secure capable teachers for the Medical College of Ohio. On 20 August 1820, he announced that the school was organized with the following faculty: Jesse Smith, M.D. (1793-1833), professor of anatomy and surgery; Benjamin S. Bohrer, M.D., professor of materia medica and pharmacy; the Reverend Elijah Slack, A.M., assisted by Mr. Robert Best (1790-1830), chemistry; Daniel Drake, M.D., professor of the institutes and practice of medicine, including obstetrics and diseases of women and children.[31]

The Medical College of Ohio, the second medical school west of the Allegheny Mountains, opened with a class of twenty-four. The president, Daniel Drake, delivered the "Inaugural Discourse on Medical Education" in the chapel of Cincinnati College, 11 November 1820.[32] Though only thirty-five years of age, Drake already had an international reputation as is shown later. His "Inaugural Discourse" was a fervent plea to raise the standards of medical education. He recommended broader preliminary training, the extension of

---

[30] [Editorial], "Medico-Chirurgical Society," *The Western Spy*, N.S., VI: p. [3]—c. [2], Jan. 8, 1820.
[31] Daniel Drake: "Medical College of Ohio," *Liberty Hall* . . . , N.S., II: p. [3]—c. [2-3], Aug. 23, 1820.
[32] Daniel Drake: *An Inaugural Address on Medical Education* (Cincinnati: Looker, Palmer & Reynolds, 1820). Reprinted with an introduction by Emmet Field Horine (New York: Henry Schuman, 1951).

CINCINNATI COLLEGE.

Fig. 6. Cincinnati College, chartered 1818, medical department opened in 1835.

the course of medical lectures from the customary four months to five, teaching at the bedside of patients, and hospital training. Probably influenced by a former teacher, Benjamin Rush, Drake insisted that the student must not confine his researches to the changes of anatomical structure alone but "must extend them to the mind itself, and to its operations and effects." [33] Many additional points in Drake's address are worthy of comment. To be appreciated, however, the "Inaugural" must be read in its entirety.

In 1876, Dr. J. C. Grubbs, then the oldest living graduate of the Medical College of Ohio, related his impressions of Drake during the 1820-21 session. The lectures were delivered in a large room over the drug store of Isaac Drake at 91 Main Street, Cincinnati:

[33] *Ibid.*, p. 8.

Dr Drake was a gentleman of the old school, and he was very pleasant and affable to all students. He was a fine and graceful writer, and well versed in all the collateral branches of medicine, as zoology, botany etc., etc. Professor Drake impressed me more than any other of the teachers, so that I always used him as my consulting physician up to the time of his death. He had a large practice and was the only man here who had a European reputation. He was the fortunate possessor of a buggy in which to visit his patients, the rest went on horseback or walked, as we had to do in our pre-vehicular day. He had a gray horse too, so that everybody knew him at sight.[34]

Drake believed that: "The laboratory is not more necessary for the study of chemistry or a garden of plants for the study of botany, than a hospital for the study of practical medicine and surgery." [35]

December 1820 found Drake in Columbus, Ohio, fathering a bill for a hospital. On 16 January 1821, the Commercial Hospital and Lunatic Asylum for the State of Ohio at Cincinnati was created and $10,000 appropriated. The township was to furnish a site and its trustees were to superintend erection. Current expenses were to be defrayed by one-half of the duties on sales at auction and by ordinary poor taxes. Paupers and Ohio boatmen when sick at Cincinnati were to be treated gratuitously. Penniless lunatics of the state were to be admitted with the counties from which they came, paying two dollars a week, "the price that is now paid for keeping them in jail." [36] The medical and surgical attendance on all the patients, both of the hospital and asylum, whether

[34] J. C. Grubbs: "Presidential Address" in *Transactions of the Society of the Alumni of the Medical College of Ohio* (Cincinnati: Cincinnati Lancet Press Print, 1880).

[35] Daniel Drake: *Introductory Lecture . . . Medical College of Ohio* (Cincinnati: Morgan and Overend, 1849), p. 15.

[36] [Editorial], "The Hospital," *Liberty Hall . . .* , N.S., II, Jan. 20, 1821: p. [3]—c. [1].

paupers or otherwise, was to be furnished by the professors
of the Medical College of Ohio. As remuneration, the professors were at liberty to admit the students of the college to
witness the treatment. The fees paid by the students for admission were to be deposited in the treasury of the Medical
College of Ohio as a fund with which to augment its library
and apparatus.[37]

As I have said elsewhere, this was the *first* hospital in the
United States established primarily for teaching purposes and
staffed exclusively by the professors of a medical school.[38] It
antedated by more than half a century the pavilion built by
the University of Michigan, once erroneously termed, "the
first university hospital in the United States." [39] The name,
"Commercial," in the title of Drake's hospital does not change
the fact that it was deliberately founded for teaching. Neither
does the contention that the Michigan pavilion was a university hospital whereas that in Cincinnati was attached to a
college alter either facts or dates.[40]

The Medical College of Ohio in 1896 became the medical
department of the University of Cincinnati. The present title
of the institution is University of Cincinnati College of
Medicine. The hospital, founded by Drake in 1821, continues
actively as the Cincinnati General Hospital. In it a bronze
memorial tablet to Drake was unveiled 10 June 1916, with
appropriate ceremonies. At this time the library received, by
gift of a descendant, the most valuable of Drake's known
holographic writings. This is the series of ten reminiscential
letters to his children, first published in 1870 as *Pioneer Life
in Kentucky.*

[37] *Ibid.*
[38] Emmet F. Horine: "Introduction" to Drake's *Inaugural Discourse on
Medical Education,* 1820 (New York: Henry Schuman, 1951), p. xxiii.
[39] Abraham Flexner: *Daniel Cloit Gilman, Creator of the American Type
University* (New York: Harcourt, Brace & Co., 1946), p. 142.
[40] Abraham Flexner: Correspondence with author, 13 Dec. 1951 and 7 Mar.
1952.

Had Daniel Drake accomplished nothing else than the founding of a medical school and a hospital connected with it, his fame would be secure. In 1952, the centennial of Drake's death, the Cincinnati Academy of Medicine and the University of Cincinnati College of Medicine joined in commemorative tributes to him. The June 1952 number of the *Cincinnati Journal of Medicine* (Vol. 33, No. 6) was issued as the "Daniel Drake Memorial Edition." On 28 May 1952, the Hamilton County Home, with its new multimillion dollar buildings used as a county home and chronic disease hospital, was dedicated as the Daniel Drake Memorial Hospital and Hamilton County Home. To pay tribute to its first duly elected honorary member, the 1952 meeting of the Kentucky State Medical Association was called "The Daniel Drake Memorial Meeting." The official program contained a biographical sketch.

8 §

No effort to form a literary establishment in a new country is entirely lost for it renders the subsequent attempt more successful.[1]

Medical College of Ohio, 1821-23–Transylvania University, 1823

THE FIRST session of the Medical College of Ohio began 11 November 1820 and terminated early in April 1821. Of the twenty-four students, seven received degrees of M.D. The Medical College of Ohio was the first in the United States to extend the curriculum to five months. Later this forward step was voided and the course of study shortened to four months, as was the custom in the other medical schools.

Even during the first session, there were indications of discord. The Reverend Slack became jealous of the superior talents and dexterity of Robert Best, his assistant in chemistry, and flatly refused to use him again. Slack was meddlesome and joined with Jesse Smith to harass Drake. The other professor, Benjamin Bohrer, admitted his own limitations in teaching materia medica and pharmacy. Why he intrigued to supplant Drake in teaching more difficult subjects is hard to understand. Bohrer joined with Slack and Smith in their conspiracies and attempted to hoodwink Drake.

[1] Daniel Drake: A *Narrative of the Rise and Fall of the Medical College of Ohio* (Cincinnati: Looker & Reynolds, 1827), p. 40.

172

The original act of the legislature had made Drake president. He was to hold office two years, after which time an election was to be held with every professor eligible. The other members of the faculty were jealous of Drake's vastly superior abilities and reputation. Each coveted the office of president. Drake slyly remarked later: "As the presidential CHAIR was not so large as to receive the whole of us at the same time, this feature of our organization proved decidedly objectionable." [2]

On 18 August 1821, announcement was made that the next session would open on the first Monday of November. Slack, Smith, and Drake were to occupy the same positions held the first year. By way of appeasement, Bohrer was given the chair of "Clinical Medicine" in addition to materia medica and medical botany.

JOHN D. GODMAN. From the start of the college, Drake had thought of securing an additional teacher. On 5 September 1821, announcement was made that John D. Godman (1794-1830), a graduate in medicine of the University of Maryland (1818), had accepted the chair of surgery and demonstrative obstetrics. Assignments were now re-arranged, with Drake relinquishing physiology to Smith and obstetrics to Godman. Smith allowed Godman to teach surgery.

Godman's abilities were on a par with those of Drake and the two became lifelong friends and admirers. Godman was one of the most talented physicians in the United States. Largely self-taught, he was fluent in Latin, French, and German, and conversant with four other foreign languages. He was the author of three volumes on American natural history, the sprightly *Rambles of a Naturalist,* many anatomical studies, and translator of Levasseur's *Lafayette in America in 1824 and 1825.* Drake wrote that Godman's lectures "were

[2] *Ibid.,* p. 15.

well received by the class, who admired his genius, were cap-
tivated by his eloquence, and charmed by the naivete of his
manners." [3]

In attendance at the second session were thirty students, of
whom seven received their degrees. Godman, thoroughly dis-
gusted with the intrigues of Slack, Smith, and Bohrer resigned
—the resignation to take effect after commencement. Drake,
at the close of the exercises frankly discussed the difficulties
which beset the college. He stressed the advantages to Cincinnati of a medical school and suggested the appointment
of a lay committee of investigation. Slack, Smith, and Bohrer
refused to meet with the committee. Bohrer resigned his professorship, which left only Drake, Slack, and Smith in the
faculty. In reporting on the college to the General Assembly
of Ohio, Drake described the faculty meeting of 7 March
1822:

> At 8 o'clock we met according to a previous adjournment
> and transacted some financial business. A profound silence
> ensued, our dim taper shed a blue light over the lurid faces
> of the plotters, and every thing seemed ominous of an ap-
> proaching revolution. On trying occasions, Dr. Smith is said
> to be subject to a disease not unlike Saint Vitus' Dance; and
> on this he did not wholly escape. Wan and trembling he
> raised himself (with the exception of his eyes) and in lu-
> gubrious accents said, "Mr. President—In the resolution I am
> about to offer, I am influenced by no *private feeling*, but
> solely by a reference to the public good." He then read as
> follows: "Voted that Daniel Drake, M.D. be dismissed from
> the Medical College of Ohio." The portentous silence re-
> curred, and was not interrupted till I reminded the gentlemen
> of their designs. Mr. Slack, who is blessed with stronger
> nerves than his master, then rose, and adjusting himself to a
> firmer balance, put on a proper sanctimony, and bewail-

[3] Daniel Drake: "Memoirs of Dr. Godman in *Rambles of a Naturalist* by
John D. Godman (Philadelphia: Thomas T. Ash, 1833), p. 25.

ingly ejaculated, "I second the motion." The crisis had now mercifully come; and learning by enquiry that the gentlemen were ready to meet it, I put the question, which carried, in the classic language of Dr. Smith, *"nemo contradicente."* I could not do more than tender them a vote of thanks, nor less than withdraw, and performing both, the Doctor politely lit me downstairs.[4]

The community was incensed over the expulsion of the founder of their medical school. Drake was re-instated but resigned immediately. The lay investigative committee at a public meeting suggested that each professor re-enter the college and that funds be solicited for a suitable building. Jesse Smith, president pro tem, and Elijah Slack, registrar, refused to follow these suggestions. Thus Drake's first connection with the Medical College of Ohio came to an end.

It seems important to record here Drake's reactions to the controversies arising directly from his efforts on behalf of the medical school:

Three charges have been often made against me, to which I propose to respond.

1. That among my medical brethren I am quarrelsome.

2. That I cultivate other branches of science than my profession.

3. That I am ambitious.

I will consider them separately.

1. The whole of my public controversies with any of the medical men, of this or any other place, have been since the year 1818; the time when I formed and expressed the design of instituting a medical school; and they have all grown directly or indirectly out of that design. From that date, in ambush or open day, they have waged upon me a predatory war; and when I have *defended* either the object or myself, they have with one voice exclaimed—*What an awful quarrelsome man! How dreadful broilsome he is! No soul can*

[4] Drake: A *Narrative* . . . , pp. 10-11.

*live in harmonious concord with him! But for him we should
be, as one might say, a body of brethren.* We have tried by
every art not to irritate him, until we are really discouraged,
and cannot do anything more! He is so pugnacious, that he
contends with a dozen of us at once; and until society will
frown him into due submissiveness, or what would suit our
interests better, drive him into banishment, they cannot expect to enjoy the sweets of peaceful tranquility!

To this effect have been the pacific and pathetic vocifera-
tions of my humble aggressors, whenever I was driven into
resistance, and happened to make reprisals upon them; and
by such appeals they have expected to perform what there
was no hope of accomplishing in any other way. Like certain
heroes of the Dunciad, they have had great faith in the power
of noise; and it must be allowed, that of all the torrents that
can be formed in society against an individual, not one is
more difficult to stem than a clamor. Whether that which
they have laboured to raise, can be made strong enough to
sweep me away, time only can determine.

2. That I have cultivated other branches of science than
my profession.

I should feel proud to plead guilty to this charge without
qualification. It is true that I believe in common with many
other physicians, that the science of medicine consists of
something more than a collection of *infallible receipts*; that
it is indeed a wide spreading branch of the great stock of
human knowledge; and that in pursuing its ramifications we
are often drawn into a temporary study of the objects with
which they are entwined—I have moreover perceived, that
our country abounds in the unopened and ample stores of
nature's productions, and have delivered an elementary course
of lectures on Botany, and another on Mineralogy, with the
sole view of inspiring my young countrymen with a taste of
those sciences; but even when thus employed—while held in
transient captivity within their magic circles—I have never
forgotten that they are but the auxillary organs of the profession, and entitled only to the homage of a secondary devo-

tion. The scientific world would be amused to learn, that such a charge has been brought against a man, who has contributed little more to their journals, than his accusers, who have contributed nothing.

I shall dismiss this allegation, and proceed to the last.

3. That I am ambitious.

The objects of my ambition have been a Public Library —a School of Literature and the Arts for the promotion of useful knowledge—a Lancaster-Seminary, with a superadded Grammar School, and a College for classical education, supervening upon this—a Museum, in which lectures on the curious productions of nature and art might be delivered—a Medical College—a Public Hospital and a Lunatic Asylum for the state. All of these have been originated within the last 10 years; and in each of them I have had the honor, with a little band of ardent and munificent spirits, to be a labourer. The difficulties we have had to encounter, have been neither new nor feeble. As old ones have been vanquished new ones have appeared; and, to borrow a metaphor, like the traveller ascending the Alps, we have only surmounted one, to be presented with the rugged front of another.

Circumstances have too often placed me in the van of this little *corps* of patriots; and involved me in the collisions, which occur between these who solicit for public institutions, and those who refuse to give, or give with reluctance. He who resists importunity, must in self defence, condemn either the applicant or the object as unworthy. Some of my fellow citizens have occasionally done both, denouncing me as ambitious, and the ends for which I laboured, as undeserving of encouragement, because they chose to *stigmatize* them as objects of an ambition. That I was ambitious of being the humble means of naturalizing the sciences in this new country, I acknowledge, without the dread of imputed vanity or the apprehension of censure.

To effect this, I was willing to forego the pursuit of loftier objects, and refrain from entering the ranks of those who press forward to the prize of glory, awarded to such as augment the treasures of human knowledge by new discoveries. I was disposed, indeed, to commute the labours of the philosopher for those of the patriot; and instead of attempting to extend the boundaries of science, to cultivate the genius so liberally bestowed on the youth of a country, whose want of literary institutions I have so much reason personally to deplore.

I was personally desirous of seeing a liberal and permanent medical school established in Cincinnati; the town of all others in the western country which has the greatest number of natural advantages for such an institution. This object, I supposed, might sanctify ambition itself; and being rigidly within the limits of my profession, I expected it to silence the clamours of the most scrupulous. No calculation was ever more fallacious, for no project could have awakened the jealousy of so many. The alarum bells were chimed in louder peals; and the cabalistic phrase "inordinate ambition," with new accompaniments, echoed through the whole community. The majority, it is true, saw no approaching harm, but only wanted a pretext to remain passive, and the clamour furnished this. The enlightened and the patriotic had already exhausted their means upon preceding institutions, and were not able to afford the assistance which their judgment dictated as necessary; and their feelings suggested as due to the undertaking. . . .

To fail under such a combination of sinister circumstances, could mortify none but a man of the sickliest self-abasement; to succeed might have gratified a nobler ambition than I am conscious of possessing, or dare to claim.

The labours of this place will not, however, be ultimately unproductive. In the cycle of changes an auspicious hour will sooner or later arrive, when the Medical College, and any of our other institutions which appear to be now prostrate, may be revived and made to shed upon society the fruits, which, in a flourishing condition, they cannot fail to produce. But before this can take place, the community must become more united; their countenance must be withdrawn from those who, out of selfish motives, array themselves in opposition; the labour and the contribution must not be exacted from a few; nor must it be a reproach to those who dedicate themselves to this service, that they are ambitious.[5]

On 16 March 1822, Godman announced the opening of his office "over Mr. Griffin's store, at the corner of Main and Lower Market Streets." [6] A subsequent "card," 22 June 1822, stated that an apparatus for sulphurous fumigation of diseases of the skin was being installed in his office.[7] Though qualified as a surgeon, Godman did not limit his practice, nor did any other physician of this period.

Through the patronage of the first exclusive book-shop owner in Cincinnati, John P. Foote, Godman issued in March 1822 the first number of the first medical journal published west of the Allegheny Mountains. The first issue of *The Western Quarterly Reporter of Medical, Surgical and Natural Sciences* had 102 pages of which Godman wrote 95. The remaining seven pages were written by his preceptor, Dr. Wm. N. Luckey. Drake gave to Godman the names of over two hundred subscribers to his projected journal of 1818.

In the Preface to the first issue of his journal, Godman announced his aims with rhetorical flourish:

> To assist in advancing the great cause of improvement and science, is a pleasing occupation under any circumstances, but more especially so in a country like this, where society is yet so young and the kingdoms of nature so partially explored. The time which has elapsed since its first settlement is so short, and the changes effected have succeeded each other with such rapidity, that credit can scarcely be given to the fact, that forty years ago, the places now enlivened by cities, towns, villages and all the active bustle of society, were

[5] *Ibid.*, pp. 36-40.
[6] [Announcement], "Doctor John D. Godman," *Western Spy and Literary Cadet*, N.S., VIII:p. [3]—c. [3], Mar. 6, 1822.
[7] *Ibid.*, N.S., VIII, No. 622:p. [3]—c. [3], June 22, 1822.

shadowed by ancient forests, re-echoing with the howls of ferocious animals—the more discordant and terrifying yells of savage men, or the sullen roar of mighty rivers rolling their tributary waters to the ocean. . . .[8]

"Article IV," by Godman, in the March 1822 issue of the *Reporter* is in Latin. Cincinnatians living in the "Tyre of the West" could not be outdone by the inhabitants of the "Athens of the West" (Lexington, Ky.). There, in 1819, Harvard graduate, William Gibbs Hunt (1791-1833), had issued *The Western Review and Miscellaneous Magazine,* containing poems in Latin, Italian, and French. For the poems in French, "the reader must supply the accents." That roving genius and delver into all knowledge, Constantine S. Rafinesque, supplied many of the poems.

Godman's essay, "De conceptu adnatationes quaedam," is a discussion of an article in Latin by Edwin A. Atlee.[9] It may have been pre-Victorian prudery that led Atlee to use Latin in reporting the occurrence of pregnancy in an atresia of the vagina which prevented entrance of the penis. Though admitting the difficulty in handling Latin, Godman did a creditable job. He incidentally reported a case similar to Atlee's which his dear friend, Drake, had brought to his attention, "quem Medicus Drake nostras, mihi amicissimus, seduliter notavit." [10]

The second issue of *The Western Quarterly Reporter* consisted of 104 pages, Godman writing 45. Drake now came to his aid and edited two articles for publication. In the third issue, Drake first publicly announced his intention of prepar-

[8] John D. Godman: "Preface," *The Western Quarterly Reporter,* I:[v], Mar. 1822.
[9] Edwin A. Atlee: "De Conceptu," *American Medical Recorder* (Philadelphia), IV:646-52, Oct. 1821.
[10] John D. Godman: "De conceptu," *The Western Quarterly Reporter* (Cincinnati), I:51-53, Mar. 1822.

ing a "Treatise on the Diseases of the Western Country." [11] The story of Drake's travels and researches in the preparation of his great classic must be told later.

In the autumn of 1822, Godman returned to Philadelphia where he delivered a series of lectures on anatomy and physiology. Three issues of *The Western Quarterly Reporter* had appeared before Godman's departure from Cincinnati. He left enough material for three additional issues of his journal. It seems likely that Drake supervised the publication of the fourth issue of Volume I, and Nos. 1 and 2 of Volume II. The late General Edgar E. Hume (1889-1952) once termed Godman's *Western Quarterly Reporter*, "the rarest American Medical Journal." [12] This is incorrect as I have shown. [13]

In December 1822, the General Assembly of Ohio amended the act authorizing its medical college. [14] The major change was the transfer of control from the faculty to thirteen named trustees. Upon organization, the trustees at once unanimously elected Drake to the professorship formerly held. He declined. [15]

On 10 February, 1823, the faculty of the medical department of Transylvania University, Drs. B. W. Dudley, Charles Caldwell, Samuel Brown, Wm. H. Richardson, and the Reverend James Blythe, unanimously recommended Daniel Drake for the Chair of Materia Medica and Medical Botany. [16] Shortly thereafter the board of trustees unanimously elected

[11] Daniel Drake: "Treatise on the Diseases of the Western Country," *The Western Quarterly Reporter*, I:307-11, 1822.

[12] Edgar E. Hume: "Early Kentucky Periodical Literature," *Annals of Medical History* (New York), N.S., VIII; July 1936:324-47.

[13] Emmet F. Horine: "Daniel Drake and the Origin of Medical Journalism West of the Allegheny Mountains," *Bull. Hist. of Med.*, XXVII:217-35, May-June 1953.

[14] Ohio General Assembly, "Medical College of Ohio—An Act," *Cincinnati Advertiser*, N.S., I, Jan. 13, 1823:p. [2]—c. [2].

[15] [News Item] *Ibid.*, Mar. 5, 1823:p. [3]—c. [2].

[16] Transylvania University, Medical Department, Faculty Letter to Trustees, Feb. 10, 1823. In Transylvania College Library.

Drake. At the same time Drake's friend, Robert Best, was elected assistant to the professor of chemistry. Each accepted.

Samuel D. Gross (1805-84), eminent surgeon, medical author, and teacher, who was intimately associated with Drake for over fifteen years, wrote:

> His great error was that he was morbidly sensitive, and that he permitted himself to be swayed by every puff of wind that swept across his path. Baseness and malignity never entered into his character. In all the difficulties and troubles, growing out of his early professional relations, I know not a solitary one in which he had not strict justice on his side.[17]

Ever solicitous of the health of his family, having lost a daughter and a son in infancy, Drake was especially perturbed over the continued indisposition of his wife. He built a rough summer home about which he wrote his friend Richardson of Lexington: "I have disposed of my family in a cabin on the top of one of the hills that fortify the town, and since their ascent to what we have denominated 'Mount Poverty' their health has been much better." [18]

With the exception of the final illness and death (1825) of Drake's wife, the years from 1818 through 1822 seem to have been his most trying ones. It had been necessary to take his only son, wayward and seemingly incorrigible, from the Lancasterian Seminary and place him (1821) in a private school known for its strict discipline. Drake's business ventures had failed and he was deeply in debt. His cherished dream of founding a medical school had led to controversies. He had been slandered by a small group of local physicians whose names are known to us, not by their scientific contributions, but almost entirely by those vitriolic letters. Only an indomitable will could have carried Drake on and upward to fame.

[17] Samuel D. Gross: "Daniel Drake" in *Lives of Eminent American Physicians and Surgeons* (Philadelphia: Lindsay & Blakiston, 1861), p. 655.
[18] Drake: ALS to Richardson, *loc. cit.*

Many of Drake's friends resembled him in strength of character and will power. In this group is Josiah Meigs, previously mentioned as one of the founders of the School of Literature and Arts. Meigs was an educator, lawyer, first professor of and president of the University of Georgia, surveyor-general of the Northwest Territory, and, finally, commissioner of the General Land Office of the United States. He once wrote Drake:

> I have always had apprehensions that your *Intellectual* man would claim too much of your *Corporeal* man. Juvenal said 2000 years ago, very properly, that it is folly
>> "propter vitam vivendi perdere causas:"—
>> [in pursuit of living to vainly destroy the purpose of living]
> a sentiment well illustrated by an old *Sailor*—he was sitting astride of the main top-gallant *yard;* his Captain on the quarterdeck ordered him to go to the extremity of the yard to reeve a halyard. Jack saw that if he attempted it he should fall, and after hearing the Curses of his Captain for some time, he said, "I'll tell you what, Captain, I have been a Sailor, man and boy, these 40 years; I always made it a rule never to kill myself for the sake of living, and by — I won't go!!!"
> I recommend the story to your attentive consideration, and I dare say that Mrs. Drake will join me. . . .[19]

[19] Wm. W. Meigs: *Life of Josiah Meigs by his Great-grandson* (Philadelphia: Privately printed, 1887), p. 99.

Seek to find your pleasures in books, and not in the gossip of the world around you.[1]

Lexington, 1823-24

ON 9 MAY 1823, Drake had accepted the professorship of materia medica and medical botany in Transylvania University. A week later he made the following announcement:

> To Debtors and Creditors
> The undersigned, being about to remove from Cincinnati, earnestly requests all those indebted to him, to adjust their accounts without delay; and those having claims against him to present them for settlement. Application for either purpose may be made at the Drug Store of B. Drake, No. 95 Main Street.[2]

Although the lectures in the Medical Department of Transylvania University were not scheduled to begin until Monday, 3 November 1823, Drake with his family started for Lexington on 5 July 1823. Accompanying them was a party of seven which included Benjamin Drake, Peyton Short Symmes (a local poet), and a young law student, John Hough James (1800-81). Dr. and Mrs. Drake were in their gig and the others were either on horseback or in hacks. Three days later the party arrived in Lexington, 82 miles from Cincinnati.

Details of the trip are found in the record of one of the

---

[1] Daniel Drake: *Introductory Lecture on the Means of Promoting the Intellectual Improvement of Students and Physicians* (Louisville: Prentice and Weissinger, 1844), p. 17; 2nd ed., p. 16.

[2] Daniel Drake: "To Debtors and Creditors," *Liberty Hall and Cincinnati Gazette*, V:p. [3]—c. [4], May 16, 1823.

Drake party, John H. James, then under treatment by the doctor. James began his diary on New Year's Day 1821, and continued it for sixty years. Now in the Library of Miami University, Oxford, Ohio, it gives impressions of persons and events not found elsewhere. This diary is the basis for an interesting biography of James: A *Buckeye Titan*.[3]

On the morning following his arrival in Lexington, Drake visited the Reverend Horace Holley (1781-1827), president of Transylvania University. Drake then called on the members of the medical faculty and his former friends. After two weeks in Lexington, Dr. and Mrs. Drake in their gig and young John H. James, on horseback, journeyed to Olympian Springs, then a popular health resort in Bath County, 47 miles to the east. They arrived on 21 July 1823, to find Henry Clay and several members of his family. Drake had taken his wife in the hope that she might be benefited. He occupied his time in studying the geology of the area, in botanizing, and in determining the chemical composition of the three springs at the resort. Later, on their return to Lexington, the Drakes and young James dined at Ashland with the Clays.[4]

Drake was again associated with three members of the medical faculty with whom he had taught in 1817, Benjamin W. Dudley, William H. Richardson, and the Reverend James Blythe. Additional members of the faculty were Charles Caldwell (1772-1853) and Samuel Brown.

HORACE HOLLEY. Horace Holley, a Unitarian clergyman and graduate of Yale (1803), had assumed his duties as president of Transylvania University, 19 December 1818. There can be no doubt concerning his executive abilities, since in a short time the academic and medical departments were re-

[3] William E. and Ophia D. Smith: A *Buckeye Titan* (Cincinnati: Historical and Philosophical Society of Ohio, 1953).

[4] John H. James: MS diary, pp. 86-107. In Library of Miami University, Oxford, Ohio.

vitalized. In addition, the law school authorized in 1799 was activated. Students were attracted from distant parts of the county and, under Holley, Lexington became the "Athens of the West."

Holley had many assets, including a charming personality and an excellent voice. He was an orator, possessing a wide knowledge of literature, metaphysics, and art. An interesting conversationalist, he always drew his listeners into participation. Some narrow sectarians accused Holley of heretical views. Consult Niels Henry Sonne for the most authoritative and comprehensive discussion of the intellectual viewpoint in pioneer Kentucky.[5]

BENJAMIN W. DUDLEY. Benjamin W. Dudley held the combined chairs of surgery and anatomy, for each of which students paid fifteen dollars. And these chairs he doggedly insisted on occupying until 1844, long after they had been separated in other medical colleges. There were apparently no squabbles between Drake and Dudley during their second association in teaching. In fact, Drake acted as mediator in a difficulty between Dudley and Brown in 1825.

WILLIAM H. RICHARDSON. William H. Richardson, friend and admirer of Drake, held the combined professorships of obstetrics and the diseases of women and children. Though poorly trained, he had learned much from observation, was a forceful lecturer, and beloved by his students. Lecture notes made by one of them, James Clayton, show that Richardson possessed a surprising amount of knowledge of the subjects taught.[6] Another student of a later date said:

[5] Niels Henry Sonne: *Liberal Kentucky, 1780-1828* (New York: Columbia University Press, 1939).

[6] James Clayton: [MS], "Records of the Lectures delivered by the Professors of the Medical Department . . . 1824 and -5," Property of Marion F. Beard, M.D., who has generously permitted its use.

"He was not scholarly nor graceful and fluent as a lecturer; but he was ardent and impressive, sufficiently learned in his special branch, and had at his ready command a large stock of ripe personal experiences. I honor his memory beyond that of most men I have known." [7]

JAMES BLYTHE. It will be remembered that James Blythe, D.D., was professor of chemistry in 1817-18. He resigned in 1818 but was re-elected in 1819 and continued to teach in Transylvania until 16 March 1831. At this time he resigned to become president of Hanover College, Hanover, Indiana. The following is Drake's estimate:

> Dr. Blythe was not a working chemist and of course had no great skill as a manipulator; but he was a classical scholar and adequately acquainted with the general principles of the science, which he presented to his class in a perspicuous manner. In his moral and social character he was honest, upright and dignified; proud but not arrogant, firm yet not obstinate—abounding in self respect, but at all times disposed to respect the rights and feelings of others.[8]

SAMUEL BROWN. Samuel Brown, a Virginian, the son of a Presbyterian clergyman, received an excellent classical education. He and Ephraim McDowell (1771-1830) studied medicine under the same preceptor, Dr. Alexander Humphreys (d. 1802), who suggested that they go to the University of Edinburgh.[9] Here Brown studied two years but took his medical degree at Aberdeen. In 1799, when the Medical Department of Transylvania was authorized, he and

[7] Lewis Rogers: "Address of the President," *Transactions of the Kentucky State Medical Society*, (Louisville: John P. Morton & Co., 1873), pp. 45-46.

[8] Daniel Drake: "Death of Dr. Blythe," *West. Jnl. Med. & Surg.* (Louisville), V:474-76, June 1842.

[9] Emmet F. Horine: "The Stagesetting for Ephraim McDowell (1771-1830)," *Bull. Hist. of Med.*, XXIV:149-60, Mar.-Apr. 1950.

"Dr." Frederick Ridgely (1757-1824) were elected professors. The board of trustees did not designate the subjects each was to teach. No accredited courses were begun and, upon leaving Lexington in 1806, Brown resigned. He did not return until his re-election to a professorship, that of theory and practice of medicine in 1819. In 1822 he founded the Kappa Lambda Society which will be described later. His friend and biographer, Réné La Roche, said: "Few individuals have presented a more rare combination of those amiable qualities, of those virtuous and cultivated feelings of the human heart, which render character estimable in life, and serve to elevate their possessor above the rest of their fellow beings." [10]

CHARLES CALDWELL. Samuel Brown wrote President Holley from Philadelphia in 1819, suggesting that Charles Caldwell be considered for a professorship. He was elected professor of the institutes of medicine and of clinical practice, and dean of the faculty. Following his acceptance, Caldwell shortly thereafter left for Lexington, 6 October 1819. With utter disregard of facts, Caldwell egotistically claimed "premiership" in establishing the Medical Department of Transylvania University, thus bringing scientific medicine to the West. With no hesitation whatever he accepted the title *Pater medicinalis occidentalis.* To paraphrase adequately Caldwell's ideas is impossible, hence this quotation:

> I had under my direction [1819] one of the most miserable Faculties of medicine, or rather the materials of which to form such Faculty, that the Caucasian portion of the human family can well furnish, or the human mind easily imagine. It consisted of five professors (I myself being one of them), among whom was divided the administration of seven different branches of the profession. And of the five, three were

[10] Réné La Roche: "Samuel Brown" in Samuel D. Gross: *Lives of Eminent American Physicians and Surgeons,* p. 246.

(as related to the duties to be discharged by them) but little else than medical ciphers. But fortunately this nullity was not altogether the result of mental deficiency. Had it been so, I need not add that the case would have been remediless [*sic*]. It arose more, perhaps, from an entire want of the proper kind and degree of mental cultivation and training. One of them [Samuel Brown] in particular, was a man of very respectable intellect, had received somewhat of a classical education, had been regularly, and, as some thought, thoroughly bred to medicine, and, as a colloquist, was fertile and uncommonly eloquent. But his nerves seemed to be made of aspen leaves, interwoven with the leaves of the mimosa sensitiva, that trembled and shrank from the slightest touch of responsibility; even from the responsibility of uttering and maintaining a medical doctrine; no matter whether it was derived from an external source, or from the internal working of his own fancy. Of the other two, one [the Reverend James Blythe] had been also, to some extent, educated; but he knew more of almost anything else than he did of the subject he was appointed to teach. The other possessed an intellect not much, if in any measure, below the middle standard; but he [William H. Richardson] was miserably letterless and untrained. The professor of it could do nothing more than converse fluently but very coarsely on such matters as he superficially knew, and on nothing was his knowledge more than superficial. To real study and investigation he was a stranger.

The fourth professor [Benjamin W. Dudley], though perhaps the most meagerly endowed of the whole by nature, was one who was qualified and resolutely determined to work. Yet he was firm in the belief and free in his expression of it, that the school was destined to have very limited classes. His avowal of this opinion I somewhat positively discouraged; requesting him in a tone not altogether, however, free from jest and playfulness, either to dismiss his prophetic spirit or bridle his tongue; for that I was determined to defeat and nullify his predictions; and that I was neither accustomed to meet nor well prepared to brook disappointment.[11]

Caldwell's *Autobiography*, from which the quotation above was taken, is teeming with vitriolic statements. One might conclude that the book was written by a senescent person with delusions of his omnipotence. Such a conclusion is negated by the fact that Caldwell's earlier writings often display similar carping criticisms. As a polemist he not only attempted to refute the statements of his adversary but sought to wound him by abuse. He was proud that he had "been more or less at war with the world of conservatives ever since the earliest remembrances of my boyhood." [12]

One reviewer of Caldwell's *Autobiography* said: "He looked upon his professional existence as sixty years of continued battle. During all that time he had never yielded a hair to any living man. Those who would not accommodate themselves to him he cast aside; as for him, he was the mountain, and Mahomet must approach." [13]

Of the six faculty members, Caldwell and Drake were the only ones known by their writings. Caldwell's contributions were prolix, much greater in quantity than quality. At the present time (1959) the most desirable of Caldwell's books and pamphlets might bring a maximum price of twenty-five dollars. The commoner Drake items bring not less than fifty dollars, while the most unusual ones are quoted at many times this amount.

There were several reasons for Drake's removal to Lexington four months before the university opened. He was fatigued and discouraged after more than a dozen years of

[11] Charles Caldwell: *Autobiography* (Philadelphia: Lippincott, Grambo, and Co. 1855), pp. 354-55.

[12] *Ibid.*, p. 439.

[13] Review of Autobiography by Charles Caldwell, *Buffalo Medical Journal*, in Western Journal of Medicine and Surgery (Louisville), N.S., IV:43-48, July 1855.

strenuous efforts to bring science and culture to Cincinnati. A student throughout life, he had access in Lexington to the largest medical library to be found at that time in the United States. There was a preponderance of volumes in Latin and French, languages with which he was familiar. Fond of pageantry, President Holley wished to make the exercises of Drake's induction as colorful as possible, hence Latin was to be used. Following investiture, Drake was to deliver an oration in Latin. Immediately thereafter, the introductory lecture to his course on medical botany and materia medica was scheduled. July through October 1823, were indeed busy months for the new professor.

In October 1823, "Curtius" wrote the editors of *The National Republican* (Cincinnati) concerning "Our public institutions":

> . . . Of the MEDICAL SCHOOL, it is scarcely too much to say that, if the citizens of Cincinnati had been, during its progress, as much awake to their own obvious interests, as they seem to have become since its prostration;—and had supported the enterprising Projector with half the zeal which he exercised in his repeated efforts for its success; they would not now have to bow to the mortifying supremacy of a rival institution, from whose surpassing progress, there is but little ground to hope that ours can ever successfully be re-organized. The head that conceived it is indeed no longer with us; the hand that might have upheld its tottering fortunes, now exercises its unwearied energies, where ever prejudice will not prove blind to its usefulness, nor conviction be dumb to its praise.—Nay—even the late hostile seat of his earliest hopes and most extensive labors is *now* resonant with his praise;— the praise of him whose persevering ardor indifference was once suffered to chill, and whose noblest efforts hostility was allowed to paralyze. . . .[14]

[14] Curtius, Senior [To the Editors] "OUR PUBLIC INSTITUTIONS," *National Republican and Ohio Political Register* (Cincinnati), I, No. 81:p. [2]—c. [4-5], Oct. 10, 1823.

On Friday, 7 November 1823, Drake was again publicly proclaimed professor of materia medica and medical botany. President Holley conducted the exercises in Latin and Drake responded in a felicitous address in the same language.* Drake alluded to his previous connection with the university and pledged anew his allegiance. He predicted perpetual growth and glory for the university through harmonious action of the professors. To this goal he and the other teachers would work unceasingly. Lunsford P. Yandell was greatly impressed:

> I was in Lexington, a student attending my first course of lectures when he [Drake] returned to the school and I saw him take the oath of office, and heard him deliver the Latin address required at that day of professors by the university at their inauguration. I am aware that large deductions must be made for first impressions on an enthusiastic youthful mind; and that much of the admiration created by new men and strange scenes is to be set down to the charm of novelty; but my conviction is still firm, after the lapse of fifty years, that I have never since seen a more splendid combination of talent than adorned Transylvania University at that day.[15]

Drake's introductory, delivered immediately after his Latin oration, was "On the Necessity and Value of Professional Industry." He was to use the theme, "industry," on many subsequent occasions. Not only were his lectures on this subject stimulating but his own unwearied exertions set an example for his students.

> You have proposed to become enlightened practitioners of medicine; and you could not have chosen a more elevated

---

* Drake's address in Latin is owned by Transylvania College whose librarian, Miss Roemol Henry, graciously supplied a facsimile.

[15] Lunsford P. Yandell: "Medical Literature of Kentucky," *Trans. Kentucky State Medical Society* (Louisville: John P. Morton & Co., 1874), p. 218.

or difficult object. With *this* object, idleness has no compatibilities; a great design and small means are preposterous; and he who may hope to achieve the former by the agency of the latter, is not insignificant but contemptible; nay, in the profession of medicine, he is criminal. True greatness, however, does not lie in the mere conception of lofty and useful designs, but in their speedy and perfect accomplishment.

. . . .

In the profession of Medicine, one of the causes of the superiority of city over country students and practitioners, is the social and scientific collision of the former. The interrogating parties, literary clubs and societies of emulation, debate and deliberation, which exist in cities, open to their members new views both theoretical and practical; defecate their intellects, and preserve in them the *raciness* of character, which is so seldom retained, under a protracted course of solitary reading.

. . . .

It is one of the most beautiful features, in the noble aspect of American society, that its sympathies are invariably bestowed on the youth who grapples with adversity; and, that none are so much respected, as those who honestly emerge from obscurity to distinction.

. . . .

It has, moreover, been supposed, that what is vaguely denominated genius, may be made a substitute for industry. . . . Genius is not the name of any faculty, but of a great though indefinite degree of mental strength. Now I would ask, how can the power of acquiring and arranging ideas, be made a substitute for the ideas themselves? *They* must be excited by external occasions, and to acquire them, application is as indispensable for a genius as for a dunce. The difference in time in which they would learn the same thing, it is true, may be very great, but *when objects commensurate with their respective positions of intellect are assigned to them, equal diligence becomes necessary.* To him, then who studies closest, the palm of merit is due; for rewards should not be connected with capacity which is of Heaven, but with diligence, which depends on ourselves. It may be said, therefore, to be disgraceful for him, on whom the Creator has bestowed a greater portion, to be equalled by one who has been sparingly endowed.

. . . .

If a provident temper of mind make you desirous of guarding against the gloomy insignificance—the sad and solitary nothingness of an ignorant old age, you must accomplish it, by industry in youth, and such industry is peculiarly appropriate to this object, since in our declining years, the knowledge acquired in early life, is almost all that remains with us. The first inscriptions on the tablets of the mind are the last to be effaced—what a resistless motive for early diligence is suggested by this important law of human nature; and from its frequent violation, how few, like Nestor in the Iliad, become in old age the living oracles of wisdom to the rising generation.

. . . .

Enterprise delights not in the path that is unembarrassed, courage is animated by danger, and genius disdains the achievement that involves no peril—the road to glory is not devoid of thorns, but they are the thorns which surround the rose.[16]

It will be remembered that John D. Godman started (1822) in Cincinnati the first medical journal published in the West: *The Western Quarterly Reporter.* Drake super-

[16] Daniel Drake: *An Introductory Lecture, on the Necessity and Value of Professional Industry* (Lexington, William Tanner, 1823). Reprinted, Chicago, 1937.

vised publication after Godman left Cincinnati. In January 1824, announcement was made:

> The publication of the Western Quarterly Reporter has been transferred to Lexington, Ky., where it will be edited by Dr. Drake, assisted by those eminent men with whom he is associated in the Medical College, and its former editor Dr. Godman, now residing in Philadelphia. It will be published by W. W. Worsley, and there is little doubt that its usefulness will be increased and its circulation extended by the change of its location.[17]

Apparently publication of this periodical was never begun in Lexington.

Drake entered fully into the social and scientific life of Lexington. In January 1823, the Kentucky Institute was established with Dr. Holley, president. The eccentric Constantine S. Rafinesque was secretary. There were twenty-four members, twelve laymen and the professors of Transylvania University. Of thirteen essays known to have been read during 1823, Rafinesque wrote three, Holley two, and Drake one: "On the Influence of Climate upon the Character of Man." [18]

In 1823, the legislature of Kentucky incorporated the Transylvania Botanic Garden Company. Drake's friend Richardson was the first president and Rafinesque, secretary. Circulars were published, stock was sold, and ten acres were bought within Lexington. In 1825, planting began but soon ceased, according to Rafinesque, as a result of "secret hostility to my undertaking, and several subscribers did not pay their instalments." [19] In the spring of 1826, Rafinesque left Transylvania with curses on it and on its president. Although Drake taught

---

[17] Literary and Scientific Notices, *Cincinnati Literary Gazette*, I:7, Jan. 1, 1824.

[18] "Kentucky Institute," *Cincinnati Literary Gazette*, I:86-87, Mar. 13, 1824.

[19] C. S. Rafinesque: *A Life of Travels and Researches* (Philadelphia, 1836), Reprinted in *Chronica Botanica* (Waltham, Mass.), VIII:291-360, Spring 1944.

botany in the Medical Department and Rafinesque in the Academic, neither mentions the other. Later, as will be told, Drake caustically reviewed Rafinesque's circular advertising his secret remedy, Pulmel, for the cure of all diseases of the lungs.

Sometime before 1803, the Lexington Medical Society was organized. There were two classes of membership: "ordinary," the students of medicine, and "honorary," the practicing physicians. Casual meetings were held until 1817 when the medical faculty of Transylvania University enlivened it by their discussions. Drake was an active member at that time and, on his return to Lexington in 1823, was elected president.[20] Closely related with the above-mentioned organization was the Kentucky Medical Society of Transylvania University, of which Drake was also president. It appears probable that this latter group was in reality the alumni association of the university. Many were the heated debates in these societies, the professors competing before their students. Drake described one:

> Professor Caldwell came forward with his heavy artillery, and opened an uninterrupted fire of two hours and twenty minutes upon one of the bastions of my little fortress. I began to return his fire, loading my blunderbuss with facts and quotations from many substantial works obtained from the library which *he* selected in Europe. It being late, the society adjourned. Last Friday night, I mounted the battery and returned his fire for two hours and thirty minutes. At ten, he commenced another cannonading and continued it for forty-five minutes. My batteries were silenced. The question was, whether plants grew up without seeds, cuttings or sprouts. I had asserted they do not, and this led to the bombarding. The doctor in his last words declared that my "learned, ingenious, ardent and eloquent speech" was lost

[20] "Lexington Medical Society," *Cincinnati Literary Gazette*, I:30-31, Jan. 24, 1824.

upon him, for I had mistaken the matter in dispute between us.[21]

In 1820, Dr. Samuel Brown founded a secret medical fraternity in Lexington, The Kappa Lambda Society of Hippocrates. Its ideals were to promote science, friendship, virtue, and honor. Many affiliated chapters were chartered in the larger eastern cities, notably in Philadelphia, New York, and Baltimore. All chapters were subservient to the parent one in Lexington. However, on 11 December 1822, the rule of subserviency was abolished. Thereafter, the first affiliate in any state or country was to be the Grand Kappa Lambda Society for that area. It was given full authority to issue charters and regulate membership.[22]

Drake and the other professors of the Transylvania faculty were members with the exception of Caldwell and Dudley. Réné La Roche (1795-1872) of Philadelphia stated that the effects of the society there were extremely salutary:

> The medical men in Philadelphia lived in an almost constant state of warfare,—quarreling, and even worse, was not uncommon among them, and now and then street fights occurred. This state of things gave way under the influence of the society. Soon after its establishment, harmony, comparative harmony, at least, was restored among its members, and before long, through their influence, among other medical men around them.[23]

At Dr. Brown's suggestion a periodical was started under the auspices of Kappa Lambda: *The North American Medical and Surgical Journal* (Philadelphia). Twelve volumes were published, January 1826 to October 1831. With its own

[21] Daniel Drake letters in Mansfield: *Memoirs* . . . , p. 163.
[22] Henry Miller: *Resolutions* . . . , *of the Kappa Lambda Society*, broadside, (Lexington, 1822).
[23] La Roche: "Samuel Brown" in Gross: *Lives of Eminent American Physicians and Surgeons*, p. 245.

journal and with many active chapters, Kappa Lambda seemed destined to exert a beneficial influence for all time. The fact that it was a secret organization led eventually to violent opposition in the 1830's, notably in New York.[24] Despite attacks, the New York Grand Chapter survived, sent delegates to the early meetings of the American Medical Association, and is known to have been active as late as 1862.[25] The founding chapter in Lexington apparently died at a much earlier date.

Early in March 1824, graduating exercises were held, with forty-six of the two hundred students receiving medical degrees. Drake stayed in Lexington during the remaining months of 1824, although occasional trips were made to Frankfort, Cincinnati, and elsewhere for consultations. His friend, Henry Clay, was a candidate for the presidency. Dr. Godman had written Clay from Philadelphia suggesting that Drake's aid be solicited: "Dr. Drake has excellent talents for composition of the kind which would be most serviceable for the present occasion. He is very friendly to you and would be rejoiced at your success. In writing to him I have stated the necessity of his becoming active in promoting our wishes. . . ."[26]

Influenced by Godman's suggestion, and, perhaps at Clay's request, Drake wrote a series of thirteen letters on "The Presidency," signed "Seventy Six." The first of these letters appeared in *Liberty Hall and Cincinnati Gazette* on 20 April 1824, and the last, 27 August 1827.[27] Widely copied, the let-

[24] [Anon.]: *A History of the New York Kappa Lambda Conspiracy* (New York: William Stuart, 1839).

[25] Philip Van Ingen: "Remarks on Kappa, Elf or Ogre?" *Bull. Hist. Med.*, XVIII:513-38, Dec. 1945.

[26] John D. Godman: ALS, Philadelphia, 1 July 1823, to H. Clay, Lexington. Clay Correspondence, Library of Congress.

[27] Letter No. II was published in Liberty Hall, Apr. 27, 1824; III:May 4, 1824; IV:May 7; V:May 14; VI:June 4; VII:June 25; VIII:July 2; IX:July 23; X:Aug. 10; XI:Aug. 13; XII:Aug. 17; and XIII:Aug. 27, 1824.

ters attracted considerable attention. In the first letter, Drake discussed the qualifications of the candidates; John Quincy Adams, William H. Crawford, Henry Clay, and Andrew Jackson. The second communication listed specific reasons for supporting Clay: "An inhabitant of the West, therefore, of necessity more national than one of the East and South, because the East and the South have united to form the West. But this is not all. The East has its interests, which are chiefly commercial, subordinately manufactural; the South has its, which are mainly agricultural to a limited degree as to the number of articles: but the West has *every* interest. . . ." [28]

Letter III enumerated further qualifications of Clay and Letters IV and V discussed his ideas on slavery. Discussion of internal improvements, sectional feelings, and answers to the *Presidential Catechism* of "S. P. H." concluded the series.

As is well known, the election of 2 November 1824 gave Andrew Jackson the greater number of votes although not a majority. Hence, the House of Representatives had to act. Here, John Quincy Adams, although second by popular vote, was chosen president on the first ballot.

Later Adams appointed Henry Clay secretary of state. Since Clay as a representative from Kentucky and speaker of the House had helped elect Adams, cries of "bargain and corruption" were started by Jackson and his followers. Drake now came to the defense of Clay by a letter to the editors of the *National Intelligencer* (Washington).[29] He stated that Mr. Clay, at different times before leaving for Washington in the fall of 1824, had told him of his intention of voting for Mr. Adams, hence accusations of a bargain were untrue.

This communication was widely copied by other newspapers and apparently carried considerable weight. The

[28] *Ibid.*, N.S., VI, No. 1032:p. [3]—c. [3-4], Apr. 27, 1824.
[29] Daniel Drake: Letter to *National Intelligencer*, Lexington, Mar. 21, 1825 in *Niles Weekly Register* (Baltimore), XXVIII:84-85, Apr. 9, 1825.

vehement attacks against it by the Jacksonians indicate its importance. For many months, in their organ, the *United States Telegraph* (Washington), efforts were made to slur Drake.[30] He finally made a dignified reply: "In the sketch of my life and character contained in your papers of the 28 ult. [should be: 9th inst.], shown to me this evening, you have fallen into some mistakes, the most important of which I claim the privilege of correcting." [31]

[30] Duff Green: "Mr. Clay and the bargain," *United States Telegraph* (Washington), I:227, Dec. 26, 1827. *Ibid.*, I:241, Jan. 9, 1828.
[31] Daniel Drake: Letter *Daily Cincinnati Gazette*, I, No. 17:p. [2]—c. [3-5], Jan. 16, 1828.

10 ♊

Lexington, 1824-27

SOMETIME AFTER the 1824 graduating exercises of the medical school, Dr. Samuel Brown left for France to visit his brother, James, the U.S. minister there. Dr. Brown arranged for Drake to assume his duties until he returned. On 8 November 1824, Drake delivered an introductory lecture to his own course on materia medica and medical botany. The next day he lectured in place of Dr. Brown on the theory and practice of medicine. There were 234 students, of whom 56 were candidates for degrees. At this period in medical education and for almost a century afterwards, the professors, in addition to delivering their official lectures, coached students privately. Indicative of his popularity, Drake's private group of students in 1824 numbered fifty-seven.

Two notebooks of the 1824-25 lectures have been located, one of an anonymous student[2] and the other of James Clayton of Kentucky.[3] Here the notes on lectures by Drake are much more extensive than those of the other professors. Apparently his clarity and felicity of expression made note-taking easy. He often enumerated the points he wished to emphasize, using short and simple sentences.

[1] Daniel Drake: [Editorial], *Western Journal of Med. and Physical Sciences* (Cincinnati), Hex. II, V:331, July, Aug., Sept. 1837.
[2] [Anonymous: student's notebook], "Drake's lectures on materia medica," 1824. In Transylvania Library.
[3] Clayton: *Record of the Lectures . . . 1824-25.*

Of the notes of more than seventy lectures of 1824-25 made by Clayton, only two lectures by Caldwell are recorded. The notes of one of these consists of three lines and the other of three pages. Caldwell taught medical jurisprudence and the institutes (a term used then for the principles of medicine including physiology, pathology, therapeutics, and hygiene). His pet obsession was phrenology, the fanciful doctrine by which mental characteristics or faculties were revealed by the shape and protuberances of the skull. Probably his frequent references to phrenology and demonstrations of it made note-taking difficult.

While in France on a trip in 1821 for the purchase of apparatus and medical books for Transylvania University, Caldwell became an ardent devotee of phrenology. In 1824, he published *Elements of Phrenology*, of which a second edition appeared in 1827.[4] He believed that phrenology "is so ample in compass, and as rich and diversified in its productions, as any that man can be invited to cultivate."[5] He prophesied: "That Phrenology will be a rock of adamant in the stream of time, inscribed with the names of Gall, Spurzheim, and Combe and their coadjutors [Caldwell, of course, being one], when the writings of its opponents shall have been washed to tatters, and buried in the rubbish as worthless as themselves."[6]

Not only did he preach the value of this fantastic "science" to his students but lectured before hundreds of lay audiences in various parts of the United States. No doubt Caldwell was sincere in his belief that, as he often announced, there were but three perfect phrenological heads in the United States, those of Daniel Webster, of Henry Clay, and modesty for-

[4] Charles Caldwell: *Elements of Phrenology* (Lexington, Thomas T. Skillman, 1824), 2nd ed., "greatly enlarged" (Lexington: A. G. Meriwether, 1827).

[5] *Ibid.*, 1st ed., p. IV.

[6] *Ibid.*, 2nd ed., p. V.

bade naming the third. Frances Trollope (1780-1863), vitriolic critic of American manners, described the outcome of a course of lectures (1828) by Caldwell at the Western Museum in Cincinnati. She referred to him as "the Spurzheim of America."

> Between twenty and thirty of the most erudite citizens decided upon forming a phrenological society. A meeting was called, and fully attended; a respectable number of subscribers' names was registered, the payment of subscriptions being arranged for a future day. President, vice-president, treasurer and secretary were chosen; and the first meeting dissolved with every appearance of energetic perseverance in scientific research.
>
> The second meeting brought together one-half of this learned body, and they enacted rules and laws, and passed resolutions, sufficient, it was said, to have filled three folios.
>
> A third day of meeting arrived, which was an important one, as on this occasion the subscriptions were to be paid. The treasurer came punctually, but found himself alone. With patient hope, he waited two hours for the wise men of the west but he waited in vain: and so expired the Phrenological Society of Cincinnati.[7]

No discussion of phrenology by Drake has been located although, unquestionably, he ridiculed it. A facetious review of Caldwell's *Elements of Phrenology* (1824) by his brother, lawyer-author Benjamin Drake, doubtless reflected the doctor's opinion. The closing paragraphs are illustrative:

> Still however we are not infallible; and as our author declares that Phrenology "is now so rooted that nothing can shake it, and that the issue will prove that its course is irresistible," we regret that he did not enrich his pamphlet with a map of the head, exhibiting the location of the various

[7] Mrs. Frances Trollope: *Domestic Manners of the Americans* (London: Whittaker, Treacher & Co., 1832), p. 71.

organs. Considering the high price at which it is sold, we think such a drawing ought to have been afforded. Seventy-five cents, in specie, for 100 pages of coarse print, on coarse paper, clumsily stitched together, would on this side of the Ohio [in Cincinnati], be considered an exorbitant charge. We should really suppose that the price had been affixed when an elegant accompanying map was in contemplation. For the great mass, of the community, such a craniological picture would have been highly acceptable. Possessed of one of these, we might have, at a single glance, a knowledge of the character of every one we meet.

For the information of that portion of our citizens, who may have prudence enough to keep out of harm's way, and who, at the same time, are disciples of the learned professor, we would observe, that the organ of combativeness is a double one, and seated just behind the ears. Dr. Spurzheim declares that this faculty "gives the propensity to pinch, scratch, bite, cut, break, pierce, devastate, demolish, ravage, burn, massacre, struggle, butcher, suffocate, drown, kill, poison, murder, assassinate and *snake-pole*."

Gentle and pacific citizens of Ohio, beware! Venture not among the Kentuckians, for this terrible organ of Combativeness is powerfully developed on all their craniums.[8]

Drake taught the interrelationship and mutual dependence of all the organs of the body. The organs varied as to their importance and subordinate ones could be removed without endangering life. "This may be illustrated by a clock or by any complicated machinery. Remove the hands of a clock, it still goes. You may remove some other inferior part, and it still is a chronometer, but stop the pendulum and all is still."[9] However, in the loss of certain organs, ovaries, testicles, etc., "some function is suspended." Though the sugges-

[8] [Benjamin Drake]: Review of Elements of Phrenology by Charles Caldwell (1824), *The Cincinnati Literary Gazette*, I:57-59, Feb. 21, 1824.
[9] Clayton: *op. cit.*, p. 12.

tion is improbable, he might have had a hazy notion of the internal secretions. The necessity of studying the "mutual dependencies and rank of the different organs of the animal economy is obvious."

He lectured at length on the classification of and the "Modus Operandi of Medicines." At least six lectures were devoted to dyspepsia. He believed there was a relationship between the heart and intestines since "palpitation of the heart is often produced from intestinal torpor, which is often relieved by a simple cathartic." [10] On 25 November 1824, Drake stated, "I have had palpitation of the heart resulting from derangement of the stomach. This palpitationis cordis has alarmed me frequently. I have been awakened in the night with a violent turbulent action of the heart. The frequent occurrence of this induced me to believe that it was not dangerous. I have not had it for years. It has left no organic derangement." [11] Today's diagnosis of such attacks would be paroxysmal tachycardia if the seizures were sudden in onset and equally abrupt in termination. His deduction that the frequency of the attacks indicated their harmless character is interesting.

In January 1825, Samuel Brown returned to Lexington and took over his duties on the twenty-sixth. Altogether, Drake had delivered twenty-six lectures for Brown on the theory and practice of medicine. Despite the great amount of time devoted to the management of his own department in addition to lecturing for Dr. Brown, Drake translated from the French a *Synoptic View of Mineral Poisons . . .* by Dr. DeSalle (Paris, 1824). This translation, with additions and a "Note on the Vegetable Poisons" by Drake, was published as a supplement to Best's *Tables of Chemical Equivalents* in Janu-

[10] Anonymous notebook, p. 82.
[11] Clayton: *op. cit.*, p. 66.

ary 1825.[12] Apparently this was the earliest of many translations which Drake made from the French.

Early in March 1825, Samuel Brown resigned his professorship, giving as reasons the situation of his children and his private affairs. He concluded: "As a Resolution of the Medical Faculty has made it the duty of Professor Drake to examine the candidates on the Practice & to sign my name in the Diplomas, I flatter myself that the Board will not hesitate to sanction this Resolution or to accept of the Resignation which I most respectfully tender to them." [13]

Brown's resignation was accepted and, shortly thereafter, Drake was elected professor of the theory and practice of medicine. By action of the medical faculty he was designated its dean.

The spring of 1825 was spent by Drake and his wife in visiting numerous watering resorts of Kentucky and Ohio, hoping to benefit Mrs. Drake. They returned to Cincinnati about May 15 for the great event of 1825, the visit of Lafayette (1757-1834) who was the "Nation's Guest" from August 1824 to September 1825.[14] Dr. Holley of Transylvania, then in New York, wrote his wife on 22 August 1824, that he planned to invite Lafayette to Lexington. "The General will literally have to shake hands with the nation, and it will be well if his hands are not worn off, like the toe of the papal image." [15]

Coming from Nashville to Louisville by steamboat on 8

[12] Robert Best: *Tables of Chemical Equivalents, Incompatible Substances, and Poisons and Antidotes* (Lexington, W. W. Worsley, January 1825). Drake's translations with additions of DeSalle, pp. 42-59; and Drake's "Notes on Vegetable Poisons," pp. 60-74 inclusive.

[13] Samuel Brown: ALS to Board of Trustees, Mar. 1825. In Transylvania College Library.

[14] A. Levasseur: *Lafayette in America,* translated by John D. Godman, M.D. (Philadelphia: Cary and Lea, 1829).

[15] Horace Holley: ALS to his wife, 22 Aug. 1824. In Library, Transylvania College.

May 1825, Lafayette's vessel was snagged by the limb of a submerged tree. He and his party were removed seconds before the boat turned over and sank. Another boat took the general up the Ohio to the town of Portland (now a part of Louisville), thence to the city by land, the route being strewn with flowers. From Louisville he went through Shelbyville, Frankfort, Versailles, and on to Lexington where he received "forty-eight hours of uninterrupted entertainment." [16]

On his visit to Transylvania University, Dr. Holley delivered a welcoming address to which Lafayette responded. An honorary degree of Doctor of Laws was then conferred on the general. Following this came an "Introductory Ode" composed by Mrs. Holley and delivered by Gustavus Adolphus Henry, of Christian County, Kentucky. The sixth and final stanza was:

> Let this temple of science, The Pride of the West,
> Assemble its sons in devout gratulation:
> Let the love of our country pervade every breast,
> Till it wake every soul to intense emulation.
> > Already its children in gladness are met
> > To raise the loud anthem to brave LA FAYETTE! [17]

The "Introductory Ode" was followed by "Musick," after which came a "Salutatory Address in French," a "Latin Ode," "An English Ode," "Musick," and a concluding "Latin Eclogue" by Adolphe Mazureau of New Orleans. The address in French is followed by this apology: "Accentuated types for the above could not be obtained."

From Lexington, the Lafayette party went through Georgetown, Ky., to Covington on the Ohio. The general was placed in a decorated barge manned by six prominent citizens as

---

[16] Levasseur, *op. cit.*, p. 170.
[17] Transylvania University, *Order of Exercises . . . in Honor of General La Fayette* (Lexington, Fayette County Kentucky, No printer, May 1825).

rowers. Landing at the foot of Broadway in Cincinnati, 19
May 1825, where thousands had gathered, he was greeted by
a salute of thirteen guns (according to Levasseur) amid cries
of: "Welcome, Lafayette." A carpet had been spread from the
boat to a waiting carriage. Walking around the carpet,
Lafayette explained that the soil of America was good enough
for him to walk on. Three years later August Hervieu (1794-
1859?), protege of the famous authoress, Frances Trollope,
began painting "The Landing of Lafayette at Cincinnati." *

In July 1825, Dr. and Mrs. Drake were in Lebanon, Ohio,
for ceremonies incident to breaking ground for the Miami
Canal. Drake had, in his *Picture of Cincinnati*, suggested
feasible locations for canals in Ohio, of which this was one.[18]
They had dinner with Henry Clay, Governor De Witt
Clinton (1769-1828) of New York, Governor Jeremiah Mor-
row (1771-1852) of Ohio, and other prominent persons.

Returning to Cincinnati in September 1825, Mrs. Drake
became seriously ill with "bilious fever and dysentery." Recognizing the danger, Drake called fellow physicians in consultation and exerted every effort to relieve her. Mansfield
states that he searched every pharmacy in the city endeavour-
ing to secure drugs of utmost purity.[19] Despite the best of
medical advice and nursing, Mrs. Drake died on 30 September
1825. The following day she was buried in the Presbyterian
grounds, adjacent to the church of his friend, the Reverend
Joshua L. Wilson. Foreseeing the rapid growth of Cincinnati
with encompassment of the cemetery, Drake, on 22 October
1851, transferred the remains of his loved ones to the new and

* Hervieu's canvas measured twelve by sixteen feet. At least forty likenesses
of prominent persons could easily be identified. There were the governors of
Ohio and Kentucky, General (later President) Harrison, Dr. Drake, Judge
Burnet, and many prominent Cincinnatians. Wide search has failed to reveal
the location of Hervieu's painting. I would greatly appreciate learning of any
clues relative to it.

[18] Drake: *Picture . . .* , pp. 221-25.

[19] Mansfield: *Memoirs . . .* , p. 179.

beautiful Spring Grove Cemetery. He never ceased to mourn the loss of his beloved Harriet. The following stanzas of 18 March 1830 express his abiding, deep, and sincere emotions:

DIRGE

1. Oh joyous flew the days
    When thou wert mine;
   Young love then shed its rays
    Almost divine;
   Thy spirit beaming eye
    Fir'd me with ecstasy,
   And charm'd away my griefs
    Harriet my dear.

2. Dreary have been the years,
    As on they crept,
   Since tossed with hopes and fears
    I watch'd and wept,
   Till o'er my trembling soul
    I felt dark horrors roll,
   And saw thee sink in death,
    Harriet my dear.

3. Oh sad have been my cares
    And not a few:
   Bitter the silent tears,
    Dropp'd with the dew,
   When in my heart's deep gloom
    I've stoop'd to kiss thy tomb
   And mourn o'er our past joys
    Harriet my dear.

4. Calm rest beneath the sod
    Thy lov'd remains,
   Thy pure soul gone to God
    Feels no more pains;

But deep thy memory dwells
In his lone heart that swells
At sound of thy sweet name
Harriet my dear.[20]

Although Drake's grief was almost overwhelming, his philosophy carried him on for the sake of his three young children and his professional obligations. His intimate friend and associate, Samuel D. Gross, states that, when first they met in 1834, Drake wore a black suit and "crepe on his hat in mourning for his wife."[21] On or near the anniversaries of her death, he set aside a day of meditation, composed verses, and visited her grave.

In addition to his French translation on poisons, Drake's only published article in 1825 was a "Geological Account of the Valley of the Ohio," written in 1818.[22] The serious illness of his wife during 1825, undoubtedly prevented his customary literary activities.

In November 1825, Drake returned to Lexington where he found 281 medical students, the peak enrollment at Transylvania during its whole history. His introductory lecture on the theory and practice of medicine was delivered in the chapel of the university at twelve noon on 9 November 1825. The lectures were continued through the first week of March 1826. Sixty-four students received medical degrees on 11 March 1826. A local news item stated that the chapel was crowded with ladies and gentlemen. The dean, Doctor Drake, delivered the valedictory address which was "peculiarly appropriate and displayed in a good degree the comprehensiveness and energy of thought as well as beauty of style for which the Professor is justly distinguished."[23]

[20] Daniel Drake: MS, book of poems, 1830-36. In author's collection.
[21] Gross: *Autobiography*, Vol. II, p. 261.
[22] Daniel Drake: "Geological Account of the Valley of the Ohio," Transactions of the American Philosophical Society N.S. II:124-39, 1825.
[23] From *Kentucky Gazette. Cincinnati Commercial Register*, I, No. 50:p. [2]—c. [1], Mar. 31, 1826.

At the time of Holley's acceptance of the presidency, there were criticisms of the liberality of his Unitarian views. The Presbyterians, first to open the attack, were soon joined by the Baptists. The Methodists apparently took no part in the attacks. As Transylvania flourished under Holley's guidance, the tempo of the attacks increased, reaching a peak in 1825-26. The welfare of Transylvania mattered little if the advocate of "fashionable vices" could be destroyed. Michael Servetus (1511-53), burned at the stake through the animosity of John Calvin (1509-64) was subjected to no greater persecution, aside from the use of faggots, than was Holley. Dozens of pamphlets, veiled and sometimes openly defamatory letters to the newspapers, memorials to the legislature of Kentucky, and even sermons from the pulpits were used to discredit him. His enemies were often guilty of deliberate misrepresentation. Holley's every movement was watched and spies among those entertained in his home reported that he gave "frequent and sumptuous entertainments while statuary, painting, music, cards and dancing attracted the young and the gay." [24]

The attacks became intolerable and Holley resigned on 23 December 1825, the resignation effective at the close of the graduating exercises in 1826.[25] The trustees begged him to reconsider and he agreed to remain for the time being. Opposition to Holley was largely sectarian although there were political overtones which involved some of the trustees.

Holley attempted neither public defense nor retaliation, hoping perhaps that time and the continued success of Transylvania under his guidance would silence his detractors. In his *Discourse* delivered after the death of Colonel James Morrison, Transylvania's greatest and most liberal early bene-

[24] Robert Davidson: *History of the Presbyterian Church in Kentucky* (New York: Robert Carter, 1847), p. 305.

[25] Horace Holley: ALS, Dec. 23, 1825, to John Bradford, Chairman, Board of Trustees. In Library of Transylvania College.

factor, Holley made a defense in summarizing the liberal
views of the deceased: "Whenever a conscience becomes so
perverted as to make the possessor think it is his duty to
persecute, it is time to resist and punish him as a common
nuisance: unless, indeed, in this free and happy country, the
best and surest of all punishments is to let him alone, or
leave him to the natural indignation of an offended people." [26] Holley was fearless and far from conciliatory at times,
as was Drake.

With the exception of the Reverend Blythe and Caldwell,
the professors in the Medical Department did not openly participate in the battle. The Reverend Blythe, a Presbyterian
clergyman, established the *Christian Register* in 1822, in
which Holley was not directly attacked. It was abundantly
clear, however, that the purpose of the publication was to
refute Holley's ideals by quoting opposite views.

Caldwell, in his introductory lecture, November 1824, discussed and defended Natural Religion as peculiarly that of
physicians and scientists. The Reverend James Fishback
(d. 1838) of the First Baptist Church, at that time a member of the Transylvania board of trustees, took violent exception to Caldwell's views. Shortly thereafter, Fishback delivered a sermon in which he sought to prove that *true* religion was based on revelation as found in the Bible and that
Natural Religion "is altogether a delusion and has not one
proposition of truth in it." [27] Seven letters passed between
Caldwell and Fishback. In the seventh, Caldwell wrote:
". . . you ought to have informed yourself better as to the
sentiments I uttered, before venturing to speak of them." [28]
The polemics of their discussion do not concern us.

[26] Horace Holley: *A Discourse Occasioned by the Death of Col. James
Morrison.*, p. 19.
[27] *Correspondence between Dr. Charles Caldwell and Dr. James Fishback*
(Lexington: Thomas T. Skillman, 1826), p. 28.
[28] *Ibid.*, p. 35.

Growing out of the Caldwell-Fishback controversy was one between Caldwell and the Reverend John Breckinridge (1797-1841), leader of Kentucky Presbyterians. Four letters written by Breckinridge and three replies from Caldwell were published in *The Western Luminary* which was edited by Breckinridge.[29] In his reply to the first letter, Caldwell wrote:

> It is our happy lot to live at a period of the world enlightened greatly beyond those that have preceded it; and to reside in a country, the spirit of whose institutions, ecclesiastical and civil, is marked, not barely by *tolerance*, but by perfect *liberality*, benevolence, and charity. The very term persecution is offensive to us in its sound, and nothing is so odious as the practice which it designates. . . .
>
> From the period of the crusades to the present moment, some part of Christendom has been perpetually shocked by scenes of persecution on account of religion, the actors in which have been *honest at heart*, but most deplorably *astray in their intellect*.[30]

The attacks against Holley were unquestionably harmful to Transylvania. Parents had no desire to send their sons to an institution headed by an "atheist," as the sectarians called its president. There was a marked decrease in enrollment in all departments in 1826-27. The medical class had ninety-one fewer students than in the preceding year.

Drake's literary output during 1826 was limited to an article published in *Cincinnati in 1826*.[31] It has been impossible to identify this contribution with certainty. He could have written Chapter V (pp. 40-48) concerning Cincinnati's literary and scientific institutions. In addition, he may have written the paragraphs on "Public Health" (pp. 52-53).

The 1826-27 session of Transylvania University was with-

---

[29] "Correspondence between Doct. Caldwell and J. Breckinridge," *The Western Luminary* (Lexington) I:641-55, Apr. 20, 1825.

[30] *Ibid.*, I:642.

[31] B. Drake and E. D. Mansfield: *Cincinnati in 1826*.

out incident except for continued attacks on its president. On 14 March 1827, Holley resigned his position. Five days later, Drake resigned his professorship of the theory and practice of medicine and the deanship. It has been impossible to find any explanation for the concurrence of these resignations. Holley's resignation was, to the academic and law departments, a blow from which they never recovered. He had built Transylvania to a point where it was the equal of any of the eastern universities. Following Holley's departure, a Baptist clergyman became president. The Baptist was succeeded in turn by an Episcopalian, a Presbyterian, and a Methodist. By the late 1850's, the university could have been classed as no more than a high school.

The Medical Department, managed by the professors, was the only one to exhibit vitality after Holley left. It was disrupted by the resignation of three of its professors in 1837, followed by a fourth in 1838.[32] Though reorganized, it failed to maintain its former status, being overshadowed in time by the growth of the medical schools in Louisville and Cincinnati. The Transylvania Medical Department was suspended in 1857, at which time there were but thirty-two students, of whom nine received degrees.

Holley left Lexington for New Orleans on 27 March 1827, "accompanied for a considerable distance by a procession of pupils, citizens, and friends testifying by every expression of affectionate sorrow, their sincere attachment to his person and character." [33] In Louisiana he was implored to start a college. To this he consented and a prospectus was issued. After this task was completed, he and Mrs. Holley sailed for New York. Shortly thereafter he contracted yellow fever to which he succumbed on 31 July 1827. He was buried at sea, a victim of a

[32] Emmet F. Horine: "History of the Louisville Medical Institute," *Filson Club History Quarterly* (Louisville), VII:133-47, July 1933.

[33] Caldwell: *Discourse on the Genius and Character of Rev. Horace Holley* (Boston: Hilliard, Gray, Little and Wilkins, 1828), p. 273.

disease to which he would scarcely have been exposed but for sectarian persecution.

Charles Caldwell summarized Holley's views:

> But too liberal to be influenced by sectarian intolerance, and holding in scorn the presumption and obtrusive importunity of the propagandist, he never attempted to force on the community, nor even on individuals, his theological opinions. Free himself to select his path to the footstool of Mercy, he was not the tyrant to throw others into chains, and attempt to drag them thither, by usurped authority, dooming them to the penalty of endless torment, in case of non-conformity to some nostrum of belief. True piety he held to be an affection of the heart, that can neither be called forth, nor extinguished, by mere doctrinal influence. Perfectly independent in his religious sentiments, and catholic in all things, to him the universe was a temple of adoration, every work of beneficence, and every instance of duty faithfully performed, an act of worship acceptable to Heaven, and the only authority to which he bowed in homage, was the recognized will of the living God. And a knowledge of that will derived alike from written revelation, and that still older revelation, the works of nature.[34]

The resignations of the president of the university and of the dean of the Medical Department were recognized as calamitous. "Amicus" in the *Kentucky Reporter* expressed keen regret at Drake's resignation and the loss to the university and to Lexington: "Nature gave him a mind strong, active, penetrating and acute. Enterprise and ambition are the natural offspring of such a mind. . . . He is distinguished for colloquial ability and amiableness of disposition, for affable manners and dignified deportment, for refined sentiment and purity of morals. . . ." [35]

[34] *Ibid.*, p. 40.
[35] Amicus: "Letters to the Editor," *Kentucky Reporter* (Lexington), XX, No. 24:p. [3]—c. [1-2], Mar. 24, 1827.

11

Cincinnati, 1827-29

THE REASONS for Drake's resignation from so lucrative a professorship in Transylvania can only be surmised. Undoubtedly he wished to be with his parents, children, and other relatives in Cincinnati. He probably anticipated the deterioration of Transylvania as a result of Holley's departure. Work on a "Treatise on the Diseases of the Western Country" projected in 1822 had to be resumed. His literary output had been curtailed in Lexington, and a desire to resume writing was doubtless a factor. Finally, as always, he believed that no city in the West had greater prospects and afforded more opportunities than Cincinnati.

In March 1827, Drake joined with Dr. Guy W. Wright (1793-1831) to establish *The Western Medical and Physical Journal*. On 1 April 1826, Wright associated with Dr. James M. Mason (1797-1837), started a semimonthly periodical in Cincinnati, *The Ohio Medical Repository*. It was the second medical journal published west of the Allegheny Mountains.[2] After the eighth issue, that of 19 July 1826, Mason retired.

In the issue of *The Ohio Medical Repository* for 21 March 1827, Wright announced that the promise of enlarging and improving the journal was being fulfilled:

[1] Drake: *Introductory Lecture, on the Means of Promoting the Intellectual Improvement of Students* (1st ed.), p. 16; (2nd ed.), p. 15.
[2] Horine: "Daniel Drake and the Origin of Medical Journalism West of the Allegheny Mountains."

It is with extreme pleasure, we have in our power now to state, that Daniel Drake, late Professor of the Theory and Practice of Medicine in Transylvania University, has united with the former editor of the *Repository*; and will, in future, devote his talents to the new series, much enlarged—assuming a new shape, and in every relation, an increased importance. In the great acquisition of talents to the editorial department, we have thought proper to alter the title and have called it "The Western Medical and Physical Journal."

The first issue of the *Journal*, a continuation of the second medical periodical in the West, appeared in April 1827. It was published monthly with the following sections: original essays and cases, selected essays and cases, original reviews, selected reviews, selected intelligence, and, lastly, original intelligence and notices. This final section consisted of sprightly editorials and comments about current essays and events. The proportion of original essays and borrowed material (selected essays and reviews) was comparable to that of journals published in the East and in Europe. Concerning borrowed material, Dr. Oliver Wendell Holmes (1804-94), once said: "The ring of editors sit in each other's laps, with perfect propriety, and great convenience it is true, but with a wonderful saving in the article of furniture." [3]

The first essay in the first issue (April 1827) was by Drake: "History of a Case of Neuralgia Facialis; with reflections." [4] Within six months the subscribers numbered over seven hundred. Drake contributed nine original articles to the first volume in addition to many book reviews and editorials.

Drake and Wright continued as joint editors for twelve monthly issues. The first publishers were N. & G. Guilford. They were replaced by Hatch and Nichols in September 1827

[3] Oliver Wendell Holmes, Chairman, Committee on Medical Literature, *Transactions of the American Medical Association* (Philadelphia: T. K. and P. G. Collins, 1848), p. 256.
[4] *Western Medical and Physical Journal*, I:13-29, Apr. 1827.

(Vol. I, No. 6). In November the firm became Hatch, Nichols & Buxton. On 26 April 1828, Edmund S. Buxton announced the commencement of a new periodical, *The Western Journal of the Medical and Physical Sciences*, with Drake as sole editor.[5] The April number of the new journal appeared shortly thereafter.

The reasons for Buxton's withdrawal from the partnership and his independent establishment of a rival journal are matters for conjecture. Wright was undoubtedly angry since he announced that the rumor concerning the discontinuance of *The Western Medical and Physical Journal* was false, that an issue would appear shortly, and that he held against two of the printers an obligation for printing the second volume.[6] Drake was not mentioned, although an unconfirmed source intimated that there had been disagreement.

In May 1828, there appeared the second number of the periodical edited by Drake and, shortly thereafter, the first issue of Volume II of *The Western Medical & Physical Journal*. Wright was now editor and also publisher. The anomalous situation of two rival medical journals in Cincinnati at this time seems to have been overlooked by previous writers. Wright, in the May 1828 number of his periodical, stated: "The Journal *will answer as a continuation* of itself, without the assistance of the *illegitimate* offspring." [7]

The two publications with titles so nearly alike has confused binders. In one file, for example, the May 1828 issue (Vol. II, No. 1) of Wright's periodical has been bound between the April and May (1828) issues of Drake's journal. In another volume, the binder placed the May 1828 issue of

[5] Edmund S. Buxton: [Ad.], *Saturday Evening Cronicle* (Cincinnati), II, No. 17:p. [3]—c. [4-5], Apr. 26, 1828.
[6] Guy W. Wright: [Announcement], *Western Medical and Physical Journal. National Republican and Ohio Political Register* (Cincinnati), VI, No. 554: p. [3]—c. [3], Apr. 29, 1828.
[7] Guy W. Wright: *West. Med. & Phys. Jnl.*, II, May 1828, back cover.

Wright's publication before the second number (May 1827) of Volume I. No issues subsequent to the May 1828 number of Wright's periodical have been located and it seems probable that he withdrew from medical journalism. As a result of illness he was absent from Cincinnati for over a year. Although Wright returned in October 1830, to resume practice,[8] his improvement was temporary and he died 24 January 1831.[9]

Drake later referred to the *Journal* started in 1828 as a continuation of the periodical he and Wright began in 1827. As is evident, this was erroneous. The following announcement of the journal with the slightly altered title is of interest:

> The plan of this work is nearly the same with that of the Western Medical and Physical Journal. To the subscribers for that work it will serve as a continuation or second volume, while to new subscribers with a different title page, to be furnished, it may be a first volume, provided they do not wish to possess the volume of the Western Medical and Physical Journal just completed. Such subscribers can, however, be furnished, with that volume by the publisher of this.[10]

The publisher's announcement of the new journal edited by Drake showed a fully opened dogwood bloom bearing the inscription, *E sylva nuncius*. Because of Drake's early experiences in the forest and his continuing love of nature, it is evident that he suggested the emblem. The use of the singular, *sylva*, appeared once, after which the plural was used, *E sylvis nuncius*. After several years Drake lengthened his motto to *E sylvis, aeque atque ad sylvas, nuncius*. Monthly

[8] Guy W. Wright: "A Card," *Cincinnati Advertiser and Ohio Phoenix*, N. S., VIII, No. 86:p. [3]—c. [4], Oct. 30, 1830.

[9] [Obituary], *ibid.*, N.S., IX, No. 8:p. [3]—c. [3], Jan. 26, 1831.

[10] Edmund S. Buxton: [Ad.], *Saturday Evening Chronical* (Cincinnati), II, No. 17:p. [3]—c. [4-5], Apr. 26, 1828.

E. Martin, sct.

*Fig. 7. Dogwood emblem adopted (1828) by Daniel Drake for his
medical journal.*

publication was discontinued with the issue of March 1829
and a quarterly three times the size of the monthly appeared
in June 1829. The quarterly was continued through the April,
May, June 1838 issue, when publication was suspended. A
year later, Drake took his journal to Louisville where it was
consolidated with the *Louisville Journal of Medicine and
Surgery* to form *The Western Journal of Medicine and Surgery,* a monthly. The first issue appeared in January 1840,
under the editorship of Drake and Lunsford P. Yandell, Sr.
Although Drake withdrew as editor early in 1849, *The
Western Journal* was continued until 1855, when it passed
into the hands of Samuel D. Gross who renamed it *The
Louisville Review.* In October 1856, Gross moved to Philadelphia where he published one additional number of *The
Louisville Review.* Gross then united it with the *Medical*

Examiner and Record of Medical Science to form the *North American Medico-Chirurgical Review* which was published from 1857 to 1861. Thus the periodical established by Wright and Mason in 1826 survived for a period of thirty-five years.

After returning to Cincinnati from Lexington in March 1827, Drake remained only a short time arranging for publication of the early issues of his and Wright's medical journal. He then went East with at least two objectives in view. Eye infirmaries had recently been established in New York and Philadelphia. He wished to inspect these institutions preparatory to starting a similar one in Cincinnati. While in New York, he doubtless went to West Point to visit his uncle by marriage, Colonel Jared Mansfield. His second purpose in going East was to secure an appointment as midshipman for his son, Charles D. This latter object was accomplished in Washington, 13 April 1827. Drake then visited Boston and on his trip home went to Middletown, Connecticut, to get his son.

CHARLES DANIEL DRAKE. Charles Daniel, then sixteen, had become a problem. Accomplishing nothing scholastically in the Lancasterian Seminary in Cincinnati, Charles had been sent to Bishop Philander C. Chase's school in Worthington, Ohio, where discipline was said to be strict. He twice attempted to run away and was apprehended. The third attempt was successful. Charles was then sent to St. Joseph's Seminary, Bardstown, Kentucky, and then transferred to a private school near Lexington. Still another school near Lexington was tried and then he was placed in Dr. Louis Marshall's school at Versailles, Kentucky. In none of these was anything accomplished and Drake brought him home where he attempted unsuccessfully to tutor him. Next Charles was sent to Captain Partridge's Military Academy at Middletown, Connecticut.

Charles in his *Autobiography* refers to himself as a midshipman, lawyer, author, senator, and chief justice. He attributes his youthful "harum scarum, wilful ways partly to lack of parental discipline and subjugation *before I was two years old*." [11] Association with children along the Cincinnati water front and undoubtedly also with the rough boatmen were factors. "Mercurial, volatile, and wayward, I was a sort of living perpetual motion." [12] "I had been sent away from home to six schools, one in Ohio, four in Kentucky, and one in Connecticut and had in reality learned but little from books, but a great deal, mostly bad, from association." [13] Drake wrote of his son: "He is not wicked but as volatile, restless, fugacious, and changeable as Will Weathercock in the farce. I have seen him personate a whole flock of wild duck at the same time." [14]

Dr. Drake believed that a "cruise of two or three years in the Mediterranean or Pacific would give him [Charles] steadiness of purpose and habits of regular and methodical application." [15] Charles left home for Norfolk, Virginia, on 31 October 1827. From this port he sailed on the "Porpoise" for Mediterranean parts. In a few weeks he was arrested for striking an "insolent" sailor with a billet of wood and, probably, for using language unbecoming a midshipman. It has been hinted that the language of the Ohio boatmen surpassed in every way the curses of the seagoing sailors. Instead of facing trial, Charles resigned and returned home. Here, his father would neither see nor speak to him.

Charles then went to Washington where Judge McLean, postmaster general in Adams' cabinet, and Judge Rowan, both

---

[11] Charles D. Drake: "Autobiography," MS owned by State Historical Society of Missouri, Columbia, p. 15. Quoted by permission.
[12] *Ibid.*, p. 22.
[13] *Ibid.*, p. 243.
[14] *Ibid.*, p. 23.
[15] *Ibid.*, p. 236.

friends of the family, interceded. Soon afterwards, young Drake was ordered to the "Hornet." Shortly after sailing and just before the vessel reached Pensacola, Charles was accused of insubordination. Whereupon he resigned, was reinstated and ordered to duty on the "Grampus." The transfer from the "Hornet" to the "Grampus" was providential, since on 10 September 1829 the former vessel sank in a storm with no survivors. However, Charles was soon in difficulties on the "Grampus," again as a result of insubordination. On 30 October 1829, his appointment as acting midshipman was revoked by the secretary of the navy. Returning home in April 1830, he began the study of law in his Uncle Benjamin's office. After admission to the bar he became a successful lawyer in St. Louis, Missouri. Later he was elected to the U.S. Senate and ultimately was appointed chief justice of the U.S. Court of Claims in Washington, where he served until his voluntary retirement.

On his return to Cincinnati in May 1827, Drake's first efforts were directed toward the establishment of an infirmary for the care of diseases of the eyes. It was announced:

> Dr. Drake one of the Editors of this Journal, in a recent visit to the East, has made the necessary arrangements, and is about to establish in this city, an Infirmary for diseases of the eye—both Clinical and Surgical. It will be modelled after the excellent institutions of a similar kind recently established in New York, by Drs. Delafield and Rogers, and in Philadelphia, by Dr. Hays.
> [Mention is made of the prevalence of diseases of the eye in the West and of the accessibility of Cincinnati.]
> According to the practice pursued in the Eastern infirmaries, those who are unable to pay, will be operated upon gratuitously.[16]

[16] [Notice], "Eye Infirmary," *West. Med. and Phys. Jnl.*, I:126-27, May 1827.

On 20 July 1827, Drake announced resumption of the practice of "Physic and Surgery" in Cincinnati.[17] Public announcement was made of the opening of the eye infirmary on 15 November 1827, although patients had been received since 1 July. Drake was the first physician west of the Allegheny Mountains to devote special attention to ophthalmology and the first to establish an eye infirmary. He stated: "By the aid of a number of benevolent citizens of Cincinnati, he will be able to defray the expenses of poor persons from the country, while they are under treatment in this city. To such his professional services will be offered gratuitously. His regular prescribing days are Wednesday and Saturdays, between the hours of ten and one o'clock; but in urgent cases he may be consulted at any time." [18]

One hundred prominent citizens enrolled as contributors to the charity fund. To be eligible for charity treatment, evidence of need was to be furnished to one of the Board of Visitors, consisting of the Reverend Joshua L. Wilson, president; Davis B. Lawler, secretary; William M. Walker, treasurer; the Reverend William Burke; Martin Baum; Peyton S. Symmes; and John P. Foote.

In December 1827, Drake sent a memorial to the Ohio State Medical Society asking their approval and support of the new infirmary. The convention unanimously adopted the following resolution:

> *Resolved* That this Convention highly approves the foundation and objects of the Cincinnati Eye Infirmary established by and now under the direction of Daniel Drake, M.D. and believe that the gentleman is qualified in an imminent [*sic*] degree, to superintend an establishment of this kind and

[17] Daniel Drake: "Card," *National Republican and Ohio Political Register,* V, No. 475:p. [3]—c. [3], July 24, 1827.
[18] "Cincinnati Eye Infirmary," *ibid.,* V, No. 508:p. [3]—c. [1], Nov. 16, 1827.

therefore recommend it to the favorable consideration of the public and the patronage of the Legislature.[19]

In the same month, the Ohio legislature granted articles of incorporation. Drake maintained the infirmary until his removal to Louisville in 1839.

Drake was the first American to report an instance of a ruptured intestine with an intact abdominal wall.[20] Previously only a few similar reports had appeared in European literature. Today, as is well known, surgeons readily recognize the symptoms and operate immediately. Before the days of anesthesia and of routine abdominal surgery, such patients died. Drake's diagnosis was correct since he concluded that "a rupture of some portion of the alimentary canal had happened; or that extensive inflammation had been suddenly developed, and would speedily terminate the scene." The diagnosis was verified by autopsy. One of his reasons for reporting the case was "that external violence *may* lacerate and rupture, one of the most empty and protected of the intestines, without doing any visible injury to the skin."

At the request of the Agricultural Society of Hamilton County, Ohio, Drake delivered A *Discourse on Intemperance*, 1 March 1828.[21] This address marked the beginning of the temperance movement in Cincinnati, perhaps in the West. Afterwards he was invited to deliver many addresses on the same subject. At one of the meetings on a warm summer afternoon, Drake had spoken at length without any end in sight. A motion was made to "adjourn awhile and take a

[19] Ohio State Medical Society: *Proceedings* (Zanesville: Adam Peters, 1828), p. 4.
[20] Daniel Drake: "An account of the death of a man from a lacerated wound of the Jejunum, the adominal parietes remaining entire," *West. Med. & Phys. Jnl.*, I:550-55, Jan. 1828.
[21] Drake: A *Discourse on Intemperance* (Cincinnati: Looker & Reynolds, 1828). This address also was published in *West. Jnl. of Med. & Phys. Sc.*, II:11-34, Apr. 1828 and II:65-91, May 1828.

drink." The motion carried and many listeners went across the street to a saloon. After their return the address was resumed.[22]

The *Discourse* is an example of Drake's logic and clarity of expression. There were six divisions (chapters), beginning with a discussion of the chemical nature of alcohol and its effects and closing with a list of possible corrections of over-indulgence. He did not anywhere advocate total abstinence but deplored especially the use of spiritous liquors at conventions, professional meetings, and social gatherings. He displayed considerable originality and presented some novel conclusions. Concerning matrimonial unhappiness as a cause of intemperance, he said:

> It is unfortunate, that so many wives mistake scolding for remonstrance; and drive their husbands into dissipation by indulging in the former, when a proper exercise of the latter would contribute so largely to preserve them from every kind of vice. That many a weak minded husband has been scolded into drunkenness, is undeniable; but others—or their friends for them—have ungenerously ascribed their intemperance, to the scolding, which it had in reality provoked. At best, moreover, it is a contemptible excuse for getting drunk, that a man is married to a *scold*—in other words to a silly, petulant or garrulous woman. It should rather animate him to increased sobriety, resolution and steadiness; that the peace and character of his family may, as far as possible, remain unimpaired. . . .
>
> An intemperate wife, who should assign her husband's moroseness, as a reason for her drinking, would find but few persons disposed to admit the validity of her excuse; and the same rule should be applied to the vices of the other sex.[23]

[22] Mansfield: *Memoirs* . . . , pp. 189-90. In another place Mansfield places the date of Drake's address as 1825. Consult "The Pioneer Church in Ohio," *Presbyterian Witness* (Cincinnati), X, Jan. 9, 1867:p. [4]—c. [4].

[23] Drake: *Discourse on Intemperance*, pp. 32-33.

During the first half of the nineteenth century the majority of physicians accepted the concept of "spontaneous combustion" in confirmed alcoholics. The adjective, "spontaneous," was erroneously used since what was implied, in most instances, was actually a greater degree of combustibility of the alcoholic than nonalcoholic. Drake's discussion of so-called "spontaneous combustion" clearly shows that contact with actual fire was a necessary prelude:

> Intemperance predisposes the body to Spontaneous Combustion. On this point facts have multiplied, until the most incredulous inquirer can scarcely retain his doubts. The bodies of corpulent inebriates, when asleep, have, in several instances taken fire, by the accidental contact of a coal or candle, and all the soft parts have been reduced to ashes, or driven off in clouds of thick smoke. To conceive of the possibility of this revolting catastrophe, we need only recollect the combustible nature of fat, and the still more inflammable quality of ardent spirits, which is composed of the very same materials; which, being swallowed daily, in excessive quantities, with reduction of food, may be presumed to alter, to a certain degree, the chemical composition of the body. Meanwhile its vital powers become greatly reduced, and thus render it an easier prey to fire or other external agents.[24]

Drake was intrigued with the idea of spontaneous combustion. He inserted a paper by Pierre-Aimé Lair on the subject as an appendix to his *Discourse*.[25] Later he translated from the *Dictionnaire des sciences médicales* an article by Marc which was published in his medical journal.[26] In 1830 another dissertation was inserted in the *Western Journal*, in which is stated that "a lean dry individual" never became a

[24] *Ibid.*, 43.
[25] *Ibid.*, pp. 71-84.
[26] M. Marc: "On the Spontaneous Combustion of the Human Body," translated by the editor [Daniel Drake], *West. Jnl. Med. & Phys. Sc.*, II:130-41, June 1828.

victim. All persons supposed to have developed spontaneous combustion have been fat and were near an open fire.[27]

The subject of spontaneous combustion has interested many other physicians. Altogether twenty-six books and approximately one hundred essays on the subject have been recorded. The latest cases reported occurred in 1937.[28]

On 31 July 1828, Edmund S. Buxton announced that as a result of illness he had disposed of the *Western Journal of the Medical and Physical Sciences* to Dr. Drake. In the August 1828 issue of the *Journal,* the editor stated he had "unexpectedly become at once Proprietor, Editor and Publisher."

> It is not without regret, that he finds himself thus situated; as his editorial duties were, of themselves, sufficient to occupy most of the time, which professional engagements left at his disposal. Inured, however, to hard labour, and deeply interested, as he has become, in the success of the undertaking, he is far from cherishing a feeling of discouragement. [Contributions were requested concerning]
>
> 1. Rare or singular cases of disease. To report all cases would be impracticable and absurd. To report the successful *only,* is uncandid. Cases which go to the suggestion of a new principle or rule of practice; which either weaken or sustain a disputed point; which terminating unfavorably, may serve as a warning to the profession; and finally, those which occur with exceeding rarity may always be published with advantage to others, and credit to the reporter.
>
> 2. New forms of disease, depending on causes, either discovered or unknown.
>
> 3. Annual epidemics. . . .
>
> 4. Brief or synoptic reports, consisting of a sort of account current with the weather and diseases, of the different seasons.
>
> 5. Accounts of new medicines. . . .

[27] "Dupuytren: Spontaneous Combustion," *ibid.,* IV:283-84, July, Aug., Sept. 1830.
[28] C. A. Forssander: "Two Unusual Cases of Spontaneous Combustion," *Middlesex Hospital I.,* XXXVII:151-52, Oct. 1937.

6. Experimental treatises on our *native* medicinal plants.

7. Chemical and therapeutick accounts of our mineral springs.

8. Comparative histories of the diseases of the negroes and whites.

9. Facts for an estimate of the peculiarities, which the diseases prevailing on board of steam boats of the Western and Southern waters may present.

10. Reports on the diseases in our penitentiaries.

11. Detached facts, in clinical medicine, which may be proper for insertion under the head of Original, Miscellaneous Intelligence.

12. Notices of the discovery in the West and South, of such minerals, as are in any way employed in pharmacy.

The Editor would not, however, absolutely restrict his correspondents to new facts; inasmuch as he believes that on many subjects a new arrangement of old ones, is imperiously required; he would be happy, therefore, to receive and publish essays and dissertations on all subjects in the profession, provided they develop, either new principles or new practical maxims.

[The rules suggested for the preparation of papers continue to be models.]

The first excellence is truth. Everything that is published in a journal of medical science, should as far as possible, be divested of error; for it may all, sooner or later, influence the treatment of the sick, whose lives might be jeopardized, in consequence of perversions or suppressions of the truth. The next great requisite is *Perspicuity:* that what the writer has observed and thought, may be readily and clearly comprehended. The next is *conciseness:* which many readers would, in reality place at the head of the column of good qualities: —And it cannot be denied, that they would have much reason on their side; for the quantity that is published, in the journals, and detached works, of the present age, is really enough to deter the timid and the indolent, from all reading. *Originality,* is another important property, which should never be wanting. Mere learning, and laborious rumination of that which has been masticated by others, will neither advance the interests of the profession, nor satisfy readers of good sense. Finally, those who write for medical journals, should not consider the minor rules of composition beneath their attention. If advanced in years and reputation, their example will be authoritative, and should, therefore, be a good one: If young, they should seize every occasion to improve themselves in the art of writing. Indeed no member of the profession, either high or low, should consider himself at liberty to disregard the laws of *orthography, etymology, syntax and collocation* in anything which he presumes to address to his brethren. Lastly, in mercy to editors and compositors, he should write (or procure to be written) an unaffected and legible hand; without which, he has, in fact, no guaranty, that the printed will be a correct copy of his written communication.[29]

Drake regarded the "labourer as worthy of his hire" and offered to give a year's subscription to the *Journal* for each short article accepted. For longer papers, one dollar a page would be paid. Finally, a prize of fifty dollars was offered for the best dissertation on any of the following subjects: diseases of the Negroes, especially "Negro Consumption"; treatment of autumnal fever on the principles of Broussais; the cause and pathology of "milk sickness"; and "the successful application of the process of Civiale, to the destruction of the calculus vesicae, established by American cases." [30]

The following announcement appeared in the September 1828 issue of Drake's *Journal:*

The great delay in the publication of this number requires an explanation. On 18th September, the day on which the printing of a number commenced, the Editor, on rescuing

[29] Daniel Drake: "To the Physicians of the Western States," *West. Jnl. Med. & Phys. Sc.* II:i-vi, Aug. 1828.
[30] *Ibid.*

one of his friends from the flames, suffered extensive burns on both hands. The accident was followed by various afflicting constitutional disorders, from which at this time, October 24, he is but beginning to recover. He was thus prevented from finishing several original articles for the number, and has been compelled to substitute selected matter; which he hopes, however, from its extrinsic excellence, will not be unacceptable to his readers.

The October number will positively be committed to the press in a few days, and issued with all possible expedition.[31]

On the evening of 18 September 1828, the bed of Drake's sister-in-law, Miss Caroline Sisson, caught fire after she had retired. He rushed into her room and succeeded in extinguishing the flames by compressing the burning bedcovers with his naked hands which were severely burned. Miss Sisson died eight hours after the accident. It was several months before Drake recovered and his hands were permanently scarred. The serious constitutional symptoms produced were described in a published report.[32]

Even though indisposed, Drake translated from the *Dictionaire de sciences médicales* the article on "Wounds of the Heart."[33] In addition he described with autopsy findings a case he had treated of softening of the heart.[34] Many editorials and reviews were composed during his convalescence. As the result of his inability to attend to the duties of his eye infirmary, he requested the visiting board to appoint a consulting surgeon. Jedediah Cobb (1800-60), professor of anatomy and physiology in the Medical College of Ohio, was

[31] Daniel Drake: "Explanation," *ibid.*, II:328, Sept. 1828.
[32] Daniel Drake: "History of two Cases of Burn, Producing Serious Constitutional Irritation," *West. Jnl. Med. & Phys. Sc.*, IV:48-60, Apr., May, June 1830.
[33] "Wounds of the Heart," translated by Daniel Drake, *West. Jnl. Med. & Phys. Sc.*, II:333-37, Oct. 1828.
[34] *Ibid.*

appointed.[35] In November 1828, Drake again apologized for the delay in issuing his *Journal* as a result of his continued indisposition, but promised that the December number would appear on time. At this time he was elected president of the Board of Health. There are two newspaper notices in which he urges the vaccination of all Cincinnatians, since several patients with smallpox had been removed from boats.

The first installment of one of Drake's choicest satirical writings, "The People's Doctors," appeared in 1829.[36] This was a composite review of five popular medical treatises: Thomson's *Botanic Family Physician*, Robinson's *Lectures on Medical Botany*, Swaim's *Panacea*, Rafinesque's *Pulmist*, and Salmon's *Compleat English Physician*. Shortly after the review appeared in the *Journal*, it was issued with additions as a pamphlet dedicated "To The People."

> This brings us to our own age—than which, with all our boasted elevation in learning and philosophy, no other has ever presented a greater *variety* of barefaced and abominable quackeries. To eradicate them would be more difficult, than to root out the sour dock and Canada thistle of our fields, while the soil continues to favor their reproduction. Planted in the ignorance of the multitude, warmed by its credulity, and cherished by their artful and unblushing authors, these impostures are fixed upon us, as the poison oak encircles the trunk of the noble tree, whose name it has prostituted. . . .
>
> When one of these quackeries is inoculated into a community nothing can arrest its speed, or limit its duration. Every dog has his day, and so has every nostrum.
>
> .   .   .   .
>
> Of these books, the first is by *doctor* Thomson, who has favored the public—(that is such part of them as have the

[35] *Ibid.*, II:394.

[36] Daniel Drake: "The People's Doctors," *West. Jnl. Med. & Phys. Sc.*, III:393-420 and 455-62, Oct., Nov., Dec. 1829.

good sense to pay twenty dollars for a patent right) with an engraved likeness of himself, which we commend to the amateurs. The first thirty pages are composed of interlarded sketches, of the author's birth, labours and persecutions; of warnings to the good people against the "regular faculty," and of his system of physiology, pathology and therapeuticks. As most of the people no doubt are ignorant on all these important points, we shall make such extracts as the occasion seems to require.[37]

As mentioned earlier, Rafinesque, who had taught at Transylvania from 1819 to 1826, concocted a secret remedy, Pulmel, which he claimed would cure every known type of disease of the lungs. "It is a peculiar compound substance, formed by the chemical combination of several powerful vegetable principles, acting on the lungs and the whole system." This marvellous remedy was marketed in 1829 in twelve forms: Syrup Pulmel, Balsam, Balsam Syrup, Lotion, Wine, Sweet Chocolate of Pulmel (cakes or liquid), Sugar of Pulmel, Honey of Pulmel, Lozenges, Powders, and Pulmelin, "or Concentrated Salt of Pulmel, dose one grain, but double price." His entry into the patent medicine field brought him no more financial returns than did his numerous other ventures. Drake wrote:

> Rafinesque is a name not unknown to our Backwoods readers; but many of them may ask, whether the Pulmist is the same fishtaker, and ancient chronicler of Kentucky? We answer, that such *appears* to be the fact; and dismal, indeed, must be the "times," that can make an apothecary's muller of such a learned head. We have not had the advantage of seeing the professor's 'doctor book', the title of which is prefixed to this article, but his 'circular' lies before us, and affords intrinsic evidence, that the *pulmist* is no other than

[37] *Ibid.*, Cincinnati, Ohio: "Printed and published for the Use of *The People*," 1829.

the distinguished *antiquary* who lately settled the limits, and *located* the wigwams, of our Indian tribes for the last three thousand years! Strange metamorphosis of genius! It was, doubtless, while inquiring into the arts and sciences of these savage hordes, long since extinct, that this extraordinary man exhumed the recipes which are to cure consumption, and all other diseases of the lungs! How clever it is, thus, to compel the tomb to give up the knowledge which enables the *doctor* and his agents, at the corner of 'Sixth and Chestnut streets,' Philadelphia, to disappoint its future expectations! This is fairly turning the tables upon the grave.[38]

[38] *Ibid.*, p. 33.

12

*The want of ambition contributes
signally to retard the progress of medical
science.*[1]

Cincinnati, 1830;
Philadelphia, 1830-31;
Cincinnati, 1831-32

APPARENTLY as an aftermath of the severe constitutional re-
actions caused by the burns resulting in enforced confine-
ment, Drake fell into a reminiscent and poetic mood in 1830.
Prior to this he had attempted no versification so far as we
know. During this year he wrote fifteen poems, approximately
half of his known output: "Sonnet to the Falling Snow,"
"Origin of Snow Flakes," "To Elizabeth," "To Harriet
Echo," "The Winds," "To Harriet Echo," "To a Solitary
Maple," "To my Mother-in-law," "The Death of Little Jane,"
"To Belle," "Childhood and Age," "Dirge" (to Harriet, see
Chapter 10), "Hymn" (Fifth Anniversary), "October Flow-
ers," and "Age and Youth." [2]

The greater number of these poems are occasional in
nature, a mixture of conventional imagery and of unpre-
tentious diction somewhat representative of the period. They
certainly disclose that he was observant and imaginative,
with an ear for meter. "The Death of Little Jane" deserves
especial notice since it tells in rhyme a simple story, the

[1] Drake: *Essays on Medical Education*, p. 82.
[2] Drake. MS, book of poems.

earliest of its type located in my brief survey of poetry. It was composed for his niece, Harriet, "Feby 14th 1830, at night sick —Written in pain and haste, To please but childhood's taste." Jane had run away from home to see a parade:

. . . .

> Now when sweet Jane, the soldiers saw,
> She screamed out loud, "La me! Oh la!
> What pretty caps the horsemen wear!
> See how their plumes dance in the air!"

. . . .

Poor Jane was now in all her glory
But hear the end of my sad story.
> On with the footmen came the drum,
> Whose thunders almost struck her dumb,
> And still, she stood, to hear it beat
> Quite in the middle of the street.
> Just then in fright a horse and dray
> Took down the street and ran away.

. . . .

> The boys and negroes by a dash,
> Escaped the dangers of the crash,
> But little Jane forgot to go,
> And on her head received a blow:
> Bleeding she fainted on the spot—
> Some thought her dead but others not.

. . . .

> A dreadful wound her forehead show'd,
> Her flaxen hair was dyed with blood,
> Her limbs had lost the power to move
> Her half closed eyes beamed no more love,
> One gasp her pale lips give for breath,
> And then she calmly sunk in death.

> Thus when the tempest rends the grove,
>   The limbs of some tall mountain ash
> Are hurled in fury from above,
>   And kill the rosebud in the crash.[3]

In the following year, 1831, these poems were written: "To Mrs. Hentz," "To my Mother on her 70th Birth Day," "Note to my Adopted Daughter," "Funeral Hymn for Sixth Anniversary," [4] "Hymn for my Mother's Funeral," and "To Belle."

Drake read widely, had a remarkably retentive memory, and echoes may have risen naturally and appropriately in his verses. It is relevant to say that his verses are both spontaneous and eclectic. Possibly influenced by William Cowper (1731-1800) or by Jane Taylor (1783-1824) or written independently, Drake's twenty-four stanzas, "To my Mother on her 70th Birth Day," review his childhood. Each stanza is answered by the refrain, "My Mother:"

> Who toiled by day, and sunk to rest
> With me upon her wearied breast
> And hush'd my cries, and called me "bless'd?"
>   My Mother.
>
> .   .   .   .
>
> Who in the floorless cabin slept,
> And round her bed the lizards crept?
> Or o'er her babies watch'd and wept?
>   My Mother.
>
> Who as she left her sleepless bed,
> The silent tear of anguish shed,
> To hear me cry in vain for bread?
>   My Mother.
>
> .   .   .   .

[3] Drake: MS, book of poems, pp. 31-36.
[4] *Ibid.*, pp. 55-56: Also Mansfield: *Memoirs* . . . , pp. 180-81; also Juettner, pp. 57-58.

Who dress'd me in my Sunday clothes
And grac'd my bosom with a rose,
And made me outward turn my toes?
                              My Mother.

. . . .

The parting came as years roll'd on,
Who now embrac'd her youthful son
And bid him go, then mourn'd him gone?
                              My Mother.
Now that disease and age have shed
Their baleful influence on thy head,
Look to thy God and feel no dread,
                              My Mother.[5]

He composed the following poems in 1832: "To Dove and
Echo," "To Echo and Dove," "To Mrs. Mansfield," [6] and
"The Lover's Winter Visit" (written on the twenty-fifth
anniversary of his marriage).[7] "The Funeral Song for Eighth
Anniversary" and "The Buckeye Tree" (a ditty) were written
in 1833.

"The Buckeye Tree" was sung to the tune of "Yankee
Doodle" on 26 December 1833, at the celebration of the
forty-fifth anniversary of the settlement of Cincinnati.[8] Following the song, Drake was toasted as "The Author of the
Picture of Cincinnati." After thanking the audience and men-
tioning a description of the buckeye tree in his book, he ex-
tolled the virtues and uses of this native tree. The climax of
his address was the suggestion that the buckeye be adopted
as Ohio's emblem. The speech was enthusiastically received
and thenceforth Ohio has been "The Buckeye State."

[5] Drake: poems, pp. 47-51.
[6] *Ibid.*, p. 71; also in Mansfield, p. 374.
[7] Drake: poems, p. 67-70; Mansfield, pp. 372-74; Juettner, p. 36.
[8] Drake: poems, pp. 75-55.

Being born in the East, I am not *quite* a native of Ohio, and, therefore, am not a Buckeye by birth. Still I might claim to be a greater BUCKEYE than most of you, who were born in the city, for my BUCKEYEISM belongs to the *country*, a better soil for rearing Buckeyes than the town.

My first remembrances are of a Buckeye cabin, in the depths of a cane break, on one of the tributary brooks of Licking river; for whose waters, as they flow into the Ohio, opposite our city, I feel some degree of affection. At the date of these recollections, the spot where we are now assembled, was a Beech and Buckeye grove; no doubt altogether unconscious of its approaching fate. Thus, I am a BUCKEYE by engrafting, or rather by inoculation, being only in the bud, when I began to draw my nourishment from the depths of a Buckeye bowl.

. . . .

From the very beginning of emigration, it [the buckeye tree] has been a friend to the "new comers." Delighting in the richest soils, they soon learned to take counsel from it, in the selection of their lands, and it never yet proved faithless to anyone who confided in it.

When the first "log cabin" was to be hastily put up, the softness and lightness of the wood, made it precious; for in those times laborers were few, and the axes once broken in harder timber, could not be repaired.

When the infant BUCKEYES came forth, to render these solitary cabins vocal and make them instinct with life, cradles were necessary, and they could not be so easily dug out of any other tree. Thousands of men and women, who are now active and respectable performers on the great theatre of western society, were once rocked in Buckeye troughs.

. . . .

To the Buckeye—yes, gentlemen, to the Buckeye tree; and it proved a friend indeed, because, in the simple and expressive language of those times, it was "a friend in need." Hats were manufactured from its fibres—the tray of the delicious "pone" and "johnny-cake"—the venison trencher—the noggin —the spoon—and the huge, white family bowl for mush and milk, were carved from its willing trunk; and the finest "boughten" vessels could not have imparted a more delicious flavor, or left an impression so enduring. . . .

Thus, beyond all the trees of the land, the buckeye was associated with the family circle—penetrating its privacy, facilitating its operations and augmenting its enjoyment. Unlike many of its loftier associates, it did not bow its head and wave its arms at a haughty distance, but might be said to have held out the *right hand of fellowship;* for of all trees of our forest, it is the only one with *five* leaflets arranged on one stem—an expressive symbol of the human hand.

·   ·   ·   ·   ·   ·   ·   ·   ·   ·   ·   ·   ·   ·   ·   ·   ·

But, Mr. President and Gentlemen, I must dismiss this fascinating topic. My object has been to show the peculiar fitness of the Buckeye to be made the symbol-tree of our native population. This arises from its many excellent qualities. Other trees have greater magnitude and stronger trunks. They are the Hercules of the forest; and like him of old, who was distinguished only for physical power they are remarkable chiefly for their mechanical strength. Far different is it with the Buckeye, which does not depend on brute force to effect its objects; but exercises, as it were, a moral power, and admonishes all who adopt its name, to rely on mental cultivation, instead of bodily prowess.[9]

"A Parting Song," [10] composed 5 January 1835, was used at a social gathering following the close of the Medical Convention of Ohio, Columbus, 5-7 January 1835. Dr. Silas Reed,

---

[9] Daniel Drake: "The Buckeye Tree," *Western Monthly Magazine* (Cincinnati), II:151-54, March 1834. Also in Appendix to Benjamin Drake: *Tales and Sketches from the Queen City* (Cincinnati: E. Morgan and Co., 1838), pp. 173-80.

[10] Drake: poems, pp. 79-82; also contemporary broadside in author's collection.

editor of *The Western Medical Gazette* (Cincinnati) describes the party:

On the evening of the final adjournment of the Convention, and after listening to an eloquent lecture from Dr. Drake, on the manner and importance of instructing the blind, delivered to both houses of the legislature and the citizens of Columbus, we repaired to his room to spend the remainder of the evening in cultivating those kindlier feelings of our nature, which the world seems determined to deny us. We proved, however, by speeches made to that effect, that we are far less quarrelsome than our enemies would have us, and that the few misunderstandings which did arise between us, were less the result of *innate* ill nature, than the officious meddlings, misrepresentations and exaggerations of the people and our patients, who often appear to take delight in seeing "the doctors by the ears." Nearly forty of the members were present, and all seemed thus set apart for the mingling of thought and feeling, and the pouring forth of vivid flashes of wit and sentiment. . . .

Before the party broke up, we were favored with a speech from our host, on the subject of the various modes of "climbing," as he was pleased to term it; or, in other words, the different and best methods to be pursued in acquiring an honorable distinction, and the manliness of climbing on the *out side* of the tree, in our efforts to obtain high places of profit and honor.

Could you have heard his natural history of various climbing animals of the West, and their several instincts in this peculiar art, you would have declared that he had taken lessons in the hunting skirmishes of David Crockett. Altogether, it was one of the most jocose and ironical affairs of pleasantry I ever heard. . . .

The author of the speech then presented his guests with a "Parting Song," composed (by himself) for the occasion, and tuned to "Auld Lang Syne;" which was sung by all in the most spirited and feeling manner.

Time will never efface the remembrance of the stirring up of the deep fountains of social emotion, which it occasioned; and in after years, those present will look back upon that meeting as one of the greenest spots of their professional recollections.[11]

"To Catherine Jameson, on her Marriage with Mr. Fisher," a poem of four stanzas, was written 28 January 1836. His final attempt at versification which I have located is a bit of doggerel, "To an Apple Pie," hastily composed on 19 November 1841. At this time he was teaching Roman history to Jane Short, daughter of his friend and associate in the Louisville Medical Institute, Charles Wilkins Short (1794-1863). Jane Short, then sixteen, gave him an apple pie which elicited the following:

> 'Tis One! as I begin this line,
> (The hour when temperate people dine,)
> And I'm about, sweet Jane, to try
> The virtues of your apple pie;—
> A classic dish, I cannot doubt,
> When cut & tasted, 'twill turn out;
> For who can let her fancy stray
> Along the noble Appian way
> Or ramble through the Parthenon,
> And then bid classic thoughts be gone,
> When, in the culinary art,
> She pauses to perform a part?
>
> . . . .
>
> One piece I've eaten, and another
> Almost as large as was its brother,
> Lies waiting on my white & smiling plate
> And when this line is finish'd, will be ate.
>
> . . . .

[11] Silas Reed: "Social Party of the Members," *Western Medical Gazette* (Cincinnati), II:465-67, Feb. 1835. "The Parting Song," pp. 466-67; also Juettner, pp. 435-36.

> Ceres, her finest flour has lent,
> Her choicest fruit Pomona sent,
> While ancient Araby the Blest,—
> Renown'd in Latin song & Story
> Has shed the spices of the East,
> As erst in days of Roman glory,
> They fell in aromatic flowers,
> (As nectar drips from summer showers)
> On pies & other nice confections
> Which graced the tables of Patricians.
>> In times to come, when pies you make
>> Sweet Jane, remember Dr. Drake.[12]

It is evident that Drake was accustomed to long hours of work. Rarely was he idle. In 1829, he had written the first of his essays on medical education: "Selection and Preparatory Education of Pupils." [13] Three months later, Essay II: "Private Pupilage" appeared.[14] And Essay III: "Medical Colleges," was published in the first issue of his *Journal* for 1831.[15] These three essays with four additional ones were issued in book form in 1832.[16]

Practical Essays on Medical Education and the Medical Profession is a medical classic, proclaimed by the eminent medical historian and bibliographer, Fielding H. Garrison (1870-1935), as "far and away, the most important contribution ever made to the subject in this country." [17] Undoubtedly no book on medical education written in the United States has had such far-reaching effects. Had Drake written

---

[12] Daniel Drake: MS in author's collection.
[13] Daniel Drake: *West. Jnl. Med. & Phys. Sc.*, III:13-27, Apr., May, June, 1829. Reprinted, *Ohio State Medical Journal*, XXXVI:636-38, June 1940 and 773-76, July 1940.
[14] *West. Jnl. Med. & Phys. Sc.*, III:317-40, Oct., Nov., Dec. 1829.
[15] *Ibid.*, V:9-23, Apr., May, June 1831.
[16] Daniel Drake: *Practical Essays on Medical Education and the Medical Profession in the United States.*
[17] Fielding H. Garrison: *Introduction to the History of Medicine* (Philadelphia: W. B. Saunders Co., 1913), p. 376; 3rd ed., 1924, p. 465.

nothing else, his fame in the annals of American medicine would be secure.

A few laudatory reviews appeared in western periodicals. East of the Alleghenies, only one review has been located, that by Elisha Bartlett (1804-55):

> This is a little volume, dedicated to the students of the Medical College of Ohio, by one of the professors in that institution and if it should have the effect to inculcate in them the elevated and generous views of the science and practice of the healing art which it presents they could not have received a more valuable token of their instructor's regard. . . . The argument and spirit of the essays are directed to the establishment of a high standard for medical education, and correct principles of taste and ethics. . . .[18]

Drake's ideas on medical education were far in advance of his time. He pointed out the necessity for careful preliminary training and insisted that an acquaintance with Latin and Greek was essential. Attendance at lectures must be obligatory, four years elapsing between commencement of studies and graduation. There should be a strict regard to the moral character of candidates. His series of recommendations closed with the following:

> The examinations for a degree should be more searching than they are generally made. This, it is true, would diminish the amount of graduation fees received by the professors, but the public would be gainers.
>
> Lastly, as a means of promoting this object, and of advancing the respectability of the profession, there should be in every medical school, a series of Sunday morning discourses by one of the professors, on the *morals* of the profession,

[18] [Elisha Bartlett, Review]: *Medical Magazine* (Boston), II:274-76, Nov. 1833.

and the virtues and vices of medical men, embracing their duties to their patients and a system of medical ethics.[19]

The leaven of Drake's ideas can be clearly traced through one of the graduates (1860) of the Medical College of Ohio, John Shaw Billings (1838-1913). As is well known, Billings' three most significant achievements were the Surgeon General's Library (now National Library of Medicine) and its monumental Index Catalogue, the Johns Hopkins Hospital, and the New York Public Library. In addition to planning the Hopkins Hospital, he was the most influential of the medical advisers for the establishment of the Johns Hopkins University School of Medicine. In a collective review, "Higher Medical Education," Billings listed twelve books on the subject, Drake's *Essays* being placed first.[20] He regarded Drake "as a man whose fame, as compared with that of his contemporaries, will probably be greater a century hence than it is today, and whose name, even now [1876], should be among the first of the illustrious dead of the medical profession in the United States." [21] As an admirer of Drake, Billings was familiar with many of his writings and especially with the *Practical Essays on Medical Education*. Necessarily, therefore, Billings had Drake's recommendations in mind when advising the committee members who adopted the standards for Johns Hopkins in 1887.

Fifteen years later (1902) reforms in medical schools were demanded by the American Medical Association, and its Council on Medical Education formulated requirements for their accreditation. There followed Abraham Flexner's famous report (1910) to the Carnegie Foundation for the advancement of teaching, and in a few years the inadequately

[19] Drake: *Practical Essays* . . . , p. 57.
[20] J.[ohn] S.[haw] B.[illings]: "Higher Medical Education," *American Journal of Medical Sciences* (Philadelphia), CLI:174-89, July 1878.
[21] *Ibid.*, CXLIV:439-80, Oct. 1876.

equipped and staffed schools closed or merged with stronger units. Within ten more years the greater number of medical schools in the United States received "Class A" ratings. Thus, ninety years after the publication of the *Essays on Medical Education,* Drake's recommendations transmitted through Billings and other studious physicians had in large part been adopted.

The pertinency of Drake's *Essays on Medical Education* is still apparent today. It is most unfortunate that studies in the humanities continue to be shouldered out of the modern medical curriculum as a glance at any set of examination papers will verify. Educators might, at the present time, reread with profit Drake's pleas and the logical reasons presented for preliminary study of Latin and Greek.

Several years ago I stated that this classic should be required reading for every student of medicine. Recently I found that Samuel D. Gross was also so greatly impressed with the *Essays on Medical Education* that he said that they "ought to be in the hands of every medical pupil and every junior practitioner in the country." [22] With forceful and entertaining diction Drake covers all phases of the subject. Not as yet has all this valuable advice fully permeated the profession.

> In the selection of boys for the study of medicine, many circumstances entirely disconnected with their fitness, too often exert a dominant influence; when their sway should be kept subordinate, or even regarded as entirely inadmissible. A neighboring physician wants a student to reside in his office; or one son of the family is thought too weakly to labour on the farm or in the work shop; he is indolent and averse to bodily exertion or addicted to study, but too stupid for the Bar, or too immoral for the Pulpit; the parents wish to have one gentleman in the family, and a *doctor* is a gentleman:—these and many other extraneous considerations,

[22] Gross: "Discourse on the Life . . . of Daniel Drake," p. 47.

not unfrequently decide the choice and swell the numbers, while they impair the character of the profession.

. . . .

The student of medicine should not only be of sound understanding, but imbued with ambition. A mere love of knowledge is not to be relied upon, for the greatest lovers of knowledge, are not unfrequently deficient in executive talents, and go on acquiring without learning how to appropriate. Let parents, therefore, not be misled by the signs which indicate a fondness for study, unless the desire involves a feeling of emulation. A thirst for fame, is indeed a safer guaranty, than a taste for learning; as it generates those executive efforts, which are indispensable to the successful practice of the profession.

Further the temperament of the youth, should be that of industry and perseverance; without which he will balk at every difficulty, and require to be goaded on through all stages of his pupilage. An indolent or irresolute student, whatever may be his genius, can never figure as a physician; and should, without delay, be apprenticed to some vocation, in which the destruction of limbs and life will not be the inevitable consequence of idleness and discouragement.[23]

. . . .

The physician should shrink with horror from the idea of prescribing on false premises, or by loose and unphilosophical analogies. He should recollect, that human life is at stake; that a human being, in extremity, is confided to his skill and honor; and that an ignorant or presumptuous stroke of his pen, may translate that confiding fellow creature—perhaps his bosom friend—from time to eternity, to confront him with damning testimony on the day of final retribution. Although such practice is not legally felonious, it deserves unqualified denunciation; for in a moral view, where lies the

[23] Drake: *Practical Essays* . . . , pp. 6-8.

248 Daniel Drake
line of distinction, between criminal prescriptions, and those which prove fatal, through the criminal ignorance of their authors? I say criminal ignorance, for although, in the abstract, there is no criminality, in being unacquainted with the truth, yet, in the practice of medicine, to be ignorant of facts and principles, which lie within the grasp of common minds under common opportunities, and still to undertake that, which they, only, who are acquainted with those facts can accomplish, is to forget the divine maxim of doing to others as we would be done unto; and, literally to wage war upon human life; not in malice prepense towards any individual, but with the senseless and fatal impartiality of an epidemic disease.[24]

In March 1830, Drake accepted the professorship of the theory and practice of medicine in the Jefferson Medical College, Philadelphia. He was the first westerner to be selected as a professor in an eastern medical college. At this time the chair of theory and practice was considered the most important in any institution. He stipulated that he would not obligate himself to teach more than one term. His reason for accepting the Philadelphia appointment was the opportunity thus afforded to select teachers for another medical school in Cincinnati.

He freed himself from the task of publishing his medical journal by selling it to Dr. James C. Finley who became the junior editor. To combat the rumor that Drake was permanently leaving Cincinnati, Dr. Finley issued a Publishers Notice:

We regret to learn that an impression has gone abroad, that Dr. Drake's association with the Jefferson Medical College, will interfere with his editorial duties. Not only will this not be the case, but his connexion with that institution will secure to the Journal a support that cannot fail to render

24 Ibid., p. 88.

its pages more interesting. We are authorized to state that Dr. Drake has no idea of leaving Cincinnati. His associations of the past and his prospects for the future, are all connected with the West, and will secure his permanent residence on this side of the mountains.[25]

On 25 May 1830, Drake was elected president of the First District Medical Society. He had been one of the organizers of this society and its secretary in 1812. Late in September 1830, he was in Oxford, Ohio, at the exercises of the fifth commencement of Miami University. Here (29 September 1830) he delivered a lecture on "Health" at 6:00 A.M. in the chapel which *was filled!* The address was "humorous" and contained much of wisdom.[26] The reporter commented that the harmful effects of tobacco were described though the speaker had finished a cigar immediately before entering the chapel.

Drake's basic reason for going to Oxford was not mentioned in the news item. As an early trustee of Miami University (1815-18) and friend of President Robert Hamilton Bishop (1777-1855), Drake went to suggest that a medical department be established in Cincinnati. He did not await action of the trustees but hurried to Philadelphia, where he arrived on 28 October 1830, registering at the United States Hotel.

During the first week of November 1830, Drake began lecturing to 111 students of the Jefferson Medical College. Six of these were taking postgraduate courses. He was enthusiastically received. The Philadelphians had not heard such oratory from a teacher of medicine since the days of Benjamin Rush.

The National Library of Medicine owns two volumes of

[25] [James C. Finley]: Publishers Notice, *West. Jnl. Med. & Phys. Sc.,* IV:160, Apr., May, June 1830.
[26] [News Item], *Cincinnati Daily Gazette,* IV, No. 1023:p. [2]—c. [1-2], Oct. 13, 1830.

manuscript notes of Drake's lectures in 1830-31.[27] Each subject is logically and concisely developed. He was well informed concerning advances in medicine and refers frequently to Laënnec, stressing the importance of auscultation in the diagnosis of heart and lung diseases.

On "Sunday morning, January 16, 1831," Drake delivered a special lecture on the "Duties of the Physician to his Patients."[28] He exhorted the students to qualify themselves thoroughly as physicians since they would be guardians of lives. Concerning consultations he held it advisable to ask for a consultant if in doubt as to the disease or treatment but not merely to share the responsibility of the death of the patient. Promptness in answering summonses to the sick and punctuality in subsequent calls are most necessary. All appointments of any kind "should be considered sacred." He insisted that, in the sickroom, "it becomes the physician's duty to cultivate a suavity of manners—a kindness of disposition. . . . He must be *suavitus in modo* but *fortior in re*."[29] He proceeded to discuss the necessity of clearness of the directions given nurses, length and frequency of visits, admission of clergymen to the sickroom, and remuneration of physicians. When a patient asks: "Am I going to die?," either remain silent or answer, if the condition is serious, "Your situation is a critical one. The judicious physician can foresee danger when it is but a speck in the horizon. If there be danger communicate it to the friends and not to the patient himself."[30]

Drake took advantage of the opportunities offered in Philadelphia by attending the meetings of the various societies. In the earlier days of the Jefferson Medical College (opened

[27] Lorenzo N. Henderson: "Notes of lectures on the theory and practice of medicine delivered by Daniel Drake in 1830-31," MSS, 2 vols., 772 pages. In National Library of Medicine.

[28] *Ibid.*, pp. 751-72.

[29] *Ibid.*, p. 758.

[30] *Ibid.*

1824), the professors in the University of Pennsylvania Department of Medicine were jealous and ridiculed it at every opportunity. Samuel D. Gross tells of a Wistar party during the winter of 1830-31, at which the professor of the institutes and practice of medicine of Pennsylvania, Nathaniel Chapman (1780-1853), deliberately turned his back on Drake.[31] Aside from the fact that Drake held the professorship of medicine in a rival institution, Chapman may have been piqued over Drake's criticism in "The People's Doctors" of the secret nostrum, Swaim's Panacea. A recommendatory letter of this quack remedy by Chapman had received wide publicity.[32] A more remote reason may have been Drake's immediate adoption of Laënnec's revolutionary teachings concerning auscultation which Chapman ridiculed for many years.

Gross also tells of two debates on medical subjects with prominent opponents in which Drake was victorious:

> His fluency and facility of language gave him great advantage as a public debator. To his ability as a profound reasoner, he added subtility of argument, quickness of repartee, and an impassioned tone and style, which rarely failed to carry off the palm in any contest in which he was engaged. During his sojourn in Philadelphia in 1830-31, Broussaism, then so fashionable in that city, formed the subject of discussion before the Philadelphia Medical Society. Being a member, he was induced to take part in the debate against the doctrine, while Dr. Jackson, the present [1853] Professor of the Institutes of Medicine in the University of Pennsylvania, and himself no mean speaker, arrayed himself on the opposite side. The discussion, which had been in progress several evenings, waxed warmer and warmer, and excited

[31] Gross: *Autobiography*, Vol. II, p. 281.
[32] [Ad.]: "Swaim's Panacea" (containing a letter of recommendation by N. Chapman), *Louisville Public Advertiser*, IX, No. 860:p [1]—c. [1-2], Jan. 3, 1827.

universal interest among the members and visitors. Dr. Drake
had the floor, and had already made a brilliant effort, when,
suddenly stopping, he exclaimed in a loud voice, and with
peculiar emphasis, addressing himself, to the chairman, the
distinguished Dr. Condie, "Sir, is it not so?" The effect was
electric. The worthy dignitary, unconscious apparently of
what he was doing, sprang upon his feet, exclaiming, "Yes
sir, I believe it is," to the great amusement of every one
present.[33]

. . . .

At Cincinnati, in 1834, in a debate with Professor Eberle
on malarial fever, he [Drake] demolished his opponent by
quotations from his own work on the practice of medicine
[John Eberle: A *Treatise on the Practice of Medicine*, 2 vols.,
1830; 2nd Ed., 1831] at that time a standard authority.[34]

On 24 January 1831, Drake delivered an oration on intemperance before the Pennsylvania Temperance Society.
The Committee on Agency of the society, headed by the
famous Mathew Carey, requested a copy of the lecture for
publication. Drake replied:

Philadelphia Jan. 27th 1831

Gentlemen,
    The discourse of which you do me the honor to ask a copy
for publication was hastily prepared, in the midst of my
collegiate duties and not intended for the press. Certain portions of it, moreover bear a close resemblance to some parts
of a published address on the same subject, which I delivered
in Cincinnati, nearly three years ago. I am willing, however,
to refrain from consulting my literary reputation since you
suppose the publication of this may do some good to the
cause of which we are the common advocate; and herewith

[33] Gross: *Discourse on Life . . . of Daniel Drake*, p. 63.
[34] Gross: *Autobiography*, Vol. II, p. 273.

place the manuscript, with all its imperfections at your disposal.[35]

During the winter, Benjamin Drake, in Cincinnati, was quietly having friends interview the trustees of Miami University to interest them in a medical department. Early in January 1831, the board authorized Daniel Drake to select a medical faculty. This commission was speedily accomplished. Having delivered all requisite lectures in his course, he resigned and left Philadelphia early in February 1831.

He went to Columbus, Ohio, where he found that trustees of the Medical College of Ohio, greatly alarmed over the possibility of a rival medical school, had attempted to induce the legislature to prohibit the establishment of one by Miami University. Drake's efforts are described in a letter to his friend, Dr. Réné LaRoche, of Philadelphia:

> I was detained 12 days at Columbus, our seat of government, by arriving, there the evening of the day, on which a memorial was presented by the Medical College of Ohio, praying the Legislature to suppress my project! The Agent of the Institution, had been 5 weeks in Columbus, preparing the minds of the members for this unholy and sordid prayer. —By 3 O'c'k in the morning, I had a remonstrance of 9 pages prepared; and just 24 hours after their petition was read, mine was announced and referred to the same committee. After a week of deliberation & inquiry, the committee reported against their request; and said, as the friends of the Med. College of Ohio are afraid of Miami University, it is well to reorganize and strengthen the former! A resolution to this end was accordingly reported, & by the vote of my friends was laid over, to the meeting of the next Legislature. Thus the gallows, which they erected for us, they are likely to enjoy themselves! As far as I can see, hear, or by any means

[35] Daniel Drake: *An Oration on Intemperance of Cities: Including Remarks on Gambling* (Philadelphia: Griggs & Dickinson, 1831), pp. 3-4.

learn, public sentiment, both in the state and city, is decidedly in our favor. Everything, indeed is, auspicious.[36]

Going to Oxford, Ohio, Drake found the trustees of Miami University ready to follow his recommendations, 22 February 1831:

> *Resolved*, That the following gentlemen be appointed to the Professorships . . .
>
> Daniel Drake, M.D., Professor of the Institutes and Practice of Medicine & Dean of the Faculty.
>
> James M. Staughton, M.D., Professor of Surgery.
>
> John F. Henry, M.D., Professor of Obstetrics and Diseases of Women and Children.
>
> George McClelan [*sic*], M.D., Professor of Anatomy and Physiology.
>
> John Eberle, M.D., Professor of Materia Medica and Botany.
>
> Thomas D. Mitchell, M.D., Professor of Chemistry and Pharmacy.
>
> Joseph N. McDowell, M.D., Adjunct Professor of Anatomy and Physiology.
>
> . . . .
>
> *Resolved*, That the Trustees be held in no way responsible or liable for expenditures of the medical department.[37]

Announcement was made immediately of the establishment of the Medical Department of Miami University.[38] The title page of an *Oration on Intemperance* delivered by Drake in Columbus designates him as "Professor of the Institutes and Practices of Medicine in Miami University." Thomas D. Mitchell wrote an essay for Drake's *Journal* as "Professor of

[36] Daniel Drake, Cincinnati, March 15, 1831, ALS to Dr. Réné La Roche, Philadelphia. Original in the Library of College of Physicians, Philadelphia.

[37] Miami University, Oxford, Ohio: *Journals of the President and Board of Trustees*, 1809-1842, pp. 225-29.

[38] R. H. Bishop, President: "Medical Department in Cincinnati," *West. Jnl. Med. & Phys. Sc.*, IV:622, Jan., Feb., Mar. 1831.

Chemistry and Pharmacy in Miami University." [39] James M. Staughton as "Professor of Surgery in Miami University" published two essays.[40] Likewise the "Professor of Materia Medica and Medical Botany," John Eberle, wrote several articles. Thus the new professors were publicizing the university as well as themselves. The only one of the teachers listed in the Miami faculty who did not accept his appointment was Dr. George McClellan.

Drake's attachment to his adopted state and to the cause of medical education is revealed in a letter to the secretaries of the district medical societies of Ohio, dated 6 May 1831:

> Gentlemen,—It must be known to such of you as have long resided in the state of Ohio, that in the year 1819, I had the honor to obtain from the General Assembly an act of incorporation for a medical college in this city: it is generally known that circumstances, which at this late period I shall not recount, separated me unwillingly from the infant institution, and united me successively with two other schools in Lexington and Philadelphia.
>
> During my sojourn abroad, however, I could not forget that Ohio was my home; and having been the first to project a medical institution within her limits, I felt myself at liberty to resume medical instruction on the spot where I had begun it. By the accompanying circular you will perceive that I have, at length, had the good fortune to acquire a body of associates, most of whom are experienced and eminent professors. Both they and myself are deeply impressed with the value of your respect and patronage; and I beg leave to say, that we shall labor unceasingly to deserve the former as the only honorable means of acquiring the latter.
>
> We have asked nothing from the Miami University—from the state—from society—from or of the existing institution

[39] Thomas D. Mitchell: Hints on the Morality of Medicine," *ibid.*, V:23-35, Apr., May, June 1831.

[40] James M. Staughton: "On the Use of Mercury in Syphilis," *ibid.*, 36-44. Also, "History of Lithotomy," *ibid.*, 57-86.

in this city. We are creating and collecting, with our own private means, the material requisite to our enterprise: and relying on nothing but our own exertions, they will, of course, be such as can scarcely fail to be beneficial to those who may become our pupils, and must contribute something to the general advancement of the profession in the west.

As a fellow-citizen of Ohio, I take the liberty of soliciting your individual confidence and support, toward a project which I shall continue zealously, if not ably, to prosecute for the remainder of my life.[41]

The trustees of the Medical College of Ohio foresaw their doom unless establishment of the new institution could be stopped. There were no teachers of prominence and no authors in their faculty. Two plans were formulated, the first being appearance before the Supreme Court in Butler County, Ohio, in which Miami University is located. An application was filed for writ of *quo warranto*, inquiring by what authority the medical department was to be started. The court's ruling was that, because of the "novelty and difficulty" of the question, it must be studied at length and decided by the judges themselves.[42] The delaying action of such a court decision ruined Drake's chances of starting the Miami medical department in 1831.

The second plan of the trustees of the Medical College of Ohio was one of intrigue by which division of Drake's faculty was attempted. This maneuver was partly successful in that Drs. Thomas D. Mitchell and James M. Staughton defected to the side of the trustees. Dr. Eberle also leaned toward them. Dr. Henry alone remained loyal. Drake, therefore, was forced to capitulate and his Miami University Medical De-

[41] Edward Thomson: "Recollections of Dr. Drake," *The Ladies Repository* (Cincinnati) XIII:105-12, Mar. 1853. Also in E. Thomson: *Sketches, Biographical and Incidental* (Cincinnati: L. Swornstedt and A. Poe, 1856), pp. 109-32.
[42] *Select Committee of Senate of Ohio: Report on Medical College*, Feb. 3, 1834 (Cincinnati: Lodge, L. Homedien & Co., 1834).

Fig. 11. Fort Washington, drawn (1791) by Major Jonathan Heart,
U.S.A. Courtesy of The Historical and Philosophical Society of Ohio.

Fig. 12. Cincinnati in 1802, from Max Burgheim: Cincinnati in
Wort und Bild. Fort Washington, flag flying, is to the right of center.
Further to the right, nearer the river, is "Dr." Goforth's home where
Daniel Drake lived for five years.

Fig. 13. Isaac Drake. (Audubon, 1820)

Fig. 14. Mrs. Isaac Drake. (Audubon, 1820)

Fig. 15. Cabin similar to those erected in 1788.

Fig. 16. "Dr." William Goforth. Courtesy of The Historical and Philosophical Society of Ohio.

Fig. 26. Alexander Hamilton Mc-
Guffey. Courtesy of Kingsland Drake
McGuffey, owner.

Fig. 27. Mrs. A. H. (Elizabeth
Mansfield Drake) McGuffey. Courtesy
of Mrs. Daniel B. Ruggles.

Fig. 28. James Parker Campbell,
from miniature owned by Miss Marion
C. Bridgman.

Fig. 29. Mrs. James Parker (Harric
Echo Drake) Campbell.

Fig. 22. Benjamin Drake. Oil by Aaron Corwine, 1826(?). Courtesy Prof. James E. Vance, owner. Print from The Ohio Historical Society.

Fig. 23. Midshipman Charles D. Drake. Oil by Aaron H. Corwine, 1827. Courtesy of Mrs. G. M. Fuller, owner.

Fig. 24. Charles D. Drake, Feb. 843. Presented to Cincinnati Art Museum by Mrs. Daniel B. Ruggles, Photograph by Edward H. Dwight.

Fig. 25. Mrs. Charles D. (Margaret Cross) Drake.

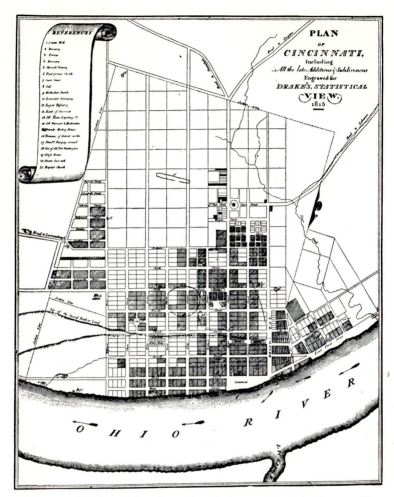

Fig. 21. Cincinnati in 1815. Frontispiece to Drake's Picture. Size of original, 12⅝ x 10¼ inches.

Fig. 17. Daniel Drake. Original owned by Mrs. Elizabeth Drake Parkinson.

Fig. 18. Mrs. Daniel Drake. Original owned by Mrs. Elizabeth Drake Parkinson.

Fig. 19. Home of Dr. and Mrs. Daniel Drake, 1812-23.

Fig. 20. Col. Jared Mansfield. Oil by Thomas Sully, courtesy of U.S. Military Academy.

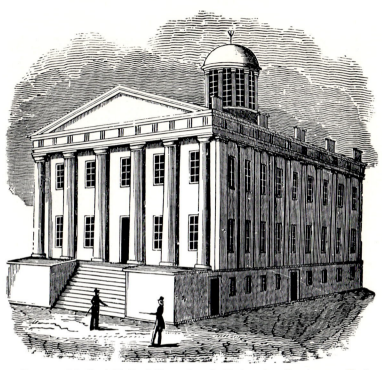

Fig. 30. *Medical Hall of Transylvania University (Lexington, Ky.).
Erected 1839, burned 1863. From Robert Peter:* History of Medical
Department.

Fig. 31. *Daniel Drake. Courtesy of
Christ Hospital, Cincinnati, owner.*

Fig. 32. *Daniel Drake. Courtesy of
Fayette County (Kentucky) Medical
Society, owner.*

Fig. 33. Daniel Drake, aet. 65, engraved by A. H. Ritchie for 1st ed. Pioneer Life in Kentucky (1870).

Fig. 34. Daniel Drake. Composite oil portrait made for the author by John T. Bauscher (1890-1951). Copyrighted.

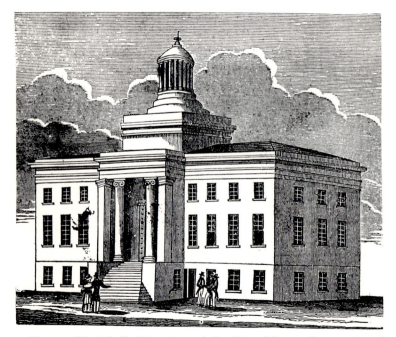

Fig. 35. The Medical Institute of the City of Louisville, completed in 1838, burned 31 December 1856.

partment died before enrolling a single student. He did obtain concessions by stipulating that all members of the Miami faculty be retained.[43] He was unable to have his arch enemy, "the foreigner" (John Moorhead) ousted. However, the two early schemers, the Reverend Elijah Slack and Dr. Jesse Smith, who had shamelessly dismissed him in 1822, were themselves expelled.

The reorganized faculty of the Medical College of Ohio, as of 13 July 1831, was as follows:

Jedediah Cobb, anatomy; Thomas D. Mitchell, chemistry and pharmacy; James M. Staughton, surgery and dean of the faculty; John Eberle, materia medica and botany; John F. Henry, obstetrics and diseases of women and children; John Moorhead, theory and practice of medicine; Charles E. Pierson, institutes of medicine and medical jurisprudence; and, Daniel Drake, clinical medicine.

With an implacable enemy, Moorhead, occupying the chair which logically and rightfully should have been given to Drake, friction was inevitable. Moorhead, Cobb, and Pierson dictated to the board of trustees. Since Mitchell and Staughton joined with Moorhead, Drake and Henry were isolated.

The size of the Commercial Hospital limited Drake's efforts to institute modern bedside instruction, of which he was an early advocate. His efforts to secure autopsies were blocked by another ignorant and prejudiced group, the Township Trustees who had charge of the hospital. Thus from the time of the consolidation, Drake was hampered by the jealous and hostile faculty which dictated not only the policies of the trustees of the college, but also those of the township. Regardless of his unhappy situation, he waited until 19 January 1832, before resigning:

[43] Daniel Drake: "Plan of Consolidation" in John F. Henry: *An Exposure of the Conduct of the Trustees and Professors* (Cincinnati: Wood & Stratton, 1833), pp. 6-7.

To the Honorable Board of Trustees of the Medical College of Ohio, *Gentlemen*—Last summer, when I suggested
and agreed to accept the chair of Clinical Medicine in the
Medical College of Ohio, as the only means in *my* power,
of effecting the union of the Medical Department of Miami
University with the College, an object which you had originated and were anxious to accomplish. My chief motive was
to prevent the interests of medical education in Cincinnati,
from being seriously injured by protracted negotiations. At
the moment of devising the professorship, I felt an apprehension, that its subjects and limits would be too restricted,
in the then existing condition of the Hospital, to afford me
an opportunity of being useful to the class; but I felt and
perceived that a state of things had been produced by others,
which left me no alternative, if my apprehensions should be
realized, to resign at the end of the first session.

When the Chair of the Institutes was declined by the
gentleman, (Dr. Pierson, of New York) to whom it was offered, unless he were allowed a year of preparation, and I
saw that branch assigned to me (*for the time being*) by the
unanimous vote of the Faculty, I cherished the hope, that
your honorable body would not grant the favor he solicited;
but at once confirm the union of the Institutes with Clinical
Medicine, and by reducing the number of Chairs from eight
to seven, afford me a sufficient amount of duties. You have,
however, preferred a different course, and I am, therefore,
compelled, to request you to accept my resignation; which I
wish to take effect immediately after the next public commencement.

Thirteen years have this day elapsed, since I had the honor
to solicit and obtain from our Legislature, the charter of the
College; and to be appointed President and Professor of the
Institutes and Practice of Medicine.—From that day down to
the present anniversary, whether belonging to it, or to other
institutions in different and distant cities, the Medical College of Ohio, has never ceased, nor can it hereafter cease,
to be with me an object of the deepest interest. Therefore,

it is that I send in my resignation before the end of this session, that your honorable body may be able to make and promulgate arrangements for the next course of lectures, before the class shall disperse.

In taking a final leave of an institution, which for so many years has been an object of affection, but to the prosperity of which I can no longer contribute the influence of my feeble exertions, I cannot forego the opportunity of expressing a hope, that it will continue to flourish until it shall reach the high distinction and impart the solid advantages, anticipated in its foundation.

I have the honor to be, respectfully,

Your ob't. serv't, Dan Drake.[44]

He was immediately accused of attempting to wreck the college, of wanting to either rule or destroy. The faculty and the trustees were panic stricken and desperate. Their spiteful treatment of Drake's loyal friend, Henry, is revealing.

JOHN F. HENRY. John Flournoy Henry (1793-1873), professor of obstetrics and diseases of women and children, was a Kentuckian who had been a surgeon's mate under General William Henry Harrison during the War of 1812. Henry had practiced in Washington, Mason County, Kentucky, near Drake's boyhood home. A graduate of Jefferson Medical College, Henry was for awhile in politics, serving as a representative from Kentucky in the Nineteenth Congress (1826-27).

After Drake's resignation from the Medical College of Ohio, the trustees sought to oust Henry. Their initial procedure was to circulate malicious rumors about his competency. Learning of this, the students issued a memorial certifying to Henry's having "perspicuously" lectured on his subjects and that "he was a credit to the instituton." Next the Township Trustees, who had supervision of the Commercial

---

[44] Liberty Hall . . . , N.S., XI, No. 1120:p. [4]—c. [2], Apr. 26, 1832.

Hospital, accused him of mismanagement of the obstetrical department. He immediately demanded an investigation which resulted in his exoneration. Foiled in their underhanded efforts to force him to resign and ignoring their pledges made at the time of the consolidation of the Miami Medical Department with their institution, the trustees arbitrarily expelled him, 7 April 1832.[45] Thus ended the connection with the Medical College of Ohio of Drake's close and loyal friend, John Flournoy Henry.

In addition to Henry's *Exposure*, numerous other pamphlets were published during the controversy, lasting until 1835. At this time a new "war" of words began. The pamphlets up to 1835 add nothing more than minor details to what has been told. A review of them, more than 150 pages, seems unnecessary and beyond the scope of this biography.[46]

---

[45] Henry: *An Exposure of the Conduct, loc. cit.* Consult [R. Ayers *et al.*, Township Trustees]: *To the Public*, Feb. 12, 1833, in which there is an attempt to refute Dr. Henry's *Exposure*.

[46] (a) Joshua Martin, Chairman: *Proceedings and Correspondence of Third District Medical Society . . . in Reference to Medical College of Ohio* (Cincinnati), Dec. 1832, 39 pages.

(b) William Corry *et al.*, Trustees: *To the General Assembly of the State of Ohio* (1833), 15 pages.

(c) Samuel W. Davies [Trustee of Medical College]: *A Refutation of Sundry Unfounded Accusations* [by] *Dr. Daniel Drake* (Cincinnati, Jan. 2, 1833), 8 pages.

(d) Daniel Drake: *To the Honorable the General Assembly of Ohio* (Cincinnati, Jan. 19, 1833), 20 pages. This is a lucid and forthright history of the controversy.

(e) [Committee of Senate]: *Report on the Medical College of Ohio* (Cincinnati: Lodge, L'Hommidieu & Co., 1834), 20 pages.

(f) Faculty . . . : *Facts Concisely Stated* (Cincinnati: F. S. Benton, 1835), 8 pages.

(g) Daniel Drake: *A Reply to . . . "Facts Concisely Stated"* (Cincinnati, Jan. 23, 1835), 6 pages.

(h) *Ibid.*, 2nd ed., considerably improved (Jan. 1835), 7 pages.

(i) *Ibid.*, 3rd ed., greatly improved (Jan. 31, 1855), 8 pages.

13

A theory to be true, must explain all facts, and be the only one that can.[1]

Cincinnati, 1832-36

REPORTS OF outbreaks of Asiatic cholera in various parts of Europe in the early 1830's intrigued Drake. He then began, it seems with prophetic insight, a study of all available literature concerning cholera. Early in 1832, he published the first of his papers on this subject.[2] When reports of cholera in Canada (8 June 1832) appeared, Drake introduced resolutions concerning preventive measures before the First District Medical Society.[3] Shortly thereafter he was appointed chairman of the Committee on Epidemic Cholera of the Cincinnati Medical Society which was to advise articles for its treatment in homes.[4] In July, 1832, Drake's book, *A Practical Treatise on the History, Prevention and Treatment of Epidemic Cholera*, was published. Contrary to prevailing concepts, he asserted that the theory of the "animalcular" origin of cholera explained more of the facts than any other hypothesis.[5] He suggested that the animalcula were disseminated by air and their ova either inhaled or swallowed with subsequent multiplication in the body.

[1] Daniel Drake: *A Practical Treatise on . . . Epidemic Cholera* (Cincinnati: Corey and Fairbank, 1832), p. 48.

[2] Daniel Drake: "Epidemic Cholera: Its Pathology and Treatment," *West. Jnl. of Med. & Phys. Sc.*, V:596-616 and 652-64, Jan., Feb., Mar. 1832.

[3] Daniel Drake: "Resolutions," *Daily Cincinnati Gazette*, VI, No. 1550:p. [2]—c. [6], June 29, 1832.

[4] Daniel Drake: [Chairman] *Cincinnati Advertiser and Ohio Phoenix*, N.S., X, No. 55:p. [3]—c. [1-3], July 12, 1832.

[5] Drake: *A Practical Treatise. . . .*

In a "Postscript," 23 July 1832, to his book, the following prediction appears: "There is no longer any ground for hoping that we shall not be invaded. Indeed, nothing is more probable than its spread over the whole of the United States, and no duty more urgent than that of preparing to meet it." [6]

On 6 October 1832, Drake reported the existence of cholera to a member of the Board of Health. This elicited neither a statement nor a response. The following day, Drake publicly announced that epidemic cholera had appeared in Cincinnati and that since 30 September 1832 there had been fifteen deaths. [7] His adversaries ridiculed such a statement but the president of the Board of Health, Samuel W. Davies, a politician and implacable foe of Drake, appointed a Sanatory Committee to investigate. As might have been expected several members of the faculty of the Medical College of Ohio and three other physicians, all unfriendly to Drake, were appointed. This learned committee, composed of Jesse Smith, M.D.; Jedediah Cobb, M.D.; V. C. Marshall, M.D.; John Moorhead, M.D.; Abel Slayback; John Eberle, M.D.; and J. M. Staughton, M.D., reported that after reviewing the cases not a single instance of cholera was found. [8] Drake's announcement of the presence of cholera caused his enemies to react in a partisan manner, seven to one. For a day the populace was confused, but only for a day, because the rapidly mounting death lists vindicated only too well the correctness of Drake's diagnosis. The Sanatory Committee must have been dissolved since it issued no subsequent report. However, the Board of Health on 10 October 1832 belatedly admitted

[6] *Ibid.*, p. 180.

[7] Daniel Drake: "Cholera in Cincinnati," *Daily Cincinnati Gazette*, VI, No. 1634:p [3]—c. [2], Oct. 8, 1832.

[8] Samuel W. Davies, President, Board of Health: "Report of Sanatory Committee," *Daily Cincinnati Gazette*, VI, No. 1635:p [3]—c. [1], Oct. 9, 1832.

that cholera had appeared. Ironically, three members of the committee died of cholera during the epidemic.

On 13 October 1832, *The Cincinnati Chronicle* issued a broadside extra, on the "Care of Cholera" written by Drake. He outlined the early symptoms and listed the customary treatment. "The Epidemic would lose all its terrors, if people would attend instantly, to the first symptoms— Go to bed, drink hot water or tea, promote a perspiration, and send for their family physician. . . . Let us unite in aiding each other, for a few days—The Pestilential Cloud will soon pass away." [9] The text of this broadside was carried in a large number of the western newspapers.

Vanquished publicly, the vindictive opponents now secretly spread malicious rumors concerning the victorious Drake, to the effect that he had lost all his patients and that then, feigning illness, he had gone into seclusion. The facts were that Drake's father had died of cholera on 14 October 1832. Yet Drake had not spared himself during nineteen days and nights of constant effort in behalf of his patients and the welfare of the community. As a result he had an attack of what his medical attendants diagnosed as an "inflammatory affection of the brain" for which they performed venesections totaling two quarts.[10] His adversaries accomplished nothing by their falsehoods. On the contrary, Drake, already widely and favorably known throughout the nation, acquired additional stature and his opinions concerning cholera were widely quoted.

Always an advocate of cleanliness, Drake insisted that in fighting cholera the municipal authorities should "remove all kinds of filth" and abate nuisances. Housekeepers "should

[9] Daniel Drake: "Cure of Cholera," broadside, Oct. 13, 1832, *Cincinnati Chronicle*—Extra. Only known copy in Library of Transylvania College, Lexington.

[10] Daniel Drake: "Epidemic Cholera in Cincinnati," *West. Jnl. Med. and Phys. Sc.*, V:321-64, Oct., Nov., and Dec. 1832.

bring their habitations and the grounds attached to them, into the utmost state of cleanliness." [11] Persons should take warm baths "once or twice weekly," occasionally showers, and, each morning, bathe the whole body with cold water, "rubbing dry with a coarse towel." [12] Drake estimated the death rate to have been approximately 4 per cent of the total population.

The most amazing suggestion, one which could have reduced or even stopped the cholera epidemic, came from a Cincinnati Negro, Henry Boyd. Charles Hammond (1779-1840), lawyer, first great journalist of the West, and famous editor of *The Cincinnati Gazette,* wrote the following editorial which is so interesting that it is copied verbatim:

CHOLERA

Although our report of the Board of Health makes more cases of fatal termination than that of yesterday, we are advised that the character of the disease is, in fact ameliorated.

It is an old saying that in every emergency *"even the weak may give some help."* Mr. Henry Boyd, a man of color, has suggested that the source of cholera is in the water, and that it may be removed by boiling all the water we use and letting it cool again before used. This is a very simple process which can produce evil to no one. Even our country friends of the market may boil and bottle their water, before they come to the city, and if the theory be well founded, bring it with them and incur no risk.

This morning we have no more than twenty-five waggons on fifth street. The country people are greatly mistaken in neglecting their business. There is as much danger in one place as in another— The disease is not contagious.[13]

[11] Drake: A *Practical Treatise* . . . , pp. 168-71.
[12] *Ibid.,* p. 172.
[13] Charles Hammond: "Cholera," *Cincinnati Daily Gazette,* V, No. 1642:p. [3]—c. [1], Oct. 17, 1832.

During the winter of 1831-32, Drake was, of course, lecturing in the Medical College of Ohio. In January 1832, he spoke before the Cincinnati Lyceum and shortly thereafter he attended a meeting of the First District Medical Society. A great deal of time during 1832 was spent in researches concerning Asiatic cholera and in writing about it, climaxed by the start of the epidemic in October 1832. On 15 December 1832, he began a series of popular lectures on anatomy and physiology before the Ohio Mechanics Institute. These lectures were delivered weekly through mid-April 1833. With his large practice, private and consultative, one is amazed that he found time to lecture, to write so much, and speak so frequently. Around Cincinnati and its suburbs, he used his gig while distant calls were made on horseback.

In 1829 there had been established in Cincinnati the Academic Institute, the members being local teachers and friends of education. It has been impossible to determine whether Drake was one of the founders of this organization. As an outgrowth of it, the Western Literary Institute and College of Professional Teachers came into existence with Thomas J. Matthews as president. The proceedings of the first regular meeting, held in Cincinnati 3 to 6 October 1832, were published in the *Academic Pioneer and Guardian of Education.*[14]

Members of this institute were influential Cincinnatians and outstanding educators of the West. Active in the meetings were such men as Albert Pickett, father of Cincinnati's public school system; Alexander Kinmont, the classical scholar; Calvin E. Stowe, husband of Harriet Beecher; William Holmes McGuffey, and his younger brother, Alexander, compilers of the famous readers. There were 135 members in 1834.

Among other addresses, Drake delivered one on "The Phi-

---

[14] "Proceedings of Western Literary Institute," *Academic Pioneer and Guardian of Education* (Cincinnati), 1:38-66, Dec. 1832.

losophy of Family, School, and College Discipline." [15] In this address ideas are expressed which are as modern as though written yesterday. In contrast to the educators of his day, he recognized and stressed the supreme importance of the home in the whole educational process. He emphasized what teachers have recently proclaimed, namely, that character is *caught, not taught,* and is the result of emulation of those who are admired. Though a firm believer in corporeal punishment, provided it were administered in fairness to the child, he nevertheless affirmed that rewards were a more effective means of discipline.

Although the public school movement was in its infancy in Drake's time, he propounded the wisdom and the validity of such a system. In 1835 before the Western Literary Institute and College of Professional Teachers, in discussing a report[16] on common schools, he said:

> I am not, sir, a civilian, but a physician; nevertheless I have ventured on the conclusion, that a law requiring all parents to educate their children, in certain branches, provided public schools be established, is in strict accordance with the spirit of our Constitution, and the most certain means of perpetuating them. . . . The only defensible ground of a property assessment for the support of schools, for the benefit of those who have no property, is that the latter, if reared in ignorance, may become dangerous to the former, by a direct physical action or by vicious legislation. . . . It is certainly not a greater stretch of power to require men to educate their children, in a school provided for them, than to compel another to yield up a portion of his earnings for the establishment of such a school. . . . Is it not a higher and nobler duty to bring into requisition the

[15] Daniel Drake: "Discussion on the Philosophy of Family, School and College Discipline," *Transactions of the Fourth Annual Meeting of Western Literary Institute* (Cincinnati: Josiah Drake, 1835), pp. 31-62.

[16] Samuel Lewis *et al.*: "Common Schools," *ibid.,* 1836, pp. 151-60.

vast mental resources of a nation, than its mineral treasures? the productions of its soil? [17]

In other discussions before this "college" he is revealed as an astute, far-sighted, and remarkably sensible educator. There were other participants equally remarkable. Examination of the *Transactions of the Western Literary Institute and College of Professional Teachers* has been extremely rewarding. Although the group was composed originally of Cincinnati teachers it soon embraced members in all the central western and southern states. Also there were representatives from the East, making it national in scope.

In an editorial titled "Extra Professional Duties," Drake wrote:

> Among the obligations imposed on medical men in this new country, by their belonging to a *learned* profession, is that of encouraging education generally. This is the duty of every man of letters in society, and physicians ought to be of this *caste*. They should know and feel, moreover, that for the profession to attain to the dignity of sound scholarship, students of medicine should be well taught and disciplined in their preparatory education; hence it becomes, in part, a professional duty for physicians to promote, by every means in their power, the academical and collegiate education of our sons, from among whom the ranks of the profession are to be replenished. It is under this conviction, that we write this article, not only to discharge our own duty, but to stimulate our brethren in the West to the discharge of theirs. . . .
>
> When the opportunity of a better academical education especially, shall be within the reach of our youth generally, our students of medicine will feel ashamed to hand in theses remarkable for nothing but violations of spelling and grammar; and our physicians not be kept from recording and

[17] Drake: "Discussion," pp. 173-74.

publishing their observations because they do not know how
to express themselves intelligibly.[18]

Drake attended the Literary Convention of Kentucky, 8
November 1833, where he spoke in the chapel of Transylvania University on the importance of promoting literary and
social contacts in the Mississippi Valley:

> Communities, like forests, grow rigid by time. To be prop-
> erly trained they must be moulded while young. Our duty,
> then, is quite obvious. All who have moral power, should
> exert it in concert. The germs of harmony must be nourished,
> and the roots of present contrariety or future discord torn
> up and cast into the fire. Measures should be taken to mould
> a uniform system of manners and customs, out of the diversi-
> fied elements which are scattered over the West. Literary
> meetings should be held in the different states; and occa-
> sional conventions in the central cities of the great valley, be
> made to bring into friendly consultation, our enlightened and
> zealous teachers, professors, lawyers, physicians, divines and
> men of letters, from its remotest sections. In their delibera-
> tions the literary and moral wants of the various regions
> might be made known, and the means of supplying them
> devised. The whole should successively lend a helping hand
> to all the parts, on the great subject of education from the
> primary school to the University. Statistical facts, bearing on
> this absorbing interest, should be brought forward and col-
> lected; the systems of common school instruction compared
> and the merits of different school books, foreign and do-
> mestic, freely canvassed. Plans of education, adapted to the
> natural, commercial, and social condition of the interior,
> should be invented; a correspondence instituted among all our
> higher seminaries of learning, and an interchange established
> of all local publications on the subject of education. In short,
> we should foster western genius, encourage western writers,

[18] Daniel Drake: [Editorial], "Extra Professional Duties," *West. Jnl. Med.
& Phys. Sc.* (2nd Hexad, I) VII:316-18, July, Aug., Sept. 1833.

patronize western publishers, augment the number of western readers and create a western heart.[19]

The text of this address seems to show that Drake was concerned over the possibility of dissolution of the Union more than a quarter of a century before the War between the States. His arguments are directed especially toward cementing the West indissolubly in order to hold the Union together. The closing paragraph of his Transylvania address was as follows:

> When these great objects shall come seriously to occupy our minds, the union will be secure, for its center will be sound, and its attraction on the surrounding parts irresistible. Then will our state governments emulate each other in works for the common good; the people of remote places begin to feel as the members of one family; and our whole intelligent and virtuous population unite, heart and hand, in one long, concentrated, untiring effort, to raise still higher the social character, and perpetuate forever, the political harmony of the green and growing West.[20]

The famous Englishwoman, Harriet Martineau (1802-76), in her *Retrospect of Western Travel,* quoted more than five pages of this address in order to give "some idea of the spirit of the man in one of its aspects, though it has none of the pithy character of his conversation." [21]

Drake was a masterful individualist, attempting to bring culture, literature, arts, and the sciences to Cincinnati and the West. He had a host of admirers and staunch supporters.

---

[19] Daniel Drake: *Remarks on the Importance of Promoting Literary and Social Concert, in the Valley of the Mississippi, as a Means of Elevating Its Character, and Perpetuating the Union* (published by the Members of the Convention: The Louisville Herald, 1833), pp. 25-26.

[20] *Ibid.,* p. 26.

[21] Harriet Martineau: *Retrospect of Western Travel* (3 vols., London: Saunders and Otley, 1838), Vol. II; pp. 226-31; also 2 vols. New York: Harper & Brothers, 1838, Vol. II; pp. 41-44.

Contrariwise, his militancy and accomplishments created a group of jealous enemies, who persistently attempted to discredit him. Some of his friends felt that he sometimes sought preferment. John Cleves Short (1792-1864) once wrote his sister Jane that he much preferred her to write of her own activities and interests than those of the "big-bugs" and "all the flosculous mysteries of the Drakean school." [22] Previously Short had written, "I shall send this evening for Drake, the only physician here I have any confidence in." [23] Dr. Charles Wilkins Short, brother of John C., wrote in a diary of a river trip to see this same sister, Jane, that "Dr. Drake dined with us on board before starting, and on that occasion gave us a sample of his queer ways, by employing the time in writing squibs for the Louisville Journal, in relation to the Medical Institute which was at that time in the height of a war with the Doctors of Louisville." [24]

John Moorhead, undoubtedly Drake's most implacable foe, apparently sought every opportunity to attack him. One illustration of his spitefulness must suffice. Mr. John B. Brooke, aged 34, on 18 January 1834, suddenly began having severe pain in the region of the liver. Dr. Robert Moorhead was called and, shortly thereafter, his brother, John. They diagnosed the illness as "colic" and prescribed purgatives! Mr. Brooke worsened and the abdomen became distended. Dr. John Eberle was called in consultation. A mixture of castor oil, spirits of turpentine, and croton oil was given! Stimulating enemas, to be frequently repeated, were ordered! The patient's doom was thus sealed. Venesection was performed and fourteen ounces of blood removed.

[22] John Cleves Short: ALS, 15 Jan. 1834, to Miss Jane A. Short. Author's collection.

[23] *Ibid.*, ALS, 25 Oct. 1829, to Dr. Charles Wilkins Short. Owned by The Filson Club.

[24] Charles Wilkins Short: MSS, "Botanical Memoranda, 1833-40" (22 May 1840). Owned by Mrs. Henry Tyler.

Four days after the onset of the illness, the Moorheads were replaced by Drs. Drake and Wolcott Richards. Their diagnosis was peritonitis caused by rupture of the gall bladder. Although the relatives were told that death was imminent, they insisted on some type of treatment. Cupping was employed in addition to the sovereign remedy of the period, calomel!

The Moorheads secured permission for an autopsy. Neither Drake nor Richards was invited. Dr. Alban G. Smith (1788-1865), at that time professor of surgery in the Medical College of Ohio, reported findings fully substantiating the diagnosis of Drake and Richards. The Moorheads refused to accept the unmistakable autopsy findings and insisted that colic was the cause of death. Their method of proving their contention was to send letters to the newspapers and to distribute handbills widely.[25] The Moorheads attacked Drake's professional and private character, asserting, moreover, that the cupping was a cruel and unjustifiable procedure which hastened death. It is strange that the newspapers should have published such wanton attacks.

Drake summarized the controversy for professional readers:

> I am almost ashamed to fill up the pages of this journal with comments on these different propositions of the Moorheads; but the distant reader will perhaps excuse me, when he is informed, that one of the gentlemen has for many years been at the head of the Medical College of Ohio, and regarded by its trustees, as one of the ablest physicians in America. The published pathological and therapeutic opinions of *such* an official, may not be authoritative with his *pupils*, but may have weight with physicians who, living at a *distance*, cherish respect for the distinguished faculty to

---

[25] R. & J. Moorhead: "To the public," *Cincinnati Daily Gazette*, VII, No. 2034:p. [2]—c. [2-3], Jan. 27, 1834; *ibid.*, No. 2043:p. [2]—c. [7], Feb. 6, 1834; *ibid.*, 2047:p. [2]—c. [3-4], Feb. 11, 1834. Drake replied in the *Gazette* to each of these communications.

which he belongs, and are, therefore, entitled to notice. I shall examine them seriatim.

1. Mr. B., it is asserted died of *Colic*. The stress laid on this word by the professor, would seem to indicate, that he regards colic as a disease not less specific than the small pox or hooping-cough. In his adherence to the antiquated nosology of the school in which he was educated, he seems to be unaware, that the word colic is vaguely applied to a group of symptoms, consisting of intermittent abdominal pain, constipation and swelling and that these symptoms may arise from a great variety of lesions, and be, or not be, accompanied by inflammation. . . .

But the Professor seems to regard an inflated state of the bowels, as characteristic of *colic*, and consequently absent, after death from any other disease . . . ! Who does not know, that acute peritonitis, when it proves fatal, is attended with abdominal distention . . . ?

2. The Professor informs us, that during the illness of Mr. B. he believed that he labored under intussusception, or displacement of the bowel, and that his colic was occasioned by that anatomical lesion. . . . Who ever heard of death from either of those affections, but by the coming on of inflammation, and who would expect to ward off that condition, by the unrelenting and unmixed administration of irritating cathartics?

3. That not less than three feet of inflated ileum was lodged in the pelvis, and that this was a displacement, and the cause of the colic, which occasioned death, is rather a startling enunciation to come from a learned Professor. I shall not inquire how *three feet of inflated* bowel could be condensed into the male pelvis . . . ! But what shall we think of a Professor, who considers a portion of the small intestines *out of place*, and the cause of death, when he finds it in the pelvis—. . . . Thus we see, that the Doctor has mistaken the *natural and constant* position of a portion of the small intestines for a displacement, and deduces from it a *mortal Colic*.

If these quotations expose the ignorance, in simple descriptive Anatomy, of a cherished professor, and thus cast a stigma on the institution of which he is one of the luminaries, the fault is not mine but his; for he gratuitously thrust himself, and rudely dragged me before the public; and if the exposure which I have made, should give offense to the state of Ohio, which is fostering him for the benefit of her sons, I shall regret it; but will say, as their friend, that, if what I have written should prove a stimulus to his improvement, and secure better teachings for them in future, I shall have something to solace me under her censure.[26]

It is not known whether Drake's friend, the Reverend Robert Hamilton Bishop, D.D., president of Miami University from 1824 to 1841, suggested his selection as one of the orators there in 1834. Drake first met the Reverend Bishop in 1817 at Lexington, when the latter was acting president of Transylvania University. They were again associated there in 1823 and 1824. From such contacts, and from having heard the address on "Health" at Miami in 1830, the Reverend Bishop was well aware of Drake's oratorical abilities. The Union Literary Society of Miami University invited him to deliver its anniversary discourse on 23 September 1834. The theme selected was his beloved West "affectionately inscribed to the native young men of the VALLEY OF THE MISSISSIPPI." This discourse was originally "Published by the Society" in 1834. It was reprinted in *Oxford Addresses* in 1835 and issued again in facsimile in 1955.[27]

Sixty years before Hamlin Garland wrote *Literary Centers*,[28] in which he suggested "revolt against the domination

[26] Daniel Drake: "Irritation and Inflammation of the Peritoneum," *West. Jnl. Med. & Phys. Sc.*, VII:489-531, Jan., Feb., Mar. 1834. The quotations are on pp. 525-28.

[27] Daniel Drake: *Discourse on the History, Character, and Prospects of the West* (Cincinnati: Truman and Smith, 1834); *Oxford Addresses* (Hanover, Ind.: Joseph G. Monfort, 1835), pp. 193-226; *Discourse . . .* (Gainesville, Florida: Scholars' Facsimiles & Reprints, 1955).

[28] J. Christian Bay: "Native Folk Spirit in Literature—Three Essays" (Cedar Rapids, Iowa: The Torch Press, 1957), *Literary Centers*, pp. 31-45.

of the East over the whole nation," Drake was advocating the
use of western themes by westerners: "The mind of the West
is at least equal to that of the East and of Europe, in vigor of
thought, variety of expedient, comprehensiveness of scope and
general efficiency of execution; while in perspicacity of observation, independence of thought, and energy of expression, it
stands on ground unattainable by the more literary and disciplined population of older nations." [29]

And almost a century before Meredith Nicholson wrote
"Stay in your own Home Town," [30] Drake said:

> The early history, biography, and scenery of the Valley of
> the Mississippi, will confer on our literature a variety of
> important benefits. They furnish new and stirring themes for
> the historian, the poet, the novelist, the dramatist, and the
> orator. They are equally rich in events and objects for the
> historical painter. As a great number of those who first
> threaded the lonely and silent labyrinths of our primitive
> woods, were men of intelligence, the story of their perils and
> exploits, has a dignity which does not belong to the early
> history of other nations. We should delight to follow their
> footsteps and stand upon the spot where, at night, they
> lighted up the fire of hickory bark to frighten the wolf; where
> the rattlesnake infused its deadly poison into the foot of
> rash intruders on his ancient domain; where, in the deep
> grass, they laid prostrate and breathless, while the enemy, in
> Indian file, passed unconsciously on his march.[31]

In the notes to this discourse, Drake criticized both James
Fenimore Cooper (1789-1851) and James Kirke Paulding
(1778-1860): "The failure of Mr. Cooper in his Prairie, and
Mr. Paulding in his Westward Ho, is conclusive evidence,
that in delineating the West, no power of genius, can supply

---

[29] Drake: *Discourse* . . . , pp. 12-13.
[30] Bay: *Op. cit.*, "Stay in your own Home Town," pp. 17-26.
[31] Drake: *Discourse* . . . . , pp. 33-34.

the want of opportunities, for personal observation, on our natural and social aspects. No western man can read those works with interest, because of their want of conformity to the circumstances and character of the country, in which the scenes are laid." [32]

Drake sent an inscribed copy of his discourse to Paulding and probably to Cooper also. Paulding in a long and cordial letter thanked Drake and admitted the correctness of his criticism:

> In a note at the end of your address, you pass a judgement on a work of mine, perfectly in consonance with my own. I became sensible in its progress, that I had undertaken a task, which could only be successfully achieved, by one brought up and as it were identified with the scenery & modes of life he attempts to describe. But I had got too far, that I did not like to lose my labour, and went on, relying on the ideas of others, rather than my own. Had I depended entirely on my own imagination, it is probable I might have been more successful. [33]

Ever active in health projects, Drake suggested in an editorial (1833) that, since the Ohio school for the deaf and dumb had been so successful, it was now time to establish a similar institution for the blind. [34] In his eye infirmary and in his practice, he had found a large number of blind children. At the time nothing came of this suggestion. With his usual persistence, he again in the following year called attention to the plight of the blind in Ohio. [35] As chairman of a committee

[32] *Ibid.*, p. 55.
[33] Ralph M. Aderman: "James Kirke Paulding on Literature and the West," *American Literature* (Durham, N.C.), XXVII:97-101, Mar. 1955.
[34] Daniel Drake: [Editorial] "School for the Instruction of the Blind," *West. Jnl. Med. & Phys. Sc.*, VII (2nd Hex., I):483-85, Oct., Nov., Dec. 1833.
[35] Daniel Drake: "School for Instruction of the Blind," *Cincinnati Mirror and Western Gazette*, III:115-16, Jan. 25, 1834.

of the Medical Convention of Ohio, 5 to 7 January 1835, Drake urged the establishment of a school for the blind.[36] On the evening of 7 January 1835, he addressed the Ohio legislature on the same subject. Having failed in arousing sufficient interest, Drake on 17 January 1835 lectured on the blind before a large audience in the Mechanics Institute of Cincinnati. At the conclusion of this address a meeting was held with General William Henry Harrison as chairman. Resolutions were offered memorializing the Ohio legislature and praying that a school for the blind be established.[37] Shortly thereafter the institution was founded in Columbus.

Another project to which Drake devoted considerable thought and attention at this time was the erection of hospitals for rivermen on the Mississippi and its tributaries. The first mention of this subject was in an editorial in his *Journal* calling attention to a similar endeavor by Dr. Cornelius Campbell of St. Louis.[38] In a longer editorial Drake stressed the need for national hospitals, not only along the navigable rivers but also in the northern lakes.[39] As chairman of the Committee on Western Hospitals of the Medical Convention of Ohio, he reported, 6 January 1835, on the necessity of national hospitals in the valley of the Mississippi and the Lakes.[40] This comprehensive report was ordered to be reprinted and copies sent to the governor of Ohio and the other governors of the Union, the president of the United States, members of Congress and the House of Representatives. This report received wide attention, being reprinted as Document

[36] Daniel Drake, Chairman: "Report on a School for the Education of the Blind," *West. Jnl. Med. & Phys. Sc.* VIII (2nd Hex., II):465-67, Oct., Nov., Dec. 1834.

[37] [Ed.] *Cin. Mirror* . . . , IV:107, Jan. 24, 1835.

[38] Daniel Drake: [Editorial], "National Marine Hospitals," *West. Jnl. & Phys. Sc.*, VII (2nd Hex., I):652-53, Jan., Feb., Mar. 1834.

[39] *Ibid.*, VIII (2nd Hex., I):301-5, July, Aug., Sept. 1834.

[40] Daniel Drake, Chairman: "Report on Western Commercial Hospitals," *ibid.*, VIII:459-64, Oct., Nov., Dec. 1834.

Nos. 195 and 270 of the House of Representatives, Twenty-fourth Congress, first Session. The report was issued later as Document No. 264 to accompany a bill, House Resolution No. 654, introduced in the Twenty-fourth Congress.[41] Action was favorable and several hospitals were built in cities along the Ohio and Mississippi Rivers and in lake ports.

Drake, in his *Picture of Cincinnati* (1815), had suggested feasible canal routes through Ohio, Indiana, and Illinois, connecting the Great Lakes with the Ohio River. With no essential change the suggested routes were those along which the canals were constructed. He lived to see many of the canals in use.

As is well known, railroad transportation was born in the 1820's. In time the railroads superseded the canal systems. The new method of travel with its amazing possibilities intrigued Drake, who became one of its early advocates.

On 10 August 1835, a public meeting was held in Cincinnati to arouse interest in a railroad from Covington or Newport, Kentucky, to Paris in the same state. At the close of the discussion, Drake proposed a far more comprehensive plan and introduced the following resolution: "*Resolved,* That a committee of three be appointed to inquire into the practicability and advantages of an extension of the proposed railroad from Paris into the State of South Carolina." [42]

The resolution was unanimously adopted and Drake was appointed chairman of the committee. At a subsequent meeting, 15 August 1835, the chairman read a comprehensive report. Drake pointed out that the proposed railroad along with the canal system would connect the Great Lakes and the bordering states with the southeastern seaboard: "The proposed main trunk [of the railroad] from Cincinnati to

[41] House of Rep., 24th Congress, 1st Session, Doc. No. 264: Daniel Drake [Report]: *National Hospitals in the West* [Washington], Blair & Rives, Printers, 1836), 5 pages.

[42] Mansfield: *Memoirs* . . . , p. 253.

Charleston would resemble an immense horizontal tree extending its roots through, or into, ten states, and a vast expanse of uninhabited territory, in the northern interior of the Union, while its branches would wind through half as many populous states on the southern seaboard.[43]

Several months after Drake's proposals had been enthusiastically adopted, E. S. Thomas (1775-1845), sometime owner and editor of the *Cincinnati Daily Evening Post,* claimed that he had first suggested a "railroad, for carrying freight and passengers . . . near the close of eighteen hundred and twelve, or the beginning of eighteen hundred and thirteen." [44] Mansfield discounts the claims of Thomas since "no public mention of it was ever heard, or movement made" until after Drake's suggestion.[45] Thomas refused to publish a letter by Drake in which his position was clearly stated. Shortly thereafter, the letter was published in the *Charleston Mercury* (South Carolina), then copied in *The Daily Cincinnati Republican* and reprinted in a booklet of six pages.[46] Drake insisted that he had never claimed to have been the only one who had thought of a railroad:

> What I do claim is this, that ignorant of what was in the mind of any other person on this subject, I offered a public resolution for an inquiry, which was adopted on the 10th of August [1835] last; that as chairman of the committee, then appointed, I embodied the facts and speculative views of the

[43] [Daniel Drake]: "Railroad from the Banks of the Ohio River to the Tide Waters of the Carolinas and Georgia" [map] (Cincinnati: James & Gazlay, 1835), p. 7.

[44] E. S. Thomas: *Reminiscences of the Last Sixty-five Years* (2 vols., Hartford: Printed by Case, Tiffan and Burnham, for the Author, 1840), Vol. II, pp. 104-11.

[45] Mansfield: *Memoirs* . . . , p. 253.

[46] Daniel Drake: (a) "To John A. Stewart, Esq., Editor of the *Mercury Daily Cincinnati Republican,*" V, No. 1656:p. [2]—c. [3-5], May 2, 1836. (b) *Railroad to Carolina from the Ohio River* (Cincinnati, March 1, 1836), p. 6.

report, received, adopted, and ordered published by the adjourned meeting of the 15th; that I wrote the address to the people of the states interested. . . . The result was the enactment of a charter by the states of South Carolina, No. Carolina, Tennessee and Kentucky.[47]

Drake was appointed a delegate from Ohio to the Knoxville Convention, 4 July 1836, which assembled to discuss the proposed railroad. He was one of the most active members, making seven motions in addition to presenting a report. At the close of the meeting, the president appointed him a member of the special Committee of Thirty-nine.[48]

Prior to the Knoxville Convention, Drake had visited friends in Huntsville, Alabama. Here on 2 July 1836, the citizens had held a preliminary meeting to discuss the railroad, "The eminent Dr. Drake of Cincinnati was present," and invited to discuss the proposition:

> He traced the origin of the scheme . . . and concluded with an eloquent and animated exhibition of the advantages of such a work, as forming a strong and indissoluble bond of National Union. His views on this part of the subject were bold, expansive and impressive in a very high degree— happily blending the ardent spirit of a patriot with the comprehensive research of the enlightened scholar and philanthropist. The audience were, without exception, delighted with the remarks of Dr. D. and separated with many new views and more favorable impressions not only with respect to the splendid project in contemplation, but as regards all works of the same enlarged scope and beneficent tendency.[49]

[47] *Ibid.*
[48] Knoxville Convention: *Proceedings . . . in relation to the proposed Louisville, Cincinnati & Charlestown Rail-road* (Knoxville, Tenn.: Knoxville Register Office, 1836).
[49] (From the *Huntsville Advocate*): "The rail-road meeting," *Daily Cincinnati Republican and Commercial Register,* V, No. 1718:p. [2]—c. [4], July 20, 1836.

Back in Cincinnati three commissioners, Dan Drake, E. D. Mansfield, and John S. Williams, were appointed to offer stock for sale. Each share was to have a value of $100 and on 17 October 1836 the Stock Book of the Louisville, Cincinnati and Charleston Rail-Road Company was opened with Drake in charge.[50]

In the Cincinnati area subscriptions for 874 shares were obtained. The total subscribed amounted to 37,909½ shares, a sufficient number to insure the issuance of charters by the various states. The charter granted by the legislature of Kentucky required that more extensive rail connections be constructed than originally planned. This stipulation, which would have necessitated many millions of additional capital, prevented the start of the railroad at this time. Years later Drake's dream became a reality.

On 16 April 1836, a meeting of the "friends of Texas" was attended by a large number of Cincinnatians. The speaker was Daniel Drake who explained the object of the meeting and appealed for contributions. He closed his address as follows: "*Resolved*, that from the best information we can obtain, the people of the state of Texas are justifiable in a political and religious point of view in the resistance they have made to usurpations of the despot Santa Anna."[51]

The speech was "enthusiastically received." Other resolutions were presented which, together with the one made by Drake, were unanimously adopted. Drake was elected the permanent chairman.

Aside from the desire of the Cincinnatians to help the cause of the oppressed Texans, many of them were acquainted with the provisional president of the newly established Republic of Texas. David G. Burnet (1789-1870),

[50] "Stock Book" in possession of the Medical Library, Cincinnati General Hospital.

[51] *Daily Evening Post* (Cincinnati), II, No. 139:p. [2]—c. [1-2], Apr. 18, 1836.

provisional president, had studied law in Cincinnati with his brother, Judge Jacob Burnet, in the early 1820's.

At subsequent meetings of the "friends of Texas," sufficient contributions were obtained with which to buy two brass cannons which, in shipment, were listed as "hollow ware." These "twins" from the "Queen City" were used with devastating effect as explained in the following letter:

Executive Department Republic of Texas
    Velasco, July 22, 1836
To Daniel Drake, M.D.: William Corry, Esq.;
    Pulaski Smith, Esq.; Nathan Leamans, Esq.;
        and W. Chase, Esq.
Gentlemen:

The two beautiful pieces of *"hollow-ware,"* lately presented to us, through your agency, by the citizens of Cincinnati, as a free-will offering to the cause of human liberty, were received very opportunely, and have become conspicuous in our struggle for independence. Their first effective operations were in the memorable field of San Jacinto, where they contributed greatly to the achievement of a victory not often paralleled in the annals of war. I doubt not that their voices will again be heard, and their power felt in the great and interesting cause to which they were dedicated by your liberality, and in the advancement of which we are so arduously engaged.

To you, gentlemen, and to the Citizens of Cincinnati, who have manifested so generous a sympathy in our cause, I beg leave to tender the warmest thanks of a people who are contending for their liberties and their lives, against a numerous nation of semi-savages, whose cruelty is equalled only by their want of spirit and of military prowess.

Should our enemy have the temerity to renew his attempt to subjugate our delightful country, the voices of the *twin sisters* of Cincinnati will yet send their reverberations beyond the Rio Grande, and carry unusual terror into many a Mexican hamlet.

Texas has no desire to extend her conquests beyond her own natural and appropriate limits, but if the war must be prosecuted against us, after abundant evidence of its futility has been exhibited to the enemy and to the world, other land than our own must sustain a portion of its ravages.

Permit me, gentlemen, to tender to you, and to your fellow-citizens who have rendered Texas much efficient aid, assurance of my profound esteem

Your ob.'t serv.'t,
David G. Burnet.[52]

[52] Wm. C. Binkley, editor: *Official Correspondence of the Texan Revolution, 1835-1836* (New York: Appleton-Century, 1936), Vol. II, pp. 881-82.

14 ☤

> *I have lived too long in the West to need a macadamized road for any journey, and look upon the difficulties that may be encountered as mere stimulants to effort.*[1]

Cincinnati, 1832-36

THE REPEATED attacks against Drake after his resignation from the Medical College of Ohio in 1832 are apparently without parallel in the annals of American medicine. Active participants were some of the professors, the majority of the trustees of the college, and their henchmen. In addition to the "regulars," various medical cults participated in the fray: steam doctors, the "eclectics," and the Thomsonians (followers of Samuel Thomson (1769-1844), the New Hampshire farmer turned herb doctor. He recommended steambaths along with herb concoctions (Nos. 1 to 6) containing as the more active ingredients, cayenne pepper and lobelia.

The Ohio Medical Reformer, of which only two issues (December 1 and 15, 1832) appeared, claimed that it sponsored the "Eclectic Sect" and that all systems of medicine were "composed of a little Truth and much Error." [2] In the first issue, Drake was satirized by "Hudibras" of Worthington, Ohio, in "Doctor Diabolus, or the Devil in Cincinnati":

---

[1] Daniel Drake: "Medical Schools in Cincinnati," supplement to *West. Jnl. & Phys. Sc.*, III (Hex. II):pp. 169-203, Apr., May, June 1835. Also separately printed, p. 33.

[2] To correspondents," *The Ohio Medical Reformer* (Cincinnati), I:8, Dec. 1, 1832.

In days of yore, when time was young,
And Birds conversed as well as sung,
In Cincinnati's western city,
North of Ohio and Kentucky,
There lived a Doctor, lank and thin,
With pointed nose and lengthened chin.
His gait was gaunt, yet debonair;
And though his looks demure were seen
His cheeks were wan, his visage grim,
With spindle shanks, and figure slim,
His withered brow and tresses grey,
Seem to have known a better day.

. . . .

His gorge was wide and he would gobble—
All fulsome praise for which some squabble.

. . . .

This learned Doctor's name you ask?—
How many years with him are passed?
His name well known to brother cits;—
For who have not heard of his wit,
His schemes, and specs, and learned puff's,
His school intrigues, and temper rough?
How he co-lectured at the College
And taught to students CLINIC *knowledge;*—
How he quarrel'd with *the seven,*
And broke the compact HE had chosen,
And thus by fate reduced their number
To that 'gainst which he'd often thundered;—
How in a case I'll soon relate,
He proved his own a simple pate?
                    To be Continued.[3]

Our curiosity concerning the "case" to be related in "Doctor Diabolus" must remain unsatisfied since the remainder of the poem was never published.

[3] Hudibras: "Doctor Diabolus," *ibid.*, I:4-5, Dec. 1, 1832.

Imbued with the highest ideals in childhood, Drake was uncompromising in their observance. He dearly loved his profession and in it found the embodiment of these ideals. The Hippocratic Oath was sacred to him. Persons with different childhood backgrounds and with less uncompromising ideals could not understand Drake. He was forthright and never a mere conformist. As previously indicated, his sensitive nature often prompted replies to attacks which should have been ignored. And his combativeness sometimes helped to prolong controversies. Drake did not seem to realize that his standing in the profession was such as to have made it unnecessary to reply to any type of attack.

Once in discussing the Medical College of Ohio, Charles Hammond of *The Cincinnati Daily Gazette* editorialized:

> It often happens that talented men, create for themselves a kind of personal atmosphere, and can breathe freely in no other. With such, *egomet* is every thing. They seem scarcely to know that there is any body else in the world.—They are never in the wrong, never unjust, never unreasonable. No matter upon what path they journey, cross them in it and they are sure to be provoked. *Nemo me tangere* is their motto. This class of men are great sufferers in their relations of life. They overflow with their troubles, and the burden of their conversation is to pour their complaints upon the ear of an auditory, and not to listen, is to aggravate their wrongs. I could name half a dozen such men without writing Dr. Drake one of them; yet it is more than likely before he has read thus far, he will say, *here is an attack upon me.* Without meaning to make the application, I may truly state that Doctor Drake's recent course has introduced this train of reflections on my mind.[4]

This assessment by Hammond brings to mind the familiar quotation from Burns: "Oh wad some power the gifties gie

[4] Charles Hammond, editor: "Men and Things," *Cincinnati Daily Gazette,* VI, No. 1746:p. [2]—c. [4-5], Feb. 19, 1833.

us. . . ." It would certainly be difficult to find two more aggressive individualists than Hammond and Drake. The latter's reaction to Hammond's editorial is unknown. However, William Davis Gallagher (1808-94), journalist, poet, and author, having observed both men for more than ten years, wrote:

> It may be asked, and we expect it will be, why we have coupled these two names [Hammond-Drake] together—the one being that of a politician and lawyer, the other that of a physician. We answer—There is great simularity in the men. Though of very different professions, and constantly engaged in very different pursuits, they both occasionally step aside, the last from his medicine to test his powers in the political arena, the first from his law and politics to dabble in theology, to the amount of now—and—then preaching a "Lay Sermon," and a censorious discourse to theological disputants. They are men of great worth in their different professions, of great talents, and of great influence; consequently, they have enemies, who magnify the errors or weaknesses of the one into great moral obliquities, and the persevering and it may be somewhat selfish spirit of the other into unbounded ambition; enemies who strike at them, in the dark and in the light, on any and every occasion,—who possess not their minds, and cannot appreciate them,—who can never reach their exalted stations, and therefore endeavor to pull them down to their own level,—who have not magnanimity to acknowledge the extent and worth of their labors, and therefore do them injustice; enemies, half a dozen of whom attack them at a time, as the proud mastiff is attacked by a pack of yelping curs, who, if he but look upon them and growl, fly off until another and more favorable opportunity offers of renewing the attack; enemies whom they both disregard till their impudence calls loudly for chastisement, and upon whom both then turn with very similar weapons, and silence for the time with very similar adroitness. . . .

Few men have been more warmly opposed in any schemes

of their own originating, or which having originated with others they were endeavoring to perfect, than Dr. Drake in some of his. But possessed of great fortitude and perseverance, he has either removed or avoided every obstacle that has been placed in his way; and though he has sometimes triumphed overmuch in victory, he has never allowed defeat to depress his active and energetic spirit. While he has been thus opposed at home, he has been universally admired and eulogized abroad; and is at this time a member of some of the principal scientific societies of this country and of Europe. . . .

As a public lecturer, it would be difficult for anybody to point out an individual anywhere, who possesses the tact of rendering himself more popular, or the talent of extemporizing with greater facility, and of making himself understood by his audience. The Doctor presents the *subject* he is handling directly to the "minds eye." . . .

It is this facility he has, of presenting his subject to an audience so as to concentrate their attention directly upon it, (altogether unassisted by his manner of delivery, for he is without gracefulness, and has an intonation of voice,—a peculiar drawl,—at the close of his sentences, which is exceedingly disagreeable,) together with the earnestness he evinces in discussing his subject, his happy allusions and apt illustrations, the piquancy of his wit and the familiarity of his style, that enables him as it were to rivet his audience to their seats, and to hold them when he chooses, (which is sometimes the case,) for a *double* lecture. . . .

To conclude: Imagine a gigantic, muscular being, with the chest of a centaur and the limbs of an Alcides, planted as firmly by the forge as Roderick Dhu on his rack, with every part of his frame braced, and every muscle in action,— imagine such a being with sledge-hammer in hand, striking with the power of a Vulcan, sending the sparks in every direction, and leaving at every stroke an impression and an evidence of the power that wields the implement,—and you will have a pretty correct idea of CHARLES HAMMOND and

DANIEL DRAKE, except that they work with pens instead of sledge-hammers, and operate upon the *mind* instead of *metal*. Or imagine, if you please, an expert and athletic swordsman, hemmed in by half a score of enemies, cutting and slashing on all sides, dealing here a flesh wound and there a death-blow, overpowering an antagonist here and frightening one with a feint there, and escaping from the unequal rencontre but slightly injured,—and you have on the field of war what these men are on the field of mental strife. This is a rough picture: they, as writers, are rough men. We trust it will not be thought too highly colored for truth. We have studied them, and thus they have appeared to our understanding.[5]

At this time (1833), Harriet Beecher, later Mrs. Calvin E. Stowe (1811-96), wrote:

> Our family physician is one Dr. Drake, a man of a good deal of science, theory and reputed skill, but a sort of general mark for the opposition of all of the medical cloth of the city (Cincinnati.) He is a tall, rectangular, perpendicular sort of body, as stiff as a poker. . . . The other evening he was detained from visiting Kate and he sent a very polite, cere-monious note, containing a prescription, with Dr. D's com-pliments to Miss Beecher, requesting that she would take the enclosed in a little molasses at nine o'clock precisely.[6]

Miss Beecher is entirely too general in asserting that "all of the medical cloth of the city" opposed Drake. Investigation shows that opposition was confined to the "small" and jealous professors of the medical college, some of their friends, and various "cults." Drake was the leader of, and extremely popu-lar with, the majority of the Cincinnati physicians. He had the largest consultative practice in the city, the neighboring territory, and across the Ohio River in Kentucky.

[5] W. D. G. [William D. Gallagher]: "Brief Notices of Western Writers. Charles Hammond, Esq.—Daniel Drake, M.D.," *Cincinnati Mirror, and Western Gazette of Literature and Science,* III:51-52, Nov. 30, 1833.
[6] Fields: *Life and Letters of Harriet Beecher Stowe,* p. 79.

Early in 1833, the Third District Medical Society and the State Medical Society joined in requesting reformation of the Medical College of Ohio. The General Assembly of Ohio then authorized the appointment of five commissioners to investigate the charges. On 12 April 1833, Dr. Joshua L. Martin, Xenia, Ohio, president of the Third District Society, handed the commissioners specific complaints against the trustees and faculty. It was stated that the character of the teaching had deteriorated at one time to the point that the medical faculty of Transylvania University refused to recognize a course of lectures. The uncalled for and reprehensible treatment of Dr. Henry by the college and Township Trustees was severely condemned. Mismanagement of funds, publication of false statements, restrictive rules concerning the library, and proscription of autopsies were cited in addition to other abuses. It was even revealed that one of the college trustees was an advocate of a quack system of medicine.[7] After three weeks of study, the commissioners issued a report which was referred to a select committee of the General Assembly of Ohio. This committee was indeed a "select" one; they lauded the faculty and trustees while heaping abuse on Drake, who was accused of having instigated the charges.

Prior to the above episode, Drake had in his medical journal at various times announced the number of students, names of graduates, and minor news items but had never referred to the deplorable status of the college. Following the report of the "select" committee, Drake could no longer restrain himself: "The Editor is determined, hereafter, to advise the distant reader, from time to time, of the character and advantages of our Medical College. . . .[8]

Concerning the report, he said:

[7] Joshua L. Martin: "Charges and Specifications," *West. Jnl. Med. and Phys. Sc.*, VII (Hex. II):625-31, Jan., Feb., Mar. 1834.
[8] Daniel Drake [Editorial]: "The Medical College of Ohio," *ibid.*, 623-51.

It is certainly quite a distinction to be made thus the subject of an elaborate and lengthened state paper, by a Committee of the most dignified branch of our Legislature! Toward the close of the Report on the conduct and character of "Drake," as the Committee courteously designate him, they declare *"That the Charges* against the Agents of the State are NOT SUSTAINED by the evidence;" consequently the "Agents of the State" are acquitted and *one* of the fifty witnesses singled out for calumniation, within the very walls, where he once personally made those explanations to the General Assembly, which led to the establishment of both the College and the Hospital! [9]

. . . .

Dr. Drake in conclusion, wishes to say, that after he was called as a witness before the Commissioners, in April last, and delivered his testimony, he left the whole matter to the Legislature, and neither by written or spoken words, advised any physician or student, in favor of Lexington or any other school, in preference to that in Cincinnati. On the contrary, six of his pupils were connected with the latter, a greater number than any of its professors furnished. Notwithstanding all this, however, it seems that Professor Mitchell has received intelligence that Dr. Drake's exertions kept away 88 pupils. This is truly paying a splendid compliment to his standing in the Valley of the Mississippi. While engaged in the drudgery of professional business, and remaining constantly in one town, to direct the choice of 88 students, scattered over ten or twelve states, is a moral influence which few men in the profession have ever wielded. No wonder the Faculty and Trustees, have invoked the aid of the General Assembly against this talismanic power! [10]

The status of the Medical College of Ohio remained unchanged until 9 February 1835. At this time 28 physicians in

[9] *Ibid.,* 631-32.
[10] *Ibid.,* 650-51.

Cincinnati and 108 additional ones of Ohio sent a memorial to the trustees requesting changes in the faculty and other reforms. A committee of three trustees sought suggestions from the memorialists and found the consensus favored complete reorganization with retention of only Professors Eberle and Cobb.[11] Under these circumstances the newly appointed board of trustees hoped that all the professors would resign. Drake was asked by a member of the board whether he would accept a professorship were Moorhead retained, to which he replied:

> When, *ex necessitate,* I was associated with him in 1831-2, I carried myself in every official interview with whatever discretion, moderation, decorum and courtesy I possess; but in the spring of 1833, when he gave testimony to the commissioners appointed by the governor, he represented me as overbearing, unjust and tyrannical. If such was my deportment then it would be bad hereafter; and the peace and dignity of the college require, that I should not come into it, in connection with one who is strongly predisposed to recognize in me those unenviable qualities.
>
> I wish to say explicitly, however, that *I do not and will not stand in the way of a successful reorganization of the college,* an object which I have much at heart, and should the Board reject me for Dr. Moorhead, but at the same time, improve the condition of the school, by the election of the able and efficient men, whose names I know to be before them, I will not only do all in my power to induce these gentlemen to accept and enter the school without me, but I will to the full interest of my humble means, do everything to advance its interests and augment its usefulness.[12]

Since the professors did not resign, the trustees attempted the embarrassing procedure of declaring the chairs vacant,

[11] Daniel Drake: "Medical Schools in Cincinnati," supplement to *West. Jnl. Med. & Phys. Sc.,* IX:169-203, April, May, June 1835. Reprinted separately as: *Reform of Medical College of Ohio,* 35 pages.
[12] *Ibid.,* p. 12.

seriatim. Despite Drake's explicit statement, he was elected to the chair of the theory and practice of medicine, although Moorhead was retained. Of course Drake refused the appointment and was again criticized. His comment was that:

> He does not cherish of himself the opinion, that his entering the college could raise it, in opposition to a dead weight of incompetent colleagues. He did not choose to venture into the water to save it from drowning, and sink with it. He presumed himself at liberty, as a citizen of Ohio, to judge while out of the school, of the propriety of entering it; and to make a decision without having his right to do so, called in question by any of the trustees; or without having his refusal denounced as dictation or obstinacy. In this, however, he was mistaken, as individual members of the Board, have felt themselves at liberty to censure him for not accepting; as though he had knocked at the door for admission, knowing who were already in, and when it was opened, had refused to enter.[13]

It is apparent that Drake would have accepted a professorship had Moorhead been dismissed. Four months passed during which the board of trustees was neither able to dismiss all the incumbents nor secure replacements for those released. In 1819, Drake had obtained a charter for Cincinnati College which suspended operations during the depression of the early 1820's. He now decided to resuscitate it with medical and legal departments in addition to its former academic status. He frankly stated that by this plan he sought to force capitulation by the Board of Trustees of the Medical College of Ohio. In this he was successful. The project uppermost in his mind for many years was the creation of an outstanding medical college in Cincinnati.

At a called meeting of the Trustees of Cincinnati College on 22 May 1835, the following resolution was adopted:

[13] *Ibid.*, p. 16.

Whereas the recent attempt of the medical profession and the General Assembly of Ohio to reorganize and improve the conditons of the Medical College of Ohio, have, as we are informed been unsuccessful . . . and whereas there is the utmost danger that Ohio will lose the advantages of a Medical institution, unless immediate measures be taken to organize a substitute for said College, therefore be it

Resolved, That the Board will proceed forthright to establish a medical department of Cincinnati College.[14]

On 30 June 1835, Daniel Drake, dean of the medical faculty of Cincinnati College, announced that the chairs had been filled as follows:

Special and Surgical Anatomy,
By Joseph N. McDowell, M.D.

*General and Pathological Anatomy, Physiology
and Medical Jurisprudence,*
By Samuel D. Gross, M.D.
(Late of the Medical College of Ohio.)

Surgery,
By Horatio G. Jamison, M.D.
(Late of the Washington Medical College, Baltimore.)

Obstetrics and the Diseases of Women and Children,
By Landon C. Rives, M.D.
(Late of the state of Virginia.)

Chemistry and Pharmacy,
By James B. Rogers, M.D.
(Late of the Washington Medical College, Baltimore.)

Materia Medica,
By John P. Harrison, M.D.
(Late of Louisville, Ky., now of Philadelphia.)

Theory and Practice of Medicine,
By Daniel Drake, M.D.

[14] *Ibid.,* p. 23.

Adjunct Professor of Chemistry and Lecturer on Botany,
John L. Riddell, M.S.
(Late of the state of New York.) [15]

The members of this faculty were distinguished for their teaching abilities and literary achievements. They were more widely known than the teachers of the Medical College of Ohio. The course of study in the Medical Department of Cincinnati College was to extend from the last Monday in October 1835 to the end of February 1836, with six lectures delivered daily throughout the session. Ever anxious in attempting to improve the moral status of the medical profession, Drake announced that: "Every Sunday morning of the last three months of session, the professor of the Theory and Practice, will deliver a discussion on the social, moral and religious duties of students and medical men; which of course the members of the class will be at liberty to attend or decline, according to their respective tastes." [16]

Drake's concluding paragraph in the pamphlet concerning the attempted reform of the Medical College of Ohio and the establishment of the Medical Department of Cincinnati College deserves quotation:

> In this and a preceding article, I have said much of myself, but let it be remembered, that others have said of me still more. I have often been compelled to grapple, single-handed, with combinations, formidable by their numbers, their influence, and their individual respectability; but, in every instance, up to the commencement of the narrative of which this is a part, I have written in my own defence against published attacks. If in any stage of this protracted controversy, injustice has been done to a single individual, I stand ready to make reparation; if I have, knowingly, falsified any public document, or perverted any important fact, let me be

[15] *Ibid.*, pp. 27-28.
[16] *Ibid.*, pp. 28-29.

convicted. Finally, I expect hereafter to write more *on* the profession, and less of it; and, instead of uttering my own *complaints*, to speak on the *complaints* of others; not, it is true in the wisdom of an oracle, but with the heart of a man devoted to the glory of his profession.[17]

The Cincinnati College building erected in the early 1820's had deteriorated through disuse. It was repaired and remodeled. In addition to the part assigned to the Medical Department, rooms were arranged for the accommodation of the Cincinnati Medical Society, the Cincinnati Literary Society, the Western Academy of Natural Sciences, and the Western College of Professional Teachers.

Drake donated a number of books as a nucleus for a medical library. Other members of the faculty followed his example. In discussing the reasons for establishing the Medical Department of Cincinnati College, Drake wrote:

> If the Medical College of Ohio had been prosperous, such a project would not have been undertaken, at least by those who *have* engaged in it. As it is not prosperous, no harm can come to the interests of the profession from a new school. The Cincinnati College has taken nothing from the Medical College of Ohio, and, therefore, deprives our students of medicine of no advantage which that institution could afford. As to anatomical subjects, it is well known that enough are attainable, for two schools. Then, who is or can be injured by the new school, but the professors of the old? the fear of which, perhaps, may impel them to greater efforts than heretofore, and thus the students who chance to return to that college will be better taught—for which they may thank the new project.[18]

The authority of the trustees of Cincinnati College to establish a department of medicine was questioned. Such a

[17] *Ibid.*, p. 35.
[18] *Ibid.*, p. 29.

question was ludicrous since the original charter of 1819 explicitly authorized Cincinnati College to grant all or any of the degrees conferred by other institutions in the United States.

There was no decrease in the frequency and number of attacks made against Drake. He replied to some of his assailants while ignoring others. Concerning past relations with the Medical College of Ohio, he wrote:

> In the dark days of adversity, which shrouded those relations, their letters [from pupils and medical friends] come like the occasional sun beams which penetrate the gloom, and fall pleasantly on the eye of him who gropes beneath although they may not illuminate the path by which he must travel out. The impression they make is imperishable, and will constitute for years to come, a most powerful stimulus to exertion in the halls of medical education, where, with many of those to whom this little effusion is addressed, not a few of the happiest hours of my life have been spent.[19]

One of the most dastardly and vitriolic attacks ever made on Drake was that sponsored by Alban G. Smith who later changed his name to Alban Goldsmith. With considerable assistance in writing, Smith issued nineteen letters published in *The Cincinnati Whig and Commercial Intelligencer* from 8 July to 7 August 1835. Each instalment was signed "Vindex." These communications were reprinted in a pamphlet which was widely circulated.[20] In the prefatory note concerning the recurring disturbances in the Medical College of Ohio will be found the following statement: "These difficulties have been created chiefly, by the agency of *one man*, who, intent upon his own aggrandisement, has adopted *what-*

[19] *Ibid.*, p. 35.
[20] [Alban G. Smith]: "An Inquiry into the Causes that have Retarded the Prosperity of the Medical College of Ohio," *Cincinnati Whig and Commercial Intelligencer*—extra, 1835, 42 pages.

ever means were best calculated to work out his own ends." [21]

Smith's attack was doubtless occasioned by Drake's discussion of the opinions of the Ohio physicians obtained by the committee of investigation of the board of trustees. Drake asserted that the majority of physicians polled regarded Alban G. Smith as of secondary rank in the faculty. Drake qualified his statement by saying that he was "speaking of the professor and not of the man." [22] Thus he was not placing Smith in the group with Moorhead whom he regarded not only as incompetent but vindictive, coarse, and vulgar. Alban G. Smith, at one time associated with Ephraim McDowell, probably had good training and was an expert surgeon, the third in the United States to perform an ovariotomy (1833). However, he was regarded as an uninspiring teacher and, therefore, not to be retained in the thorough reorganization of the medical college.

The Vindex pamphlet is a boringly repetitious, pedestrian tirade crammed with innuendoes, erroneous and palpably false statements, and surmises against Drake. It is asserted that as a result of a quarrel with "Dr. Bligh [*sic*], Drake left Lexington in 1818." [23] This is absurd since there is ample evidence to the contrary in friendly letters from the Reverend Blythe to Drake.

Vindex quotes Dr. Jesse Smith's testimony concerning Drake's "intrigues" which resulted in his dismissal from the Medical College of Ohio in 1822. In describing these events he alludes to "the amiable and quiet dispositions of Drs. [Jesse] Smith and Slack." [24] Alban G. Smith is unaware of a contemporary letter of Jesse Smith to his wife's parents revealing "dispositions" far from tractable:

[21] *Ibid.*, p. 2.
[22] Drake: *Reform of Medical College of Ohio*, p. 19.
[23] [Smith]: *An Inquiry* . . . , p. 14.
[24] *Ibid.*, p. 9.

If the Trustees do not treat us better, than they have done; & consult us, & let us do what we have a mind, for we have all the labour, & responsibility no body else, for the present at least, can carry it on against us—This may seem boasting; but I appeal to the event for its truth—My branch & Mr. Slack's are far the most important—we have both laboured & contributed far more than others, the State, Trustees, & Professors collectively; [at this time, 1823, the only professors were Dr. Jesse Smith and the Reverend Elijah Slack] we are determined to have the Col. on a permanent basis, & with a prospect of flourishing, before we will enjoy the honor of being Professors in it. But enough of this—[25]

Alban G. Smith alleges that John D. Godman was incensed with Drake and resigned from the Medical College of Ohio. This is still another absurd statement. Godman referred to Drake as his "dear friend." Later he had Drake supervise the publication of several issues of his medical journal. In 1823, Godman wrote a cordial letter to Henry Clay concerning Drake's abilities (see reference 26, Chapter 9). Drake and Godman corresponded regularly until the latter's death. The eulogy by Drake at this time most certainly does not disclose the slightest evidence of there having been disagreement between them.[26]

The statement by Vindex that, in 1833 on the death of Dr. James M. Staughton, professor of surgery, Drake sought the chair is palpably preposterous. Alban G. Smith attributed Drake's enmity to his own election to the professorship of surgery. "The war we have seen, has lasted three years, and

[25] J.[esse] & E. B. Smith, ALS, Cincinnati, 29 April 1823, to Mr. & Mrs. J. & E. Bailey. Graciously lent by Mrs. Malcolm McAvoy, granddaughter of Dr. Smith.

[26] Daniel Drake: "Biographia Medica," *West. Jnl. of Med. & Phys. Sc.*, IV:597-611, Jan., Feb., Mar. 1831. Reprinted in Godman's *Rambles of a Naturalist*, pp. 13-36.

has been prosecuted with vigor and ability, by the assailants." [27]

It is difficult to separate fact from fiction in the Vindex pamphlet. Were it free of erroneous and false statements, the following letter quoted in it would not be suspect:

Cincinnati, December 30th, 1834

Dear Sir—

I understand that you are about to attend the Medical Convention at Columbus. If such be the fact let me advise you as a friend, to curb your propensity for telling lies, so that you may not disgrace yourself among strangers, and bring discredit on the Convention. I do not of course [here a word is omitted in the copy which I have—it is probably the word, "suppose"] that you can refrain entirely—but a strong resolution may enable you to hold in a little. I hope this advice will not be lost upon you.

Your Obed't Serv't.
Daniel Drake[28]

Prof. Mitchell

Categorical denial that Drake wrote this letter is impossible. Of course, it should not have been written despite ample provocation as the result of Dr. Thomas D. Mitchell's lurid testimony against Drake before the commissioners appointed by the governor. The fact that it is not signed, "Dan Drake," as had been his invariable custom for many years, adds to the doubt of its authenticity.

Toward the close of the Pamphlet Vindex asks:

In what does Dr. Drake's reputation consist? Where are his Medical works? Where are his operations—his cases? He has made it by *thrusting* himself continually before the public, and if he could not come before it in the character of a

[27] [Smith]: *An Inquiry* . . . , p. 19.
[28] *Ibid.*, p. 38.

physician, he has Proteus-like assumed that of the politician, the school-orator—the 4th of July stump speaker, the founder of female schools; in short he has sought and gained that sort of notoriety, which every man of tolerable talents may attain, by laying aside the garb of self respect, and propriety, and interfering in every body's business, without any body's permission.[29]

Drake did not immediately reply to the scurrilous pamphlet —primarily because the letters were anonymous and the greater number of the accusations had been previously made on several occasions and refuted. As the first class of the Medical Department of Cincinnati College was assembling, prior to the start of the formal lectures, Drake defended himself in a speech. The class requested copies of the documents refuting the charges of Vindex. Drake declined but addressed a letter to the students which they published along with resolutions endorsing him and claiming that the wholly false accusations were made under the auspices of *"interested persons of the Medical College of Ohio."* [30]

Alban G. Smith did not write clearly, a fact amply confirmed by the Vindex diatribe. And the assistance of some of the professors of the Medical College of Ohio did not improve the diction. Drake stated that Raphael Semmes (1809-77), then a midshipman and nephew of Smith's wife, claimed authorship of the first of the Vindex articles. This is the same Raphael Semmes so conspicuous during the War between the States as commander of the celebrated privateer "Alabama."

Regardless of any assistance Smith may have had, Drake

[29] *Ibid.,* p. 41.
[30] [Ezra Read, President, Medical Students of Cincinnati College]: *Medical Department of Cincinnati College* (Cincinnati, 1835). Drake's reply to the students in this pamphlet was first published in the *Cincinnati Whig and Commercial Intelligencer,* N.S., I, No. 1342:p [2]—c. [2-5], Nov. 5, 1835; concluded in No. 1343:p [2]—c. [3-5], Nov. 6, 1835.

blamed him for instigating the articles: "I, therefore, say to you, that Dr. Alban G. Smith, of the Medical College of Ohio, is the author of "Vindex"—and as such, I pronounce that he has uttered a black catalogue of falsehoods. . . ." [31]

Drake was informed by the printer that the Vindex pamphlets were ordered by Samuel Yorke Atlee:

> Now who is Samuel Yorke Atlee? A lawyer, who never had business, and advertised the people of Cincinnati, in 1832, that if they would not patronize him better, he should return to the east—who, however, changed his mind, and became the editor of the Chronicle, till he was discharged by the publisher in a few months; who then went to St. Louis, and became a stage player—but failing in that, returned to Cincinnati, and entering as a pupil of the Medical College of Ohio, became the open and reckless eulogist of the professors, whom he used to ridicule in doggerel rhymes—who at the end of the session re-opened a lawyers office, and having no business, got out a new edition of Vindex.
>
> Such is the pennypost whom Dr. Smith has employed to circulate his anonymous libels, in the taverns, canal boats and coffee houses of the city! Mr. Atlee has at last found his proper level, and I shall there leave him, to subscribe myself,
>
> Most respectfully,
your obed't servant
Dan. Drake[32]

[31] *Ibid.*, p. 10.
[32] *Ibid.*, p. 11.

15

Most of your libels have been so often put forth, within the last 20 years, that I can nearly tell what beggar wore the rags from which the paper was made, on which they are printed.[1]

Cincinnati, 1836-39

IN THE Medical Department of Cincinnati College, Drake had gathered a distinguished faculty. It was probably second to none in the United States at that time. Leaders in their respective fields, each admired the abilities of his associates. There were apparently none of the petty jealousies and bickerings which produced so much turmoil in the Medical College of Ohio.

HORATIO G. JAMISON. The first full professor to resign from Drake's group was Horatio G. Jamison (1778-1855) who taught surgery. It is evident that his resignation after one session in the school was not the result of any disagreement. He was not the fluent teacher that Drake and some of the others were, and he may have been embarrassed. However, the illness of his wife was probably the primary reason for his wish to return to Baltimore.

WILLARD PARKER. Jamison was succeeded by Willard Parker (1800-84), a graduate of Harvard (A.B. in 1826 and M.D. in 1830) and one of the most distinguished teachers

[1] Daniel Drake: *The War not Exterminated!* Broadside, 29 March 1839, column [4].

of surgery in America. He was ambidextrous and was said to have operated without the use of glasses when eighty. Like Drake he was greatly interested in public hygiene and in the cause of temperance. During the summer of 1837, he went to Europe, where he bought books, manikins, anatomical preparations, chemical apparatus, and appliances for Cincinnati College. From Paris, on 17 May 1837, he wrote an extremely interesting letter concerning the hospitals and medical conditions there.[2] Though Parker wrote a number of articles, principally case reports or descriptions of operations, there is only one book by him which was posthumously edited by his son: *Cancer: a Study of Three Hundred and Ninety-seven Cases of the Female Breast* (1885). Leaving Cincinnati in 1839, he became professor of the principles and practice of surgery, College of Physicians and Surgeons at Columbia University, New York City, where he remained until his retirement. The Willard Parker Hospital for Contagious Diseases in New York City was named for him.

JOSEPH NASH McDOWELL. The most erratic personality among the faculty of Cincinnati College was Joseph Nash McDowell (1803-68), nephew of Ephraim. He was a brother-in-law of Drake, having married Amanda Virginia Drake. McDowell obtained his classical education at Transylvania University and likewise his medical, receiving an M.D. degree in 1825. He had taught large private classes in anatomy and surgery in Lexington, Philadelphia, and Cincinnati before becoming professor of special and surgical anatomy. An able orator, he illustrated lectures with a varied assortment of anecdotes. It was said that he had a story for every structure of the body, whether it was a bone, a muscle, or a nerve. After suspension of the Medical Department of Cincinnati College in 1839, he went to St. Louis where he

---

[2] Willard Parker: Letter (Paris, 17 May 1837), *West. Jnl. Med. & Phys. Sc.*, XI:161-62, Apr., May, June 1837.

founded the Medical Department of Kemper College which
was called the Missouri Medical College ("McDowell's College.")

It is related that McDowell constructed the college building as a fortress in which he stored some fourteen hundred
muskets and several brass cannons, preparatory to an invasion
of Upper California. No documentation was offered in confirmation of this story or of several others equally bizarre.
The U.S. government took over the college building in 1862.
Samuel D. Gross stated that during the Civil War, McDowell
"embraced the Southern cause, fled to Europe, and finally,
with the reputation of an erratic genius, he died in a state
of utter bankruptcy." [3]

SAMUEL D. GROSS. The combined chairs of general and
pathological anatomy, physiology, and medical jurisprudence
were occupied by Samuel D. Gross, a graduate of Jefferson
Medical College (1828). Before the close of 1830 he had
translated three books from the French, one from German,
and had authored one: *The Anatomy, Physiology and Diseases
of the Bones and Joints.* During his four years in Cincinnati
College, he wrote the first systematic treatise on pathological
anatomy in the English language.[4] This book was inscribed
"To Daniel Drake, M.D."

> Distinguished alike as an accomplished and successful
> teacher, an erudite and skilful physician, a zealous promoter
> of science and literature, and an ardent friend of patholog-
> ical anatomy, the following pages, intended to illustrate one
> of the fundamental branches of medical science, are respect-
> fully inscribed, as a testimony of esteem for his excellent tal-

---

[3] Gross: *Autobiography,* Vol. I, p. 70.
[4] Samuel D. Gross: *Elements of Pathological Anatomy* (2 vols., Boston:
Marsh, Capen, Lyon & Webb, and James B. Dow, 1839).

ents and attainments, and as a token of sincere regard for
his character,

By his obliged friend
and servant, THE AUTHOR.[5]

This book, important for its time and scope, was re-issued
in 1843, a second edition appeared in 1845 and a third in
1857, each inscribed to Drake. Shortly after the suspension of
Cincinnati College, Gross was elected to the chair of surgery
in the Louisville Medical Institute (now the School of Medicine, University of Louisville). After sixteen happy years in
Louisville he accepted the professorship of surgery in his
alma mater, Jefferson Medical College, where he remained
until his death. The *System of Surgery* (1859) by Gross went
through six editions, and portions of it were translated into
Japanese. Of the professors in Cincinnati College, Gross
was second only to Drake in literary output.

JAMES BLYTHE ROGERS. The professor of chemistry
and pharmacy in Cincinnati College, James Blythe Rogers
(1802-52), was the oldest of the extraordinary "Brothers
Rogers," a unique family in American science. He was the
eldest son of Patrick Kerr Rogers, M.D. (1776-1828), professor of natural history and chemistry in the College of William
and Mary. The second of the famous brothers, William
Barton (1804-84), was a geologist, chemist, founder, and
first president of the Massachusetts Institute of Technology.
Henry Darwin Rogers (1808-66), also a geologist, made important surveys of New Jersey and Pennsylvania. Finally
(1858) he became professor of natural history in the University of Glasgow. The youngest brother, Robert Empie Rogers
(1813-84), a University of Pennsylvania graduate in medicine,
taught chemistry successively in the University of Virginia,
the University of Pennsylvania, and finally, in Jefferson Medi-

[5] *Ibid.* (1st ed., 1839); reissue, 1843; 2nd ed., 1845; 3rd ed., 1857.

cal College. James Blythe Rogers was professor of chemistry in Cincinnati College during the four years of its existence. With his brother, Robert Empie, he wrote notes and additions to the seventh edition of Edward Turner's *Elements of Chemistry*. Gross said of James Blythe Rogers that "he was a brilliant teacher, and decidedly the most excellent lecturer on chemistry I have ever listened to." [6] He was dean of the faculty of Cincinnati College during the 1837-38 session. When this institution seemed destined to close, James B. Rogers resigned and went to Philadelphia where in 1847, he was elected to the chair of chemistry in the Medical Department of the University of Pennsylvania.

LANDON CABELL RIVES. Landon Cabell Rives (1790-1870), of a prominent Virginia family, was the professor of obstetrics and diseases of women and children. His academic education was obtained at the College of William and Mary. In 1821 he wrote a thesis, "Turpentine in Disease," and was graduated from the Medical Department of the University of Pennsylvania. Unlike his associates he rarely wrote for publication. He edited John Lizars: *Anatomy of the Brain* (Cincinnati: H. W. Derby, 1854). He was the last dean of the Medical Department of Cincinnati College, 1838-39. Gross stated that Rives "discharged well the duties of his chair, was popular, and commanded general respect by the gentleness and urbanity of his manners." [7]

JOHN POLLARD HARRISON. John Pollard Harrison (1796-1849), a native of Louisville, was professor of materia medica. In 1815, he had begun the study of medicine under the most prominent physician in Louisville, John Croghan, M.D., a graduate (1813) of the University of Pennsylvania.

[6] Gross: *Autobiography*, Vol. I, p. 67.
[7] *Ibid.*, Vol. I, p. 69.

After four years apprenticeship, Harrison entered the University of Pennsylvania from which he was graduated, M.D., in 1819. His thesis was entitled "Analogies of Plants and Animals." Active in the formation of the Louisville Hospital, Harrison began in it a series of formal medical lectures, the first of their kind advertised in Louisville.[8] Early in 1835, Harrison went to Philadelphia to practice and teach. Shortly thereafter, he accepted a professorship in Cincinnati College where he taught until its suspension. He then accepted a professorship in the Medical College of Ohio in which he taught until his death. Though not approaching either Drake or Gross in the amount and scope of his writings, Harrison was easily third in output of the faculty of Cincinnati College. His *Elements of Materia Medica and Therapeutics* (2 vols., 1845) received considerable attention. Unfortunately it was redundant and based on many previously discarded theories. Gross stated that Harrison ". . . had culture, with enthusiasm and earnestness in the lecture room, and was popular with the students; but he was essentially a weak man, an imitator, as a writer and lecturer, of the inelegant styles of Caldwell and Chapman, and like them, a hide-bound solidest—men who do not think it possible for the blood to be endowed with the slightest vitality." [9]

JOHN LEONARD RIDDELL. Believing that botany should be taught as a special branch to medical students, Drake recommended the appointment of John Leonard Riddell (1807-67) as lecturer on botany and adjunct professor of chemistry. Riddell was especially well qualified, having received both A.B. and A.M. degrees from the Rensselaer Polytechnic Institute. His appointment to the lectureship on

---

[8] John P. Harrison: "Medical Tuition," *Louisville Public Advertiser,* IX, No. 876:p. [2]—c. [5], Feb. 28, 1827.

[9] Gross: *Autobiography,* Vol. I, p. 69.

botany undoubtedly resulted from several papers on the subject published in Drake's medical periodical and on his
Synopsis of the Flora of the Western States (Cincinnati,
1835), a book of 116 pages. While teaching, Riddell at the
same time matriculated in the college and was graduated,
M.D., in the first class (1836). Shortly after graduation he
accepted the professorship of chemistry in the Medical Department of the University of Louisiana (now Tulane University), a position he held until his death.

Even though only a few months elapsed between the
announcement of the establishment of the Medical Department of Cincinnati College and its opening, sixty-six students
matriculated. An interesting side light to the practice of pad-
ding the number of students attending medical colleges is
shown by the following announcement by Drake:

> The reader is informed, that the Medical Faculty of the
> Institution, report none but pupils who are engaged in the
> study of Medicine with a view of becoming physicians, and
> such graduates as matriculate for the purpose of revising their
> studies, by an attendance on the lectures; consequently visiting
> physicians, druggists, dentists, teachers, portrait painters, and
> amateurs are not embraced in this catalogue.[10]

The stimulating influence of Drake and his associates is
apparent in the accomplishments of certain of the graduates.
Of the eighteen members of the first class (1836) to graduate,
four attained considerable prominence. William J. Barbee
(1816-92), after practicing medicine in Cincinnati for ten
years, became a teacher, a clergyman, and an author: *Physical and Moral Aspects of Geology* (1861); *The Cotton Question* (1866); *The Scriptural Doctrine of Confirmation*; and
many others. William K. Bowling (1808-85) became one of

[10] Daniel Drake, Dean: *A Catalogue of the Officers and Students in the
Medical and Law Departments of Cincinnati College; First Session: 1835-6*
(N. S. Johnson, Feb. 1836), p. 6.

the founders of the Medical Department of the University of Nashville. He started (1851) the *Nashville Journal of Medicine and Surgery* and in 1875 was president of the American Medical Association. After practicing medicine for several years, Edward Thomson (1810-70) entered the Methodist ministry, was later elected a bishop, and became president of Ohio Wesleyan College. In 1853, he wrote a deeply appreciative biographical sketch of Drake.[11]

As previously mentioned, a fourth member of the 1836 class, John L. Riddell, was elected to the professorship of chemistry in the Medical Department of the University of Louisiana. Here he continued his botanical studies, of which several reports were published. A genus of plants was named for him. In 1838 he made a scientific exploration of Texas and, shortly thereafter, was appointed melter and refiner of the New Orleans mint. So far as I have been able to determine, Riddell was the first in the United States to devise a binocular microscope.[12] By the use of both eyes he apparently obtained stereoscopic effects. His descriptions indicate that the magnifications were not great. He speaks of observing, instead of "amorphous" masses, the "delicate superimposed membranes, with intervening spaces, the thickness of which can be correctly estimated. . . . In brief, the whole microscopic world, as thus displayed, acquires a tenfold greater interest in every phase, exhibiting, in a new light, beauty and symmetry indescribable." [13] Riddell's work in the development of microscopic technique was recognized in the United States and also in Europe.

The second session (1836-37) of the Medical Department

[11] Thomson: "Recollections of Dr. Drake."
[12] J. L. Riddell: "Notice of a Binocular Microscope," *American Journal of Science and Arts* (New Haven, Conn.), 2nd. Series, XV:68, Jan. 1853. His paper read before the American Association for the Advancement of Science appeared in *New Orleans Medical and Surgical Journal*. X:321-27, Nov. 1853.
[13] *Ibid.*

of Cincinnati College opened with a class of eighty-five.
There were 125 students on hand for the third session and
112 for the fourth. In 1836, the board of trustees re-established the academic department. Drake's vision was that of a
large university with many departments. Through his influence the Reverend William Holmes McGuffey was elected
president. He also became professor of "Intellectual and
Moral Philosophy and the Evidences of Christianity." There
were at this time seven full professors and an assistant in the
medical school; as well as a professor of law and others from
the academic department. In the "academical" section, ten
professors (three of whom taught in the Medical Department) and two instructors are listed. The catalogue for
1837-38 listed 325 students in all departments. Commenting
on the flourishing condition of the institution, Wm. R.
Morris, president of the board of trustees, stated that among
the students:

> Order, subordination, morality, and love of study, prevail,
> in a degree equal to any previous example. The various pro-
> fessors and tutors are working men, of high capacity, untir-
> ing diligence, and warm devotion, to their respective duties.
> They consider themselves as permanently attached to the
> College—destined to sink or swim with its fortunes;—and,
> every circumstance seems to announce, their efforts must
> speedily raise it to the rank of the highest Universities in the
> union.[14]

Two factors hampered Cincinnati College from its opening, lack of funds and hospital facilities. There were a few
small donations from the townspeople but almost the entire
cost of renovating the dilapidated college building and equip-
ping it was borne by the professors in the Medical Department. The trustees attempted to secure admittance of their

[14] Cincinnati College: *Catalogue* (2nd ed., Cincinnati: N. S. Johnson,
1838), p. 16.

medical students to the Commercial Hospital on an equal basis with the pupils of the Medical College of Ohio. The latter would have benefited since the student admission fees to the hospital went into the college funds. However, the professors of the Medical College of Ohio bitterly opposed admission of students of Cincinnati College and the Township Trustees, in charge of the hospital, acquiesced.

At this time the U.S. Treasury Department had a commission in the area investigating suitable sites for "marine" hospitals in the Mississippi Valley. A contract was obtained from the secretary of the treasury by which the surveyor of the Cincinnati port was ordered to send sick boatmen to the Cincinnati College Hospital. The medical faculty immediately rented a commodious building across the street from Cincinnati College and converted it into a hospital. Drake now consolidated his eye infirmary with the new hospital. The need for a teaching hospital connected with the college was thus adequately met. However, within less than a year sufficient political pressure was brought by the Medical College of Ohio group to have the surveyor of the port given discretionary power over the boatmen. Since he was responsive to the wishes of those in control of the Medical College of Ohio, boatment were no longer sent to Drake's hospital, and the result was loss of revenue. The faculty continued the hospital, financing it from fees received from their students. The burden finally became too great and, in February 1839, the Cincinnati College Hospital closed along with Drake's eye infirmary. The latter especially had benefited hundreds of indigent persons during its existence, 1827-39.

The next plan pursued by Drake and his associates was to petition the General Assembly of Ohio for an amendment to the Commercial Hospital Act whereby the faculty and students of Cincinnati College be admitted on an equal basis with those of the Medical College of Ohio. The amendment, after undergoing considerable discussion and alteration, was passed with the proviso that the Cincinnati Township Trustees be given discretionary powers. The incumbent trustees opposed the admission of the faculty of Cincinnati College. In April 1838, an election for Township Trustees was scheduled and two groups were nominated: one favoring the Medical College of Ohio and the other, followers of Drake. Electioneering was bitter and, during it, a scurrilous broadside (herewith reproduced) against Drake was issued. Trustees, openly opposed to Cincinnati College, were elected by a wide margin.[15]

Whether the initials "E. R. T.—J. B." on the slanderous handbill are those of its authors is an unsolved problem. No self-respecting person would have written it. Cincinnati directories furnish no clues as to the identity of "E. R. T." The "J. B." may have been Joseph Bonsall, a carpenter in 1828, a lumber merchant in 1831, and later a real estate agent. A Quaker, he seems to have forgotten his early training in associating with Medical College of Ohio group.

While Drake was in Columbus, Ohio (February 1839), petitioning the assembly, a private letter he had written in 1837 to Dr. Reuben D. Mussey, professor of surgery in the Medical College of Ohio, was published in the Cincinnati newspapers and copies were posted in public places.[16] The object of the publication was to prevent favorable action on the hospital petition. Although publication of the letter and the false emphasis placed on it failed in its primary object, it did serve to increase animosity toward Drake.

Reuben D. Mussey and Drake had been students at the University of Pennsylvania. In 1837, when Mussey was offered the professorship of surgery in the Medical College of

[15] Joseph Bonsall: *Controversy in Relation to the Medical Schools of Cincinnati* (Cincinnati: Isaac Hefley & Co., 1839), p. 19.
[16] Daniel Drake: "Letter To Professor Mussey," *Daily Advertiser and Journal* (Cincinnati), I, No. 107:p [3]—c. [1-2], Feb. 2, 1839.

To every Voter of Cincinnati Township:

Haste to the polls, my friend!
Our freedom is at stake!
You must the boon defend,
Against one DOCTOR DRAKE.

Rub open both your eyes,
For dreadful to relate,
The town is fill'd with spies
Employed by DOCTOR DRAKE.

Their persons they disguise,
While in the streets they wait
Like spiders catching flies—
The tools of DOCTOR DRAKE.

Unstop and turn your ears
At every step you take,
Till each good patriot hears
The schemes of DOCTOR DRAKE.

These schemes I long have known,
They've often made me quake, —
Indeed, I weep and moan,
To think of DOCTOR DRAKE.

The city is his prey,
Its blood his thirst can't slake,
Then to the polls to-day,
And *do up* DOCTOR DRAKE.

Let every shop be bolted,
Hang up the hoe and rake,
Or else we shall be *dolted*,
And sold to DOCTOR DRAKE.

The town will ne'er have peace,
Nor any comfort take,
'Till from among our *geese*,
We thrust out this Wild DRAKE.

But hard he is to drive,
On land he glides—a snake
With many joints and eyes,
The cunning DOCTOR DRAKE!

On water see him swim,
And not the surface shake,
All smooth and light and trim—
The treacherous DOCTOR DRAKE!

You take a deadly aim,
Your fouling-piece don't shake,
He sees the flashing pan
And dives! oh, DOCTOR DRAKE!

Deep in the stream he sinks,
No ripples mark his wake—
You watch till each eye winks,
But see no DOCTOR DRAKE,

Again your gun you charge,
And swear his neck you'll break;
Down stream you gaze at large,
Up stream pops DOCTOR DRAKE.

Then try percussion caps,
No flash, you know, they make;
Shoot all at once, my chaps,
And kill off DOCTOR DRAKE.

E. R. T.
J. B.

Fig. 8. *Broadside distributed in Cincinnati in April 1838.*

Ohio, he wrote his friend, the Reverend Calvin E. Stowe, inquiring about the stability of the college in comparison with that started by Drake. The Reverend Stowe requested that Drake answer, which he did on 15 August 1837. The letter was an honest and lucid, though brief, history of the situation with which the reader is already familiar. Drake's first cousin whom he had befriended and trained, John T. Shotwell, M.D. (1807-50), then dean of the Medical College of Ohio, brazenly asserted that his preceptor's letter evidenced that *he* was waging a war of extermination. Drake's comment was:

> Thus, by absolute falsification, my letter, which simply announced the *existence* of a war, between the two schools, a fact of public notoriety, is made to declare that *I* had waged it. Did any man of honor, ever before, resort to such a barefaced perversion of a printed document, to maintain an odious monopoly? Who ever before, saw a student, unblushingly falsify the plain language of his *own* preceptor, for the purpose of degrading him, in his absence, and that too, for selfish and sinister purposes . . . ? [17]

Juettner, in quoting Drake's letter, states that it was "ill-advised" and that, if Mussey permitted its publication, "it was an unpardonable breach of confidence." [18] It does not seem that simple and truthful statements of facts made at the request of an acquaintance should be termed, "ill-advised." The publication of the letter under the tense circumstances was without doubt a shameless "breach of confidence." Its truthfulness was no doubt what aroused the opposition to such fury.

It is difficult to single out from the many writings of Drake one which should be given first place for cogency, clarity and

[17] Daniel Drake: *The War of Extermination* (Cincinnati, 25 Mar. 1839), pp. 7-8.
[18] Juettner, pp. 166-67.

reasoning. Any one of a dozen would be in competition with the others. Garrison thought Drake's *Narrative of the Rise and Fall of the Medical College of Ohio,* "one of the choicest bits of medical humor in existence," and that the essays on medical education were the best ever written on the subject.[19] In addition to these and others which could be mentioned is *The War of Extermination,* occasioned by the publication of the letter to Mussey. Alban G. Smith, in the Vindex pamphlet, had declared that "war" had been prosecuted against him. Drake on his part, in *The War of Extermination,* showed that, from the day the Medical Department of Cincinnati College was started, attacks were constantly being made against it and more especially against him. He accepts the challenge and describes the fray lucidly with logical conclusions which are unanswerable. He pointed out that during the four years (1835-39) of Cincinnati College, medical students in Cincinnati were double their previous numbers. The Medical College of Ohio, therefore, had not been injured but had probably benefited by competition.

> [While seeking to advance faster than our rival] we stopped not to throw obstructions in *her* way; if we saw her rowers become weary and desert her for other vessels, we found, in the fact, no moral reason why we should relax in *our* exertions; if, in the third year of our existence we were ahead of her in the race, and in the fourth continued there, it was not that *we* went *too fast* but *she too slow.* This, then, is our offence, the crime for which we are arraigned before the public. We plead guilty, to the charge, but give in palliation, that the destinies of Cincinnati repose on the enterprise of her citizens, and that they in whose hearts the fires of emulation burn most glowingly, must always contribute most to the common glory.[20]

[19] Garrison, 3rd ed., pp. 465-66.
[20] Drake: *The War of Extermination,* p. 15.

Mr. Joseph Bonsall attempted to answer Drake, who replied in an article titled: *The War not Exterminated*. It is equal, if not superior, to the last-mentioned one. A single quotation will suffice:

> Sir, let me say that you have meddled with strife which concerned you not—that you have enlisted in the little trained band of calumniators, who have for a long series of years sought to raise themselves into distinction by assaulting my reputation, and let me tell you further that your fate will be like that of your predecessors. Four generations of them have already passed away, and that to which you belong, will strut its hour on the public stage and disappear. I am not to be put down by calumny, nor will I remain silent under it. My contempt for the charge of being quarrelsome, when I am but defending my right and reputation, is only equaled by the scorn, with which I look upon you and the faction you serve.[21]

The faculty of the Medical Department of Cincinnati College formed a partnership by which each held interest in the building, the apparatus, anatomical museum, library, and hospital. In 1837, Drake transferred his medical journal to the college, with Drs. Harrison, Gross, and himself acting as the editorial committee.[22] This arrangement continued in effect until the temporary suspension of the periodical with the issue for May, June, July 1838.

One aspect of the protean mind of Drake is seen in his awareness of the need for publicity and of proper public relations. In 1836, he and his associates in the Medical Department purchased the subscription list of a Cincinnati newspaper, *The Mirror*. The name was changed to *The Cincinnati*

[21] Drake: *The War not Exterminated*, column [4].
[22] Daniel Drake: "New Prospectus of the West," *West. Jnl. Med. and Phys. Sc.*, Hex. II, V:159-60, Apr., May, June 1837.

Chronicle, the organ of the college. Being unsuccessful, it was sold within less than a year.

Drake's hatred of his enemies did not always cease even after they had left the scene. In 1837, Alban G. Smith (Vindex) accepted the chair of surgery in the College of Physicians of New York. A portion of Drake's comment concerning him was:

> A smatterer in Anatomy—in Surgery a mechanic; a man whose fondest friends have not claimed for him either talents or science; who is profoundly ignorant of the grammar and orthography of his mother tongue; who is *not a graduate,* and could not, *on examination,* receive a degree, *even* from the college from which he was taken, or in which he was placed; who was elected into the former, on a recommendation designed as a hoax, who could not, and did not, sustain himself, even in *that* institution; who has been three times published as a liar in Cincinnati; and who left it without disclosing to his colleagues or the Trustees of the College to which he belonged, that he was about to decamp. It has been reported, *mirabile dictu,* that he had been *sent for* by the good people of New York, to supply the place of Mott and Bushe! Verily, to borrow an idea from Peter Pindar, medical skill must have been at a low ebb in that city, when they were driven to make *such* an importation. But New York is an importing city, and may sometimes mistake brass for gold.[23]

John Bell (1796-1872), editor of *The Eclectic Journal of Medicine* (Philadelphia), took exception to Drake's editorial by saying that he did not remember to have ever seen "such harshness of invective, or, rather virulence of abuse, directed against any individual. . . ."[24]

[23] [Daniel Drake], Editorial: "College of Surgeons . . . New York," *West. Jnl. Med. and Phys. Sc.,* 2nd Hex.: V:163-65, Apr., May, June 1837.
[24] [John Bell, editor]: "Medical Journals," *Eclectic Journal of Medicine* (Philadelphia), II:17, Nov. 1837.

Drake's reply to Bell's censure follows:

Exhortation to gentility of style.

Our friend, the Editor of the Philadelphia "Eclectic Journal of Medicine," in his November number, has read us a lecture for calling things by their right names. Now, this is in violation of all the laws of nomenclature and classification. Suppose a naturalist were to call "dog fennel" by the name "rose," would not all distinction be confounded? If we wrote in a certain style of a certain *quassi* [*sic*] professor, who in his floatings floated, *ex necessitate*, from this city to some other, we wrote according to the *fact*, and were not at liberty to employ any but appropriate terms. If some of these were coarse, they might, to use the language of Junius, be unworthy of *us*, but not inapplicable to the individual to whom they were applied. Our friend of the Journal of Medicine was once a straight-forward, up-and-down Tennessee Backwoodsman, and could have endured, without flinching, the utterance, upon a contemptible object, of whatever epithets might have been necessary to a just delineation. We fear that the taste of our friend is losing its backwoods simplicity, by long residence in a great city. It is flattering to us, however, that he still retains an affection for the West, and is willing to read homilies of gentility and refinement to his benighted and half civilized brethren of the Valley of the Ohio. We hope that having done this, he will turn his attention to the western adventurer, whom he has volunteered to blow up into a great man, and try to improve *his* language a little. He who spells hemorrhage in *four* different modes on one page, and winds up with a *flannen* roller, needs the tuition of our friend or some other school-master, and we hope for the honor of the institution to which he is now attached, will receive it. Our friend of the Journal has charged us with "virulence of abuse." Now, there *can* be no abuse as long as facts are stated. Our friend then virtually tells his readers, that we have not confined ourselves to facts! But how does he know this? Was he in Cincinnati during the sojourn of *his* friend among us? Is he prepared to point out a single statement made by us that is not literally true? If so, we invite him to do it. He shall have a reply, containing our proofs, to put in his Journal, that its readers may see the difference between our averments and the testimony under which they are made. That is the way to disgrace us. . . .[25]

As a member of the Medical Convention of Ohio, 1 to 3 January 1838, Drake was extremely active. Of thirty-five motions made during the meeting, he introduced fifteen. He was on eight of the committees reporting, being chairman of five. The most remarkable of the reports was that made by Drake: "On Defects in the Organization and Administration of the Medical Schools in the United States." Not a single one of the resolutions in the report has failed of fulfilment, though over half a century elapsed before they were all in force:

1. *Resolved,* That, in the opinion of this Convention, the sessions of the different Medical Schools, throughout the Union, are too short, and that they ought to be extended one month, and the students required to stay to the end of the term.

2. *Resolved,* That the number of Professorships is too few, and that ampler provision should be made for teaching Physiology, Pathological Anatomy, Pharmacy, and the Natural History of Medicines, Botany, comparative Anatomy, Meteorology, Medical Jurisprudence, and Mental Physiology.

3. *Resolved,* That, if practicable, our Medical Schools should be so organized, as that Students in their first course, would have their attention chiefly directed upon special Anatomy, Physiology, Chemistry, Pharmacy, and the other elementary branches; and their second upon Pathological Anatomy, Therapeutics, the practice of Physic, Surgery and Obstetrics.

4. *Resolved,* That, in admitting Candidates to examination

[25] [Daniel Drake]: "Exhortation to gentility of style," *West. Jnl. Med. and Phys. Sc.*, 2nd Hex., V:499-500, Oct., Nov., Dec. 1837.

for degrees, a stricter regard than is at present shown, should be had to their preliminary education.

5. *Resolved*, That the practice of graduating young men before they are 21 years of age should be abandoned.

6. *Resolved*, That no Pupil ought to be graduated before the end of four years, from the time he commenced the study of Medicine.

7. *Resolved*, That, if the various Schools of the Union, were to send representatives to a meeting at some central point, to confer together, many of their existing defects, by a simultaneous co-operative effort, might be successfully remedied, and that we, respectfully, recommend such a Convention to be held. Till when it would not be practicable, nor should it be expected that any single institution will attempt the reforms which are here proposed.

8. *Resolved*, That the corresponding Secretary be instructed to send a printed copy of the proceedings of this Convention, to all the Medical Institutes of the United States, with a letter, calling the attention of their Professors to these Resolutions.[26]

After four years, the Medical Department of Cincinnati College closed, having enrolled a total of 388 students. No other institution in the United States has achieved such success in so short a time. It was successful, yet it failed. Various theories for its closing have been advanced, the simplest one being lack of funds. Basically this reason was only partly correct. There is contemporary proof that Samuel D. Gross is wholly wrong in his discussions of the closing. In his *Autobiography*, Gross wrote:

> The retirement of Dr. Drake caused angry remarks on the part of certain members of the Faculty, chief of whom was McDowell, his brother-in-law. Drake knew how difficult it would be to build up a great school in the existing state of

[26] Medical Convention of Ohio: *Journal of the Proceedings*, 2nd. Session, Jan. 1838 (Cincinnati: Pugh & Dodd, 1838), p. 17.

affairs, and the offer from Louisville, with the promise of rapid reward, was too tempting to be resisted. He was poor, had had numerous reverses, and needed assistance. Besides, he had lost nearly all his practice, and was not likely to regain it if he should remain in Cincinnati.[27]

Gross wrote in another place in his *Autobiography*: "After a successful career of four years this school Cincinnati College was permanently suspended—a result due mainly to the withdrawal of its originator, who, influenced by a guarantee, accepted a chair in the Louisville Medical Institute, thus leaving in the lurch all his late colleagues." [28]

The only possible explanation for these erroneous statements accusing Drake of deserting the others is that Gross at the time was senile. He certainly had no cause whatever during their years of intimate association to doubt Drake's honesty and uprightness; hence he could not have written such slander had he been normal. He completely ignored the fact that he *himself* had resigned (21 August 1839) before the Trustees of Cincinnati College suspended its Medical Department and, of course, while Drake was still a professor therein.

The events leading up to the suspension of the medical school are a matter of record. Shortly after the 1839 commencement, 3 March, Drs. Rogers and Parker went East after each had intimated he might resign since the Commercial Hospital had been closed to the faculty. On 16 July 1839, the resignation of the professor of surgery, Willard Parker, was received. Drake immediately made efforts to secure a replacement but was unsuccessful. Samuel D. Gross resigned on 21 August 1839 and on the following day Landon C. Rives sent in his resignation. On 24 August 1839, the trustees: "*Resolved*, That all the professorships in the Medical section

[27] Gross: *Autobiography*, Vol. I, pp. 65-66.
[28] *Ibid.*, Vol. II, pp. 266.

of this College, be and the same are hereby declared vacant." [29]

At the same time a committee of the trustees was appointed to secure suggestions from the former Professors concerning plans for re-organization. The committee reported the consensus to be that "the re-organization of the Medical Department is wholly impracticable. . . ." Drake resigned his professorship on 27 August 1839 and on this same day the trustees: "*Resolved*, That the Medical Department of the Cincinnati College, be and the same is hereby suspended." [30]

The news of the suspension of the Medical Department of Cincinnati College probably reached Louisville on 28 August 1839. The professors of the Louisville Medical Institute took immediate action to secure the services of Drake. The trustees sent the dean, Dr. Charles Wilkins Short, to Cincinnati to personally try to secure Drake's acceptance of a professorship. Following the report of Short's successful interview, Drake was unanimously elected, 7 September 1839, professor of clinical medicine and pathological anatomy, a chair especially created for him. The Louisville Medical Institute thereby had eight full professors, the largest number in any western school and more than most of those in the East.[31]

Study of contemporary source material reveals conclusively that at least three factors entered into the dissolution of the Medical Department of Cincinnati College:

1. Lack of endowment, with steadily increasing deficits and no hope of a reversal of the trend.

2. The failure to secure hospital affiliation for bedside instruction.

---

[29] Cincinnati College: "Suspension of Medical Department," *Cincinnati Chronicle*, III, No. 5:p. [2]—c. [1], Sept. 14, 1839.

[30] *Ibid.*

[31] Horine: "A History of the Louisville Medical Institute . . . 1833-1846."

3. The institution would doubtless have continued the struggle for existence for a few more sessions had it not been for the calamitous resignation of the professor of surgery in midsummer. It was manifestly impossible to secure a successor for this important professorship in time for the 1839-40 session.

The outstanding success of the Medical Department of Cincinnati College focused attention on the deplorable condition of the Medical College of Ohio. The trustees of the latter institution were forced to make drastic changes. Even with the re-organization, bickerings and intrigues in the faculty continued, though the calibre of medical instruction was greatly improved.

From 1819 through 1839, the malicious mastermind instigating the repeated attacks on Drake was John Moorhead. From his open declaration of "war" in 1819, he harassed Drake both openly and covertly. His vindictiveness was boundless. His name is known to us today, not because of one even mediocre contribution to medical progress, but as the consequence of his harassment and persecution of Daniel Drake.

Throughout the whole course of these controversies we find Drake placed on the defensive, never their instigator. The fact that he was so aggressively resourceful in outwitting Moorhead and his associate calumniators has doubtless led to the erroneous assumption of Drake's quarrelsomeness. As stated elsewhere, I have yet to find a single instance in which he was the aggressor.[32] When aroused, he fought tenaciously and used all types of ammunition except falsification. He did not easily forget and sometimes followed the trail of a defeated enemy.

[32] Emmet F. Horine: "Cincinnatian Unique: Daniel Drake," *Cincinnati Journal of Medicine*, XXXIII:200-10, 222-38, May 1952.

16

*[There is no era in the life of a physi-
cian] in which his self-complacency is so
exalted, as the time which passes between
receiving his diploma with its blue rib-
bon, and receiving crepe and gloves, to
wear at the funeral of his first patient.*[1]

Louisville, 1839-46

THOUGH TEACHING in Louisville, Drake maintained his official
residence in Cincinnati. During the winters in Louisville, he
went at least once a month on week ends by boat to visit his
daughters. The older, Elizabeth Mansfield, had married
(1839) Alexander Hamilton McGuffey (1816-96), lawyer,
author, and brother of the originator of the famous readers.
The younger daughter, Harriet Echo, was the wife (M., 4
June 1839) of James Parker Campbell (1806-49), a businessman and packer of meats. Since 1825, Drake had fathered as
well as "mothered" his children and his interest in and affection for them were indeed great.

Drake's acceptance of a professorship in the Medical Institute of the City of Louisville was wise. John Moorhead and
his spiteful friends were left behind. With much larger classes
Drake's income was far greater than it had ever been from
previous professorships. He was again associated with industrious and competent teachers. Compared to the storm-
wracked Cincinnati experience, the Louisville period was like
sailing into the calm sea of a well-protected harbor.

Three of his associates in Louisville, Charles Caldwell, John

[1] Daniel Drake: "Traveling Letter from the Senior Editor," *West. Jnl. Med.
& Surg.*, N.S., II:355, Oct. 1844.

Esten Cooke (1783-1853), and Charles Wilkins Short were graduates of his own alma mater, the University of Pennsylvania. The other members of the faculty were Joshua B. Flint (1801-64), a Harvard graduate; Henry Miller (1800-74) of Transylvania; Jedediah Cobb (1800-60), A.B. of Bowdoin and M.D. of Harvard; and Lunsford Pitts Yandell, Sr., of the University of Maryland.

In Transylvania University, Drake had lectured with Caldwell and Short and, in the Medical College of Ohio, with Cobb. Lunsford P. Yandell, Sr., had been one of his pupils in 1823-24. Drake had known Miller in Lexington. Therefore, the only members of the institute faculty with whom he was unacquainted were John Esten Cooke and Joshua Barker Flint.

In Louisville as in Lexington, Charles Caldwell claimed to have founded the medical school. In neither place was this true though, in both places, he was helpful. The Medical Institute of the City of Louisville was chartered in 1833. It was not opened then since a full faculty could not be obtained. In the mid-1830's, Benjamin W. Dudley, professor of surgery and anatomy in Transylvania University, secretly proposed transferring the Medical Department to Louisville since he was having increasing difficulty in obtaining anatomical material. When this suggestion leaked from a faculty meeting, the trustees and other Lexingtonians voiced vehement disapproval. Dudley disavowed the plan and preferred charges against Caldwell and Yandell as conspirators. Caldwell was summarily dismissed. Following this action, the trustees then declared all chairs vacant in the medical school. As the turmoil was beginning, Caldwell went to Louisville where, on 30 March 1837, he delivered a stirring address on the advantages of a medical institution. The mayor and City Council immediately furnished a site and $30,000 for a building and an additional $20,000 for laboratories, apparatus, and a library. Angry with the trustees for declaring all chairs vacant, John Esten Cooke and Lunsford P. Yandell, Sr., accepted professorships in Louisville. Thus the upheaval in Lexington in 1837 resulted in the immediate opening of the Louisville Medical Institute, now the School of Medicine of the University of Louisville.

Rivalry between the Lexington and Louisville institutions became intense. The Louisville school rapidly forged ahead and during the 1849-50 session enrolled 376 students compared to 92 in Transylvania. At this time the Lexington faculty, aided by Joshua B. Flint who had resigned from the Louisville Medical Institute in 1840, "invaded" Louisville and established the Kentucky School of Medicine. Summer sessions were held in Transylvania and winter courses were given in Louisville, with several of the professors teaching in both institutions. In 1857, the Medical Department of Transylvania was closed. The separately managed Kentucky School of Medicine in Louisville was continued until it merged with the University of Louisville in 1908. The claim repeatedly made by the Kentucky School of Medicine during its latter years that it was the "lineal descendant" of the Medical Department of Transylvania cannot be substantiated. To claim descent merely through having employed several professors in common for a few years is ridiculous. The fact is that the Kentucky School of Medicine was from 1850 to 1852 the "Medical Department of the Masonic University of Kentucky." The college in Lagrange, Kentucky, sponsored by the Masonic Fraternity, was closed, leaving the Louisville "Department" without sponsorship. Then it was that the General Assembly of Kentucky granted articles of incorporation to the Kentucky School of Medicine as an independent institution.[2]

[2] Kentucky School of Medicine: *Annual Announcement for Session 1852-53* (J. B. Flint, Dean), p. 3.

The trustees of Transylvania University never at any time had any connection whatever with the Louisville school.

In 1838, Charles Wilkins Short resigned from Transylvania and accepted the professorship of materia medica and medical botany in Louisville. At the time he wrote a letter of explanation to his brother-in-law, Benjamin W. Dudley. This letter is in the possession of The Filson Club (Louisville), with a notation stating that Dudley refused to accept delivery. This is somewhat typical of Dudley who was easily angered and usually expressed himself with considerable heat. Operating before the discovery of anesthetics, he is reported to have said: "Let them scream—it is a relief of nature." However, if the patient struggled, his voice changed to a stern command: "Be still, Sir, or I'll send your soul to Hell in half a second!" [3]

JOSHUA BARKER FLINT. Joshua Barker Flint, the professor of surgery, received an A.B. from Harvard in 1820. He then became the private pupil of Dr. John Collins Warren who later (1846) publicly demonstrated the use of ether in surgical operations. Flint was graduated in medicine from Harvard in 1825 and was one of the founders of *The Medical Magazine* (Boston) in 1832. Through the recommendation of his preceptor, Warren, who declared Flint was one of the best qualified surgeons in the United States, he was given a professorship in Louisville. In 1838, Flint was sent to Europe for the purpose of purchasing a library and apparatus for the institute. The late Captain Alfred Pirtle (1837-1926), president of The Filson Club, who had been acquainted with Flint, once told me that he was "a perfect gentleman with a most pleasing personality." Somewhat frail in health, Flint's

---

[3] Waller O. Bullock: "Dr. Benjamin Winslow Dudley," *Ann. Med. Hist.* N.S., VII:201-13, May 1936.

practice, studies, and professional duties were so onerous that little time was left for writing. At least six of his introductory addresses were printed in addition to his presidential address before the Kentucky State Medical Association in 1859. He edited and prepared notes of the second London edition of Robert Druitt's *Principles and Practice of Modern Surgery* (Philadelphia, 1842). From his preceptor, John Collins Warren, Flint learned of ether and became the first surgeon in the West to use it in operating.

JEDEDIAH COBB. Quiet, unassuming, and capable, Jedediah Cobb entered the Medical College of Ohio in 1824 as professor of the theory and practice of Medicine. The following year he became professor of anatomy and taught the subject for the remainder of his life. His part in Moorhead's war against Drake is not clear, though of necessity he had to co-operate with the trustees of the Medical College of Ohio. He once furnished them with a letter, 4 December 1833, replete with rumors. Drake quoted the letter and commented as follows:

> Professor Cobb's certificate is a choice mess of stuff for a gentleman to put his name to. Several students, whose names are not given, in a tavern not designated, told a Mr. Ford, who told Mr. Guilford, who told Dr. Cobb, who told the Trustees, who told the General Assembly, who told the Public,—that Dr. Drake had advised them to go to Lexington, for that the Cincinnati School was in a sinking condition and would not have 25 pupils! The whole is utterly false, whether these unknown students, a Mr. Ford, Mr. Guilford or the Professor was the original author.[4]

It is quite evident that Drake held no grudge against Cobb since they worked harmoniously in Louisville. In 1844, Cobb

[4] [Daniel Drake, ed.]: "The Medical College of Ohio," *West. Jnl. Med. & Phys. Sc.*, Hex. II, V, I:623-51, Jan., Feb., Mar. 1834.

was elected dean of the Louisville Medical Institute, a position held until 1852, when he resigned in order to return with
Drake to the re-organized Medical College of Ohio. Cobb was
not a writer; I have been unable to find any essay of importance written by him.

HENRY MILLER. Kentuckian by birth and education,
Henry Miller had been elected to a professorship in the Louisville Medical Institute when chartered in 1833. He resigned
in 1837, but was immediately re-elected professor of obstetrics
and diseases of women and children. Miller was a forceful
but not a voluminous writer. His *Theoretical and Practical
Treatise on Human Parturition* (Louisville) appeared in
1849. A second edition with the title changed to *The Principles and Practice of Obstetrics* (Philadelphia) was published
in 1858. He was the first Kentuckian to make use of anesthetics in parturition. In 1859 Henry Miller was elected president
of the American Medical Association.

CHARLES WILKINS SHORT. Charles Wilkins Short, of a
prominent Kentucky family, became acquainted with Drake
about 1812 through his brother, Judge John Cleves Short.
Their uncle, William Short, "received from Washington,
with the unanimous approval of the Senate, the first appointment to public office conferred under the Constitution of the
United States." [5] During Thomas Jefferson's residence in
France, William Short was his private secretary and his
"adopted son." Short succeeded his "second father" as chargé
d'affaires at the Court of Louis XVI. Later he was minister
president to the Netherlands and, finally, commissioner pleni-
potentiary to Spain. During his residence in France, William
Short became "the hero of the most romantic love affair in

[5] S. D. Gross: *Biographical Sketch of Charles Wilkins Short* (Philadelphia:
Collins, 1865), p. 15.

which an American ever engaged." It was with Rosalie, Duchess de la Rochefoucauld, and lasted forty years without any suggestion of sordidness.[6]

In August 1816, Drake gave Charles Wilkins Short a copy of Correa da Serra's digest of Dr. Muhlenberg's catalogue of American plants. Dr. Short had this sixteen-page pamphlet bound with seventy-two blank pages upon which he wrote extracts from Jussieu's *Genera Plantarum secundum Ordines Naturalis*. The handwriting is uniform and easily legible, the extracts being in Latin and Short's notes in English.[7] His interest in botany continued throughout his life. At least six plants bear his name. He had succeeded Drake as professor of materia medica and medical botany when the latter was transferred (1825) to the chair of the theory and practice of medicine in Transylvania University. In 1828, Short, with John Esten Cooke as co-editor, established the *Transylvania Journal of Medicine and the Associated Sciences*. They continued it for four years when Lunsford P. Yandell, Sr., succeeded them. Short's most important writings were a series of essays on the plants of central Kentucky.[8]

JOHN ESTEN COOKE. The professor of the theory and practice of medicine, John Esten Cooke, taught haltingly although with candor, earnestness, and zeal. As early as 1827 he began to teach that all diseases had a common origin with accompanying derangement of the liver. Though fantastic, the simplicity of Cooke's theory and the uniform treatment

[6] Marie Goebel Kimball: "William Short, Jefferson's only Son," *North American Review*, 223:471-86, Sept., Oct., Nov. 1926.

[7] [Correa da Serra]: *Reduction of all the Genera of Plants . . . of the Late Dr. Muhlenberg* (Philadelphia: Solomon W. Conrad, 1815), with MS addendum by Charles W. Short, 1817. Author's collection.

[8] Charles Wilkins Short: "Prodromus Florulae Lexingtoniensis, secundum florendi aetatem digesta," *Transylvania Journal of Medicine and the Associate Sciences*, I:92-99, Feb. 1828; I:205-65, May 1828; I:407-22, Aug. 1828; I:560-75, Nov. 1828; and II:438-53, Aug. 1829. Short published four additional supplements.

with large doses of calomel and cathartics appealed to many
of his students who acclaimed him a discoverer. His *Treatise
on Pathology and Therapeutics* (Lexington, 1828), of which
only two (of three) volumes were issued, reveals a wide
variety of knowledge but no factual studies upon which to
base his theory. The reservoir is large, the overflow is absurd
speculation. Elisha Bartlett, the medical philosopher, wrote:

> The Cookite would be utterly at a loss, in regard to the
> state of his patient if he should be deprived of the aids which
> are furnished him by a daily and nightly inspection—ocular
> and nasal—of the stools. They constitute his guiding star, his
> rudder and his compass, they shed a clear light on all his
> pathway which but for them, would be darkness and uncer-
> tainty itself. . . . Professor Cooke's doctrine . . . is quite
> perfect . . . in its comprehensiveness, and simplicity. None
> of its predecessors, from methodism to homoeopathy, can
> rival it in these respects. . . .
>
> It can hardly be considered singular, that a pathological
> and therapeutical "ready reckoner" of such facile application,
> should have come into pretty general use. . . .[9]

Cooke's theories had been criticized from the start of his
lectures in Transylvania. The first of his colleagues in Louisville to publicly criticize them was Henry Miller:

> Enough has been said to prove that calomel is not *always*
> indicated, or the liver *always* deranged in disease; and al-
> though it may appear to some that such self evident truths
> should be stated as a proposition that cannot be gainsayed,
> rather than a corollary regularly deduced from premises;
> others we apprehend, will require additional argument, be-
> fore they can be prevailed on to abandon a theory and prac-
> tice, which so greatly economizes time and intellect. Physi-
> cians in abundance are known, who, having ample capacity

---

[9] Elisha Bartlett: *Essay on the Philosophy of Medical Science* (Philadelphia: Lea & Blanchard, 1844), pp. 237-41.

for higher attainment, rest satisfied with *bilious* and mercurial exclusivism in medicine; who as regularly prescribe a
dose of calomel whenever they are consulted, as they take
their daily meals; whose pathology never penetrates deeper
than the liver or ascends above the diaphragm.[10]

Cooke was a voluminous writer, especially on "fever" and
epidemics. Though an ardent Presbyterian, he defected and,
after six weeks of intensive study, wrote an essay of 216 pages
on *Presbyterian Ordination.*[11]

Cooke's queer theory could not long survive in a group of
such talented and progressive physicians as were his colleagues.
He voluntarily resigned in 1843.

LUNSFORD PITTS YANDELL, SR. The youngest mem-
ber of the Louisville faculty was Lunsford Pitts Yandell, Sr.,
classical scholar, educator, medical editor, geologist, paleontol-
ogist, and first dean of the Louisville Medical Institute. At
one time in later life, he held a pastorate in a Presbyterian
Church. The son of a physician, young Yandell received
early schooling at the side of his talented mother and later
at Bradley Academy, Murfreesboro, Tennessee. Obtaining
his degree in medicine, he practiced for about four years in
Murfreesboro, followed by a year in Nashville. In 1831 he
became professor of chemistry in Transylvania University.
He edited the *Transylvania Journal of Medicine* from 1832 to
1837. With Henry Miller and Theodore S. Bell (1807-84),
Yandell founded the *Louisville Journal of Medicine and
Surgery*, of which only two issues appeared, January and
April 1838. Late in 1839, Yandell joined with Drake to
establish *The Western Journal of Medicine and Surgery*, a

[10] Henry Miller: "Vulgar Errors in Medicine," *Louisville Journal of Medicine and Surgery*, I:268-75, Apr. 1838.
[11] John Esten Cooke: *Essay on the Invalidity of Presbyterian Ordination*
(Lexington: Reporter Office, 1829).

monthly. The first issue of this periodical appeared January 1840, with Drake the senior and Yandell the junior editor.[12]

Drake reached Louisville early in November 1839 and, on the evening of the ninth, delivered an introductory lecture, of which the following are the opening paragraphs:

Young Gentlemen—

We are not only strangers to each other, but strangers in Louisville, as most of us including myself, have sojourned in the city but a single week. We have come here to enter its new Medical Institute, you as pupils—myself as a teacher. Under such circumstances, I may be permitted, in the opening of my Introductory lecture to say a few words relative to the school.

The Medical Institute of the City of Louisville possesses three indestructible elements of prosperity:—First—Permanent and expanding hospital advantages; Second—equally permanent and ample means for the study of practical Anatomy; Third—such a relative geographical position as makes it easily accessible to the students of the Mississippi Valley, already numbering at least one fourth of the whole width the United States afford.

These are strong guaranties of rapid and continued growth, aside from the professors who compose its Faculty, and the large appropriations of money which have been made for its establishment. Of the former delicacy forbids my speaking; but of the latter, I must declare that they are unrivalled in the United States, and have this striking peculiarity that they have been made by the city in its corporate capacity. Louisville is indeed the only city in the U.S. that has founded a medical school. She may feel proud of this enlightened & liberal policy while every physician and student of medicine who loves his profession in the West & South, should honor it with an expression of praise.

It must be gratifying to the distinguished physicians and

[12] Horine: "Daniel Drake and the Origin of Medical Journalism West of the Allegheny Mountains."

civilians, who have guided the public spirit of the city upon this noble object, to find, that in the first three years of its existence, the Institute has attracted more numerous classes; than ever before assembled, in the three earliest sessions of any other medical school of the new world. The City of Louisville will henceforth through an indefinite period of time continue an emporium of medical learning—a prouder distinction in your opinion and mine than any conferred by her extended commerce—more than this I need not say— less, I could not do her justice.[13]

Early in 1840, Charles Caldwell preferred charges of incompetence against Joshua B. Flint, professor of Surgery. He was acquitted by the board of managers.[14] Caldwell covertly continued attacking him. At a meeting of the board of managers, with six members present on 13 April 1843, three voted to dismiss Flint and three were opposed. Later, two of the three members voting against his dismissal openly declared that he ought to resign.[15] Learning of the sentiments of the board, Flint resigned. Charles Caldwell in his *Autobiography* does not mention his connection with the affair and merely states that Flint was "removed by the Board of Managers, not on account of incapacity, but on account of a want of sufficient exertion and self-training."[16]

A bitter newspaper controversy followed the resignation of Flint. On 22 May 1840, twenty-one physicians attended a "Meeting of the Medical Faculty, of Louisville" with William A. McDowell (1795-1853), chairman, and Lewis Rogers (1812-75), secretary.[17] A preamble declared that the resident

[13] [Daniel Drake]: "Introductory," 9 Nov. 1839. MS in Library of Cincinnati General Hospital.

[14] [News item], *Boston Medical and Surgical Journal*, XII:159-60, Apr. 15, 1840.

[15] Daniel Drake, ALS, 17 April 1840, to Norvin Green. In author's collection.

[16] Caldwell: *Autobiography*, p. 405.

[17] William A. McDowell, Chairman: *Meeting of the Medical Faculty of Louisville*. Broadside owned by The Filson Club.

and practicing physicians of Louisville had been "injured and insulted" by "the most unjust and unprovoked aspersions" upon their "professional and personal character." Fourteen resolutions were adopted in which the potentialities of the Medical Institute were praised but the management and professors were severely censured. Efforts were made by the Louisville physicians to oust the managers and all of the professors. For a while the future of the institution was doubtful as is implied by Drake's editorial entitled "Our Delay":

> Dr. Franklin, or some other sage, has said, that he who is good at an *apology* is seldom good for any thing else. That we may dodge the point of this sarcasm, we shall take care not to make the best apology in the world, for the suspension of our enterprise from January to June. Such as it is—here it comes. When our first number was *in transitu* from the printing to the post-office, some *premonitory symptoms of disease* in the LOUISVILLE MEDICAL INSTITUTE, began to show themselves, and soon became so threatening that our publishers, with the prudence of sound business men, were inclined from the connexion between the *Journal* and the *Institute*, to lie by, till they should see whether the *forming disease*, was likely to inflict serious *organic lesion* on the latter. The *morbid action* took its course, the *vis conservatrix* awoke, a *crisis* occurred, *convalescence* followed, and *sound health* is restored. The first fruits of this recovery are four numbers of the journal at one birth, with the prospect of a regular monthly delivery, for an indefinite time hereafter.[18]

The selection of Samuel D. Gross to replace Flint did not lessen the attacks against the institute. Gross is definitely the target of the eighth resolution adopted by the Louisville physicians on 22 May 1840: *"Resolved,* That no physician

[18] [Daniel Drake]: Editorial, "Our Delay," *West. Jnl. Med. & Surg.,* I:359, Feb. 1840.

or surgeon, whose professional qualifications are not such as will enable him to subsist by the *practice* of his art, is fit *to teach it*."[19] In later years, Gross became internationally famous as a surgeon. However, prior to his appointment in Louisville, he had been in general practice in Cincinnati while teaching pathological anatomy, physiology, and medical jurisprudence.

Flint was unsuccessful in an attempt to establish "The Louisville Academy of Medicine," designed to give a comprehensive course of medical instruction. An editorial in the *Boston Medical and Surgical Journal* commented on this "Academy": "Some how it looks very much like the incipient of a rival institution to the Medical Institute. There is something a little war-like in the appearance, since Drs. *Flint* and *Bullitt* are prominent members of the board of control."[20]

In 1942, by a series of astonishing and accidental happenings, narrated shortly thereafter before The Filson Club, a collection of important Flint-Drake-Louisville Medical Institute items was obtained from the attic of an abandoned residence on the property of the Churchill Downs Race Track in Louisville.[21] The printed material obtained consisted of medical journals, pamphlets, and newspapers dating from 1840 through 1854. A number of statements of account, many receipted, and a packet of six letters were found under a covering of plaster from the ceiling. A few of the items were in good condition, though much was torn and badly stained. The blowing rains, snows, and dust of a century had entered through cracked and broken gable windowpanes. School boys had been caught ransacking the attic—the odors as well as the disorder were indescribable.

[19] *Medical Faculty*, broadside.
[20] [Editorial], "Louisville Academy of Medicine," *Boston Med. & Surg. Jnl.*, XXVI:257, May 25, 1842.
[21] Horine: "A Collector goes to the Race Track. . . ."

Among dozens of important historical items found were many sheets of a hitherto unknown pamphlet of twenty pages containing six numbered essays, each signed, "Vindex." [22] The author was answering a pamphlet which had been issued by the faculty defending themselves and the board of managers of the institute.[23] Vindex, in Essays One and Two, discussed the origin and lack of progress of the institute. In the third essay Henry Miller was scathingly censured for remaining in the faculty with a colleague while criticizing his erroneous theories. Miller was quoted as stating in 1836 that "Cooke's possession of the chair of Theory and Practice was a serious defect in the Lexington school." Vindex asked: "How is it here Dr. Miller? What made it a more serious defect for Dr. Cooke to have a chair in the Transylvania school than in the Louisville Medical Institute? You complained *very privately* not long ago, that the old man taught the same things here that he did at Lexington, and that there was no such thing as improvement in him. Why don't you cry out then . . . ?" [24]

Vindex, in Essay Four, is especially vitriolic in his remarks concerning Charles Caldwell and Lunsford Pitts Yandell, Sr.:

> The chair of "Institutes of Medicine" rejoices in the incumbency of the distinguished Dr. Caldwell, who complacently styles himself the "Father of the Institute," and with the proverbial sincerity of the speaker, has been nicknamed by one of his colleagues, the "Ajax and Ulysses" of the Faculty.

[22] [Wm. A. McDowell *et al.*]: Vindex: *Some Account of the Faculty of the Louisville Medical Institute, Supplementary to an Anonymous Pamphlet by the Same, Entitled "Some Account of the Institute"* (Louisville, City Gazette Office, 1842).

[23] Medical Institute of Louisville: *Some Account of The Origin and Present Condition* (Louisville, Prentice and Weissinger, 1842).

[24] Vindex: *Some Account* . . . pp. 8-9.

> *Distinguished* he certainly is, and that advantageously, in many respects, among his associates in the College, as Gulliver was among the Lilliputians—*distinguished* on both sides of the Alleghenies as a kind of Medical Ishmael—*distinguished* all over the country as an able pamphleteer: but distinguished nowhere and never, as a competent teacher or practitioner of medicine.[25]

. . . .

> When Dr. Yandell was appointed to the chair of chemistry in Transylvania, old Professor Troost of Nashville, from whom he had received a few preparatory lessons, used to boast, in a strain half humerous [*sic*] and half satirical, that he had done what no other man of his age had done—he had made a Professor of chemistry in *three weeks*.[26]

Through five and a half pages the invective of Vindex is turned on Daniel Drake and Samuel D. Gross. It is evident that while writing, the Louisville Vindex had before him the pamphlet of his Cincinnati predecessor. Vindex of Louisville is also repetitive, though he is a somewhat better grammarian, rhetorician, and logician than the one in Cincinnati. Many of the innuendos, erroneous statements and surmises against Drake are repeated by the Louisville writer. Without any proof whatever, it is asserted that Drake's occupancy of a chair in Transylvania caused a decrease in the number of students there from 281 in 1825 to 190, the following year. No mention is made of the tempest, then at its height, against President Holley.

The first paragraph of Essay Five follows:

> In an evil hour, under the influence of that *dementia* which proverbially portends destruction the Faculty of the Institute introduced into the School, that notorious DR.

[25] *Ibid.*, pp. 9-10.
[26] *Ibid.*, p. 11.

DANIEL DRAKE, having created for him, a new chair, with the title of *"Pathological Anatomy and Clinical Medicine."* We are not disposed to employ opprobrious epithets, but when a man has spent his life in the pursuit of notoriety—and Dr. D's aspirations never seem to rise above this—it is but due to his talents, to conclude that he has obtained his object, and become *notorious.*[27]

. . . .

It was said by some sagacious wag in Cincinnati, upon the accession of Gross to the Louisville School, that as Louisville had taken the head [Drake] away from the Cincinnati Medical College, she was welcome to its other extremity, Dr. Gross. Having devoted a great deal of space to the head, we shall now content ourselves with a very summary notice of the other extremity.[28]

The sixth section contained less severe criticism of the two other members of the faculty: Jedediah Cobb and Charles Wilkins Short. The essay closed by quoting the thirteenth resolution adopted at the meeting of the Louisville physicians on 22 May 1840:

> *Resolved,* That we do protest against the issue attempted to be made, that *dissatisfaction* with its present Faculty is synonymous with enmity to the Medical Institute; on the contrary, most sincerely do we desire that it may flourish and endure as a glorious monument of the enlightened liberality of the city, long after its now existing Professors shall have passed into oblivion.   V*index*[29]

My curiosity concerning the identity of the Louisville Vindex led to a careful comparison of his pamphlet with that published in Cincinnati and to a search for all possible clues.

[27] *Ibid.*, p. 12.
[28] *Ibid.*, p. 17.
[29] *Ibid.*, p. 20.

Manifestly Alban G. Smith, then in New York, was not the
author. Of the physicians in Louisville, the accumulated
evidence pointed strongly toward William Adair McDowell,
nephew of Ephraim, as our Vindex. No doubt he was ably
assisted by Joshua B. Flint and by his associate, Henry M.
Bullitt (1817-80). In addition, some evidence pointed toward
Theodore S. Bell as an adviser. The many loose sheets of the
scurrilous pamphlet were among items bearing Flint's name;
hence he doubtless arranged for its publication and distribution.

Flint, a Bostonian, sent copies of the Vindex essays to
friends in the East. A copy of the pamphlet fell into the hands
of the editor of *The Boston Medical and Surgical Journal*
who commented:

> *Faculty of the Louisville Medical Institute:–*
>
> A pamphlet of twenty pages, double columns, in small
> type, has come to our address, having for its title *Some
> Account of the Faculty.* . . . That it is cowardly to attack
> a respectable body of men anonymously, will be admitted,
> even by those who may envy the faculty of the Institute
> as much as the author of this cut-and-thrust pamphlet. . . .
>
> Such dastardly thrusts, however, as the maker of this
> pamphlet aims at their vitals, will never affect any changes
> for the better. We are offended with him for abusing the
> English grammar of our friend, Dr. Gross. Should the pro-
> fessor be roasted over a smelting furnace for not dotting an
> *i*, or forgetting to cross a *t*? It is a spirit of little criticism
> that prompted Mr. Anonymous thus to abuse his superior.
> It is a mosqueto [*sic*] stinging an elephant. Dr. Caldwell will
> bear long shots. Pomposity like his is bullet proof. Dr. Cobb
> is exceedingly amiable, and is therefore let off with only a
> few stripes. All the rest are pelted in a mass in some parts.
>
> Our own individual opinion upon the subject is, that some
> one or two disappointed, ambitious, intriging [*sic*], second
> rate medical men of Louisville, are expecting to raise them-

selves to distinction by overthrowing the present faculty. . . .[30]

No reply to Vindex by any member of the faculty of the Louisville Medical Institute has been found. Thomas W. Colescott, junior editor of the *Western Journal,* commented with approval on the Boston editorial and indicated that a "knavish triumvirate" had written the "filthy and leprous" pamphlet.[31]

On 23 December 1841, Drake organized the Physiological Temperance Society of the Louisville Medical Institute, with Lunsford P. Yandell, Sr., as its first president.[32] The objects of the society were: "To study and make known the causes of the excessive use by the people of intoxicating drinks and other narcotic stimulants; to inquire into the diseases of body and mind produced by them; devise remedies for the same, both curative and preventive; and to discourage intemperance by the example and influence of its members individually not less than their labors as a corporation." [33]

Members of the society pledged "total abstinence from all intoxicating drinks, for five years after subscribing the Constitution." [34] By early 1847, 7 officers of the institute and 610 students had joined. Honorary members were well-known workers in the cause of temperance. No mention of this society has been found after Drake left Louisville in 1849.

HENRY CLAY LEWIS. In 1844, Henry Clay Lewis (1825-50), from Yazoo City, Mississippi, on matriculating in the

---

[30] [Editorial]: "Faculty of the Louisville Medical Institute," *Boston Med. & Surg. Jnl.,* XXVIII:125, Mar. 15, 1843.
[31] [Thomas W. Colescott]; editorial, "Anonymous Pamphleteers," *West. Jnl. Med. & Surg.,* VII:319-20. Apr. 1853.
[32] Physiological Temperance Society, *Proceedings* . . . (Louisville, N. H. White, 1842).
[33] Reuben Anderson: *Annual Oration* . . . , Feb. 6, 1847 (Louisville, Prentice and Weissinger, 1847), p. 3.
[34] P.T.S.: *Proceedings,* p. 6.

Louisville Medical Institute, joined the Physiological Temperance Society and delivered the annual oration in February 1846, shortly before graduating.[35] Failing to obtain a practice on his return to Yazoo City, he moved to Madison Parish, Louisiana, where his home was on the Tensas River. Here Lewis began a series of semiautobiographical articles of a humorous nature under the pseudonym of "Madison Tensas, M.D., the Louisiana Swamp Doctor." These were published irregularly in the *Spirit of the Times* (New York) from 1846 to 1850. They were later issued in book form.[36]

Dr. John Q. Anderson of the Agricultural and Mechanical College of Texas has written three interesting articles concerning Lewis and, in addition, has a biography in process of publication.[37] Dr. Anderson believes that Lewis "ranks among the best of the Southwestern humorists." [38] Our interest in Lewis, of course, stems from his description of a medical student's life in the Louisville Medical Institute during Drake's connection with it. It is readily apparent that Drake made the deepest and most lasting impression on Lewis.

During the winter sessions of the institute, Drake occupied an apartment arranged for him in the college building at Eighth and Chestnut Streets. Occasional references indicate that he ordinarily went for meals to the home of his friend, Dr. George W. Bayless. At other times he may have prepared meals in his apartment; at least, we know he once enjoyed an apple pie there. In "Frank and the Professor," Lewis de-

[35] Anderson, *Annual Oration* . . . , p. 4.

[36] [Henry Clay Lewis]: *Odd Leaves from the Life of a Louisiana "Swamp Doctor,"* by Madison Tensas, M.D. (Philadelphia: A. Hart, 1850).

[37] John Q. Anderson: (a) "Henry Clay Lewis, alias Madison Tensas, M.D., The Louisiana Swamp Doctor," *Bulletin of the Medical Library Assn.,* XLIII:58-73, Jan. 1955; (b) "Folklore in the Writings of 'The Louisiana Swamp Doctor,'" *Southern Folklore Quarterly,* XIX:243-51, Dec. 1955; and (c) "Henry Clay Lewis, Louisville Medical Institute Student," *Filson Club Hist. Quart.,* XXXII:30-37, Jan. 1958.

[38] *Ibid.* (a): p. 72.

scribes Frank's trip to Drake's lodgings. Dr. Anderson rightly states that "the incident may well be largely fiction." [39]

Without knocking, Frank opened the door of Drake's apartment: "I found the old gentleman very complacent and easy, standing up in his night-shirt and making whisky-tod in a teapot, whilst he gave the last touch to an introductory oration for the P. T. S. [Physiological Temperance Society.]" [40]

Drake went to his bedroom to dress and Frank drank the "whiskey-tod." On the professor's return: "I asked him how long his wife had been dead, and whether there was any truth in the report that he was courting a widow on Fifth street; also, if he bought his Irish whiskey by the gallon or cask; he apparently did not hear these kind inquiries, but asked if I had a letter of introduction." [41]

Learning that Frank was from the South, where there was "plenty of chill and fever," Drake read several pages from his book. "He commenced reading a description of the Mississippi augur [*sic*], and cuss me if it wasn't so natural, I shivered all over; and the tears pop't out of my eyes like young pigeons out of a loft, when I thought of the last shake in far distant Massassip, sitting on a log fighting mosquetoes. . . ." [42]

During the reading a knock was heard which proved to be that of a beggar woman. "The widow commenced her piteous appeal again, when, quite overcome, I rushed from the room, followed by the voice of the ruined professor who feared that his reputation was forever gone." [43] The clear implication is that this was an assignation, especially since Frank, in introducing his tale, states that the name [Drake] ought now be

[39] *Ibid.* (a): p. 65.
[40] Lewis: *Odd Leaves* . . . , p. 72.
[41] *Ibid.*, p. 73.
[42] *Ibid.*, p. 73.
[43] *Ibid.*, p. 74.

written "without the first letter." The insinuation is clearly ridiculous. Had there ever been even the slightest evidence of lack of virtue, Drake's enemies would have vociferously published it. We can without hesitation dismiss this story by Lewis as malicious fiction.

17

Louisville, 1840-49

IN THE EARLY 1840's, as is well known, Abraham Lincoln became greatly concerned over his health, both mental and physical. He was at that time the roommate of Joshua Fry Speed, to whom he read a portion of a letter to Dr. Daniel Drake:

> Lincoln wrote a letter (a long one which he read to me) to Dr. Drake of Cincinnati discriptive [*sic*] of his case. Its date would be in Dec. 40 or early January 41.—I think he must have informed Dr D of his early love for Miss Rutlidge [*sic*]—as there was a part of the letter which he would not read. . . .
>
> I remember Dr Drake's reply—which was that he would not undertake to priscribe [*sic*] for him without a personal interview—
>
> I would advise you to make some effort to get the letter.
>
> Your friend tc
J. F. Speed[2]

I have followed unsuccessfully the advice of Speed. Not only have inquiries been made of many librarians but an appeal was made to collectors of manuscripts.[3] This, the most

---

[1] Drake: *An Introductory Lecture, on the Means of Promoting the Intellectual Improvement of the Students* (2nd ed., 1844), p. 13.

[2] J. F. Speed, Louisville, 30 Nov. 1866, ALS to W. H. Herndon. In MS Division, Library of Congress.

[3] Emmet F. Horine: "Daniel Drake and the Missing Lincoln Letter," *Manuscripts* (New York), IX:31-34, Winter 1957.

important of Lincoln letters, may have been destroyed by Drake on receipt or, if not, probably by his children.

In Louisville as in Cincinnati, Drake continued to address varied groups on scientific subjects. During the winter of 1841-42, he delivered a series of popular lectures on physiology, in which he described the different methods of teaching the blind. He urged that a school be established for them as had been done in Ohio. Soon after, one of his hearers introduced in the Kentucky legislature a bill for this purpose, which was passed.[4] The suggestion made by Drake thus resulted in the establishment of the Kentucky School for the Blind in Louisville on 5 May 1842, which school is still in existence.

In December 1840 Drake publicized the suggestion of the Medical Association of North Eastern Kentucky that a state convention be held.[5] A group of sixty-nine physicians met in Frankfort, Kentucky, on 11 January 1841. Officers were elected and a comprehensive constitution and bylaws were adopted. Drake was nominated as first vice-president but declined.[6] No scientific program had been arranged but, by request, James C. Cross (1798-1855) of Transylvania University delivered a discourse on "Geology" and Drake, one entitled, "A Memoir on the Disease Called by the People Trembles, and the Sick-Stomach or Milk Sickness. . . ."[7] This is the most exhaustive of several essays by Drake on this local malady. Fielding H. Garrison included it in his list of important texts illustrating the history of medicine. Drake's "Memoir" is indeed remarkable and, at the same time, dis-

---

[4] D.[aniel Drake]: Editorial, "Kentucky School for the Instruction of the Blind," *West. Jnl. Med. & Surg.*, V:237, Mar. 1842.

[5] D.[aniel Drake, editorial]: "Medical Convention of Kentucky," *West. Jnl. Med. & Surg.*, II:480-81, Dec. 1840.

[6] Convention of the Physicians of Kentucky: *Journal of* . . . (Frankfort, A. G. Hodges, 1841).

[7] Daniel Drake: "A Memoir on the Disease Called by the People Trembles," *West. Jnl. Med. & Surg.*, III:161-226, Mar. 1841. Also reprint.

appointing. Admittedly this evaluation is based partly on our present knowledge.

The disappointing feature of the "Memoir" is that although discussing white snakeroot (*Eupatorium urticaefolium*), one of the plants now known to cause the poisoning, Drake failed to investigate it sufficiently. An Ohio farmer, John Rowe, in 1838 had produced the disease in animals by administering a fluid extract of white snakeroot and also by feeding them the fresh plant. Drake spent a day with Rowe, who unfortunately had no written accounts of his experiments and observations. Drake arbitrarily dismissed the studies as "defective and inconclusive" since they "differed too widely from that in which the animal is likely to eat the poisonous plant in the woods; and the decision that the animals killed by it, *had* the Trembles, is far from conclusive or binding." [8] The additional fact that white snakeroot grew so luxuriantly and widely over the whole district accentuated his skepticism.

Despite the auspicious organizational meeting of the State Medical Society of Kentucky and the fact that the second meeting, scheduled for 12 January 1842, was given wide publicity by Drake, a quorum was lacking. The failure to carry on is the more deplorable since the bylaws stipulated only twenty as a quorum. Not a single officer was present. Drake and Gross from Louisville waited at the convention hall for half the day and then went to Lexington to see their friends at Transylvania. There is no record of any subsequent effort to vitalize the 1841 association. It was not until 1 October 1851 that another group of physicians meeting again in Frankfort organized the Kentucky State Medical Society which has had a continuous existence except for the period of the war between the states. [9]

[8] *Ibid.*, 213-16.
[9] Emmet F. Horine: *Sketch of the Kentucky State Medical Society* [in] *Papers Presented before . . . Centennial of . . .* (Bowling Green, Ky.: J. G. Denhardt, 1952).

Drake's life in Louisville was a busy one, occupied by lecturing, prescribing for his numerous students, in consultations and in writing. During vacations he was either travelling over the broad Mississippi Valley seeking material for his monumental work or writing in Cincinnati. His plans were announced either in the newspapers or in his *Journal:* "Dr. Drake wishes to inform those who may desire to communicate with him professionally or otherwise, that he will not return to Louisville till the commencement of the Medical Lectures, the first of November; till when he may be found at the home of his son-in-law, Alexander H. McGuffey, Third Street, opposite the Bazaar." [10]

Drake's lectures introducing his classes to the subjects to be taught each year were stirring appeals for industry, perseverance, and observation. His high ideals are always apparent. Many of his "introductories" were published by his classes. One of the best of these was delivered 4 November 1844: *On the Means of Promoting the Intellectual Improvement of the Students and Physicians of the Valley of the Mississippi.* Approximately half the lecture, arranged under ten subdivisions, is addressed to the students ("the juniors") beginning their formal medical studies. The remainder of the discourse, likewise divided into ten sections, is beamed especially toward the seniors.

> The love of pleasure and the love of science may coexist, but cannot be indulged at the same time; though in fact they are seldom united. A student should draw his pleasures from the discovery of truth, and find his amusements in the beauties and wonders of nature. He should seek for recreation, not debauchery. The former invigorates the mind, the latter enervates it. Study and recreation, properly alternated, bring out the glorious results of rich and powerful thought,

[10] Daniel Drake [card]: *Louisville Daily Journal,* XI, May 17, 1841:p. [2]—c. [7].

original conception and elevated design; dissipation wastes the whole, perverts the moral taste and impoverishes the intellect. One makes great men—the other wild men. One creates the sun—the other the comet of the social and scientific heavens. A fixed luminary, spreading life and light on all around us, is one—a wandering flashing and vanishing meteor, is the other.

. . . .

The case of a student who comes to the school with idle habits, is not hopeless; but he who *goes* from it without their being corrected, is incurable, and should be banished from the ranks of our noble profession.

. . . .

To gain knowledge, a man must observe; to get understanding, he must think.[11]

Drake's first published contribution to medical literature was the germ plasm of his medical classic on the diseases of the Mississippi. His *Some Account of the Epidemic Diseases which Prevail at Mays-Lick in Kentucky* (1808) is a significant and a very early contribution to epidemiology in the United States. It was the first discussion of the subject by a physician living west of the Allegheny Mountains. His second publication, *Notices Concerning Cincinnati,* appeared in 1810. In this small book not only was there a description of the city and surrounding territory but there was also an important section on the diseases of the region. A greatly expanded version of the 1810 booklet was his *Picture of Cincinnati* issued in 1816.[12]

In the third number of Godman's *Western Quarterly Reporter,* Drake announced (1822) his intention of writing a

[11] Drake: *Introductory* . . . , 1844 (2nd ed.), pp. 5, 6, 21.
[12] The imprint of the *Picture of Cincinnati* is 1815 although no copies were for sale until 16 February 1816.

"Treatise on the Diseases of the Western Country." [13] He requested information concerning twenty-six subjects. He wished to learn of the effects on health "produced by the soil, climate, diet and drinks, occupations and pursuits" of the people. He wanted to learn about premature decay of teeth as influenced by climate, negligence, indigestion, and tobacco. What were the effects of premature marriages and what prolongation of life resulted from migration to the western states? Drake also sought information concerning diseases observed among Indians and Negroes. What special diseases, if any, occurred at lead mines and salt works? Details of autopsies were requested.

It is clearly apparent that Drake's book was projected upon the broadest possible foundation. It included sociological studies in relation to diseases as well as geographical, topographical, hydrological, geological, meteorological, and botanical relationships. He fully recognized the value of the well-known principle that health is influenced by geographical conditions and climate. Drake's concepts were many times more comprehensive than were those of that historic figure of the fifth century, B.C., Hippocrates, in his justly famous essay on the influence of climate, water supply, and environment on health entitled: "On Airs—Waters—Places."

Unduly optimistic concerning the time required to complete his investigations, Drake concluded his request of 1 September 1822 as follows: "Communications made at any period before the end of the year 1823, will be in time to answer the purposes intended." However, as things were to turn out, Drake would have been safe in fixing a far later deadline than the end of 1823 for receiving information. No doubt his appeal for facts evoked only a limited response; but over the years there were also to be many other deterrent influences. These began with the machinations of his jealous enemies, his

[13] Drake: "Treatise on Diseases of the Western Country."

acceptance (1823) of a professorship in Transylvania University, and especially the death of his accomplished and beloved wife in 1825.

Not until March 1827 did Drake again publicly refer to his projected book:

> DISEASES OF THE WESTERN COUNTRY.—The undersigned, some time since, issued a circular letter to the physicians of the Mississippi states, soliciting from them such facts and observations as would aid him, in the composition of a history of the diseases which occur between the Gulph of Mexico and the lakes. He wishes now to say, that the work which he then announced, has not been abandoned, though deferred in consequence of various official duties; but that having divested himself of these, he hopes, at no distant time, to engage seriously in the undertaking. He returns his thanks to the gentlemen who have favoured him with communications, and will thankfully receive from others what may be adapted to the plan of such a work.
>
> DANIEL DRAKE, M.D.
> *Cincinnati, Ohio, March,* 1827.[14]

Drake's burns of 18 September 1828 followed by prolonged convalescence certainly delayed work on his cherished project. Following his recovery another hindrance arose from the acceptance of a professorship in Philadelphia. On his return to Ohio, the attempted establishment of the Medical Department of Miami University and, in 1835, the re-activation of Cincinnati College prevented any writing, except editorials and defensive pamphlets. Also his medical practice required a great deal of time. On 1 April 1836 Drake again announced plans for a "Medical History of the West." By this time he had begun to realize the magnitude of his undertaking and the impossibility of securing assistance from a sufficient number of reliable correspondents. He stated that he intended to

[14] *West. Med. & Phys. Jnl.*, I:69, Apr. 1827.

resort "to travelling as the only mode on which reliance can be placed. By visiting the principal localities on the great platform between the Lakes and the Gulph of Mexico, several important acquisitions can be made, either by direct personal observation, or by intercourse with gentlemen resident in different places. . . ." He promised that full credit would be given to all those assisting him and, therefore, the book would be "from the physicians of the West—a work of reciprocal instruction—somewhat novel in the manner in which it is gotten up—limited to the diseases of the region of which it professes to treat—not dependent on the written archives of the profession for facts, but copious in its acquisitions from contemporary observers."

Drake announced that he would leave Cincinnati about the middle of May 1836 and would first pass through Indiana, Illinois, and on into Missouri. From there he planned to go to Alabama, then Tennessee, Kentucky, and on into eastern Ohio, whence he would return to Cincinnati. For a man past fifty, this was a strenuous itinerary, considering the wretched accommodations and modes of travel: ". . . in skiffs, on rail roads, in stages, buggies, common wagons, on horseback, muleback and on foot, by night and by day. . . ." [15] We are fortunate in having accounts of many of the places visited, since Drake embodied some of his observations in editorials, "Traveling Memoranda, Traveling Editorials," which were published in his medical journal. Of these captions he once wrote that they might be interpreted in one of three ways: ". . . editorials for the benefit of travellers; editorials of such excellence and interest, that they will travel far and wide among the profession; or editorials written while travelling. It is in the last sense that we use the expression." [16] His alert-

[15] Daniel Drake: "Traveling Letters from the Senior Editor, No. X," *West. Jnl. Med. & Surg.*, N.S., II:545-48, Dec. 1844.
[16] Daniel Drake: Traveling Editorials, *West. Jnl. Med & Surg.*, VII:235-40, Mar. 1843.

ness to every phase of human activity and his keen powers of observation are clearly revealed by these editorials. Lucidly written and uniformly interesting, they were widely copied by editors of eastern medical periodicals.

Writing from St. Louis, on 6 June 1836, Drake gave an interesting description of the city, its inhabitants, the physicians and their Medical Society of Missouri, the first established west of the Mississippi. The St. Louis Hospital, managed by the Sisters of Charity, was "furnished and kept in a style of great comfort and neatness." He was not blind to general conditions: "The city is built on a gentle declivity, highly favorable to cleanliness; but its municipal authorities do not seem to pay any special attention to the 'art and mystery' of scavengering. . . ." [17]

By 15 July 1836, Drake was at the health resort of Monte Sano, two miles east of Huntsville, Alabama. [18] He was enthusiastic concerning this section of the state but critical of its use of feather beds:

> It is bad enough to sleep in feathers in summer, when one lives far in the north; but to be delivered over to such a fate, in the latitude of 34° is deplorable. Every where in this region, the traverns, and, in general, the houses of the people, are furnished with feather beds, for June, July and August, not less than for January. The medical gentlemen of this country should raise their voices against this absurd and enervating custom. A hard bed for hot weather referring rather to health or comfort, should be the motto of the whole South. [19]

He noted that many of the practicing physicians were not graduates of any institution, a situation which, of course, he deplored. Among those with degrees there were more graduates of the University of Pennsylvania than of Transylvania

[17] Daniel Drake: Traveling Memoranda, *West. Jnl. Med. & Phys. Sc.*, 2nd Hex., IV:311-19, July, Aug., Sept. 1836.
[18] *Ibid.*, p. 315.
[19] *Ibid.*, pp. 317-18.

University; and this surprised him. He had other remarks on the state of the medical profession:

> The practitioners south of the Ohio river, receive much better fees than those to the north; but then the price of everything in the former, is higher than in the latter. Nevertheless, even its ablest members are perpetually leaving it for more lucrative pursuits. . . . This premature renunciation of what men have laboriously qualified themselves to prosecute, is manifestly not without a cause. . . . The period of greatest usefulness, in the life of a physician, extends from 40 to 60—he is not a man of wisdom before the former, nor of energy, after the latter term. . . .[20]

A trip of 114 miles from Huntsville, Alabama, by stage-coach, brought him to Nashville, Tennessee, whence he wrote on 21 July 1836. The scenery and geological formations along the way are described. He mentioned the physicians of Nashville and suggested that a medical department should be organized as part of the university. He was especially warm in his praise of Gerard Troost (1776-1850), professor of chemistry, geology and mineralogy in the University of Nashville, whose collection of minerals was, at that time, the largest privately owned one in the United States.[21]

By 27 July 1836, Drake was in Harrodsburg, Kentucky, at Graham's Springs, whose "hundred lights, distributed throughout the immense group of cottages and illuminating the surrounding shrubbery, gave it the appearance of fairyland. . . ." [22] Incidentally, this, the most popular watering resort in the United States at that period, was owned by Christopher Columbus Graham who later, in his ninety-second year, wrote erroneously of the Richardson-Dudley duel. Drake tarried for a week at the springs and then went

[20] *Ibid.*, pp. 318-19.
[21] *Ibid.*, pp. 469-76, Oct., Nov., Dec. 1836.
[22] *Ibid.*, p. 474.

on to Lexington. From there, on 8 August 1836, he wrote of Transylvania University, of the medical societies, and of the Lunatic Asylum of Kentucky which he suggested as a model for similar institutions. Not only was the asylum excellently managed by its trustees and the experienced physician in charge but also "the accommodations are extensive and well arranged; the warming and ventilation are effected by proper means [and] cleanliness, quiet and order, are obvious in every part. . . ."[23]

Following the trip outlined above, Drake was too busily engaged in his professional work and that in behalf of Cincinnati College to continue actively gathering information for his book. In 1839 he left the turmoil of Cincinnati to find haven in Louisville where he could devote much more time to literary pursuits. In an editorial exhortation to the physicians of the Mississippi Valley to publish the results of their observations, experience, and experiments, he wrote: "There is not in the 'wide world' a nobler and richer field for original Medical and Physiological observation, than our beloved West and South."[24]

Drake made no further extensive trips until the summer of 1842 when he surveyed the Great Lakes and their bordering states. One result of this trip was a beautifully descriptive essay: "The Northern Lakes, a Summer Resort for Invalids of the South." With a moving and artistic touch, he pictured the lake region, methods and routes of travel, principal cities, and scenic grandeur. Originally published in his medical journal, it has been twice reprinted.[25]

After a strenuous winter in 1842-43, during which he usu-

[23] *Ibid.*, p. 476.
[24] Daniel Drake [editorial]: "Contributions to our Journal by Societies," *West. Jnl. Med. & Surg.*, IV:75, July 1841.
[25] Daniel Drake: "The Northern Lakes a Summer Residence for Invalids of the South," *West. Jnl. Med. & Surg.*, VI:401-26, Dec. 1842. Reprinted, Louisville: J. Maxwell, Jr., 1842; also with *Introduction* by J. Christian Bay (Torch Press: Cedar Rapids, Ia., 1954).

ally lectured eight hours each week, Drake left by boat for New Orleans. From here his letter again referred to the "Diseases of the West" which he believed could not be written "without extensive and patient personal observation." [26]

Drake was still in New Orleans on 10 March 1843, and mentions in his letter of that date (a portion of which was reprinted in the *Boston Medical and Surgical Journal*)[27] that he had auscultated the chest of the dying Seminole chief, Tiger Tail, and heard "the palpitations of his savage but patriotic heart." By the 30 March 1843, he had reached Pensacola, Florida, where he was impressed with its naval base. He then wandered through the tributaries of the Mobile River and on up to Tuscaloosa, Alabama, where he visited the university and was "introduced to its respectable Faculty." Everywhere he went the greatest hospitality was shown him. He was impressed with the harmony in the profession throughout the South, with the exception of New Orleans.

He described a peculiar method of using snuff which even today is occasionally practiced:

> The toilet vocabulary of this country has been enriched with the new and elegant word "dipping." A lady or a miss chews the end of a stick [preferably a section of a twig, one-fourth inch in diameter and four inches long, of green plum or cherry] until she converts it into a kind of brush or fibrous mop, with which she rubs her teeth and gums. At first she presses the powdered weed with a gentle hand, but becoming enamoured, at last touches so deeply as to consume a small bottle of snuff in a week. Whole families and whole schools of girls are said, with a small number of cleanly exceptions, to be given to this method of titillating their nervous systems; and by the time they are full grown, have

[26] Drake: Traveling Editorials, *West. Jnl. Med. & Surg.*, VII:235-40, Mar. 1843.

[27] Daniel Drake: "Diseases of the West," *Boston Med. & Surg. Jnl.*, XXVIII:308, May 17, 1843.

become so thoroughly impregnated with the powder, that their apparel might hang in a hot room the whole summer, without being touched by the moths. We know of but two advantages from the habit. 1st. It may render them insensible to the breath of the other sex, who begin the use of tobacco with the study of grammar. 2d. It can be made a substitute for whiskey (now falling into discredit) by those who are in affliction. . . . In our inquiries into the diseases of the sex of the south, we have already collected satisfactory evidence, that "dipping" is the cause of some and an aggravation to many more. We might refer to its effect on their breath, complexion, and cleanliness, but this we shall leave in the hands of the gentlemen who are immediately interested.[28]

In the spring of 1844 Drake again started southward and wrote from Mobile, Alabama, on 23 April. Next his itinerary carried him to New Orleans, thence into the Indian territory, Missouri, Illinois, and to the upper reaches of the Mississippi River whence he wrote on 11 October 1844. Five days later he was on a steamboat on the Ohio River, nearing home after a summer's journey of 6200 miles.[29]

During the winter of 1844 he began the actual composition of his book. On 9 December 1844 Drake wrote to his friend, Dr. John F. Henry, then living in Bloomington, Illinois, urging his removal to Kentucky. In closing he said: "My health is good. My duties in the school are heavy, being before the class 8 hours a week. I have at last got to work on my long contemplated book, but during the winter cannot get along fast." [30]

The vacation periods of 1845 and 1846 Drake spent in Cincinnati, actively engaged in writing his book. He appears

[28] Drake: Traveling Editorial, *West. Jnl. Med. & Surg.*, VII:472-73, June 1843.
[29] *Ibid.*, N.S., II:547, Dec. 1844.
[30] Daniel Drake, Louisville, 9 Dec. 1844, ALS, to Dr. John F. Henry. In author's collection.

to have been extremely methodical in all he did—and equally indefatigable. He was described as: "Seated at a large table, which was covered with opened volumes—journals from every section of the country, and embryotic manuscripts in every stage of development, from skeleton field notes, up to the perfected copy ready for the hands of the compositor. . . ."[31]

In September 1846 he wrote by request from Cincinnati an "Editorial Letter" to his colleagues in Louisville. He discussed "Coup de Soleil," autopsies he had witnessed of victims of typhoid fever, the summer heat, and "Quackery":

> The Queen City seems to have prostituted itself to the foul embraces of empiricism. Behold the gorgeous and glittering TEMPLE OF QUACKERY. On its dome there sports a gigantic black snake, fit emblem of cunning, and a silly coot (still fitter emblem of credulity,) is fluttering into the open jaws of the wily fascinator. Let us enter the upper halls of the mansion of imposture.
>
> Turn to the east; there is the den of the *"Reformed Medical College of Ohio"*, where doctors are manufactored out of the *raw* material. (N.B. The wool may be either coarse or fine, black, white or grey: the rolls warrented [sic] equally good and the same size.) Now turn to the west; there is the den of the rival *"Eclectic Medical Institute,"* whose lathe can *turn* dunces into doctors and not destroy the natural grain of the wood. The worthies who labor in these precious establishments agree in one thing only, that of slandering the regular profession; beyond this, they show their impartiality by villifying, that is, telling the truth, on each other.[32]

The summer of 1847 found Drake again assiduously seeking information in the field. He went through the mountains

---

[31] Thomas Wood: Review of A *Systematic Treatise* . . . , *Western Lancet* (Cincinnati), XV:685, Nov. 1854.

[32] Daniel Drake: Editorial letter, *West. Jnl. Med. & Surg.*, N.S., VI:357-64, Oct. 1846.

of West Virginia and Pennsylvania, then into western New York and on to Quebec, Montreal, and Toronto. While on the St. Lawrence River between Quebec and Montreal, he wrote his colleague, Charles Wilkins Short, that his journey, "now in its 10th week has been without any accident or sickness; and not, I think, unprofitable in reference to the objects for which it was undertaken." [33] He mentioned the kind reception he had received at the hands of the physicians and surgeons of Quebec. On Grosse Isle, thirty-three miles below Quebec, he visited the "Irish immigrant's quarantine ground:"

> The approach to it [the island] is picturesque and romantic; but the sights of human wretchedness, which open around you after landing, are most sad and revolting. I did not go among those who are counted well. The sick, with Fever, Small pox & Dysentery, amounting to more than two thousand, were more than sufficient to occupy my time. I passed thro' sheds and tents, which sheltered about half that number and made such examinations as were practicable. From necessity, they are very much crowded. All ages and both sexes are indiscriminately blended. The dying along side the living are a common sight. As many as 250 & even 300 have been buried in a single week. They are all lying in the very clothes they had worn on the voyage. . . .[34]

Returning to Louisville in November 1847, Drake busied himself with lectures and in arranging the notes of his summer's trip. In December 1847, he fell into a reminiscent mood from which emerged a remarkable series of letters to his children describing his boyhood, portions of which were used in Chapter 2. The summer of 1848 was spent in Cincinnati, where he continued work on his *Diseases of the Interior Valley of North America.*

[33] Daniel Drake, Saturday night, Augt 28th, 1847, ALS to Dr. Short. In author's collection.
[34] *Ibid.*

At the close of his lectures in Louisville, March 1849, Drake resigned his professorship. Five factors prompted this action: (1) He was nearing the age of retirement in the university; (2) He wished to have more time for writing; (3) The Medical College of Ohio was being reorganized (a perennial affair) and he had accepted the professorship of special pathology, practice, and clinical medicine (Moorhead had permanently returned to Ireland); (4) Both his daughters and their families were in Cincinnati; (5) Since his book was to be printed in Cincinnati, he felt it advisable to see it through the press.

Early in 1849, printing of his classic was started. When page 528 was completed, cholera again visited Cincinnati. Drake lost several members of his family and many of his friends. He himself became ill from what he described as "a protracted attack of my old malady of the brain." [35] These recurring attacks may have arisen from a chronic sinusitis as rhinologists suggest.

Printing was resumed by mid-September 1849 and on 24 April 1850, a copyright was obtained by depositing the volume in the Clerk's Office of the Ohio District.[36] This volume had 894 pages, containing four sections of sixteen, five, four, and eleven chapters respectively. The first section included a detailed description of the topographical and hydrographical features of the valley. In addition to a folding frontispiece map of the area, there were seventeen full-page plates showing various localities: Pensacola, Mobile, New Orleans, Montreal, Quebec, and intermediate points. In the second part, the climate, variations in the barometric pressure, winds, rain, snow, humidity, and electrical phenomena were carefully catalogued. In this part there were two plates and dozens of care-

[35] Daniel Drake, Cincinnati, 21 Sept. 1849, ALS to Dr. Charles Wilkins Short. In author's collection.

[36] Frederick R. Goff, chief, Rare Books Division, L.S. letter to author, 9 June 1947.

A

SYSTEMATIC TREATISE,

HISTORICAL, ETIOLOGICAL, AND PRACTICAL,

ON THE

PRINCIPAL DISEASES

OF THE

INTERIOR VALLEY OF NORTH AMERICA,

AS THEY APPEAR IN THE

CAUCASIAN, AFRICAN, INDIAN, AND ESQUIMAUX VARIETIES OF
ITS POPULATION.

BY DANIEL DRAKE, M. D.

CINCINNATI:

WINTHROP B. SMITH & CO., PUBLISHERS
PHILADELPHIA: GRIGG, ELLIOT & CO.
NEW YORK: MASON & LAW.

1850.

Fig. 9. Title page to first volume of Drake's medical "classic."

fully prepared tables to elucidate the text. Preparation of the tables alone must have required a prodigious amount of labor. The third section dealt with diet and drinks, clothing, bathing, lodgings, shade trees, occupations, pursuits, exercise, and recreations. The fourth section, which introduced febrile diseases, had been intended as the first part of the second volume and, as such, it was incorporated with additions in that volume, published posthumously at Philadelphia in 1854.[37]

Drake had been brought to Kentucky when the entire region was thinly populated and subject to Indian raids. He had observed the vast tide of immigration from Europe, the advent of steamboats, and the rise of many large cities throughout the valley. Pondering the effects on future generations, he wrote: "The world has never before witnessed such a commingling of races. . . . The GREAT CENTRAL VALLEY OF NORTH AMERICA is the *last* crucible into which living materials, in great and diversified streams can be poured for amalgamation." [38]

Drake had advanced ideas concerning the etiology of cholera and malaria. He asserted positively that the manner in which cholera spreads "was more fully explained by the animalcular hypothesis than any other" although he added that vegetable germs might be responsible. With reference to malaria, when most physicians believed it due to marsh emanations, he taught that either animalcular or vegetable germs might be assumed as causes. He listed fourteen points in support of these theories. He observed that the variable incidence of malaria from year to year was similar to the abundance of vegetable or insect forms one year and their scarcity in other years. To quote: "It has often happened that musquitoes [*sic*] have been absent from the banks of the middle portion of the Ohio river, for a year, and in the next appeared in immense numbers. We have but to suppose insect forms of parallel size, to live under corresponding laws, and the hypothesis now before us, offers an explanation of sickly and healthy seasons." [39]

[37] Daniel Drake: A *Systematic Treatise* . . . , edited by S. S. Hanbury Smith and Francis G. Smith (Second Series, Philadelphia: Lippincott, Grambo & Co.).

[38] Drake, A *Systematic Treatise* . . . (Cincinnati: Winthrop B. Smith & Co., 1850), p. 647.

[39] *Ibid.*, pp. 726-27.

Not only was the book based on the widest possible original investigations but it represented the most advanced American thought of the period. It was not surprising that the work was enthusiastically received in the United States and in Europe. Dr. David Condie (1796-1875), well-known Philadelphia author, praised it through twelve pages of the *American Journal of the Medical Sciences*, of which the following is an extract:

> We hail with pleasure the appearance of this long expected work of Dr. Drake, on the medical topography and diseases of the valley of the Mississippi. Our anticipations in relation to it, founded upon the known abilities and untiring industry of the author, and the time and labour he is known to have devoted to the collection of the materials required for its successful execution, have always been in the highest degree favorable. These anticipations have not been in the least disappointed, now that the work has appeared. It will, we are convinced, be ranked as the most valuable and important original production, of a strictly professional character, that has yet appeared from the pen of any of our physicians. . . . No American physician will consider his library complete without a copy of the work of Dr. Drake. . . .[40]

Dr. J. V. C. Smith (1800-79), the versatile editor of *The Boston Medical and Surgical Journal*, wrote:

> . . . The embodying of the medical topography, hydrology, geology, etc., of its interior valley, including the principal diseases incident to its climate, is an undertaking of great labor, which few would possess the hardihood to undertake, and still fewer have the happy faculty of rendering such researches interesting, instructive and practical. The profession are much indebted to Dr. Drake for his indefatigable exer-

[40] David F. Condie: Review, *Amer. Jnl. Med. Sc.*, N.S., XX:109-20, July 1850.

tions in producing a work of such magnitude and importance. . . .[41]

Other American reviews were equally laudatory.[42]

Shortly after the publication of the first volume, the American Medical Association held its annual meeting in Cincinnati. Drake received an ovation after Dr. Alfred Stillé (1813-1900) read the report on recent medical literature in which he stated: "[Dr. Drake's work] belongs to the very highest rank of our medical literature, and may very probably come to be regarded as the most valuable original work yet published in America. . . . Its distinguished author has raised a durable monument to his own name, and to the medical reputation, not only of the Great Valley, but to the greater Union. . . ."[43]

The first review in a foreign periodical appeared in November 1850 in the *Monthly Journal of Medical Science*, published in Edinburgh:

This is a very remarkable volume, constituting perhaps the most extensive and able work on medical topography that has ever issued from the press. A description of diseases peculiar to the tract of country beginning with the tropics and terminating with the polar circle, having an area of six million square miles and inhabited by numerous races of men, may well be considered a gigantic undertaking. Yet long journeys of observation, during a period of forty years, and personal examination carried through eighteen degrees of latitude and

[41] J. V. C. Smith, editor: *Boston Med. & Surg. Jnl.*, XLII:357-58, May 29, 1850.

[42] S. S. Purple: Review, *New York Journal of Medical and Collateral Sciences*, N.S., V:94-95, July 1850.

Lunsford P. Yandell: Review of *A Systematic Treatise . . .* , *West. Jnl. Med. & Sg.*, 3rd Ser., VI:288-56, Sept.; 350-60, Oct.; and 408-38, Nov. 1850.

Austin Flint: Review, *Buffalo Medical Journal*, VI:62-64, June 1850.

[43] Alfred Stillé, chairman, Standing Committee on Medical Literature, A.M.A., Cincinnati Meeting, *Transactions*, A.M.A., III:166.

nearly as many of longitude, have enabled the author to publish the present work.

The contents of the book are so varied and extensive as to defy analysis. . . .

To the medical practitioners of the region described, Dr. Drake's labours will prove invaluable. . . .[44]

The British and Foreign Medico-Chirurgical Review (London) devoted thirty pages to summarizing Drake's book which was called "an elaborate work." Extracts were quoted to "exhibit not only the extreme care and minute detail with which the topography and medical history of each place is given, but also the very important information which is profusely scattered through the whole work. . . . It would do honor to any country. . . ."[45]

No French reviews have so far been located, but two laudatory ones in German have been found. The earlier one, by the well-known geographer and journalist, Dr. Karl Andree (1808-75), did not attempt an appraisal of the work but merely gave a digest of its contents.[46] The later review, by Dr. Joseph Finger, author and prominent physician in Prague, devoted twenty-five pages to a careful analysis and appraisal of the first volume.[47] He emphasized the need for such works and praised Drake's industry in having personally investigated so much of the vast Mississippi Valley. Attention was rightly called to the paucity of autopsies, a lack which Drake himself deplored. In conclusion Finger stated that:

> The general practitioner in America, for whom the [work] is in fact written, may find therein without doubt much use-

[44] Review: *Monthly Journal of Medical Science* (Edinburgh), XI:442-43, Nov. 1850.
[45] Review: *British and Foreign Medico-Chirurgical Review* (London) VII: 302-32, Apr. 1851.
[46] Dr. Karl Andree: "Das Innere Thalbecken von Nordamerika," *Das Westland* (Bremen), I:99-208, 1852.
[47] Dr. Joseph Finger: Review, *Viertel jahrschrift fuer die praktische Heilkunde* (Prag.), XI Jahrg., 1854, Bd. I:27-52.

ful instruction, and that it contains much interesting information for the European physician.—The first section appears to us in any case the better part of the work, wherein the subjects are discussed with much accuracy; only it is surprising, that the author after the ample appreciation which he bestows on the physical conditions and their laws of action nevertheless persists in so erroneous and for the greater part teleological conception of nature as so many of the opinions clearly show. [Translation mine.][48]

The American and foreign reviews from which extracts have been made clearly show the high regard of contemporaries for Drake and his book. Moreover, it was not only in reviews that the praises of Drake's work were sung. Both at home and abroad, in circles which were inclined at that time to be skeptical of American scientific ability, Drake's book was a much-quoted reference. August Hirsch (1817-94), professor of medicine in the University of Berlin, in his *Handbook of Geographical and Historical Pathology*, refers to Drake's classic forty-five times in addition to using four quotations from it.[49]

Despite the enthusiastic reception by eminent physicians and the favorable reviews of Drake's book, not enough copies were sold to defray the costs. Although it "fell stillborn from the press," Dr. Samuel D. Gross rightly stated: ". . . the work will in the future, I have no doubt, shed lustre upon medical literature and confer an enviable immortality upon the name of its author." [50]

Current appraisal of Drake's masterpiece is in full agreement with that of his contemporaries. Indeed our amazement grows. As we leaf through the 1900 pages, study the interest-

[48] *Ibid.,* p. 52.
[49] August Hirsch: *Handbook of Geographical and Historical Pathology,* translated by Charles Creighton (3 vols., London: New Sydenham Society, 1883).
[50] Gross: *Autobiography,* Vol. II, pp. 269-70.

ing maps and precise tables, we cannot but marvel that such a monumental and original medical work could have been written by one whose formal education was so rudimentary. We cannot fail to observe the breadth of mind which conceived diseases as a phase of natural history to be studied against the background of environment. We are amazed at the fortitude of a man who in his sixth decade personally investigated, despite primitive modes of travel, more than a third of the total area of the United States and a large part of Canada. A keen and philosophical spirit set a goal which, after forty years of unremitting toil, was reached amid the applause of his confreres. This work, "one of the greatest masterpieces of medico-geographic research," [51] continues to be prized and consulted by the student of social history as well as by the historian of medicine. Thus it would seem that the prophecy made in 1876 by John Shaw Billings has been fulfilled in less than the allotted time:

> This work is the '*magnum opus*' and results of the life-long labour, including extensive personal observation, literary research, and matured reflection, of a man whose fame, as compared with that of his contemporaries, will probably be greater a century hence than it is today, and whose name, even now, should be among the first on the list of the illustrious dead of the medical profession of the United States. . . .[52]

[51] Henry E. Sigerist: *American Medicine* (New York: W. W. Norton & Co., 1934), p. 93.
[52] John S. Billings: "A Century of American Medicine," *Amer. Jnl. Med. Sc.*, CXLIV:439-80, Oct. 1876.

18 ℘

Among the therapeutic agents not to be found bottled up and labelled on our shelves, is Travelling; a means of prevention, of cure, and of restoration, which has been famous in all ages.[1]

Visitors to Cincinnati

WHEN TWENTY-FIVE years of age, Drake published *Notices Concerning Cincinnati* and, thereby, became the city's most noted citizen. This position was enhanced by his many other activities in various civic enterprises. With the publication of his *Picture of Cincinnati*, he acquired a national reputation. Visitors either had letters of introduction to him or sought an interview. He welcomed everyone and arranged parties for many.

The Reverend Timothy Flint (1780-1840), nominally a Presbyterian, pioneer, missionary, editor, and author, wrote of Drake in 1816:

> Dr. D.[rake], a man, I am told, like Franklin, originally self-taught, has made very laudable effort for the promotion of science. He is himself, a scientific physician, a respectable scholar, and natural historian. He has written very accurate and detailed "Sketches of Cincinnati," and the region in its vicinity. His book conveys very exact and specific information upon the subjects, on which it professes to treat. I would refer you to it for more detailed and exact geographical and statistical information about this region.[2]

[1] Daniel Drake: "Thoughts on Modern Travelling; Designed for Valetudinarians," *West. Med. & Phys. Jnl.*, I:305-10, Sept. 1827.
[2] Timothy Flint: *Recollections of the Last Ten Years* (Boston: Cummings. Hilliard and Co.), p. 51.

In W. H. Venable's *Beginnings of Literary Culture in the Ohio Valley*, there is another allusion to Drake as Franklin: "So many good works did he undertake, so much did he accomplish, so effectually did he stimulate exertion in others, both friends and enemies, that I think he may be called with propriety the *Franklin of Cincinnati*. Much of what he did for this western metropolis reminds us of the philosopher who aided in founding the early institutions of Philadelphia." [3]

The visits of Thomas Nuttall in 1816 and in 1818 have been mentioned. Likewise the story of Bishop Philander C. Chase's visit and the organization of Christ Church (Episcopal) in Drake's home have been told.

David Thomas (1776-1859), engineer, distinguished florist, and pomologist of Aurora, New York, in his *Travels through the Western Country in the Summer of 1816* frequently mentioned Drake. He stated: "In '*the Picture of Cincinnati*' there is much to admire and approve; and our respect for the author is heightened by his exemplary modesty." [4] That Thomas "admired and approved" the book is further evidenced by the fact that he used thirteen direct quotations from it. [5]

Thomas Hulme, an Englishman, toured the Central West in 1818. He wrote:

> June 14th and 15th—Called upon Doctor Drake and upon a Mr. Bosson, to whom we had letters. These gentlemen shewed us the greatest civility, and treated us with a sort of kindness which must have changed the opinion even of the English officer whom we saw at Pittsburgh, had he been with us. I could tell that dirty hireling scout, that even in this short space of time, I have had the pleasure to meet many

[3] W. H. Venable: *Beginnings of Literary Culture in the Ohio Valley* (Cincinnati: Robert Clarke & Co., 1891), p. 304.

[4] David Thomas: *Travels through the Western Country* (Auburn, N.Y., David Rumsey, 1819), p. 32.

[5] *Ibid.*, pp. 111, 113, 158, 201, 203, 249, 276, 296, 299, 301.

gentlemen, very well informed, and possessing great knowledge of their own country, and hospitality and kindness in
all their demeanour.[6]

Another visitor entertained by Drake was Major Stephen H.
Long (1784-1864) who had orders from the Secretary of War
to make a reconnaissance of the Rocky Mountains in 1819.
He left Pittsburgh on 1 May 1819, accompanied by topog-
raphers, a diarist, a physician and surgeon (Dr. Baldwin), a
zoologist, a geologist, a naturalist, and an artist. The party
reached Cincinnati on 9 May 1819. Here repairs to the machinery of their boat were made, and Dr. Baldwin, who had
been seriously ill, was taken ashore and placed under the care
of Dr. Drake. Nine days later, Dr. Baldwin had recovered
sufficiently to resume the journey.

> During our stay at that place [Cincinnati], we have been
> gratified by the hospitable attention of the inhabitants of
> the town. Mr. Glen [to whose home the patient had been
> taken] was unremitting in his exertions to promote the re-
> covery of Dr. Baldwin's health; to him as well as to Dr. Drake,
> and several gentlemen of Cincinnati, all the members of our
> party were indebted for many friendly attentions.[7]

. . . .

> Whilst we were at Cincinnati, Dr. Drake exhibited to us,
> in his cabinet of Natural History, two large marine shells,
> that had been dug out of ancient Indian tumuli in that
> vicinity. These shells were each cut longitudinally, and the
> larger half of each only remained. From this circumstance it
> seems probable that they have been used by aborigines as

[6] Thomas Hume: "Journal," in William Cobbett, *A Year's Residence in
the United States* (3rd ed., London, 1828), pp. 275-76.
[7] Major Stephen H. Long: *Account of an Expedition from Pittsburgh to the
Rocky Mountains* (2 vols., Philadelphia: H. C. Carey and I. Lee, 1823),
Vol. I, pp. 21-23.

drinking cups; or consecrated to superstitution, they may have been regarded as sacred utensils, and either used in connection with the rites of sacrifice, or in making libations to their deities; they may, however, like the Cymbricum of the Archipelago, have served a more useful and salutary purpose in bathing. . . .[8]

Drake's *Picture of Cincinnati* once served as a convenient reference for a correspondent whose heart was turned from travel to passion. An anonymous tourist in *The Port Folio* described Cincinnati:

We arrived at Cincinnati in the morning—but when I inform you that we remained here only a few hours, and that the greater part of this time was spent with a friend—and that friend a lovely female, a companion of *my dancing days,* you will not be surprised if I add, that I have nothing to relate concerning this town. Those days may be over with me, in which the violin could have lured me from the labour of study, and the song from the path of duty—but never, if I know myself, will that hour come when woman shall cease to be the tutelary deity of my affections, the household goddess of my bosom! Think me an enthusiast, or a great dunce, if you please, but never I pray if you love me, believe that I could think of statistics with a fair lady at my side, or that I could hoard up materials for a *Letter from the West,* while a chance presented itself to talk over my old courtships, and dance once more my old cotillions. . . .

I had only time, therefore, to discover that I was in a town of ample size, and goodly appearance; where I met genteel forms and busy faces. The harbour was crowded with boats, the wharves covered with merchandize, the streets thronged with people. The indications of wealth, of business, and of refinement, were too striking to pass unobserved by one who reflected how recently the forest frowned upon this

[8] *Ibid.,* Vol. I, p. 64.

spot. See Dr. Drake's Picture of Cincinnati, for further particulars, as the auctioneers phrase it.[9]

The visit of the most famous of numerous persons to Cincinnati, General Lafayette, has been mentioned previously. The Cincinnatians arranged for lavish entertainment, climaxed by a ball attended by about 500 persons.[10] It is known that Drake and his wife were present but no comments by either have been located.

Few of the books written by travellers from 1816 through the 1840's fail to mention Drake and his *Picture of Cincinnati*. Mrs. Trollope who reached the city on 10 February 1828 is one of the few who fails to mention either him or his book. His friends were among the leaders in Cincinnati and she was never noticed by them. She arrived under more or less of a cloud, unaccompanied by her husband, but attended by a young French artist, August Hervieu. As is well known, Mrs. Trollope built a "Bazaar," which along with all her household effects, was seized by the sheriff for the benefit of her numerous creditors in March 1830. Her embitterment, which led to the spiteful *Domestic Manners of the Americans*—so amusing to the Cincinnatians—must have been intense.

A correspondent from Portland, Maine, thus described Mrs. Trollope's "Bazaar" as it appeared in 1833:

> It is an odd looking concern, part church, part jail, part bank and part dwelling house—wanting just enough of each to make you wonder what on earth it could be—out of shape —without form or comliness. No wonder the Cincinnatians stared when such a structure was thrown up among them. It is deserted now; and as the ancients speak of Cleopatra's Needle, so we may call this Mrs. Trollope's Bell top, for the

[9] [Anon.]: "Letters from the West.—No. XIII," *The Port Folio* (Philadelphia) XVIII:194, Sept. 1824.
[10] "Visit of Lafayette," *Cincinnati Advertiser*, N.S., III, No. 42:p. [2]—c. [1-5] and p. [3]—c. [2-4], May 25, 1825.

cupola is in the shape of a bell. Mrs. Trollope is well known here. They say she was intelligent, skillful in sketches, and corresponded with distinguished men abroad, but wished to figure here as a Madam de Stael. But Mrs. Trollope was a vulgar woman, gross in a thousand things, with so much of the equivocal in her character, that she could seldom or never meet with the good society of Cincinnati.[11]

Captain Basil Hall (1788-1844) and his wife, on their tour of the United States, arrived in Cincinnati early in June 1828. Captain Hall of the Royal Navy was the grandson of Lord Selkirk and Mrs. Hall, the daughter of Sir John Hunter, British consul general to Spain. As a result of their visit to the United States two books were written, the one by the captain and the other by his wife.[12] That by Mrs. Hall, consisting of a series of letters to her sister, is much more intimate and revealing than that of her husband. In both books Dr. Drake is favorably mentioned. Mrs. Hall, writing from Cincinnati on 3 June 1828, stated: "At three o'clock yesterday we went out under the chaperonage of Dr. Drake to see all that we had left unseen of the town and its vicinity and had a very pleasant drive and got home just in time to escape a violent thunder storm."[13] Captain Hall refers to Dr. Drake as follows:

> Our researches, however, were all cut short at this stage of our journey, by the illness of our little girl, whose long exposure to the noxious air of the great rivers, had given her a complaint very fatal to children in that country, and called by the ominous name of Cholera Infantum. We were above all things fortunate, however, in meeting, just at the moment

[11] *Portland Maine Daily Advertiser:* "Things in Cincinnati," *National Intelligencer* (Washington), No. 4919:p. [1]—c. [5], June 8, 1833.
[12] Capt. Basil Hall: *Travels in North America* (3 vols., Edinburgh: Cadell & Co., 1829).
Mrs. Basil Hall: *The Aristocratic Journey*, edited by Una Pope-Hennessy (New York: G. P. Putnam's Sons, 1931).
[13] *Ibid.*, p. 286.

of need, with a medical gentleman of distinguished abilities, to whose kind attentions and extensive information, we had already been greatly indebted. He at once advised us to proceed to the North—to get away from the rivers, and to climb the Allegheny mountains without delay.

Accordingly, on the 4th of June, we reluctantly took leave of Cincinnati, where there was so much to tempt us, not only in the way of local curiosity, but also of an agreeable society.

[Seven days later we] began to ascend the lower range of the Allegheny mountains, so well named the Backbone of America. The effect of the pure air of the hills on our invalid was very striking. . . .[14]

A young engineer, John Sharkey, stopped for a few hours in Cincinnati, 18 July 1829. He looked around the town while repairs were being made to the steamboat:

I was honored with an introduction to Dr. Drake, author of the "Picture of Cincinnati," who hearing me express a desire to see the work presented me with a copy of it. The present was so gratifying as it was unexpected and I felt the compliment heightened by his having told me but a moment before that he had only a few copies remaining which he intended to keep for his family as the work was now nearly out of print.[15]

Alexis de Tocqueville, the great sociologist who predicted the "mass age," was in Cincinnati during December 1831 but did not meet Drake. It appears that French travelers had bad luck in trips on the Ohio and Mississippi Rivers. De Tocqueville with his companion left Wheeling on 1 December 1831. There was much floating ice around them and their boat struck a rock at midnight. It sank immediately in shallow water. They were rescued, and arrived in Cincinnati on the

[14] Capt. Hall: *Travels* . . . , Vol. III, pp. 389-90.
[15] John Sharkey, MS diary: "10 July 1829-10 November 1829." Photostat in The Filson Club, Louisville.

following day. They continued the fight against the bitter cold which forced them to leave on 3 December 1831. Again large masses of ice plagued the boat down the river and at Westport, Kentucky, twenty-five miles above Louisville, they were put ashore. Unable to secure any type of conveyance, de Tocqueville and his friend walked to Louisville through the dense woods, which were covered with six inches of snow. Further hardships were encountered during a stagecoach journey to Memphis. New Orleans was not reached until 1 January 1832.[16] Regrettably, de Tocqueville did not describe his personal experiences in the United States in addition to his deservedly celebrated *Democracy in America*.

It is generally agreed that of visitors to the United States during the first-half of the nineteenth century, Harriet Martineau (1802-76), prolific authoress, wrote the best and most appreciative account of her impressions.[17] She reached Cincinnati on 15 June 1835. Two days later Dr. Drake, "the first physician of the place, called."

> Dr. Drake and his daughter proposed to call for us for an afternoon drive, and take us home to tea with them; a plan to which we gladly agreed. . . . Dr. Drake took us a delightful drive, the pleasure of which was much enhanced by his very interesting conversation. He is a complete and favorable specimen of the Westerner. He looks with a sort of paternal complacence on the 35,000 inhabitants, scarcely one of whom is without the comforts of life, the means of education, and a bright prospect for the future. Though a true Westerner, and devoutly believing the *buckeyes* (natives of Ohio) to be superior to all others of God's creatures, he hails every accession of intelligent members to his darling society. . . .
>
> Dr. Drake must be much older than he looks. He appears

---

[16] Alexis de Tocqueville: *Memoir, Letters and Remains* (2 vols., Cambridge: Macmillan and Co., 1861), Vol. I, pp. 25-29.

[17] Martineau: *Retrospect of Western Travel*.

vigorous as ever, running beside his stout black gig-horse in difficult bits of forest road, head uncovered and coat splashed like a farmer making his way to market. His figure is spare and active; his face is expressive of shrewdness, humour and kindliness. His conversation is of a high order. . . .[18]

The tea-table was set in the garden at Dr. Drake's. We were waited upon, for the first time for many months, by a free servant. The long grass grew thick under our feet; fire-flies were flitting about us, and I doubted whether I had ever heard more sense and eloquence, at any old world tea-table than we were entertained with as the twilight drew on.[19]

A few days later, Miss Martineau was invited to a party at Dr. Drake's:

An enormous buckeye bowl of lemonade, with a ladle of buckeye, stood on the hall table; and symbolical sprigs of the same adorned the walls. On entering the drawing-room, I was presented with a splendid bouquet, sent by a lady by the hands of her brother, from a garden and conservatory which are the pride of the city. My first introduction was to the catholic bishop [John Baptist Purcell, 1800-83]; my next to a lady whom I thought then and afterwards one of the cleverest women I met in the country. [Probably Mrs. Caroline Lee (Whiting) Hentz, 1800-56.] There was a slight touch of pedantry to be excused and a degree of tory prejudice against the bulk of the human race which could scarcely be exceeded even in England; but there was a charming good-humour in the midst of all, and a power both of observation and reason which commanded high respect.[20]

During the efforts of Drake and other Cincinnatians to establish a railroad to Charleston, South Carolina, a delegation from the latter city came north. The visitors were warmly

---

[18] *Ibid.*, London ed., Vol. II, pp. 222-25; New York, Vol. II, pp. 39-40.
[19] *Ibid.*, London ed., Vol. II, p. 234; New York, Vol. II, p. 45.
[20] *Ibid.*, London ed., Vol. II, p. 243; New York, Vol. II, p. 50.

welcomed. The most distinguished of them was General
Robert Y. Hayne (1791-1839), U.S. Senator, Governor of
South Carolina and father of the doctrine of nullification. He
had ably opposed Daniel Webster in one of the most famous
debates preceding the War between the States. One of the
visitors, in describing the entertainment in Cincinnati, mentioned "the perils of a liberally dispensed hospitality." Courteous attention to guests had contributed, "by kindness and social converse, to wing with pleasure the flight of time."

About eight o'clock, P. M., our "last, not least" visit was
paid to Dr. Daniel Drake, a distinguished physician and influential citizen of Cincinnati, at whose house we were again
hospitably entertained, and treated with the feast of reason
and the flow of soul. Here a large number of citizens, comprising much of the worth and intelligence of the place, was
assembled to receive us. In the assemblage was Judge McLean
of the Supreme Court of the United States, in form a noble
model of our species, and possessed of a fine address and
suavity of manner, and Judge Hall, formerly the celebrated
editor of the *Western Review,* and author of "Letters from
the West," and "Western Sketches," and numerous other
literary and distinguished men. On entering, we had observed
rather an unsightly stump in our host's reception room, but it
soon became manifest that there was both humor and design
in it. The Doctor had resolved on both giving and getting a
stump speech, and had therefore providently supplied himself with the stump of the Buck Eye tree—a tree from which
Ohio derives the name of "the Buck Eye State." In the
course of the evening the Doctor regularly mounted the
stump, and delivered an address, and with much humor and
tact contrived to place General Hayne as his successor on the
Buck Eye Rostrum, and to draw from him an admirable
epitome of the Barbacue Speech, demonstrating the practicability and advantages of the great enterprise which promises

the commercial and social union of the South and West.—
After General Hayne had finished speaking, Dr. Drake again
mounted the stump and gave—

"The Charleston and Cincinnati Bar.—May they soon exchange work."

He offered this sentiment with a view to draw a speech
from some member of the South Carolina bar, but a cry
soon arose that Mr. John C. Vaughn, formerly of Camden,
South Carolina, but now of Cincinnati, was the proper person to respond to the toast, as he was a member of both the
South Carolina and Cincinnati bars. Mr. Vaughn accordingly
took the stump, and after a brief but felicitous address, gave
the following appropriate toast—

"May the Palmetto be soon engrafted, by means of the
Railroad, on the Buck Eye Stump." [21]

In 1833, Drake inaugurated private literary parties at regular intervals to which were invited such local celebrities as
General Edward King, Judge James Hall, Professor Calvin E.
Stowe, Edward Mansfield, Misses Harriet and Catherine
Beecher, Mrs. Caroline Lee Hentz, and many others, including always the distinguished visitors to Cincinnati. These
gatherings were apparently instituted for the benefit of his
children, Charles D., Elizabeth, and Harriet Echo Drake.
Mansfield described the meetings:

> We used to assemble early—about half past seven—and,
> when fully collected, the doctor, who was the acknowledged
> chairman, rang his little bell for general attention. This
> caused no constraint; but simply brought us to the topic of
> the evening. Sometimes this was appointed beforehand.
> Sometimes it arose out of what was said or proposed on the
> occasion. Some evenings essays were read on selected topics.
> On other evenings nothing was read, and the time was
> passed in the discussion of some interesting question. Oc-

[21] E. S. Thomas: *Reminiscences of the Last Sixty-five* Years, Vol. I,
pp. 100-1.

casionally a piece of poetry or a story came in to relieve the conversation. . . . The subjects were always of a suggestive and problematical kind; so that the ideas were fresh, the debates frank and spontaneous. There, in that little circle of ladies and gentlemen, I have heard many of the questions which have since occupied the public mind, talked over with an ability and fulness of information which is seldom possessed by larger and more authoritative bodies. . . . [Dr. Drake's] suggestive mind furnished topics for others, and he was ever ready to revive a flagging conversation. He was a man of real genius whose mind was fresh, active, ambitious, and intellectually enterprising.[22]

These parties were continued regularly until 1839 when Drake's daughters married and he accepted a professorship in the Louisville Medical Institute.

Even early in his career, Drake's prominence was sufficient for collectors to seek his autograph. That promising journalist whose death came so early, Cyrus P. Bradbury (1818-38), recorded (3 June 1835): "Noticing a communication of Dr. Daniel Drake, in the *Whig* of this morning, in relation to the subject [cholera], and passing the office I called in and rescued it from the grate for my autograph book." [23] Bradbury, incidentally, condemned the chronological approach to history writing: the enumeration of the kings, potentates, the generals, the battles, and rebellions of nations. He insisted that authentic history must include a discussion of the sciences, arts, habits, morals, and manners of the people in the effects on men individually and on nations collectively. Drake later voiced a similar idea: "The history of a nation is not to be read in the lives of its generals and politicians merely, but comprehends, as its necessary elements, the history of all

[22] E. D. Mansfield: *Personal Memories* (Cincinnati: Robert Clarke & Co., 1879), pp. 262-63.
[23] Cyrus P. Bradbury: Journal, *Ohio Archaeological and Historical Publication* (Columbus), XV:207-70, Apr. 1906.

classes of the people, and all *branches* of intellectual, moral, religious, and physical industry." [24]

We are indebted to two of Drake's students in the 1835-36 class of the Medical Department of Cincinnati College for evaluations of his social traits. Edward Thomson wrote: ". . . Dr. Drake's social qualities were remarkable, his acquaintance being extensive, his threshold was often crossed by guests, whom he always treated hospitably. Indeed, his house was almost always open; and whenever a notable stranger was in the city, it was usually the scene of a party. . . ." [25]

And William J. Barbee considered Drake to be exceedingly "agreeable":

> Dr. Drake is exceedingly agreeable. His sociability is not excelled by any of his professional brethren in the city [Cincinnati] and, in truth, you rarely meet with an individual in the social circle who combines as many excellent qualities as the doctor. He is fond of rational amusement; and it is truly amusing to see him (a man of nearly sixty) engage in the pastimes of the young. He is expert at battledore or the hoop, and at a cotillion party he can lead out a young lady on the floor with the ease and elegance of a French dancing master. In his conversation he is generally animated, oftentimes witty. He is dignified in his deportment, without being morose. He is warmly devoted to his friends, and as warmly inveterate to his avowed enemies. . . . [26]

Another student, William K. Bowling, of the 1835-36 class of Cincinnati College, wrote in 1851 following a visit by Drake to Nashville that "his zeal for the promotion of his profession still burns with an ardor which the labors of half a century could neither quench nor dampen." [27] In reviewing

[24] Drake: *Discourses* . . . , p. 35, note.
[25] Thomson: *Recollections* . . . , p. 113.
[26] W. J. B. [arbee]: "Letters from the West. No. V," *Boston Med. & Surg. Jnl.*, XXI:96-98, Sept. 18, 1839.
[27] William K. Bowling [Ed.]: "Dr. Drake," *Nashville Journal of Medicine and Surgery*, I:128, Apr. 1851.

Drake's *Principal Diseases* . . . , Bowling paid tribute to him as "the man who had fired our soul with the love of medicine. . . . The man who taught us to hate physic as a trade—and worship it as philosophy. . . ." [28] A tabulation of the classes taught by Drake in his career as a teacher of medicine from 1817 through 1852 shows a total of approximately ten thousand. To have "fired the souls" of even a small percentage of such a number of students was a notable achievement.

In the previous chapter reasons have been given for Drake's resignation in 1849 from his lucrative professorship in the University of Louisville. Possibly the most important factor prompting his action was his undying love for the Medical College of Ohio which he had founded. Triumphantly received, he delivered one of his finest introductory addresses. He discussed the science of medicine, the beginnings of medical education in the West, the founding of the Medical College of Ohio, quoting liberally from the inaugural discourse which he had delivered at its opening on 11 November 1820.[29] His concluding words were:

> The first moments of reunion are always passionate, and wisdom places little confidence in what is then promised; nevertheless, I must declare to you, that I stand ready to pledge the remnant of my active life, and all the humble talents with which the Creator has endowed me, to her future elevation; and were I to put up the prayer of Hezekiah, for length of days, it would be to devote them to her aggrandizement; and, for the pleasure of seeing her halls overflowing with inquiring pupils, attentively listening to ardent, learned, and eloquent professors. With this pledge, those who watch over her welfare, and those who govern the Hospital which she caused to be erected, are now silently mingling theirs; while you, I trust, are resolving that your own lives

---

[28] William K. Bowling: Review of Drake's A *Systematic Treatise* . . . ," *Nashville Jnl. Med. & Surg.*, I:230-40, Aug. 1851.
[29] Drake: An *Inaugural Discourse on Medical Education.*

shall spread abroad its fame. Thus will she rise, and grace-fully move onward and upward, until she stands in beauty and honorable rank, among her distinguished sisters of the Union—the pride of her sons, and a blessing to society.[30]

The 1849 session of the Medical College of Ohio had barely begun when Drake's optimism, ambition, and hope were shattered by intrigue and faculty squabbles. Again sorely disillusioned, he resigned at the close of the session. He was soon importuned to return to the chair of pathology and the practice of medicine in Louisville, made vacant by the illness and resignation of Elisha Bartlett (1804-55), one of the ablest teachers of medicine in America. Drake re-entered the University of Louisville and taught through the 1850-51 and 1851-52 sessions.

During Drake's second connection with the University of Louisville and after the publication of the first volume of *The Principal Diseases* . . . , his thoughts turned to slavery. He regarded it as a great evil, one which was separating the North and South into hostile groups. Having travelled over the whole Mississippi Valley, from the states bordering the Gulf of Mexico to the "Lake States" and Canada, he was probably more familiar with the slave question than any other person. Greatly alarmed over the rapidly mounting tension, he fore-saw armed conflict. His efforts to prevent further deterioration of an extremely tense situation deserve study.

On 21 December 1850 Drake sent a memorial to the convention then in process of adopting a new constitution for Ohio. He stated unequivocally that the "ingress and residence of emancipated slaves in the free States lies at the bottom of the difficulties . . . now carrying dismay into the heart of every patriot . . . [which have] brought us, apparently, to the

[30] Daniel Drake: *An Introductory Lecture,* Nov. 5, 1849 (Cincinnati: Morgan and Overend, 1849), p. 16.

verge of civil war." [31] Many cogent arguments were listed in his "Memorial" which appear entirely valid. Were all states to adopt laws excluding manumitted slaves, the door to colonization in Africa would open wide.

> Those who desired to emancipate would become missionaries in the cause of liberty, so as to create a public opinion in favor of State appropriations and other facilities for transporting the manumitted to Africa. . . .
> The slave States would themselves keep the way clear; and should the anti-slavery benevolence of the free States expend itself on the same object, the North and the South, in part from the same, and in part from different motives, would be brought to unite in a common labor instead of cherishing dangerous hostilities, and presenting themselves before the world as a great and noble family, at variance with itself. [32]

He petitioned that the Ohio legislature enact laws prohibiting future ingress of emancipated and fugitive slaves and additional laws to promote colonization in Africa of the existing colored population. This memorial of Drake accomplished nothing.

Still hoping that the slavery question might be amicably resolved, Drake addressed three long letters to Dr. John C. Warren of Boston. These communications were published in *The National Intelligencer* (Washington) on 3, 5, and 8 of April 1851. They have been considered of such importance as to justify reprinting in book format. [33] Several reasons prompted Drake to address Dr. Warren. At this time Warren was not only one of the most prominent surgeons of the United States but had completed, a few months before, a term as president of the American Medical Association. War-

---

[31] Daniel Drake: [Memorial], "To the President of the Convention," *Ohio State Journal*, Jan. 4, 1851, p. 2—c. [1].
[32] *Ibid.*
[33] Daniel Drake: *Letters on Slavery*, with an Introduction by Emmet F. Horine (New York: Schuman, 1940).

ren had on 26 November 1850 presided at a "Union" meeting in Boston at which the preservation of the Constitution and the upholding of all regularly enacted laws were stressed. Drake agreed with Warren on "the absurdity of attempting to compel the Slave States to emancipate the colored people by any sudden or violent process, as it must infallibly terminate in dissolving the Union." [34]

No student of American slavery can ignore the Drake letters. At the time of publication they attracted wide attention. Upon publication of the first letter, editorial comment was in part as follows:

> The high character of the author (whose name and virtues are household words throughout the Valley of the Mississippi, and honored in every part of the Union) as well as the great ability and originality of these letters on a subject at present of universal interest, will commend them to serious consideration of all candid, thoughtful, and patriotic men. . . .
>
> The friends of the colored race will find, in the clear and well considered statements of the first of his letters, the best reasons for encouragement and hope; while the rash and misguided will, we trust, be induced to consider whether it be wise, by an overheated zeal in the cause of the enslaved, to disturb not only the good order of society, but defeat the humane purpose now cherished and increasing towards the colored population of the South. Certainly it would be difficult to place too high an estimate upon the merits of a gentleman who amid arduous professional duties, has found time, from no motive but that of service to his country and his race, to present in so able a manner his views on so great and difficult a question to the American people.[35]

In the first letter Drake discussed the housing, clothing, diet, work, habits, amusements, diseases and treatment, care

[34] Edward Warren: *Life of John Collins Warren* (2 vols., Boston: Ticknor and Fields, 1860), Vol. II, p. 64.

[35] Editorial, *Daily National Intelligencer*, XXXIX, No. 1, 883:p. [3]—c. [1], Apr. 3, 1851.

of the aged and of children, marriage, and religion of the slaves. In over half a century of observation he had noticed gradual improvement in all these areas. He firmly believed that ultimately slavery would be abolished. He asked:

> If censure cannot produce reform, and provokes retaliation through the slave, and makes his condition worse—if it disturbs the peace of our common country, and brings forth no good to anyone, why, in the name of humanity, should it be continued?[36]

. . . .

> We should realize that great changes cannot be accomplished in a moment, and that all important national reforms to be harmless and permanent, must be made slowly. It is sufficient to know that they are in progress to perceive that the causes which are in operation are of the right kind, and not temporary in their duration; all of which is, obviously, true of those to which I have referred. Again, therefore, I say, let us rely on those causes for the immediate and ultimate relief of the slave, and not attempt, unauthorized either by God or man, to cut asunder his fetters; or by irritating, without controlling his master, to retard their falling off.[37]

Drake's second letter was a much expanded and detailed discussion of the contents of his memorial to the constitutional convention of Ohio. In the third letter, advantages of colonization were stressed. Having studied slavery from many aspects and having been at one time the owner of a collection of books and documents on the subject, it is my considered opinion that had Drake's approach to the problem been adopted the War between the States might well have been averted; certainly we would not then have many of the racial difficulties which plague us today.

[36] Drake: *Letters on Slavery*, p. 8.
[37] *Ibid.*, p. 9.

If the morning sun shines more brightly on some, the evening beams of that impartial luminary fall in greater mellowness on others.[1]

Drake's Versatility

ENOUGH HAS BEEN said of Drake's activities to show that his interests were universal. He had both a natural inquisitiveness and a journalist's perception. Had he devoted himself to history and historical writing he would have been as outstanding in this field as in medicine. A recognized leader in the teaching of medicine, his oratorical abilities led to invitations to address many and varied organizations. His analytical mind would have permitted him to excel as a lawyer or judge. In any pursuit requiring nimbleness of thought and apt repartee he was a leader. Only in the business field did Drake apparently fail. Even here he might have succeeded had he not, at the same time, been engaged in many other pursuits.

Drake had a way with words: "Evils often seem gregarious." "It is the sacred duty of every writer to improve rather than corrupt the language." "Every dog has its day, and so has every nostrum." "Mankind love the luxury of delusion in physic, as well as in politics and religion." "What is a hoax but a falsehood." "As old age is ruminant, youth ought to prepare for it as many savory cuds as possible." "In styling himself 'lord of creation,' man has, perhaps, consulted his pride more than his powers." *

[1] Drake: *Pioneer Life in Kentucky*, p. 106.
* Drake's eminently quotable sayings have proved to be so numerous that I am incorporating them in a separate work.

It is of course not surprising that Drake should have been widely quoted in the newspapers and periodicals of his day. Noah Webster (1758-1843), our earliest and most renowned lexicographer, and William Holmes McGuffey, of "reader" fame, each used extracts from Drake. Webster, in his revised *Instructive and Entertaining Lessons for Youth,* inserted a long extract (over five pages) from the *Discourse on the History, Character and Prospects of the West.*[2] The closing paragraph of Webster's direct quotation follows:

> I shall not anticipate your future researches into our early history, by narrating other incidents; but commend the whole subject to your keeping, and hope to see you emulate each other in its cultivation. You will find it a rich and exhaustless field of facts and events, illustrating the emotions of fear and courage, patience and fortitude, joy and sorrow, hope, despair and revenge; disclosing the resources of civilized man, when cut off from his brethren, destitute of the comforts of life, deficient in sustenance, and encompassed around with dangers, against which he must invent the means of defence or speedily perish; finally exhibiting the comparative activity, hardihood, and cunning, of two distinct races, the most opposite in manners and customs and arts, arrayed against each other, and with their respective weapons of death, contending for possession of the same wilderness.[3]

McGuffey in the earlier editions of his *Eclectic Fourth Reader* used two extracts from Drake. One, "Patriotism of Western Literature," was from the same *Discourse* used by Webster and the other, "Natural Ties among the Western States," from Drake's address (1833) before the Literary Convention of Kentucky.[4] In the Permanent Stereotype Edition

---

[2] Noah Webster: *Instructive and Entertaining Lessons for Youth* (New Haven: S. Babcock and Durrie & Peck, 1835), pp. 162-68.

[3] Drake: *Discourse . . . on Prospects of the West,* pp. 39-40.

[4] William H. McGuffey: *The Eclectic Fourth Reader* (6th ed., Cincinnati: Truman and Smith, 1838), pp. 228-30, 272-75.

of the *Fourth Reader* McGuffey continued to use the extract
from the *Discourse* but deleted the one from the address
before the Literary Convention of Kentucky. No extracts
from Drake's writings have been found in the later and mod-
ernized series of the McGuffey "readers."

Chapter VIII on "Climate and Diseases" in Baird's *View
of the Valley of the Mississippi* is by Drake.[5] The portion of
the chapter on "Climate" appeared originally in Drake's
Western Journal.[6] It seems probable that Drake gave Baird
permission to use this article and added the section on "Diseases." In many other instances, portions of Drake's writings
have been used, sometimes without even giving him credit.

One book containing Drake material which has thus far
apparently eluded the notice of antiquarian book dealers was
written by John C. Gunn (1800-63): *Domestic Medicine, or
Poor Man's Friend*. This book designed as a household medical guide went through more than "230 editions" and was
translated into German. The first edition (1830) contains
nothing by or about Drake. In the one so-called Second Edition published in Knoxville, Tennessee (1833), there is a
letter on cholera by Drake, dated "Friday, Oct. 26, 1832."[7]
This communication, published originally in the *Cincinnati
Chronicle*, was one of several by him to allay the fears of the
populace and to give directions concerning treatment pending
the arrival of the physician. Another "Second Edition" of
Gunn, published at Madisonville, Tennessee, in 1834, does
not carry the Drake letter. Editions after the Madisonville
printing contain either two paragraphs or the entire text

[5] [Robert Baird]: *View of the Valley of the Mississippi* (Philadelphia:
H. S. Tanner, 1832), pp. 55-75; 2nd ed., 1834, pp. 67-87.
[6] Daniel Drake: "A Sketch of the Climate of the Valley of the Mississippi,"
West. Jnl. Med. & Phys. Sc., VI:9-22, Apr., May, and June 1832.
[7] John C. Gunn: *Domestic Medicine* (2nd ed., Knoxville, Tenn., F. S.
Heiskell, 1833), pp. 522-24.

which includes a discussion of "Relapse," "Neglect of the First Stage," and "Cholera and the Steam Doctors." The Drake letter will be found in the various editions until that of 1857 (*Gunn's New Domestic Physician: or, Home Book of Health*). It appears reasonably certain that Drake did not approve of the use of his letter by Gunn. Although some of the professors of the Louisville Medical Institute (Cobb, Yandell, and Short) recommended the book as a family guide, Drake did not. In fact, he seems always to have been wary of recommending anything though we have found him publicly endorsing certain schools, one book, and one medical appliance.

Drake's meticulous methods of investigation are clearly shown by two volumes of notes upon which he based an address at the semicentennial celebration of Cincinnati's founding, 26 December 1838.[8] In preparing for this address he sought information of the pioneers and their descendants, of businessmen, of the members of various professions, and of other persons in all walks of life. In 1923 these unpublished notes were edited by Dr. Beverley W. Bond, Jr., and issued as "Dr. Daniel Drake's Memoir of the Miami Country, 1779-1794."[9] The editor exercised considerable freedom and left out some material undoubtedly used by Drake in the address, which "enchained" the audience for three hours. Dr. Bond deletes the graphic description of the ordeal of the pioneers in their arduous trip over the mountains and down the river. He also leaves out the glowing tribute to the wives of the pioneers which Drake dramatically recited as an interlude:

[8] State Historical Society of Wisconsin: Draper Manuscript Collection, O., Drake Papers, 2 vols.
[9] Daniel Drake: "Memoir of the Miami Country, 1779-1794," *Quarterly of Historical and Philosophical Society of Ohio*, XVIII:37-117, Apr., Sept. 1923.

Who heard, dismayed from either shore
The hidden cataract's distant roar,
Float o'er the echo of the oar?
                    The Mother.
Who, startled in her midnight dream
As o'er the surface of the stream
The panther sent his hideous scream?
                    The Mother.

. . . .

Who shuddered when the Indian yell,
Rose horrid, from the gloomy dell
And told the bleeding infant's knell?
                    The Mother.[10]

In using these stanzas (twelve in number), Drake is again describing incidents of his own journey from New Jersey in 1788. Some of the stanzas were identical with those he set down for his mother on her seventieth birthday (see Chapter 7).

Dr. Lyman C. Draper deserves our gratitude for obtaining and preserving the two volumes of notes used by Drake for the Cincinnati semicentennial address. In contrast, Drake's executor apparently wantonly and thoughtlessly destroyed practically all of his manuscripts and correspondence.

As the result of seeing a public demonstration of hypnotism, Drake, Lunsford P. Yandell, Sr., and eight others formed a committee to examine the subject in 1844. The young lady performer who had appeared publicly was hypnotized by her sponsor and a series of questions was propounded by the committee. The answers were carefully analyzed by Drake and Yandell.[11] In addition, Drake wrote an essay in

[10] Draper MSS, I, O:7214-15.
[11] Daniel Drake and Lunsford P. Yandell: "Report of a Series of Experiments on the Alleged Mental Sympathy of a Person said to be in a State of Mesmeric Somniloquism," *West. Jnl. Med. & Surg.*, N.S., I:193-219, Mar. 1844.

which the findings were discussed philosophically.[12] The report along with Drake's conclusions was issued in pamphlet form, incidentally one of the rarer of his numerous publications.[13] The closing paragraph of his "Speculations" deserves republication, especially in view of the present interest in hypnosis and ESP:

> In conclusion, the variety of aspects which the phenomena of Mesmerism have exhibited, deserve to be regarded in connection with the hypothesis of a specific agent or influence, as producing them. The phenomena of the known agencies of nature, such as light, caloric and electricity, are invariable. Science multiplies them to our observation, but the new do not supersede the old—they are cumulative, and every succeeding year swells the aggregate. Time exerts on the phenomena of Mesmerism a very different influence. There is change but no cumulation, progression without aggregation—the snowball rolls on, but melts at the same time and grows no larger. The soil does not bring forth a more abundant harvest, as it becomes more thoroughly impregnated with the same seeds, but a new plant supersedes the old, to be in turn displaced by another. The first phenomena of Mesmerism, consisted chiefly in various agitations of the muscular system—in spasms, hysteria, syncope, coughs and vomiting; to these succeeded somniloquism, with a vision so quickened, that the individual could see deeper into a millstone than he who picks it:—a *clairvoyance* of the eye, which could discover what was then transacting in distant places; a *clairvoyance* of the mind, that enabled the somniloquist to penetrate the arcana of science; a *prevoyance* that could perceive the shadows of coming events, when other eyes could descry nothing! But this brilliant coruscation on the face of humanity, like a meteor in the heavens, soon passed away,—

[12] Daniel Drake: "Speculations on the Facts in the Analytical Report," *West. Jnl. Med. & Surg.*, N.S., I:285-313, Apr. 1844.
[13] Daniel Drake: *Analytical Report on . . . Mesmeric Somniloquism* (Louisville: F. W. Prescott & Co., 1844).

and is now succeeded by the phenomena of metempsychosis. From a state of beatific inspiration, the devoted somniloquist is degraded to a condition of a mere passive and unresisting recipient of the thoughts, feelings and will of those in communication. Her ideas are no longer her own;—she is compelled to feel what others feel;—she cannot move but at their bidding. The barriers of her mind are broken down, and "blue spirits and black, white spirits and gray," enter without opposition, and revel in its mansions without molestation. Her personal conscientiousness has become a *tertium quid*, composed of her own and another united. She is transformed into a spiritual hybrid, and loses her accountability to God and man, as the laws of neither recognize such personality.[14]

As is well known the American Medical Association was organized in 1847. Drake was not one of the founders nor did he attend either the 1848 meeting in Baltimore nor the one in Boston in 1849. At the latter meeting Cincinnati was selected as the convention city for 1850. Although not then a member of the association, Drake was selected as chairman of the standing Committee of Arrangements. The Cincinnati meeting, 7 to 10 May 1850, was well attended under the presidency of John Collins Warren of Boston. On the first day of the meeting Drake and the other members of the committee of arrangements were elected "permanent members." As might be inferred, Drake was quite active throughout the meeting. It was not an invariable rule, but certainly one which, at the time, ordinarily prevailed, that the chairman of the local committee of arrangements be elected president. In this instance, though Drake was nominated, another Cincinnatian, Reuben D. Mussey, not even a member of the local committee, was elected. Extensive search has unearthed only cryptic comments concerning the nomination of Mussey.

---

[14] *Ibid.*, pp. 55-56.

Dr. John C. Warren in a letter of 7 May 1850 to his home folks commented: "We have not succeeded in electing a new President, so that I am still tied down very closely. The division is between Dr. Drake and Dr. Mussey: the latter will probably be elected." [15]

With reference to the confirmation of the nominee, N. S. Davis (1817-1904), first historian of the association, wrote: "The unusual reluctance which was manifested by a portion of the members, to confirm the report of the Nominating Committee, making Dr. R. D. Mussey President of the Association, arose from no personal dislike, or want of respect for Dr. M., but from their strong attachment to Dr. Drake. It was not because they loved Caesar less, but they loved *Rome more*." [16]

Gross stated that Drake "might easily have been elected President for the ensuing year. But he declined to let his name go before the Nominating Committee; and the consequence was, much to the annoyance of his friends, that a man far his inferior in ability and reputation obtained that honorable post." [17] If the statement in Warren's letter is correct, Drake's name was before the nominating committee and Gross is again confused.

During the Cincinnati meeting the report on medical literature was read in which Drake's book on the diseases of the Mississippi Valley was lauded highly. He received an ovation and it is reported that he wept, saying he wished Harriet could have been there. Thus, though denied the presidency, in some instances a political "plum," he was accorded a much higher and more lasting honor, the result of his own innate abilities.

Drake continued an active member of the American Medi-

[15] Warren: *Life of John Collins Warren*, Vol. II, pp. 39.
[16] N. S. Davis: *History of the American Medical Association* (Philadelphia: Lippincott, Grambo & Co., 1855), p. 86.
[17] Gross: *Autobiography*, Vol. II, p. 271.

cal Association, participating in the meeting in Charleston, South Carolina, in 1851, and that in Richmond, Virginia, 1852. At the Charleston meeting he was appointed chairman of a committee to report at the next meeting on "Milk Sickness, so called." At Richmond, the earliest paper on the occupational hazards of photographers which has come to my notice (written by "Dr. Wright of Ohio") was read by Drake: "On the Influence upon the Health of Daguerrotypists of their Occupation." [18]

At the Richmond meeting, Drake also read an essay on the "Influence of Climatic Changes on Consumption." Although referred to the Committee of Publication, he, for some unexplained reason, refused to allow its printing. The only information available is contained in a letter from Dr. George R. Grant of Memphis. He had discussed the subject with Drake who informed him that his preconceived idea and that of others were erroneous. Instead of being less prevalent in the temperate latitudes of the Mississippi Valley than to the North, tuberculosis was infinitely more prevalent than in the rigorous climate of Canada.[19]

Drake's earliest religious training was in a group of Baptists. His mother, a Quakeress, was "excommunicated" because of her marriage to one of another sect. His wife, Harriet, was an Episcopalian. One of his most devoted friends in Cincinnati was the Reverend Joshua L. Wilson, pastor of the First Presbyterian Church. Hence, Drake had been "exposed" to many different religious influences. The Reverend William Jackson (1793-1844), first rector of St. Paul's Church (Episcopal), Louisville, in writing his brother on 22 June 1840, showed elation over the recent baptism of Drake:

[18] American Medical Association: *Transactions*, Vol. V, p. 29.
[19] George R. Grant: Letter, *Peninsular Journal of Medicine* (Ann Arbor, Mich.) I:514-16, May 1854.

It was my happiness to present to the Bishop twenty-two persons for confirmation within a few months past, and the remainder communed the same day. Among this number was Dr. Drake, one of the first medical men of the West, and a Professor of the Medical College of this city. I baptised him about two months since, and received him to the communion at the next opportunity, and I trust from his standing, decision in religion, and moral courage, that he will be found a useful member of the church.[20]

Drake was no more upright morally after uniting with the church. However, it was reported that he sought out all those with whom he had exchanged sharp words and apologized.

Drake's return to Louisville in 1850 to teach did not prevent summer vacations in travelling or in visiting Cincinnati. He was in the latter place during part of the summer of 1851. Continually interested in civic improvements, he wrote a letter to the *Daily Cincinnati Gazette* extolling the advantages of a public park. He suggested an area of approximately thirty acres lying between Sycamore and Vine Streets and extending to Mount Auburn. He stressed especially the value and advantages of a park to the poor. In conclusion he even discussed its financing:

It is not necessary that the city should in any degree oppress, or even embarrass herself by the proposed purchase. There would be no justice in making the present generation pay the whole for that which all coming generations are to enjoy. The city need only issue bonds or scrip bearing interest, and provide a small sinking fund. Thus the expenses would be distributed through many years, and not perceptibly felt in any one.[21]

[20] Margaret A. Jackson: *Memoirs of the Rev. William Jackson* (New York: Protestant Episcopal Society, 1861), p. 271.
[21] Daniel Drake: "A City Park," *Daily Cincinnati Gazette*, XXV, No. 7447:p. [2]—c. [2], July 29, 1851.

Temperance was one of the many causes to which Drake devoted much time. There are allusions to his lectures in this field during his trips throughout the Mississippi Valley. Of these lectures (fully a hundred in number), a few were published and a few others still exist in manuscript notes. The establishment of the Physiological Temperance Society of the Louisville Medical Institute has been previously mentioned. Probably it was his most extensive and persistent effort in the temperance movement. Drake believed that the drunkard started as only a social drinker. The thoughtless adoption of any custom merely because of its vogue not only disturbed but angered him:

> We accept customs, because they are customary things; and pursue them, because others lead us on. . . .
>
> Age claims respect from youth and should in return, bestow upon it the blessing of a good example—not the curse of a bad one. . . .
>
> Temperate drinking, the fruitful mother of drunkenness, is a harlot, which peoples and pollutes the land with drunkards, and yet she sits at almost every fireside! Foul and half naked in the rude cabin, painted and decked out with gaudy trappings in the splendid mansion, she accommodates herself to all conditions and, like Satan, assumes all shapes. The world absurdly despises her offspring; while its eyes are closed to the elements of pollution, which have their origin in her own system. . . .[22]

Drake's recognition of the value of reading lead to his interest in the formation of the first circulating library in Cincinnati. Further, hoping that the Western Museum Society might become a center of culture, he was one of the first to donate books for its library. Through his efforts the Medical

[22] Daniel Drake: *"Causes and Consequences of Temperate Drinking,"* in James Young: *The Lights of Temperance.* (Louisville, Morton and Griswold, 1851), pp. 169, 172, 173.

Department of Cincinnati College, during its meteoric career, accumulated over two thousand volumes. In 1851, Drake fathered the Cincinnati Medical Library Association and gave more than a hundred volumes as a nucleus for its establishment. When its reading rooms were opened, Drake was the speaker, and in two addresses scored (I believe) two "firsts." [23]

The earlier address, 9 January 1852, was entitled, "Early Physicians, Scenery and Society in Cincinnati." In so far as I have been able to determine this is the first attempt in the United States to record the medical history of any city. The second discourse, 10 January 1852, "On the Origin and Influence of Medical Periodical Literature; and the Benefits of Public Medical Libraries," was apparently the first attempt at a bibliography of the periodical literature of the country.

No speaker could have been better qualified to discuss early medicine in Cincinnati than Drake, having a few weeks before passed his fifty-first year in that city. He had either personally known or had first-hand information of the army surgeons stationed at Fort Washington in Cincinnati. Therefore he wished to manifest his gratitude, "by rescuing from oblivion the names of those who were my predecessors, and my compeers of that by-gone age." [24] He vividly recalled his own initiation into the mysteries of medicine and to the "doctor's shop" where he, no doubt, slept sometimes "beneath the greasy counter." To the extracts used in a previous chapter, the following is added:

> But medical recollections which go back half a century, admonish me, that the characteristic propensities of age may not be without their influence. Every epoch of life should be allowed to illustrate itself. You yourselves will successively follow me; and with the privilege of a senior, permit me to

[23] Drake: *Discourses.* . . .
[24] *Ibid.,* p. 9.

remind you of the maxim of Hippocrates: "Life is short—art is long—occasion brief—experience fallacious—judgment difficult." At whatever age you may be gathered to your fathers, many of your plans will be left unfinished. I pray that the time may be far off; and, still more, that when it comes, each of you may be able, in faith, to lay hold of the cheering declaration of the inspired apostle—"Blessed are the dead who die in the Lord: they rest from their labors, and their works do follow them." [25]

[25] *Ibid.*, p. 58.

20 ℞

The causes of failure generally lie in our own weaknesses, of which the greatest is the want of unfaltering constancy.[1]

Drake's Personal Appearance

DRAKE WAS erect, approximately six-feet tall, with curly auburn hair and penetrating, yet kindly, blue eyes. Agile, with great powers of endurance, he was often seen running to keep appointments. Always neatly dressed, he usually wore around his neck a gold chain, to which his watch was attached. For many years after his wife's death, crepe was worn on his hat. Henry Stuart Foote (1804-80), U.S. senator, lawyer, governor of Mississippi, author, and orator, wrote:

> He was of a healthful and commanding aspect; of a stature nearly approaching to six feet; of singularly regular features; of a most intelligent and benignant countenance; and of manners remarkably sociable, unassuming and attractive. His conversational powers were most extraordinary, and it was to me absolutely delightful to listen to his rich mellifluous tones; to drink in the mingled instruction and entertainment which constantly flowed from his lips and to behold that beaming and genial smile which lent lustre to his visage. . . . I very much doubt whether as a lecturer, upon subjects appertaining to his own profession, that he has ever had an equal upon the continent.[2]

Gross described Drake as "a handsome man, with fine blue eyes and manly features." An entirely different impression

---

[1] Drake: *Discourses*, p. 93.
[2] H. S. Foote: "Reminiscences. Dr. Drake," *Washington Chronicle*, Nov. 10, 1874:p. [2]—c. [1-2].

came from Gorham A. Worth, a banker in Cincinnati from 1817 to 1821:

> I knew Doctor Drake by reputation long before I had the pleasure of knowing him personally, and as a matter of course, I had drawn his picture in accordance with my notion of his character. I had given him a fine person, an easy, dignified address, classic features and a capital head. When I came to see him, father Abraham! said I to myself, what a mistake is here! With the exception of that small, thinking gray [*sic*] eye of his, there was nothing under heaven of an intellectual appearance about him, nor did the sound of his voice so flatter the ear as to make amends for the disappointment of the eye. The same mistake might be made in drawing a picture of Mr. Clay from a knowledge of his character. There is not a feature in the great statesman's face, there is nothing in his appearance, air or manner (except when speaking) that would lead one to connect with him any idea of talent or eloquence.[3]

That Drake had a characteristic and forceful style of speaking is apparent from dozens of descriptions. One of the best is by an anonymous writer, "Sojourner," in 1834:

> They [College of Teachers] have now met, and Dr. Drake has just arisen to pronounce the opening address.
>
> The doctor is a scientific man, but he does not believe in the doctrines of phrenology—at least, I have heard him say, that he sees no reason why he should believe in the details of the science. Look at his head, and perhaps you will find a cause for his scepticism about that. He has a great mind, but his brain must lie very compactly, or he has not much, for the frontal region is not wonderfully capacious. His forehead is of but medium height, narrow and knotted as was Michael Angelo's—and would become a veteran Xantippe of three score, just as well as it does him. Beneath those

[3] Gorham A. Worth: *Recollections of Cincinnati* (Albany: Charles van Benthuysen, 1851), pp. 65-66.

spectacles is a well fixed, kindling, bluish-gray eye, which can look as far into a mill stone, as any other eye in the land, despite the laughing wrinkles about it. . . .

In every thing which concerns the "great West," the Doctor takes special interest. He is now lecturing upon the proper discipline to be observed in families and the literary institutions of the country. He is in favor of a judicious system of flogging and emulation to be observed in schools. Mark his lectures! He begins, "The universe is a system of worlds, and the Creator is its ruler." He comes down from the heavens step by step, and is at last on the face of the earth. He now gives you the division of his subjects, and forthwith proceeds to demonstrate the correctness of his views. Now an anecdote—then some profound logic—here a truism insisted on with all the ardor of recent discovery—then an idea, grand and original, which assures you of the greatness of his intellect—now a sprinkling of poetry—and here a rapid declamation, replete with interesting points. He stops in the midst of his discourse, and while every body wonders what is the matter with him—he tells a story, or is witty, or is not, as the case may be—but always humorous. . . . His voice —ay, that belongs to himself; it is agreeable, and is not without its own peculiar music—particularly that draw-l-i-n-g at the vicinity of a period, as if he were afraid to approach it.[4]

Drake's friendships were ordinarily lasting ones; once formed they were maintained either by personal contact or by correspondence. His sociability attracted many friends and admirers. Though he was a voluminous letter writer, few letters by him survive. In my thirty-two years of collecting Drake material, only a hundred letters from him have been located, all of them being in my files either in the original, in photostat, or as typed copies. The destruction of letters from him might have been expected, but the wholesale burn-

[4] Sojourner: "Epistles from Cincinnati," *Cincinnati Mirror and Western Gazette*, IV:9-10, Oct. 18, 1834.

ing of those to him is lamentable. Of those destroyed were the priceless Lincoln letter and many hundreds of others from notable persons of the United States and of Europe.

The friendship with Josiah Meigs, begun in 1812, carried through at least the fourth generation. William Montgomery Meigs in 1887 wrote an interesting life of his great-grand-father[5] in which there is important information concerning the letters (1814-22) between his ancestor and Drake, whom he regarded with the greatest respect.*

One of the sons of Josiah, Charles Delucena Meigs (1792-1869), a graduate of the University of Pennsylvania and professor of obstetrics in the Jefferson Medical College, was a warm friend and correspondent of Drake. His *Obstetrics* was dedicated: "To the Eminent Western Physician, Philosopher, Gentleman and Scholar, Daniel Drake, M.D., of Cincinnati." [6] In this book, there is also a three-page letter addressed to Drake which discusses the origin and plans of the work. Meigs's *Obstetrics* went through three editions: 1849, 1852, and 1856.

Concerning Josiah's son, Samuel D. Gross wrote:

> Of the great men with whom during the period of half a century I have been brought prominently in contact, I regard Charles D. Meigs, for six years my colleague in the Jefferson Medical College, as one of the extraordinary, whether we consider his versatility, his learning, his talents, his enthusiasm, his eccentricity, his dramatic power, and his love for his profession, or the reputation which he attained as an obstetric practitioner, as an author, and as a teacher.[7]

[5] Meigs: *Life of Josiah Meigs.*

* The writing of this biography was delayed almost two years while an unsuccessful search was made for the Daniel Drake-Josiah Meigs correspondence. Should any of my readers know of the present location of these letters, I will greatly appreciate having the information.

[6] Charles D. Meigs: *Obstetrics; the Science and the Art* (Philadelphia: Blanchard & Lea, 1849).

[7] Gross: *Autobiography,* Vol. II, p. 339.

Since Drake was an associate member of the College of Philadelphia, a memoir was delivered by Charles D. Meigs, vice-president of the college.[8] The address was based on a forty-year acquaintance, on documents loaned by the family, on Drake's writings, and on personal "recollections and convictions." This brief biography is the best of those in my collection and contains remarkably few errors.

Apparently the last public committee upon which Drake served as chairman consisted of thirty-two members instructed to arrange for proper ceremonies attending the arrival in Cincinnati of the body of his friend, Henry Clay, who had died in Washington on 29 June 1852. Within a few days, the body of Clay in a funeral coach was started on its circuitous route to Lexington. In the larger cities through which the train passed, the casket was removed and ceremonies were held. In Cincinnati, 8 July 1852, "After the coffin had been placed under the canopy, Dr. Drake remarked that it was thought a fitting ceremony, ere the remains of the illustrious man were borne forever away, that Bishop McIlvaine, should read a portion of the 'Order for the burial of the Dead,' from the service of the Church of which Mr. Clay was a communicant." [9]

A few weeks later, Drake called his committee together to confer with the president of the Clay Monument Association. The Cincinnati committee no doubt approved of plans for the monument, though no details are available. The monument was not completed until approximately nine years later at an estimated cost of $58,000.[10]

Early in 1852, Drake had resigned his professorship in the

---

[8] Charles D. Meigs: *A Biographical Notice of Daniel Drake* . . . read July 1853 (Philadelphia: Lippincott, Grambo & Co., 1853).

[9] [News item], "Remains of Henry Clay," *Daily Cincinnati Gazette*, LX, No. 13, July 9, 1852.

[10] J. Winston Coleman: *Last Days, Death and Funeral of Henry Clay* (Lexington: Winburn Press, 1951), p. 22.

Medical Department of the University of Louisville, again
to accept a position in the Medical College of Ohio. During
the summer of 1852, spent in Cincinnati, he was busily engaged in writing the second volume of his *Diseases of the
Mississippi Valley*. In October 1852, he began a preliminary
course of lectures in the Medical College of Ohio. Later in
October he was invited to attend the second annual meeting
of the Kentucky State Medical Association in Louisville.
Here he was elected the first honorary member of the association.[11] While in Louisville, he slept in an unheated room and
contracted a severe cold which gradually grew worse on his
return to Cincinnati. Though ill, he continued lecturing and
visiting the hospital. His last public appearance was made at a
memorial meeting for Daniel Webster (1782-1852), held in
Cincinnati on the evening of 26 October 1852. Because of a
quarter of a century of friendship with Webster, Drake was
called upon to address the meeting. The daily newspaper
reported:

> The venerable Dr. Drake being called upon, rose in his
> place and remarked that, having recently taken a conspicuous
> part—because it was assigned him—in the funeral ceremonies
> of another illustrious American [Henry Clay], he would not
> yield to an expression of his emotions on the present occa-
> sion.
>
> But before he sat down, he would point attention to the
> manner of this illustrious man's death, and to those utterances
> which, from the solemnity of the occasion, and because they
> were the last words of DANIEL WEBSTER, would forever stand
> out among the most prominent, and those most frequently
> turned to by posterity. "As an humble professor of the Chris-
> tian religion," continued Dr. D., "I call the attention of the
> *young men* of this country to DANIEL WEBSTER's dying declara-
> tion of the inestimable value of the Christian religion—of

[11] Kentucky State Medical Society: *Transactions . . . 1852* (Louisville:
Webb & Levering, 1853), p. 16.

man's utter dependence on Divine mercy. To the example of the mightiest intellect of the age, let me point those who have thought religion not meet for men of culture and genius. Who shall say that the simple utterance of the departed Statesman—*Thy Rod, Thy Rod—Thy Staff, Thy Staff—They Comfort me!*—does not constitute the greatest act of that life of great acts![12]

Upon retiring that evening (26 October 1852), Drake suffered a severe and protracted chill. In spite of this, he was at the hospital and in the lecture room the next morning. That evening (27 October 1852) he had another chill and the following day was too weak to leave home. In addition to a cough, pain in the right lower chest, and irregular heart action, he had almost constant and intense frontal headache. Hoping for relief he decided that venesection might help and, without assistance, withdrew enough blood to produce fainting. Afterwards, the physicians in attendance discovered "some symptoms of inflammation in the right lung." Drake then sent for a "cupper" who succeeded in withdrawing half a pint of blood from over the painful area of the chest. Purgatives were given daily. On Sunday, 31 October 1852, talking was so difficult that only two or three words could be uttered at a time. Though extremely weak he signed his will, "Dan Drake," without much tremor.

By Monday, 1 November 1852, though much weaker, his book was uppermost in his mind: ". . . . to complete it had been his only earthly ambition, and he hoped God might spare him for that end." On the following day he "no longer desired to live to finish his book . . . and death itself [would be] most welcome." Wednesday found him weakening steadily, though still attempting to speak. Death occurred at 6:00 P.M., Friday, 5 November 1852.

[12] Charles D. Drake: *Funeral Oration . . . on the Occasion of the Obsequies of Daniel Webster* (St. Louis: Charles & Hammond, 1852), p. 35.

The description of the last illness is summarized from the notes of his son-in-law, Alexander Hamilton McGuffey, made on the day after death.[13] The treatment outlined will exemplify the crudeness of the customary methods employed over a hundred years ago.

The physicians, Dr. Wolcott Richards (1803-71) and Dr. Landon C. Rives, who were in constant attendance, concluded that an arachnitis (congestion of the brain, according to the burial certificate) was the cause of death. No autopsy was held. For many years Drake had had what he referred to as attacks of "my old malady of the brain." As my rhinological friends suggest, these illnesses may have been exacerbations of a severe sinusitis. It is of interest to speculate concerning the nature of the terminal illness. This could have been an exacerbation of a sinusitis which, with a bronchiectasis, was followed by a patchy pneumonia of the right lower lobe and, terminally, a cerebral abscess.

Cincinnati had lost its most distinguished citizen. There were special meetings of the various medical societies and medical schools at which resolutions of condolence were passed. On the day before the funeral at a called meeting of all Cincinnatians, after appropriate resolutions had been adopted, the suggestion was made that "our fellow-citizens close their places of business tomorrow, Wednesday, 10th inst., at half-past 2 o'clock and during the funeral." [14] Thus it was that on the afternoon of 10 November 1852, in Cincinnati, the stores were closed, the streets were silent, and mourners crowded into Christ Church where the Reverend Dudley Atkins Tyng (1825-58) closed the sermon, "The Honor of Godliness," with these words: "May God in mercy

[13] Alexander H. McGuffey: "Particulars concerning the last illness, and death of Daniel Drake, M.D.," MS. in Historical and Philosophical Society of Ohio, Cincinnati.

[14] [Resolutions of Citizens]: *Daily Cincinnati Gazette*, LX, No. 119, Nov. 10, 1852.

grant that this death we so much mourn may be the seed of Life to many souls; & that all who feel his loss may follow his example!" [15]

Drake was buried by the side of his wife in the Cemetery of Spring Grove, Cincinnati, Section 77, Lot 79. The inscription on his monument of limestone gradually disintegrated until it was almost indecipherable by the late 1940's. In 1951 the physicians of Cincinnati purchased a bronze replacement of the original inscription.

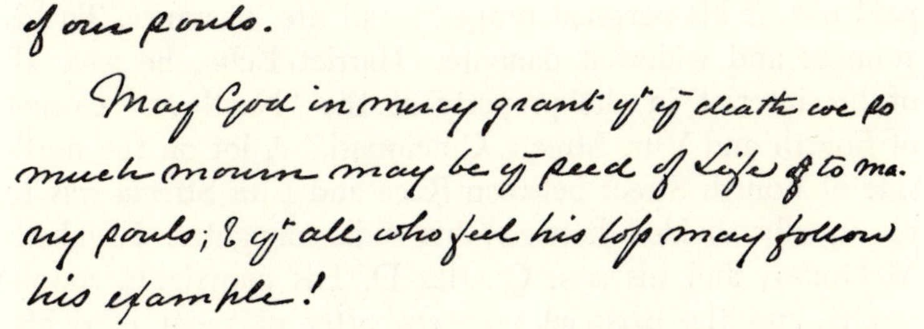
of our souls.

May God in mercy grant yt ye death we so much mourn may be ye seed of Life to many souls; & yt all who feel his loss may follow his example!

Fig. 10. From mss. of sermon preached at the funeral of Daniel Drake, Nov. 10, 1852.

Two days after Drake's death, Rufus King (1817-91), a young lawyer in Cincinnati and grandson of Governor Thomas Worthington of Ohio, wrote to his mother in Philadelphia:

> You will probably have heard before this of the death of Dr. Drake, a loss truly deplorable to Cincinnati and which will be lamented not only throughout the country but by physiologists and men of science everywhere—He leaves his great work unfinished. . . .

[15] Dudley A. Tyng: "The Honor of Godliness," preached at the funeral of Dr. Daniel Drake, Nov. 10, 1852. MS. owned by Miss Marion Bridgman, a great-granddaughter.

His family are in sad affliction, more especially Mrs. Campbell [his younger daughter, Harriet] who has borne the loss of her husband with great difficulty apparently, and under the constant support of her father. The Doctor died of a typhus attack superinduced by disease of the brain—in which it is understood *privately* that against the positive remonstrances of his physicians he bled himself so profusely as to faint and exhausted his system.

Harriet would no doubt be greatly consoled if you write to her. . . .[16]

Drake's will was a simple one, ordering that all debts be paid out of his personal property and life insurance. To his younger and widowed daughter, Harriet Echo, he gave all of his interest in the property at the "Northwest Corner of Fourth and Vine Streets, Cincinnati." A lot on the north side of Fourth Street between Race and Elm Streets was to be equally divided between his older daughter, Elizabeth McGuffey, and his son, Charles D. His copyrights, manuscripts, and the personal property, after payment of debts, were to be divided equally among his three children. His son-in-law, Alexander H. McGuffey, was appointed executor without bond and with unlimited authority in disposing of all property. The will was "Admitted to Probate, November 20, 1852." [17]

There were numerous notices of his death in the newspapers and, of course, in all the medical journals. Jerome V. C. Smith, editor of the *Boston Medical and Surgical Journal*, referred to Drake's death on several occasions in addition to reviewing Gross's and Meigs's biographical sketches. Smith closed the review of Meigs's address:

It was not his forte to waste the precious hours of existence in frivolous pursuits. Great thoughts having in view the

[16] Rufus King, ALS, in King Collection, Vol. II, No. 23, Historical and Philosophical Society of Ohio.

[17] Original in Hamilton Probate Court, Hamilton County, Ohio.

progress of society in knowledge, virtue and happiness, occupied his disciplined mind. The little dogs that barked as he passed along the highway, jealous of his progress, but unable to curb or control the indomitable force which carried him beyond the sphere of their influence, have retired to their lurking places, while Daniel Drake will be referred to, in future times, as a bright star of the first magnitude in our Western firmament.[18]

In 1853 at the meeting of the American Medical Association in New York, the following resolutions were passed unanimously by a rising vote:

Whereas, By the dispensation of an inscrutable Providence, Dr. DANIEL DRAKE has been removed since the last meeting of this Association, from the scene of his labors,

Resolved, That in the death of Dr. DRAKE, the American Medical Association has lost one of its most honored members, and the American Medical profession, one of its brightest ornaments.

Resolved, That his steady devotion to his profession through a long life, and his zeal, activity, and unceasing efforts to advance its interest, afford an example worthy of the imitation of every young physician.

Resolved, That this Association will cherish the memory of Dr. Drake for his many virtues, and for his labors, which have adorned and elevated our profession.[19]

Thomas Wood, editor of *The Western Lancet* (Cincinnati), stated that a large portion of the first volume of Drake's *Systematic Treatise* was purchased by eastern and European physicians.[20] Drake had practically completed the initial draft of the manuscript of the second volume before his

[18] Jerome V. C. Smith [ed.]: "Biography of Daniel Drake," *Boston Med. & Surg. Jnl.,* XLIX:45-46, Aug. 10, 1853.

[19] American Medical Association: *Transactions* . . . *1853,* Vol. VI, p. 42.

[20] Thomas Wood: Review of "A *Systematic Treatise,*" Second Series, *Western Lancet* (Cincinnati), XV:683-95, Nov. 1854.

death. His executor found three thousand pages of manuscript which were turned over to Drs. Samuel Hanbury Smith
(1810-94), then of Cincinnati, and Francis G. Smith (1818-
78) of Philadelphia. Editing the manuscript and preparing
it for the printer were accomplished in about a year.[21] Apparently the second volume or "series," as it was called, did
not create as much interest as the initial one. Reviews were
laudatory but not to the same extent as with the first volume.
Actually, the second "series" does not have the same lively
spirit as the first—no doubt lost in the editing was Drake's
especial gift for pungent and forceful phrasing.

It is hoped that the reader by this time has not gotten the
idea that Drake was without faults. He was indeed human.
As an ambitious leader he may have chided the less aggressive
followers, sometimes arousing their antagonism. Kindly at
heart and unusually solicitous of family, friends, and patients
he, nevertheless, presented an opposite face to his enemies.
They were attacked with unflinching valor from all sides as
the doggerel stanza so truly implied:

> *Down* stream you gaze at large
> *Up* stream pops *Doctor Drake*.

His inherent ability to arouse all sorts of people to extraordinary activity shows his superior leadership. By dogged deter-
mination and an uncompromising attitude toward his enemies
and the foes of his high standards of medical education, he
kept and multiplied friends and admirers alike. It is apparent
that Drake's friends, both cultural and scientific, were outstanding leaders. In selecting teachers for the medical schools
founded by him, he attempted to choose the most capable
men rather than those less able than he, believing that competition would spur him as well as his associates to greater
endeavor. This policy, whereby he bypassed the less competent

[21] Drake: A *Systematic Treatise.* . . .

men, accounts for many of his difficulties. His superiority was so evident that his jealous inferiors called him egotistical and unduly ambitious.

Daniel Drake had achieved much and in 1852 stood at the head of the profession, the most widely known and respected physician in the United States. It appears fitting to close with a summary of the more important events and accomplishments in the life of this pioneer of midwestern medicine.

As the earliest student of medicine, Drake received the first certificate of proficiency in the profession in the Northwest Territory. He was the first student of medicine from Cincinnati to matriculate at the University of Pennsylvania. Drake's *Notices Concerning Cincinnati* (1810) was the earliest book with a medical section printed west of the Allegheny Mountains. It contained the initial listing of the plants of the region, and described a hitherto unknown local disease: milk sickness. A leader in founding Cincinnati's first circulating library, he became its president. In medical teaching, Drake was elected a professor in the earliest active faculty of the pioneer university of the West. A leader in forming the first museum of antiquities in the West, he served as secretary of the Board of Managers. Working alone, he secured a charter for Cincinnati College (1819) and, in 1835, organized its distinguished Medical Department. He founded the Medical College of Ohio, at present the University of Cincinnati College of Medicine. By personal solicitation he persuaded the Ohio legislature to charter the first hospital for medical instruction in the United States, staffed exclusively by the professors of a medical college. As the author of the most important book on medical education in the United States, he thereby initiated the movement for higher standards in the profession. He conceived and arranged for the Medical Department of Miami University which was consolidated with the Medical College of Ohio. Through lectures Drake incited movements to establish schools for the blind in both Ohio (1833) and in Kentucky (1842). He guided the successful efforts to establish marine hospitals in the Mississippi Valley; proposed a railroad linking Cincinnati and the West with the Atlantic seaboard at Charleston, South Carolina; and was a leader in the movement in Cincinnati to assist the Texans in their fight for freedom. For twenty-two years Drake edited the most influential medical journal in the West. He authored the classic, *Pioneer Life in Kentucky*. Although abhorring slavery, he wrote a factual, objective, and philosophic account of it. His most notable achievement was the writing of "one of the greatest masterpieces of medico-geographic research."

Drake was a man who inevitably left his mark on his times. Indeed, today, his influence is alive, important, and imperishable.

Index

413